United States
Merchant Shipping
Policies and Politics

United States
Merchant Shipping
Policies and Politics

SAMUEL A. LAWRENCE

The Brookings Institution
Washington, D.C.

© 1966 by

THE BROOKINGS INSTITUTION
1775 Massachusetts Avenue, N. W., Washington, D. C.

Published July 1966

Library of Congress Catalogue Card Number 66-24070

THE BROOKINGS INSTITUTION is an independent organization devoted to nonpartisan research, education, and publication in economics, government, foreign policy, and the social sciences generally. Its principal purposes are to aid in the development of sound public policies and to promote public understanding of issues of national importance.

The Institution was founded December 8, 1927, to merge the activities of the Institute for Government Research, founded in 1916, the Institute of Economics, founded in 1922, and the Robert Brookings Graduate School of Economics and Government, founded in 1924.

The general administration of the Institution is the responsibility of a self-perpetuating Board of Trustees. The trustees are likewise charged with maintaining the independence of the staff and fostering the most favorable conditions for creative research and education. The immediate direction of the policies program, and staff of the Institution is vested in the President, assisted by the division directors and an advisory council, chosen from the professional staff of the Institution.

In publishing a study, the Institution presents it as a competent treatment of a subject worthy of public consideration. The interpretations and conclusions in such publications are those of the author or authors and do not purport to represent the views of the other staff members, officers, or trustees of the Brookings Institution.

BOARD OF TRUSTEES

Foreword

The United States merchant marine is a small industry that has played a disproportionately large role in national and international affairs. Twice during the past fifty years, the United States has been compelled to undertake massive shipbuilding programs to meet military needs overseas. Following each World War, the U.S. government has attempted to foster the development of a privately owned and operated U.S. merchant marine that would carry a substantial portion of the nation's peacetime trade and be available in future emergencies. On both occasions, it has encountered severe difficulties and achieved only partial success.

The root of the problem is that the operating and construction costs of American ships are higher than those of any other major maritime nation, whereas the productivity of American and foreign flag ships are approximately equal. The U.S. merchant marine, therefore, requires some form of direct or indirect government assistance to compete in foreign trade.

Many techniques to assist American shipping companies have been devised, but none has been entirely satisfactory. The government's most ambitious experiment, initiated in 1936, provided a comprehensive system of operating and construction subsidies to qualified companies that were willing to submit to intensive public supervision. The 1936 act was billed as a model for effective partnership between government and private industry, but its results have not fulfilled expectations. Although frequently amended, it has remained the basic framework for the government's post-World War II subsidy program. In its efforts to sustain American shipping, the government has supplemented its direct subsidy program with a variety of indirect aids.

During the past year there has been encouraging evidence of a new determination to correct deficiencies in the government program and to revive and strengthen the American merchant marine. Much disagreement exists regarding how this can be accomplished. It is hoped that this study will contribute to the effort to find constructive solutions to long-standing problems. Although the problems encountered in developing an American merchant marine are in some respects unique, they are illustrative also of more general dilemmas which must be faced in efforts to mold private economic activity to public purposes, a field in which Brookings has had a continuing research interest.

This book provides a comprehensive survey of the government program to develop an American merchant marine to serve U.S. foreign trade. It undertakes an interpretation of the manner in which various shipping programs are related to one another and to characteristics of the government's policy-making machinery as well as to national interests and the industry's needs. The study identifies strengths and weaknesses of the government's programs, calculates their cost, and weighs their effectiveness for meeting changing national needs. Principal emphasis is on description and analysis, but the concluding chapter also presents the author's proposals for updating the government program.

The manuscript was reviewed by a committee composed of Dr. Emmette Redford, professor of government, University of Texas; Dr. Daniel Marx, professor of economics, Dartmouth College; and Dr. Paul M. Zeis, director of research, Norfolk and Western Railroad, and author of the 1938 book *American Shipping Policy*. The author wishes to acknowledge particularly the helpful assistance of George A. Graham, director of the Governmental Studies Program, Brookings Institution, and Laurin L. Henry and John E. Moore, former members of the Brookings staff; William D. Carey, Sam R. Broadbent, and Walter Boehner of the U.S. Bureau of the Budget; Paul Sitton and Ira Dye of the U.S. Department of Commerce; Chester B. Earle, Marvin L. Fair, Robert E. Goosetree, and Harold H. Roth of the faculty of the American University, and former Under Secretary of Commerce Louis S. Rothschild. Former Maritime Administrator Donald W. Alexander arranged access to the agency's files and personnel, a pattern of cooperation helpfully continued by his successor, Nicholas Johnson. The author also wishes to note his particular gratitude to David E. Bell, Director of the Bureau of the Budget in 1961-62, whose consideration and interest in employee development made this study possible, and to his successors, Kermit Gordon and Charles L. Schultze, who have also assisted in this project. Alice Carroll edited the manuscript and Jean Kyle prepared the index.

Mr. Lawrence became interested in American shipping during the period 1959 through 1962, while assigned to maritime problems as an examiner in the U.S. Bureau of the Budget. The research on which the study is based was largely performed in 1963 during an eight months leave of absence from the Bureau of the Budget as a Federal Executive Fellow of the Brookings Institution.

The views expressed in this study are those of the author and do not purport to represent the views of the staff members, officers, or trustees of the Brookings Institution or the Bureau of the Budget.

Robert D. Calkins
President

January 1966
Washington, D. C.

Contents

xi

Introduction

THIS IS A STUDY of U.S. government programs to develop and maintain American merchant shipping in U.S. foreign trade and of the administrative policies and political pressures affecting these programs. The study compares the circumstances in which U.S. shipping subsidies were adopted with present circumstances and needs and considers steps which might feasibly be taken to update existing programs.

The problems besetting America's foreign trade merchant shipping industry are both economic and political. For more than one hundred years American seafaring wages and ship construction costs have been higher than those of other nations, necessitating some form of government assistance or incentives to persuade American entrepreneurs to invest in ocean shipping and to register their ships under U.S. flag. Regulations to safeguard the government's investment in the national flag fleet have imposed additional costs on subsidized American operators and have weakened some of the disciplines associated with the free enterprise system.

American foreign trade shipping depends on public support for survival. Thus, U.S. flag companies must be able to convince both the shipping public and the government that they offer services or support facilities which are important to the nation's economy, its foreign commerce, or its defense, and which are not available from other sources. Defense considerations have been the most important factor in development of U.S. maritime policy, although programs have been geared to developing a fleet suitable to service U.S. foreign commerce. American maritime policies also have been influenced by memories of the days when Douglas Mackay's clippers paced America's leadership at sea. To many Americans, it is unthinkable that the United States should not have a functioning, healthy merchant marine. National flag ships are regarded as a source of national power and prestige; unfortunately, they can also be a prolific source of trouble in international affairs.

Over the past half dozen years government maritime policies have

1

been intensively scrutinized by a number of public and private groups.†
Studies have been conducted to examine the industry's labor relations,
its services to foreign commerce, its contribution to the U.S. balance of
payments, and its contribution to national defense. An analysis of the industry's economic value has been published by the Northwestern University Transportation Center and a major inquiry into the industry's
business and competitive practices conducted by the Anti-trust Subcommittee of the House Judiciary Committee. The Joint Economic
Committee has held hearings and published extensive materials on the
relationship of U.S. maritime policies to the structure of international
freight rates and their impact on U.S. foreign trade. At the request of the
Secretary of Commerce, a blue-ribbon panel of business leaders undertook a broad review of the promotional program during 1963. In January
1965, President Lyndon B. Johnson announced his intention to propose
new maritime policies. Since then, efforts to develop new policies and
defend old ones have intensified, and studies have been published by a
presidentially sponsored Maritime Advisory Committee (which includes
both public and private members), an Interagency Task Force on Maritime Affairs, and by industry groups.

Except in the field of international shipping regulation, studies have
failed to lead to action, despite general dissatisfaction with present policies. This in itself is a challenging problem for investigation. What is it
about the government's program to assist merchant shipping which has
made success so elusive? Why should there be such wide disagreement
as to the nature of underlying problems and remedies for their correction?
Why has revision of even patently unsatisfactory policies proved so
difficult to achieve? If these questions could be answered, a strategy
might be devised for implementing desirable improvements in a field
in which current policy appears in some measure to be unsatisfactory
to everybody.

The ways in which a national flag merchant fleet can serve national
needs vary with changing circumstances. For example, it is generally
agreed that U.S. military dependence on privately owned vessels has
eased gradually since World War II. Concurrently, it has probably become more important to the United States that its subsidized shipping industry be as efficient and self-reliant as possible.

† The studies noted in the text have been sponsored chiefly by either government or the maritime industry and are cited in the Bibliography. Independent research on maritime matters has been directed principally at problems of maritime
law.

The nation's official maritime policy, as expressed in the Merchant Marine Act, 1936, is directed to both defense and commercial objectives, and emphasizes the need for an efficient industry which will contribute constructively to the nation's economy and foreign affairs. These objectives are at least partially inconsistent with one another, as well as with the primary objectives of the principal parties in interest. Furthermore, the government's promotional program must somehow be harmonized with its efforts to regulate competitive practices in the ocean freight industry and to protect American interests in American-owned vessels registered under foreign flags. The difficulty of formulating realistic and attainable policies from these varied objectives has retarded development of new programs to meet changing needs. The problem of defining, synthesizing, and updating public maritime policies to keep pace with the industry's changing economic and political environment is accordingly one of this study's principal concerns.

The study's second major concern is with techniques. The most persistent problems in the government's maritime program have been to establish proper boundaries between the public and private sector, and to define the roles, obligations, rights and privileges of the various parties in interest so that each can operate effectively within its area of responsibility. These tasks have been complicated by the proliferation of indirect supplements to the direct subsidies authorized by the 1936 act which have thrust the government into an increasing variety of industry problems and further blurred the demarkation between public and private spheres.

The government's ability to meet these problems depends on the effectiveness of its machinery for public policy development and administration, the quality of its personnel, and the political environment within which they operate. Sound organization is particularly important to a program as extensive and complex as government aid to merchant shipping. Appropriate administrative procedures are required to assure that the right problems are brought before the right people at the right time, and that a fair hearing is given to all legitimate interests. Most importantly, there must be mechanisms which will draw the program into the government's mainstream, so that it will be responsive to the flow of events and the nation's changing needs. The politics of the government's shipping program consequently constitute the study's third major interest.

This study is presented in three semi-independent parts. Part I provides a brief introduction to the industry and examines the setting and objectives of government shipping programs. It concludes with a chapter which describes the terms of the 1936 act and the machinery established for its administration.

The 1936 statute has survived without major modification for thirty years despite revolutionary changes in the industry's economic and political environment; in its technology, financial status, labor relations, and operating practices; and in its relationship to broad public objectives and to more specific defense and commercial needs. Part II reports on these developments and the manner in which government policy-makers have responded to them during the post-World War II years. This part concludes with an assessment of the costs, accomplishments, and general adequacy of the postwar promotional program in relation to postwar needs.

Part III shifts the focus from substantive policy issues to the techniques through which government has attempted to devise solutions to them. The first chapter of this part describes the formal policy-making machinery and assesses its impact on program development. The second chapter describes the principal groups interested in the program, how they are organized, how they operate, and the extent to which they have influenced the political process. The third examines operation of the broad political-administrative process in relation to the maritime program. Part III concludes with a brief analysis of the reasons so many reforms have been stalemated in this area of public policy over the past ten years.

The study's concluding chapter summarizes the problems currently facing America's maritime industry, assesses the prospects for constructive change, and advances specific proposals for improvement. Several broad alternative courses of action are considered. Attention is directed principally to those actions which appear to be politically feasible. The study assumes that it is not realistic to consider either an abrupt termination or sharp expansion of the subsidy programs. It further assumes that bringing the privately owned merchant fleet under direct public control or under control of a government corporation are politically unacceptable alternatives.

Several other limitations on the study's scope should be noted. First, the study is directed solely to consideration of U.S. government programs dealing with dry cargo shipping in foreign trade. Domestic services, passenger operations, tankers, American-owned ships registered abroad, the regulation of foreign-owned ships in U.S. foreign trade, foreign regulatory and subsidy practices, and matters concerning safety at sea, labor regulations, documentation, tonnage and registry taxes, consular services, and the like are considered only to the extent necessary to elucidate public policy bearing on the development of an American dry cargo, foreign trade merchant marine.

Second, government aids to the U.S. shipbuilding industry, including construction subsidies awarded under the 1936 act, are also considered only in relation to programs to aid shipping operations. Their impact on these programs is substantial, since for all practical purposes American ship operators are now required to obtain their ships from American shipyards at prices approximately double those in foreign shipbuilding centers. These restrictions have seriously burdened the operating industry and severely limited its growth potential. However, there is no necessary logical linkage between ship construction and operating aids which compels continuing the present system for assisting American yards. In fact, the public policy considerations applicable to subsidizing ship operations are in many respects quite different from those applicable to subsidizing the yards. Furthermore, the present system, which gears shipyard aid to the operating industry's need for new equipment, provides no assurance that American shipbuilding is maintained at the scale required to meet mobilization needs. Continued coupling of the two programs appears instead to represent a political marriage of convenience, which contains serious disadvantages for both partners. This study therefore adopts the position that the claims of American shipyards for government aid can and should be considered separately from ship operating subsidies, so that each program can be tailored to that industry's particular situation and to national needs.

A third limitation is the cut-off date for entry of new material into this study. The study was conceived in 1961. The historical and statistical research underlying its conclusions was accomplished chiefly in the first half of 1963. The succeeding three years have proved to be an extremely active period for the U.S. merchant marine. For the most part, the events of this period have confirmed the earlier analysis. Although statistics have not been updated, the most important events affecting the government's maritime programs occurring through December 1965 have been reflected in the study.

Government aid to merchant shipping was originally conceived as a temporary stimulus to assist in establishing an American merchant marine. The 1936 act placed the subsidy program on a permanent but limited basis. Postwar policies have gradually eroded many of the controls built into the 1936 program and liberalized its terms to give American shipping additional protection against foreign flag competition. Moderation of competitive pressures has permitted costs to increase and has thus compounded the basic problem. This trend appears likely to continue if a positive effort is not made to check it.

This study therefore argues for increased competition, fewer governmental controls, and a simpler, comprehensive subsidy system designed to permit relatively efficient, low-cost American companies to compete successfully in foreign trade. Implementation of its proposals would require that the parties in interest look beyond their immediate advantage to long-run needs. A thoroughgoing restructuring of the present program is a prerequisite to the constructive relationship between industry and government which is needed to fulfill the nation's maritime goals. Furthermore, the situation now is such that the survival of a genuinely private U.S. shipping industry may be considered to be at stake.

PART I

*Origins and Objectives of
The Government's Shipping Program*

The ocean freight industry operates in an arena of sharp international rivalry and interest. Historically, national control of shipping services has been regarded as one of the keys to national power. In mercantilist theory, a national merchant marine was valued both for the revenue it produced and as a means of enforcing control over distant colonies. It was one of these colonies, the United States, which contributed most to breaking the mercantilist's grip in order that merchant shipping might develop as a truly international industry.

The first act of the First Congress of the United States was aimed at promoting industry, trade, and shipping. During the next forty years, over fifty additional statutes and commercial treaties were approved to protect and promote an American merchant marine. A reciprocity act of 1828 offered to remove all barriers to the shipping of any other nation which would accord equal treatment to ships of U.S. registry. It was followed twenty-one years later by repeal of the British navigation acts. By 1860 the spread of free trade principles had opened virtually all of the world's major ports to ships of all nations to compete equally for the world's trade. Shipments within nations and to their territories, however, were excluded from these trade agreements and continue to be reserved by many nations, including the United States, to national flag ships.

The international character of the ocean freight industry makes conventional economic controls ineffective. Instead, sanctions and incentives to promote national interests must be tailored to the unique rules and customs of international shipping. Internal economic and political demands also significantly influenced the development of U.S. maritime policies.

The chapters in Part I identify characteristics of the international shipping industry which have been particularly relevant to U.S. national interests and describe the development of policies to promote these

7

interests during the years preceding World War II. The statutes which were enacted during this prewar period set the course and to a large extent have also provided the instruments for the United States' postwar maritime programs. The purpose of this part is to identify the needs to which these prewar programs were directed and assess the adequacy of the foundation which they laid for future policy development.

1

The Merchant Shipping Industry

THE ATTENTION which the U.S. flag merchant marine has received from government and in the public press is extraordinary for such a small industry. Seafaring employment provides only about 70,000 jobs. The industry's gross investment, although approximately $2 billion, is dwarfed by the assets of the Ford Motor Company or U.S. Steel. Ship operators can enter the industry through charter or ownership of a single freighter, typically costing only $4–$6 million to construct abroad. Many entrepreneurs, who obtained fully depreciated war-built tonnage at modest prices, entered the industry on far less capitalization.

Ship operations, however, are only the nucleus of the far-ranging complex of services loosely covered under the term "maritime trades." Ships must be loaded, provisioned, and fueled. Shipyards provide repair services and dry-docking as well as facilities for construction of new vessels. Ship chandlers stock specialized marine hardware and stores. In fact, only about half of the out-of-pocket costs of a typical transatlantic dry cargo shipment is incurred in port-to-port transportation.

Most of the shoreside components of America's maritime industry would continue whether or not a single ship were operated under U.S. flag. The economics of the situation compel it. Economic forces are also important in shipping operations. However, during the past thirty to forty years, sponsorship of national flag ships in international shipping has become largely a political matter.

The Economics of Ocean Shipping

Economic activity typically is so varied and unstable that its dynamics are seldom fully understood even by persons participating in the industry. This characteristic severely limits the possibilities for public under-

9

standing of industry problems and creates a major obstacle to effective regulation. In the case of merchant shipping, there is not even an accepted terminology for describing the industry's operations and the statistics which are available, though copious, can be misleading.

Types of Ships and Services. Ocean-going merchant ships are commonly divided into five broad classes: passenger liners (accommodating 200 or more travelers), combination freight and passenger ships (carrying 13 to 199 passengers), general cargo freighters, dry bulk carriers, and tankers. These classifications, however, are both imprecise and over-lapping. Thus, tankers can be used to move dry bulk cargoes; bulk carriers often are referred to as tramps (though "tramp" properly describes not a ship, but a service); and many ships are equipped to carry both bulk and packaged cargoes. A gauge of the composition of the world's merchant fleets can be gained from Table 1.

TABLE 1.   *Merchant Fleets of the World, 1965*
(Number of ocean-going ships, 1,000 gross tons or over)

Registry	Total	Passenger and Combination	General Dry Cargo	Dry Bulk	Tankers
Total, all registries	18,096	1,094	11,606	1,873	3,523
U.S., privately owned	954	31	585	59	279
U.S., government reserve and other	1,495	207	1,215	1	72
Foreign registries	15,647	856	9,806	1,813	3,172

Source: U.S. Maritime Administration, Office of Statistics, "Merchant Fleets of the World," June 30, 1965.

The dominance of dry cargo shipping both in U.S. and foreign registries is immediately evident. Dry cargo ships offer three types of services —liner (or berth), tramp (or irregular), and industrial. The most important service, both in numbers of ships employed and revenues earned, is the liner. Ships offering liner services operate as common carriers on a regular schedule between specified ports. In contrast those offering tramp services are available for hire as a whole, by time or voyage charter, to load such cargo and carry it between such ports as the charterer may require. Carriers providing industrial services are engaged primarily in movements of proprietary cargoes, often on a regularly scheduled basis and sometimes with nonproprietary goods providing cargoes for the backhaul.

In actual fact the distinctions between tramp, liner, and industrial services are not well defined. Liner schedules are frequently violated, itineraries may be adjusted on short notice to meet the trade, and cargoes may be carefully selected. The public obligations of an ocean liner have not been nearly as completely spelled out as those of common carriers in certificated domestic transportation.[1] Furthermore, some liner companies also engage in trading operations, carrying purchased cargoes for their own account, or shift their ships to tramping when the liner trade is light.

The tramp is a contract carrier. Charter contracts (or "fixtures") are arranged through ship brokers or on the Baltic Shipping Exchange, a London auction market which operates very much like a commodity or security exchange. From time to time there have been attempts to stabilize the tramp market by withdrawing tonnage during shipping depressions or releasing ships from reserve to check inflation when shipping is short. But because supply and demand are so difficult to control on a worldwide basis, these schemes have met only limited success. At least since World War II, the tramp business has been marked by sharp oscillations in rates and profits.[2]

Industrials are private or captive carriers. The ships in this category are for the most part dry bulk carriers and tankers, although ships owned by Alcoa, United Fruit, and Bethlehem Steel have also offered limited

---

[1] Common carriers are legally defined as "carriers that hold themselves out or undertake to carry persons or goods of all persons indifferently, or of all who choose to employ it" (*Merchants Parcel Delivery* v. *Pa. Public Utility Commissions*, 150 Pa. Super. 120, cited in *Black's Law Dictionary* [St. Paul: West Publishing Co., 1951], p. 229); they are subject to certain privileges and obligations under the common law. The public obligations of steamship lines are defined in the Shipping Act of 1916, as amended, whose terms are applicable only to "common carriers in domestic and international ocean transportation." The act contains several clauses specifically prohibiting carriers from discriminating among shippers, which have generated a moderate volume of litigation dealing chiefly with handling of perishable goods and with shipping contracts providing discounts to large volume shippers or in reward for exclusive patronage. Generally it has not been sufficient in these cases to show the carrier has failed to provide a satisfactory service. Rather it must be demonstrated that it has discriminated unfairly between shippers.

[2] Between World Wars I and II tramp rates were steady except during the 1926 British coal strike. During these years a large number of privately owned ships in lay-up could be quickly and cheaply commissioned to take advantage of any significant upturn in demand. Since World War II the number of privately owned ships in lay-up has been smaller. While tonnage can be broken out of the U.S. reserve fleet, the government has been reluctant to act rapidly to brake charter prices, which more than doubled during both the Korean and Suez crises.

general liner service. The industrial concerns may own their ships out-right, control them through a ship operating subsidiary, or engage ton-nage on long-term charter. Oil companies typically use a mix of these arrangements plus voyage charters so that they will be able to adjust to changing needs quickly and at minimum expense.

Shipping Rates and Customer Services. The premise of most rate-mak-ing in the ocean freight industry is "to charge what the traffic will bear."[3] This depends upon the value of the commodity to be shipped, the rela-tive importance of transportation costs to sales price, the urgency of the shipment, the competition on the route, and the relationship between carrier and shipper. However, shipment costs are also a factor, particu-larly when handling the cargo creates identifiable expenses (e.g., cargoes creating stowage problems, requiring special cargo handling equipment, or designated for pickup or delivery at a nonscheduled port). Rates also may be influenced by political and public relations considerations, even where there is no formal regulatory scheme.

In tramping the most important determinant of rates is the overall level of demand for ships. Most tramp cargoes are low value commodities which can be cheaply stored and moved at the convenience of the ship-per. Because transportation frequently accounts for 30-60 percent of the delivered cost of the product, bidding is highly price competitive. Few, if any, continuing ties exist between shippers and shipowners providing tramp services.

Liner cargoes, in contrast, run heavily to high value, "break-bulk" goods.[4] Rapid, reliable services are important both to keep inventory expenses down and to meet delivery commitments to foreign customers. Shipment costs are only a small portion of the cargoes' delivered value (13 percent in 1960) and competition tends less to price than service. Liner rates include costs of cargo handling and are usually computed on the basis of "revenue tons," which permits the carrier to charge by either weight or volume, whichever is greater.

---

[3] *The Ocean Freight Industry*, H. Rept. 1419, 87 Cong. 2 sess., pp. 122 ff., con-tains descriptions by various industry officials of the manner in which rates are established in liner trades. An analytic study of steamship rate-making has been published by W. L. Grossman, *Ocean Freight Rates* (Cambridge, Maryland: Cornell Maritime Press, 1956).

[4] About 25 percent of cargo tonnage moved by liners in U.S. foreign commerce is classified by the Maritime Administration as bulk—i.e., cargo which is loaded without mark, line, or count. However, these bulk cargoes make only a minor con-tribution to the overall revenue of the lines.

A critical problem of liner operators is retaining the loyalty of their customers. This may be accomplished by minimizing cargo loss and damage, giving fair and speedy service on claims, offering fast and reliable schedules, and performing special favors and services to the client and his family. A few lines have built their fortunes on allowing a standard price discount below their competitors. This practice has been countered by "dual rate" contracts, which offer shippers who agree to route their entire business via the contracting conference or line a substantial discount from published tariffs. In 1961 dual rate contracts were brought under government regulation and the discount limited to a maximum of 15 percent.

Indirect price competition also appears to be widely practiced in the ocean freight industry through special "contract" rates, rebates, and various under-the-table arrangements. These practices have also been discouraged by the U.S. government, which has feared that they will be used to discriminate against small shippers, ports, and carriers. However, no reliable means have been found to bring this form of competition under government control.

Steamship Conferences. The associations through which shipping lines conduct their rate-making activities are called conferences. These associations developed during the latter part of the nineteenth century, as owners of expensive and capacious new steamships faced the necessity of protecting themselves against raids on their customers if they were to maintain any kind of regular schedule. The system spread rapidly, and by the turn of the century, conferences had been established in most of the world's major trade routes. Currently there are roughly one hundred active conferences operating in U.S. foreign trade alone. They handle the major portion of the liner business on all major U.S. foreign trade routes.

The membership of conferences serving U.S. ports ranges from two to sixty firms. In almost every case the conference embraces both national and foreign flags. As a result there is a substantial identity of interest and similarity in the services offered by the principal lines of all flags.

Conferences are basically rate-making bodies. Rate schedules are developed and adjusted through a continuous process of collective bargaining between carrier and shipper associations and among factions within each group. In addition to establishing rates the conferences usually handle complaints and monitor the business practices in the trade. Frequently conferences coordinate services and sailing schedules offered by their member lines. Ordinarily, however, steamship conferences do not undertake to apportion profits, revenues, customers, or cargoes among their members.[5] They are not organized on an industry-wide basis, but separately in each trade. A large company operating worldwide may be a member of several dozen conferences. Separate conferences, each headquartered at the major terminus of the trade, handle inbound and outbound traffic on a single route; little is known about the extent to which they coordinate their affairs with one another and with other conferences which might be potentially competitive.

The conference, therefore, is an imperfect cartel. Unless it can be organized over a broad trading area or make suitable arrangements with other conferences, it faces competition from lines able to serve its customers through different routing. Even if tie-ups can be arranged to reduce this threat, the conference must take care that its rates do not price exports out of their markets and thereby kill the trade. Each conference also is permanently threatened by the possibility that nonmember vessels—both liners and tramps—might enter its trade, or that one of its own members might defect to capitalize on the profit opportunities inherent in an inflated rate structure or dissatisfied clientele. Conferences serving U.S. trades have been prohibited by statute from barring new applicants from membership on "fair and equal terms."[6]

Conferences have been the focus of a great deal of comment and controversy over the years. It is generally acknowledged that conferences have caused rates to be stabilized at a level higher than would otherwise prevail and that they permit the lines collectively to discriminate in the charges made for different categories of cargo. Supporters of strong conference organization argue that the overall level of rates at best is only marginally adequate to finance replacement of equipment and improvement of services; that the stability of ocean freight rates is more important to export-import business than their amount; and that only a stable, self-regulated conference system can protect ocean commerce against unfair discrimination between ports and shippers. The system's supporters further contend that any weakening of the confer-

---

[5] The content of typical conference agreements is reported in Daniel Marx, *International Shipping Cartels* (Princeton University Press, 1953), pp. 141 ff., and in H. Rept. 1419, Chap. 4. Some conference agreements are supplemented by subsidiary agreements among all or a portion of the members to pool revenues or cargoes or to cooperate in some other respect within the general framework of the conference agreement. See note 9 *infra*.

[6] Provisions to guarantee freedom of entry and resignation from conferences have long been required by the government as a condition to its approval of conference agreements. This requirement was enacted into law in 1961 (P.L. 87-346, sec. 2 [75 Stat. 764]).

ence system will lead to violently oscillating tariffs, which over a period of time would prove more costly to shippers than the present system.

Critics of the conference argue that rate stability is overvalued (commodities whose transportation accounts for the highest percentage of delivered cost typically move by tramp); that the rates are arbitrary and often maintained despite opportunities to expand trade by rate reduction; that uniformity of rates is illusory; that rate increases are sometimes effected without adequate notice; and that monopoly power inevitably leads to abuse. Economists have concluded that the conference system tends to increase shipping costs, as well as rates, by making it possible for high cost operators to continue in business (cost disparities of ship lines, all participating profitably in a single trade, sometimes run as high as two to one) and by retarding the transfer of ships between trades in response to shifts in demand. Finally, there has long been concern in the United States that the preponderantly foreign membership of most conferences operating in U.S. foreign trade may result in systematic discrimination against U.S. exports. However, this is very difficult to prove because of the extreme complexity of tariff and freight classifications, the unwillingness of many conferences carrying goods inbound in U.S. foreign trade to provide rate reports, and the complete absence of data on the rates and practices of conferences which deliver European goods competitive with U.S. exports to African, Asian, and South American ports.

The economics of shipping, and particularly the conference system, have been the subject of a number of exceptionally thorough official and unofficial studies.[7] Each of these investigations has concluded that whereas there are risks that the conferences may abuse their economic power, stability in the industry necessitates some form of cooperation among the lines. U.S. policy consequently has been to exempt shipping conferences from the antitrust provisions of the Sherman Act if the

---

[7] The investigations sponsored by the U.S. government have been: (1) the Alexander investigation, 1913-14, reported in *Steamship Agreements and Affiliations in the American Foreign and Domestic Trade,* Hearings before the House Merchant Marine and Fisheries Committee, Vol. 4, 63 Cong. 1 sess.; (2) the Celler investigation, 1959-62, reported in H. Rept. 1419; (3) Congressman Bonner's *Steamship Conference Study,* Hearings before the House Merchant Marine and Fisheries Committee, 86 Cong. 1 sess. (1959); (4) Senator Douglas' investigation of the impact of the conference system on U.S. foreign trade, reported by Joint Economic Committee, *Ocean Freight Rates and the Balance of Payments,* S. Rept. 1, 89 Cong. 1 sess. (1965); and (5) the Federal Maritime Commission's Fact Finding Investigation No. 6, initiated in 1964 and still in progress the following year. Similar studies have been made by the Canadians, British, Australians, the Organizaton of American States, and the United Nations Educational, Scientific, and Cultural Organization.

conference agreements are not specifically found to be detrimental to U.S. foreign commerce and the conferences submit to minimum public controls.

Regulation of International Shipping

The United States is the only nation in the world which has attempted unilaterally to enforce a comprehensive regulatory scheme over shipping serving its trade. Despite this nation's enormous economic power, this effort has enjoyed only limited success. In fact, for many years the statutory program was virtually inoperative. In 1961 the regulatory statute was substantially revised and a new organization, the Federal Maritime Commission, created to enforce it. Experience since this date has demonstrated that vigorous administration can yield tangible results, but that the potential for effective regulation remains severely limited by the international character of the shipping industry.

Obstacles to Regulation. The basic difficulty in regulating shipping is accommodating the divergent interests of U.S. and foreign shippers and carriers. Obviously, if the industry is to be regulated at all, there must be some way of resolving intergovernmental conflicts. This has been achieved in such areas as air carrier operations, radio communication, postal services, marketing of certain raw materials, and patent protection, in which relatively effective public regulation has been established. Some international regulation has also been accomplished in ocean shipping, particularly in matters relating to safety and the law of the sea; economic regulation, however, has been stoutly resisted.

There are several factors which have impeded the development of means for bridging divergent national interests in ocean shipping. First and most important, shipping interests enjoy a powerful position in the governments of all major maritime nations and are unalterably opposed to any regulation which might limit profits or inhibit their traditional freedoms.

Second, regulation of shipping rates and practices is made particularly difficult by the extreme complexity of the industry's operations. Even though liners operate over relatively fixed itineraries, there is an almost infinite combination of ports they might serve. Cargoes are classified differently by different carriers. A single conference may maintain several thousand separate commodity rates, each of which is subject to a variety of "arbitraries" and surcharges to compensate for extra handling costs, ports of loading and destination, and so forth. Simply keeping track of ocean freight rates is burdensome; to evaluate such a plethora of tariffs would probably be impossible. Furthermore, to impose centralized controls over rates and routing would almost surely decrease the efficiency of the industry's operations significantly.

Third, in order to be effective, shipping regulation has to be completely comprehensive. The ease with which ships can be transferred from flag to flag and control of shipments shifted from buyer to seller necessitates that all maritime nations subscribe to the program. If any significant portion of the shipping industry were permitted to take shelter under exempted registries or if shipments could be arranged outside the program's jurisdiction, international regulation would almost surely break down.

Fourth, effective enforcement, and hence the success of regulation, requires that participating states not only subscribe to the program but actively enforce it within their boundaries. Active cooperation of the participating states is necessary to gain access to costs and documents, and to serve legal processes in order to assure compliance with the law.

Finally, there appear to be irresolvable contradictions for a nation wishing both to maintain a national flag merchant fleet and to regulate ocean freight rates and services in its export trade. Unless a truly comprehensive regulatory scheme is achieved, governmental restraints will tend to fall more heavily on national flag ships than on their foreign competitors. A very real practical difficulty is also encountered in arranging for representatives at international conferences who have the confidence of both the shipping and shipper sectors of the national economy.

Indirect Regulatory Techniques. The many obstacles to regulating international shipping have not caused governments to abandon their efforts to assure adequate and reasonably priced transportation services for their import-export trade. Obstacles to direct, unilateral regulation have forced experimentation with a variety of indirect approaches to achieve national objectives.

One of the most common approaches has been placement of government contracts for specific "national interest" services. These contracts can at least in theory be distinguished from promotional subsidies designed to nourish national merchant marines, but because contracts are usually placed with national flag lines, their commercial and promotional objectives become intertwined. However, there are instances of governments and quasi-governmental shipper associations contracting with foreign flag lines to assure that specified shipping services, sometimes at specified rates, will be available to carry the nation's foreign trade.[8]

A second technique for controlling freight rates and services is through a bilateral trade agreement which restricts shipments of the covered commodities to the ships of the trading partners. During the past decade a significant number of such intergovernmental agreements has been concluded. In other cases shipping "pools" made up exclusively of lines representing the two trading nations have been privately negotiated.[9]

Efforts have also been made to establish multilateral regulation of ocean shipping. Following World War II a comprehensive code of fair competition in ocean shipping was developed as an annex to the convention to establish an International Trade Organization, which failed to win approval. A more modest statement was included in the charter of the Inter-Governmental Maritime Consultative Organization (IMCO), which was organized in 1948 as an advisory group to the United Nations. The functions of IMCO are to encourage removal of discriminatory and unnecessary governmental restrictions on ship operations, provide a forum for international consideration of unfair practices of shipping concerns, provide machinery for intergovernmental cooperation in technical matters of all kinds, and encourage adoption of the highest practical standards in matters concerning maritime safety and efficiency of navigation. The balanced representation of shipping and shipper interests built into IMCO's charter has, however, limited its ability to tackle and solve the industry's really important economic problems.[10]

Recently the maritime nations of Western Europe have shown in-

[8] For examples see Marx, *op. cit.*, pp. 90-104.

[9] The term "pool" refers to an agreement between two or more lines to cooperate through joint use of facilities, complementary scheduling, sharing or apportionment of cargoes, or, in most cases, a pooling and apportionment of revenues or profits. The incentive for pooling has usually been to protect the business position of the participating lines. These pools may contravene free trade principles and impose serious economic penalties by restricting competition and forcing shipping services into a rigid mold. However, they are a vehicle through which regulation might be indirectly effected.

[10] The annual report of IMCO for 1962 reports such activities as studies of means to facilitate trade and travel through document simplification, studies of methods of tonnage measurement, work on a draft convention to control oil pollution of the seas, and so forth. One of the reactions to IMCO impotence in critical economic matters has been organization of the Maritime Trades Committee of the Organization

terest in multilateral mechanisms to enforce at least a minimum code of fair practice in shipping, and officials of U.S. shipping agencies have reported occasional informal overtures. However, apprehension that negotiation of such an agreement would only exacerbate issues which could not be resolved has prevented any formal international conferences on economic matters from taking place.

United States Unilateral Regulation. European willingness to discuss possible international regulatory mechanisms appears in part to be a product of their distaste for unilateral U.S. regulation. The U.S. program applies only to liner operations and is only a very mild version of the rate and service regulation applied to common carriers in domestic trade. Nonetheless, foreign antipathy has been so severe that in 1963 five foreign governments ordered firms operating ships under their flags not to cooperate with U.S. authorities, even in response to formal subpoenas. The following year the British government, in response to a U.S. court order which exposed noncooperating lines to $100 per day penalties, applied the same fine to any of its nationals which complied with the regulatory order. By 1965 a few beginning steps had been taken toward compromising these differences, but the future of certain key elements of the U.S. regulatory program remained clouded.

The difficulties in implementing the U.S. regulatory program have centered largely on government powers to review shipping rates and rate contracts. Ever since the enactment of the first regulatory statute in 1916, U.S. shipping administrators have asserted a right to receive and review reports of rates charged pursuant to approved conference agreements in order to ascertain that they were not detrimental to U.S. foreign commerce.[11] However, until 1961 the government made no at-

---

for Economic Cooperation and Development. This quasi-governmental group is strongly shipowner oriented, since its membership consists entirely of strong shipping nations including the United States.

[11] Section 15 of the Shipping Act of 1916 (39 Stat. 733) required all conference, pooling, and related agreements to be submitted to the U.S. Shipping Board and provided that the board might "disapprove, cancel, or modify any agreement . . . which it finds to be unjustly discriminatory or unfair as between carriers, shippers, exporters, importers, or ports, or between exporters from the United States and their foreign competitors, or to operate to the detriment of the foreign commerce of the United States." General orders were issued by the board under this authority to require reporting of all conference rates by outbound conferences; some inbound conferences also reported voluntarily or pursuant to specific terms of their conference agreement. However, there was no enforcement program, no practical penalty which

tempt to challenge any generally applicable conference rate or even to obtain a complete reporting of amounts charged.[12]

The revisions to the 1916 act, enacted in 1961 as Public Law 87-346, strengthened the earlier law in several important respects. For example, the new law specifies the terms and conditions which must be met in any dual rate contract offered by a conference or independent carrier to secure its trade.[13] Each conference is also required to establish "reasonable procedures for promptly and fairly hearing and considering shippers' requests and complaints."[14] This requirement has been amplified by regulation to require that action on complaints be reported to the Maritime Commission for its review.[15] Another significant innovation is a requirement that all common carriers by water in U.S. foreign commerce file, publish, and observe a schedule of tariffs which may not be

---

could be applied to non-complying associations, no reporting at all by independent lines, and no organized data processing system permitting rate analysis.

[12] The formally docketed activity of the Shipping Board and its successor agencies has been summarized by Warner W. Gardner in "Steamship Conferences and the Shipping Act, 1916," *Tulane Law Review*, Vol. 35 (Dec. 1960), p. 135. Gardner reports that 127 proceedings dealing with rates and practices of carriers engaged in foreign commerce were docketed between 1916 and 1960; of these only half resulted in any kind of regulatory order, including four reparations orders and six referrals to the Department of Justice for criminal prosecution. Perhaps because of inadequacies in the record transmitted or perhaps because of the difficulties inherent in these types of cases, none of the referrals were ever actually prosecuted by Justice.

[13] The 1916 act had prohibited use of discriminatory contracts and deferred rebates. Dual rate contracts, which impose penalties on shippers who violate the contract terms, had frequently been alleged to be designed to accomplish the same purpose as deferred rebating and to be discriminatory. It was a 1958 Supreme Court decision invalidating the dual rate contract used by the Japan—Gulf and Atlantic Conference which precipitated the hearings and investigations which led to enactment of the 1961 statute (see Chapter 7). The statute's concentration on the dual rate issue was in part a consequence of this circumstance, in part a result of a realization that the allowable terms of shipping contracts were a key element in the competition between conference and independent carriers, which in turn provided perhaps the most effective check against discriminatory or excessive conference rates.

[14] Use of so-called "neutral bodies" was urged by the steamship conferences as the only practical method of policing steamship rates and practices. These arbitration bodies are supported by and responsible to the conferences but are intended to exercise completely independent judgment. Properly constituted, they should be analogous to international admiralty claims courts. However, it is most unlikely that they will ever attempt systematically to review steamship rates or even to influence the conferences to adopt rate-making and accounting procedures needed to permit individual charges to be examined in relation to objective criteria.

[15] 28 *Federal Register* 9257. The rule asserts the commission's power to review cases heard before neutral bodies at its own initiative or on appeal from one of the parties.

increased on less than 30 days notice.[16] Finally, the new statute also provides that:

> The Commission shall disapprove any rate or charge filed by a common carrier by water in the foreign commerce of the United States or by a conference of carriers, which, after hearings, it finds to be so unreasonably high or low as to be detrimental to the foreign commerce of the United States.[17]

Interpretation of the commission's powers and responsibilities under this subsection has proved particularly troublesome. The statutory language implies comprehensive U.S. government supervision of international shipping rates. However, Senator Kefauver, who sponsored the subsection quoted above, acknowledged that "no one could seriously advocate international rate control by the Commission" and explained that his amendment merely codified the maritime agencies' long-standing implied power to review conference rates.[18] Senator Engle, speaking for the Senate Commerce Committee, accepted Kefauver's proposal subject to the understanding that it was intended only as a check on rates which were "irrationally" out of line.[19]

How the language will actually be interpreted by the Federal Maritime Commission and the courts is not yet known. During its first two years of operation (1961-63), the regulatory commission made no attempt to investigate or disapprove rates. However, in May 1963 this passive policy was attacked by Senator Paul H. Douglas in a formal statement in which he charged the commission with "gross negligence . . . in their duty to protect American industry and the public interest."[20] Douglas' denunciation was keyed to the effect which disparities between inbound and outbound rates might be supposed to have on the competitiveness of U.S. exports and hence on the nation's balance of payments, a matter which was currently of grave concern to the Administration.

A presidential message in July 1963 pledged that the Administration would take action to overcome rates detrimental to U.S. foreign com-

---

[16] Prior to 1961 reports filed consisted simply of rates actually charged; the only obligation on the carrier was to carry all similarly classified shipments loaded on board the same ship at the same rate. The tariff provisions of the 1961 act therefore constitute a major innovation which has not been resisted by the lines.

[17] P.L. 87-346, sec. 4 (75 Stat. 764).

[18] *Index to the Legislative History of P.L. 87-346*, S. Doc. 100, 87 Cong. 2 sess. (1962), p. 427. Actually the language, which applies to independent lines as well as conferences, goes beyond powers asserted under the 1916 act. *Cf.* note 11 above.

[19] *Ibid.*, p. 456.

[20] *Congressional Record*, Vol. 109, No. 69 (May 9, 1963), p. 7743.

merce.[21] This pledge was followed by appointment of a new chairman, new executive director, and a solicitor to the Federal Maritime Commission, and by institution of several major rate investigations which in 1965 were still being processed by the commission.[22] However, the cases had proceeded far enough to reveal that the commission's capacity for influencing conference rate structures depends more on diplomacy than adjudicatory findings.

National Interests in National Flag Fleets

The difficulty for even the most powerful nations of influencing the rates and practices of foreign flag shipping lines is the most common incentive to government support of national flag fleets. A second incentive to government promotional programs, which has been particularly important for the United States, is to assure that ships will be available to meet civil and military needs in time of war. Finally, for some nations, merchant shipping provides an important complement to domestic industry, providing employment, taxable income, and a means for earning foreign exchange.

Merchant Shipping's Commercial Role. National flag shipping can be treated as an extension of national sovereignty to the seas. Ships have

[21] President John F. Kennedy, *Special Message on Balance of Payments*, July 18, 1963.

[22] The Federal Maritime Commission has instituted a number of actions to explore and test its new rate-review responsibilities. It is sponsoring a general, non-adjudicatory, fact-finding proceeding into conference rate-making practices and their impact on U.S. foreign commerce (Docket 1111); an investigation of conference rates on iron and steel products (Docket 1114, initiated by the commission at the urging of the congressional Joint Economic Committee; an examiner's report has found no violation of the 1916 act); a number of more specific investigations of conditions in certain trades (Dockets 1098, 1155, 1157, 1171, 1176, and others, most of which have been at the application of injured parties and which have in some instances concluded that the conference rates were in violation of the act); and an expanding program of non-adjudicatory statistical and economic analyses.

For all of these activities, availability of reliable basic data on foreign shipping operations is needed. Orders to foreign flag lines and conferences have been resisted but sustained in U.S. courts. In December 1964 an agreement was reached between fourteen European governments, the United States, and Japan to exchange data pertaining to operations on forty-eight trade routes. The data included: total conference revenues, overall number of revenue tons handled by conference carriers, tonnage of the ten largest revenue-producing commodities and revenues derived from these shipments, and tonnage and revenues on ten additional designated cargoes believed important to the trade. The data were made available confidentially subject to an understanding that they would not be used by the United States in litigation until there had been appropriate consultation with affected governments.

been used since antiquity as an instrument for commercial penetration. Merchant shipping backed up by naval power (both to protect the commercial fleet and to enforce its patronage) provided the basis for the power and wealth of Phoenicia, Venice, Holland, Spain, and England. As recently as 1914 President Wilson reported to the Congress that so long as the United States depended on British and other foreign ships for transport of its foreign trade, "our merchants are at their mercy, to do with as they please"; Wilson argued that this condition compromised the nation's freedom of action, and that without a national flag merchant fleet our independence existed "only on land and within our borders."[23]

In the years since World War I the growth in world trade and in the number of flags and fleets available to serve it has diminished the danger that any nation or group might develop sufficient power to use merchant shipping as an instrument for commercial exploitation. Many nations believe, however, that a national flag fleet is necessary to protect their commerce from more subtle forms of discrimination; others give this objective low priority. For example, Russia has embarked on an ambitious program of fleet expansion to provide enough ships to carry 75 percent of her trade; on the other hand, both Communist China and Cuba (a nation dependent on oceanborne freight for its existence) have been content to rely on charters of foreign flag ships.

Within the United States, opinions vary on the importance of national flag ships to the nation's foreign commerce. At one extreme, a study conducted under steamship auspices at the Northwestern University Transportation Center came to the "gloomy conclusion . . . that there appears to be little net economic contribution to the United States by the subsidized liner firms or deriving from the subsidy program."[24] At the other pole, the U.S. Chamber of Commerce has taken the position that "an American flag merchant marine is absolutely essential to the maintenance and development of our foreign commerce."[25]

The government's maritime agencies usually have taken an intermediate position. The U.S. Maritime Commission's 1937 *Economic Survey of the American Merchant Marine*, for example, concluded that "an American merchant marine is of material value in development of our

[23] Woodrow Wilson, "Message to the Congress," cited by P. M. Zeis, *American Shipping Policy* (Princeton University Press, 1938), p. 81.

[24] Allen Ferguson *et al., The Economic Value of the U.S. Merchant Marine* (The Transportation Center, Northwestern University, 1961), p. 470.

[25] *Merchant Marine Studies,* Hearing before the Senate Committee on Interstate and Foreign Commerce, 83 Cong. 1 sess. (1953).

foreign commerce," even though it reported that it had found no evidence either that foreign flag lines discriminated against U.S. exports or that U.S. lines per se protected American shippers against exhorbitant rates.[26] However, the *Survey* did find that the establishment of U.S. flag carriers following World War I had substantially improved the quality, convenience, and reliability of shipping services in U.S. foreign commerce, and that the American lines constituted an important assurance that service would be maintained regardless of events overseas.

National flag lines may also be used as a vehicle for representing national interest in conference negotiations or as listening posts for monitoring conference affairs. Opportunities may exist for national flag ships to provide leverage to improve conference rates and practices, although the practicality of this policy is highly controversial.[27] Subsidized shipping lines may be used to pioneer new routes and services in order to develop new overseas markets or sources of supply. Finally, ships held in reserve can be placed in operation during shipping shortages in order to brake runaway freight and charter rates.

Merchant Shipping's Military Role. A crucial characteristic of merchant shipping is the ease with which the industry's facilities can be converted for military use. Until outlawed by the 1856 Declaration of Paris, privateering was frequently practiced by shipowners as an adjunct to their normal business. Through World War I, merchantmen were commonly converted to use as naval vessels during periods of open conflict. In World War II only a few merchant ships were equipped to perform specific tactical missions but dry cargo, passenger, and tank ships all operated as essential components of the military transportation and supply systems.

The U.S. merchant fleet contributes to national defense in several ways. The role described in the preface to the Merchant Marine Act of 1936 is that of a "naval or military auxiliary." This terminology assumes

[26] Pp. 5-9.

[27] Proposals to use national flag ships for "trade leverage" by underwriting rates below those normal to the trade are superficially attractive but contain several dangers. Most important, the practice would invite retaliatory action by the injured parties and possibly precipitate a "subsidy war." Even if overt retaliation were avoided, it is likely that the disruption which such a policy would cause to the trade would result in the withdrawal of some privately owned shipping, which over the long term would increase upward pressure on rates. If foreign flags refused to meet the subsidized American rate, the result would be to give preferential terms to those shippers who could use government-supported vessels.

that its principal defense utility is as a supplement to ships and other facilities already operated by the military services and anticipates that during national emergencies, commercial facilities will be absorbed directly into military operations in either a combatant or logistics role.

During World War II, however, only 15 percent of the United States' huge 3,500 ship dry cargo fleet was placed in the custody of the armed services; only half of the outbound cargoes carried by the remaining 3,000 freighters assigned to the civilian War Shipping Administration were for direct troop support. Of the remainder 60 percent were Lend-Lease shipments of military and civilian goods to Britain and Russia and the balance (20 percent of the overall outbound total) "strategic trade" with non-aligned nations.[28] The necessity for continuing some level of international exchange of civilian goods even under the most severe conditions creates a second defense-related role for the U.S. flag merchant marine.

The third and perhaps most important contribution of the U.S. flag fleet to national defense is as a training and proving ground for maritime personnel and equipment. The active, commercial fleet provides the basic skills and organization for mobilization of additional ships drawn from mothballed reserves, from new construction, or by transfer from friendly foreign flags.

It is noteworthy that each of these three roles of the U.S. merchant marine is the concern of a separate government agency. Thus, the adequacy of the fleet to discharge its auxiliary role is of primary interest to the Department of Defense; its adequacy to meet civilian shipment requirements during national emergencies is the responsibility of the Department of Commerce; and its adequacy as a base for wartime mobilization is the responsibility of the Office of Emergency Planning in the Executive Office of the President.

[28] Data from War Shipping Administration, Division of Research, *Shipping Review* (Maritime Administration Library, mimeograph, 1944). The 1944 outbound tonnage is reported as follows: Army, 22.7 million tons; Navy, 6.6 million; Lend-Lease, 16.4 million; commercial and other, 11.8 million. The following commodity breakdown is given for inbound movements: sugar, 4.8 million tons; molasses, 2.0 million; coffee, 1.2 million; ores and metals (now stockpiled), 4.1 million; other, 6.5 million. Inbound dry cargo tonnage, which in 1944 amounted to only one-third outbound tonnage, served chiefly to support U.S. civilian consumption and secondarily to supply its heavy industry with raw materials. Loading of back-cargo frequently required diversion to other ports, sometimes at considerable loss of time, in addition to the time required for loading and discharge of the cargo. Therefore, the necessity to import perishable and strategic commodities during World War II placed an important drag on U.S. shipping resources.

Because commerce is the normal employment for merchant ships, the U.S. flag fleet's commercial roles have dominated the structure of the U.S. maritime program. However, at least since World War II the defense requirements for a national flag merchant marine have been widely believed to be far more compelling than the fleet's commercial justifications.

Other Economic and Political Roles. For some nations, ships are an important source of foreign exchange; for others, a major source of employment. For example, shipping services are Norway's largest export and account for one-third of that nation's entire foreign exchange earnings. The British industry provides seafaring employment for over 140,000 Englishmen. The Greek industry employs 60,000 Greek citizens and contributes importantly to that nation's foreign exchange. Revenues from tonnage taxes and registry fees meet 7 percent of Liberia's annual budget.

The U.S. merchant marine also fulfills an economic role by providing both jobs and foreign exchange earnings. However, as a general rule ship operations contribute to the national economy only if they are relatively efficient compared to other export industries. If relatively inefficient, as is the case of U.S. flag shipping, they burden the nation's economic resources. Nevertheless, in some instances (for example during periods of high unemployment or critical balance of payments deficits), even an uneconomic merchant marine may fill an economic role.

The U.S. flag fleet has also from time to time been vested with political or foreign policy roles. For example, during the 1930's President Franklin D. Roosevelt directed the establishment of a Good Neighbor Line to link the United States and South America more closely. More recently the government has indicated its interest in having U.S. flag services operated to uncommitted nations, particularly in order that U.S. foreign aid can be delivered in U.S. bottoms. According to one source the government has even used a shipping firm as a "cover" for intelligence activities.[29]

Finally, national flag ships have a representational role. In international politics some value has always been placed on "showing the flag." Many public officials have felt strongly that national prestige required that the United States, as the world's greatest industrial power, be creditably represented among the world's merchant fleets. President Franklin D. Roosevelt, for example, conceived competition between merchant fleets to achieve the fastest, most modern, and efficient facilities

[29] Daniel Wise and Tom Ross, *The Invisible Government* (Random House, 1964), p. 330.

to be "a manifestation of wholly desirable and wholesome national ambition."[30] Mr. Roosevelt continued:

> In such free competition the American people want us to be properly represented. . . . Their Government owes it to them to make certain that [American] ships are in keeping with our national pride and our national needs.[31]

Promotion of National Flag Fleets

The various ways in which a national flag fleet can support national interests have led many nations to assume an important role in merchant fleet operations. Governments watch over their trading fleets, foster them, protect them, subsidize them, assist them in obtaining cargoes, and in some instances directly administer their affairs. Any government that wishes to maintain its national flag fleet has little choice but to adopt these practices. As a result the international shipping business, although conducted as a commercial enterprise, has many of the marks of a political contest.

More than half of the world's merchant fleets—though a much smaller percentage of gross tonnage—is either wholly or partially government-owned.[32] These fleets are operated as commercial enterprises through public or mixed public-private corporations. In some cases their operations are practically indistinguishable from wholly private enterprises. In other cases there is a direct application of national resources and national power to maintain and employ the government-owned merchant fleet as an instrument of national policy.

Most of the remainder of the world's shipping is aided by some form of direct or indirect subsidy. Substantial direct assistance is given by

[30] *Message from the President of the United States,* H. Doc. 118, 74 Cong. 1 sess. (1935), p. 31. It was in this message that President Roosevelt proposed the legislation later enacted as the Merchant Marine Act, 1936.

[31] *Ibid.*

[32] In addition to eleven communist countries, there are eight South and Central American states and several Afro-Asian countries which have nationalized their merchant fleets. Mixed ownership is common in Europe. Of the eighteen merchant fleets with more than 1 million gross tons registered shipping, three—the U.S.S.R., Argentina, and Brazil—are completely under government control. Four others—France, Italy, India, and Spain—are partially government-owned. In view of the size of its Military Sea Transport Service and reserve fleet, the United States might also be considered among the major maritime nations which have a partially government-owned merchant marine. (Data from files of the Office of Statistics, U.S. Maritime Administration.)

France and Italy. Other maritime nations, including even Britain and Japan, provide credit incentives for new ship construction, allow acceler-ated depreciation, grant special tax concessions, and support special contract or mail route services.[33] Prior to World War II, France, Italy, Britain, Germany, and Japan all granted subsidies to their national flag ships which, in relation to those nations' basic operating costs, approxi-mated amounts paid by the United States.[34] Since the war, foreign sub-sidies have been much less than U.S. payments but nonetheless signifi-cant.[35]

Despite the strenuous efforts of the great European maritime nations to preserve the "freedom of the seas," financial concessions to national flag operators are frequently supplemented by flag discrimination—i.e., the use of governmental power to reserve certain cargoes or a stipulated portion of the trade to national flag ships. Such practices are prevalent among the South American states and certain Asian countries trying to develop national flag merchant marines. Many persons believe that the European states and Japan also engage in a subtle and hence more dan-gerous form of favoritism toward national flag shipping. Interrelationships between producing, trade, financial, and shipping interests are typically more tightly knit than in the United States, where antitrust considerations and sheer size have limited the growth of an industrial establishment. In shipping circles, the great industrial and financial houses of Europe and Japan are still widely believed to exert a powerful, though hidden in-fluence over the development of the shipping industry.[36]

Reservation of coastal and colonial commerce is another way in which nations give preference to national flag ships. This reserved trade, if sub-stantial or far-ranging, can provide a springboard from which to extend

[33] The most complete and up-to-date data on foreign shipping aids has been com-piled by the Committee of American Steamship Lines, *Government Aids to Foreign Competitors* (Washington, D.C., multilith, 1964).

[34] Data from J. E. Saugstad, *American Ships and Foreign Trade,* S. Doc. 224, 74 Cong. 2 sess. (1936).

[35] The largest operating subsidies per ton appear to be granted by the Italians to their government-controlled Finmare lines. The total payment in 1961 was $38 million in support of about 300 passenger and cargo ships, or $100,000-$150,000 per ship. The average U.S. subsidy is calculated in Chapter 8 to be $2.3 million per pas-senger vessel and $300,000-$700,000 per freighter.

[36] European dominance in international shipping and trade has, of course, receded since World War II, so that these fears may be not only undocumented, but also unfounded. A dated, but still interesting, discussion of how informal influences have governed the development of world shipping was published under the auspices of the National Foreign Trade Council, Inc., by J. E. Otterson, *Foreign Trade and Shipping* (New York: McGraw Hill, 1945).

services into unrestricted markets as well as assure operation of at least a nucleus national flag fleet. During the first half of the nineteenth century these restrictions, called "cabotage," were the commonest means of promoting national flag operations. The United States' cabotage law, passed in 1817, still stands. Most of the European cabotage restrictions, on the other hand, have been repealed in order to facilitate operations and demonstrate dedication to the "freedom of the seas."

The United States offers what is probably the world's most substantial and comprehensive assistance to shipowners choosing its registry; it also imposes the severest and most costly restrictions. In order to qualify for U.S. registry, an applicant must be a U.S. citizen or a U.S. corporation controlled by U.S. citizens.[37] All officers and at least 75 percent of the crew must also be citizens. In order to qualify for most of the privileges of registry, the ship must also be U.S. built.

The so-called flags of convenience present the opposite extreme. Liberia, for example, will enroll any sea-going vessel for a modest registry fee (about $20,000 for a 40,000 deadweight-ton tanker) regardless of ownership, place of build, or intended area of operation. Panama requires at least part ownership by Panamanians but facilitates incorporation of foreign-owned firms. Lebanon, now the third-ranking convenience flag, requires only that the shipowner train or employ a partially Lebanese crew and list a Lebanese city as its *port d'attache*.

Practices followed by other nations on these matters are highly variable. Almost all require some citizen participation in the ownership or management of the ships carrying their flag. Some require that the captain, officers, or men, or some portion of any of these groups, also be citizens. Hardly any restrict registries to nationally built vessels, and even these restrictions are only partial.[38]

Nationalism Versus Internationalism in Shipping

Strong national interests tend to create strong rivalries between national flag fleets. These rivalries are fueled by the desire of each government to minimize the costs of its promotional program and of

[37] 46 U.S.C. 11. The maritime laws include several definitions of citizenship. The definition which applies for the purpose of most promotional legislation (Shipping Act, 1916, sec. 2 [39 Stat. 729]) also requires that controlling financial interest in the corporation be held by U.S. citizens and that control be firmly in U.S. citizens' hands.

[38] Registry rules have been summarized by B. A. Boczek, *Flags of Convenience: An International Legal Study* (Harvard University Press, 1962).

each subsidy recipient to demonstrate that the payment of aid yields tangible benefits to the nation's commerce. As a result each national flag fleet must respond both to the demands of domestic politics and to the pressures of international competition.

International shipping is exceedingly sensitive to the manner in which governments express their national interests and react to the actions of others. Attempts artificially to build up a national flag merchant fleet through subsidies or trade restrictions can easily lead to retaliatory restrictions against those whom they are designed to aid or to a reduction in trade.

The conference system, because it tends to mute conflicts between national flag carriers, helps to lessen the abrasion of international politics. It is quite possible for severe competitive struggles to develop within conferences. In numerous instances block voting by national flag lines has followed a national policy pattern. However, while each line and each national flag group is interested in enhancing its own profit and advancing its own national interests, it also has an important stake in maintaining the integrity of the conference, which may require that both individual and national interests be set aside in favor of the common good. Experience since World War II in fact suggests that when a choice must be made, conference carriers are more likely to identify their interests with the conference system than with the government which has registered their ships.

Sufficient checks and balances surround the conference system to yield at least some rough justice, with the result that the system has proved unusually durable. However, these checks and balances have not been able to eradicate all abuses nor to contain the resentment and suspicions, particularly of the smaller nations, that the system has been discriminatory and inimical to national interests. The result has been to pour fuel on national efforts to establish national merchant marines and on the United States' effort unilaterally to regulate shipping rates and practices in its foreign trade.

Promotion of a national flag fleet and regulation of ships of all flags serving its foreign commerce offer alternative techniques for advancing the nation's maritime interests. These two alternatives can be regarded as mutually reinforcing. For example, effective and even-handed enforcement of a rule of fair competition should both tend to remove the incentive for engaging in predatory tactics and facilitate the development of an American merchant marine. However, if the impact of regulation falls more heavily on U.S. than foreign flags, it will impede the development of the U.S. flag fleet. Conversely, too enthusiastic support for the national flag merchant marine can potentially undermine regulatory objectives.

From either point of view it is essential that national maritime policy harmonize promotional, diplomatic, and regulatory considerations. Balancing off these competing objectives poses a continuing challenge for public policy-makers and administrators. The industry plainly must operate in an environment which is in large measure beyond its control. The unique and complex nature of that environment has had a crucial impact on the political process and on the development of public policy in support of a national flag merchant marine.

2

Development of Maritime Policy

UNITED STATES MARITIME programs are the product of a long period of evolution, punctuated by wars and economic depression. The objectives of the government's promotional and regulatory activities were identified more than fifty years ago and have been shaped, adapted, and sometimes obscured by the passing needs and politics of almost three generations. Each of the programs organized to meet these needs has been built upon the institutions and experience of its predecessors. Only on a few occasions, such as the enactment of the 1916, 1920, and 1936 Merchant Marine Acts, has there been even an attempt to set the program on a new course. The statements of purpose contained in these statutes remain, with minor modifications, the official basis for the government's contemporary maritime activities.

Historical Setting

In the post-revolutionary history of the United States, three stages of economic development may be identified. Each had a demonstrable impact upon U.S. flag shipping. During the first phase of national development, from the Revolution to the Civil War, the wealth of the United States lay in its shipping and commerce. Americans were a seafaring people, whose courage and enterprise were reinforced by natural economic advantages. Aided by a sympathetic national administration, American shipping grew and prospered. In 1855 American yards delivered over 2,000 new ships, and the U.S. flag fleet, although only half the size of Great Britain's, seriously threatened Britain's traditional supremacy at sea. This period of maritime greatness is the source of many Americans' affection and nostalgia for the sea.

The Civil War proved to be the turning point for the U.S. merchant marine. Large numbers of ships were transferred to British flag to avoid the Confederate raiders. Others were sunk. By the end of the war the U.S. foreign trade fleet had fallen from 2.5 million to 1.5 million gross tons.

The second phase of U.S. economic development, following the war, was directed principally to opening the nation's western frontier and expanding its domestic manufacturing capacity. Capital investment shifted to railroads with little new investment being made in overseas shipping. Consequently, America's maritime technology fell further and further behind the propeller-driven British steamships. One serious attempt was made to overcome this handicap through subsidy. The collapse of this promotional program in scandal created a profound distrust for any kind of direct government involvement in the shipping business.

By the end of the nineteenth century, the great tasks of internal development were largely accomplished and America entered a third phase of her national development—an era of wealth and economic power based upon a balanced and nearly self-sufficient economy. In 1896 the United States for the first time in many years achieved a favorable balance in trade, a condition which has persisted for more than half a century. The nation had attained a position which allowed discretion in the disposition of its resources. If the United States wished empire, wished trade, or wished a merchant marine, it appeared now to be within her power.

Revival of U.S. Maritime Interests. Beginning in the late 1890's, the United States, suddenly awakening to its "manifest destiny," began to look to the unexploited territories of Central and South America and the Far East for new markets for its rapidly expanding industrial plant. Three events of this period—the Spanish American War, the Boer War, and the 1908 cruise of President Theodore Roosevelt's Great White Fleet—gave dramatic stimulus to the adoption of a promotional policy for an American merchant marine.

The Spanish-American War was the first test of U.S. naval strength in foreign waters since the War of 1812. The U.S. Navy, particularly its detachments in the Philippines and those maintaining the blockade of Cuba, was seriously embarrassed by the lack of colliers, scouts, and supply vessels. To accomplish its mission, the Navy was forced to purchase and charter foreign vessels.[1] It is said that the victory of Manila

---

[1] To prepare for the Santiago expedition, the Army and Navy chartered every American vessel which could be obtained in Atlantic ports but were successful in securing only 36 ships totaling 90,000 tons. This and other difficulties are recounted

Bay would have been lost had Admiral Dewey not been able at the critical moment to obtain a British collier.[2]

The following year the Boers revolted, engaging Britain in its first major war since the Crimea. In order to supply this action, the British withdrew a large number of merchant ships from the North Atlantic trade. The impact on freight rates and services was so severe that a congressional commission later claimed that American exporters had "paid for the Boer War."[3]

Deficiencies in America's merchant marine were underscored again during the cruise of the Great White Fleet. After the fleet was assembled, it developed that the necessary auxiliary ships could not be obtained from the American merchant marine. As a result, this grand demonstration of American power was attended by a motley array of colliers, tankers, and tenders bearing the flags of the world.[4]

These experiences provided hard, tangible evidence that the country had better look to its merchant marine if it were serious about fulfilling its manifest destiny as a great world power. They occurred, furthermore, at a time when American businessmen were feeling the pinch of inadequate shipping services and when the country's political leaders were eager to enlarge the nation's foreign trade and overseas business commitments. Their effect was to revive public interest in maritime affairs and to kindle an animated debate regarding the government's appropriate role. The central issues, defined by President Theodore Roosevelt in a 1903 message to the Congress, were to determine "the advantages to the country" of a strong merchant marine and "an exact knowledge of the costs and proper method of carrying it on."[5]

Free Ships Versus Subsidies. At the turn of the century the principal obstacle to operating U.S. merchant ships in foreign trade was a statutory

---

in the report of the U.S. Merchant Marine Commission, *Development of the American Merchant Marine and American Commerce*, S. Rept. 2755, 58 Cong. 1 sess. (1903), p. 4.

[2] Steward R. Bross, *Ocean Shipping* (Cambridge, Maryland: Cornell Maritime Press, 1956), p. 249.

[3] S. Rept. 2755, Chap. 2.

[4] The return of the Great White Fleet was celebrated by a grand assembly of official Washington gathered at Hampton Roads. Among those who witnessed the scene and felt outraged at the dependence of the American fleet on the merchantmen of Britain, Italy, and Sweden was Schuyler Otis Bland, then a young Newport News lawyer, who later chaired the House Committee on Merchant Marine and Fisheries from 1933 almost continuously until his death in 1950.

[5] President Theodore Roosevelt, *Message to the Congress*, as quoted in S. Rept. 2755, p. 1.

requirement that they be constructed in American yards. When first enacted, in 1789, the restriction had provided an effective stimulus to an infant and potentially valuable U.S. shipbuilding industry. One hundred years later it proved an insurmountable hurdle for American shipowners wishing to engage in foreign trade. The higher cost of steel caused U.S. production costs to be 40-75 percent over those of Great Britain and Germany. American vessels were also generally believed to be less efficiently designed for ocean voyages. The result was that American shipping capital flowed overseas to purchase foreign-built ships for registry under foreign flag.[6]

The bar to importing foreign-built ships for U.S. registry provided the "free trade" elements of the Democratic party an ideal illustration of the evils of the Republican tariffs. It appeared a clear-cut case of protection granted one industry destroying another. The solution which the Democrats proposed was a free ship policy, to permit imported vessels to be operated (at least in foreign trade) under American registry. The alternative urged by the Republicans was to extend the protective system covering steelmakers and shipbuilders to include ship operators through an operating subsidy or "tariff in reverse."

The Republican ship subsidy proposal was premised on an economic philosophy rejected by low-tariff Democrats. In addition, the very suggestion of a shipping subsidy evoked memories of the 1872 Pacific Mail Line Scandal—an episode which remained fresh in the memories of many senior members of Congress.[7] The result was complete deadlock between Republicans, who proved unable to enact a shipping subsidy, and Democrats, who were equally unsuccessful in their efforts to admit foreign-built ships to American registry.

In 1910, free trade Democrats captured control of the House and together with progressive Republicans enjoyed *de facto* control of the

[6] J. E. Saugstad, in *Shipping and Shipbuilding Subsidies*, U.S. Department of Commerce, Trade Promotion Series No. 129 (Government Printing Office, 1932), pp. 31 ff., reports that registry under a flag other than that of the owner's nationality was a new phenomenon in maritime history, pioneered by Americans at the turn of the century. In 1901, U.S. interests owned and registered abroad 136 ships of 672,000 gross tons. This equaled U.S. registered tonnage in foreign trade and exceeded the tonnage of any other nation but Britain, France, Germany, and Norway.

[7] Following the Civil War, several packet lines were authorized by the Congress to be operated under government contract. The largest of these, the Pacific Mail Line, received $500,000 annually to provide monthly service to the Orient; this was raised to $1 million per year in 1872 to provide bimonthly service. Later it was learned the firm had spent $900,000 in lobbying for this change. While bribery was never proved, neither was the disposition of a large portion of the fund ever determined. See P. M. Zeis, *American Shipping Policy* (Princeton University Press, 1938), pp. 23-24.

Senate. Two years later, their long struggle for a "free ship" policy was climaxed in a hollow victory. A rider to the first Panama Canal Act granted American shipowners the right to acquire foreign-built ships on a duty free basis for operation in foreign trade (foreign-built vessels were and are still excluded from domestic transport) and removed duties from all shipbuilding materials used in construction of any U.S. flag vessels. However, the legislation included no incentives to transfer fleets to U.S. flag or to build new ships for American registry. Inasmuch as a shift in registry involved some disruption in operations and somewhat higher wage costs (to staff with American officers), no vessels were brought under U.S. flag as a result of its enactment.

The following year, Congress made ship operation under U.S. flag more attractive through a more favorable tariff structure. The 1913 Underwood Tariff, which roughly halved duties on commodity imports, also established (for the first time since 1815) a discriminatory tariff on behalf of U.S. flag ships by allowing a 5 percent tariff reduction on goods imported on American vessels. In effect U.S. flag inbound freight rates were reduced 20-30 percent. This indirect subsidy was more liberal than most of the direct subsidy proposals rejected during the preceding decade. The statute, however, stipulated that the tariff discount should not be "construed to interfere with the reciprocal commercial relations between the United States and foreign nations."[8] Litigation on the point was initiated immediately after the bill's enactment. In 1915, the Supreme Court found the system to conflict with U.S. treaty obligations and declared it null and void.[9]

Wilson's New Freedom. Woodrow Wilson's 1912 election to the presidency provided opportunities to explore new approaches toward the merchant marine. Wilson's program was chiefly directed at correcting deficiencies in American foreign trade and shipping operations rather than attempting to offset these deficiencies through discriminatory duties or subsidies. Later, when outbreak of war in Europe increased the urgency of building up a U.S. foreign trade fleet, Wilson proposed direct government action rather than subsidies to private corporations.

The international shipping industry at this time was relatively free of mandatory flag preferences, subsidies, and regulation. (Britain's leadership of course reflected her naval and commercial power as well as British business and operating skills.) The industry, furthermore, drew upon an international labor pool. Even on ships in the U.S. domestic

[8] 38 Stat. 114.
[9] *Five Percent Discount Cases,* 243 U.S. 97 (1916).

trade, only the watch officers were required to be U.S. citizens. Roughly two-thirds of the crews were foreign born; half were foreign nationals.[10]

Working and living conditions aboard ship were deplorable. Government regulation of health and safety was ineffective. More important, navigation laws generally denied sailors the legal status necessary to assert basic rights. While at sea, seamen were unconditionally responsible to the ship's master. In port, they were entitled to wages only when signing off articles and subject to imprisonment for desertion.

Although all seamen shared the hardships of the seafarer's craft, men working out of U.S. ports earned somewhat higher wages than others. The International Seamen's Union argued that the scarcity of labor in U.S. ports caused this differential and that wage rates could be equalized if penalties for jumping ship were removed. Congress removed these penalties in the Seamen's Act of 1915.[11] The same act also specified that 75 percent of ships' crews should speak the language of their officers. Although no citizenship requirement was imposed, this provision laid the basis for later restrictions on seafaring employment.

The most significant application of Wilson's New Freedom to shipping affairs was the extension of economic regulation to the ocean freight industry. The regulatory program grew out of a thorough investigation of industry practices, initiated by the Congress in 1912 to head off legal actions against three conferences filed under the Sherman Act by the Department of Justice. The study, conducted by the House Merchant Marine and Fisheries Committee, chaired by Joshua Alexander of Missouri, covered monopoly practices in both foreign and domestic trade. Despite claims of discriminatory and unfair practices, the committee concluded that the advantages of the conference system outweighed its disadvantages.[12]

[10] The nationalities represented aboard U.S. flag ships in 1910, as reported in a special survey conducted by the Commissioner of Navigation, were as follows: U.S. native born, 32%; naturalized, 19%; Spanish, 15%; British, 11%; Scandinavian, 9%; German, 4%; and others, 10%.

[11] 38 Stat. 1164. Wage equalization was operative only during World War I, inasmuch as the legislation was ruled by the Supreme Court in 1920 to be inapplicable to foreign flag vessels. A report prepared after the war indicated that under wartime conditions, equalization had occurred. See testimony of Andrew Furuseth, *The Merchant Marine Act, 1935*, Hearings before the Senate Commerce Committee, 74 Cong. 1 sess. (1935), p. 358.

[12] *Steamship Agreements and Affiliation in the American Foreign and Domestic Trade*, Hearings before the House Merchant Marine and Fisheries Committee, Vol. 4, 63 Cong. 1 sess. (1913). Somewhat over one-third of 227 shippers canvassed reported that some form of unfair discrimination had been practiced against them, and some responses were "characterized by a spirit of intense bitterness toward steamship interests." *Ibid.*, p. 1403.

The committee recommended that conferences be permitted to continue but only under public supervision. Specifically, it recommended that all conference agreements and liner rates be filed with the Interstate Commerce Commission (ICC) to be approved unless found to be discriminatory in character or detrimental to U.S. commercial interests; that published tariffs be strictly observed; and that deferred rate rebates and "fighting ships" be absolutely prohibited.[13]

The shipowners' reaction to the committee's recommendations was so hostile that no action was taken on the investigatory report for several years. Regulatory legislation was finally enacted (as an adjunct to the Shipping Act of 1916), but its legislative history stressed that positive control of international shipping rates was not intended. Government supervision of rates in domestic trade was retained.

World War I and Its Aftermath

The Alexander committee's regulatory proposals were built on the assumption that the needs of American shippers could be met through U.S. supervision of foreign flag lines and conference practices. The outbreak of war in Europe in 1914 precipitated a crisis in trade and shipping which demonstrated again the hazards of depending on foreign flag ships and established the basis for a large-scale promotional effort to build up the U.S. foreign trade fleet.

Neutrality Measures. In 1914, U.S. flag ships were employed almost exclusively in coastwise and intercoastal trades. One line provided service under a government mail contract between the Pacific Coast and the Far East; other U.S. flag services were operated in the Caribbean and to Canada. But for transport to Europe, the Near East, Africa, and most of South America, U.S. merchants depended chiefly upon British, German, French, and Italian shipping.

Withdrawal of most of the belligerents' ships from U.S. foreign commerce, therefore, created a problem of national proportions, forcing prompt government action. Two statutes were enacted immediately to encourage U.S. shipowners to place ships in the trades being vacated by

[13] *Ibid.,* p. 419. "Deferred rebates" were at the time used by many conferences as a method of forcing shippers to give the conference their exclusive patronage. The term "fighting ship" refers to a vessel whose operations are underwritten by a combine of carriers expressly to capture cargoes which might otherwise be routed via a competitor whom the combine wishes to turn out of the trade. The rate powers which the committee believed should be vested in the ICC included cancellation of discriminatory rates and fixing rate maxima, but not setting a minimum rate floor.

the belligerents: the first authorized the Treasury to write war risk insurance on American-owned ships; the second liberalized the terms under which American owners might transfer vessels registered abroad to the safety of American registry.

These actions yielded immediate results. At the outbreak of war over 500,000 tons of U.S.-owned shipping was registered abroad. By the end of September 1914 more than half of this tonnage had transferred to U.S. flag. In addition some foreign tonnage was purchased and shifted to U.S. registry before restrictions on sales were applied by other governments. Suitable vessels operating in domestic trades were also transferred to foreign service.

These adjustments were not enough, however, to brake soaring shipping rates, and further action to bring ships into the trade was deemed essential. The administration recommended organization of a government corporation to acquire and operate a fleet of approximately fifty vessels.[14] At President Wilson's request, legislation was introduced early in September 1914 to authorize the program.

The House acted rapidly to approve Wilson's proposal. However, the Senate balked at the government-ownership feature. Men who only a few years earlier had been the strongest proponents of a maritime subsidy program now argued that "it is not necessary to have a *government* merchant marine either from the point of view of the economy or national defense."[15] As time passed, their argument appeared to be strengthened by a spurt in private orders for new ships to take advantage of the high rates on U.S. export cargoes. This business completely saturated U.S. shipyards.

Wartime Programs. The consequence of these developments was to delay enactment of the Shipping Act until 1916. However, the legislation finally enacted provided many important new powers.[16] It established a

[14] The chief architect of the ship purchase program was Secretary of the Treasury William McAdoo. His arguments for government ownership were threefold: first, that private capital would not be forthcoming on reasonable terms; second, that by owning the vessels the government could protect against avarice; and third, that since public investment was required to support ship operations, title to the ships should reside with the public. To these arguments President Wilson added a fourth, that government-owned ships could be used in a positive program of foreign trade promotion.

[15] Minority views of Congressman Greene, ranking minority member of the House Merchant Marine and Fisheries Committee, in *Report to Accompany H.R. 18666*, H. Rept. 1149, 63 Cong. 2 sess. (1914), p. 12. (Emphasis added.)

[16] The Shipping Act of 1916 is composed of 36 sections: sections 1 and 2 set out basic definitions, including a definition of citizenship for purposes of the act; the next two sections authorize establishment of a Shipping Board and define its

five-member Shipping Board as a permanent independent agency with broad promotional, investigatory, regulatory, and administrative powers. It authorized the board to organize and take a majority interest in a government corporation to implement its programs. It included an open-end authorization to purchase and construct vessels and established strict controls over transfer of privately owned U.S. flag ships to foreign flags.

The 1916 act was designed primarily to equip a neutral United States to carry on peaceful commerce in a wartorn world. However, because the board was not actually organized until January 1917, it did not have an opportunity to test the program's effectiveness to meet commercial needs.

The United States declared war April 6, 1917. Two more months passed before a decision was reached to undertake an emergency ship building program. That program was probably the most extraordinary industrial undertaking ever attempted by the United States. It was a task for which the government was almost totally unprepared, to which it devoted enormous resources, and which entailed enormous waste. Of the more than 3,000 vessels authorized for construction by the board, less than one-sixth were completed before the armistice. By the time the program finally came to its untimely conclusion in May 1922, some $3.3 billion had been expended.

When finally launched, the Shipping Board's fleet was the world's largest merchant marine. Major vessels (1,000 tons or over) under U.S. flag in 1922 totaled 13.5 million gross tons, roughly five times prewar U.S. flag tonnage and 22 percent of the world fleet. More than half of this massive merchant fleet, however, was owned by the government, which had had no experience whatsoever in commercial ship operations.

Postwar Policies. The existence of such a fleet compelled the government to formulate long-range policies toward its national flag merchant marine. The authority vested in the Shipping Board by the 1916 act to own and operate ships was limited to the duration of the war plus five years. The legislation failed to provide any guidance either as to the terms and conditions under which government-owned ships might be transferred to private operation or as to the peacetime role of a national flag merchant marine.

---

basic organization; sections 5-13 authorize the board to purchase, build, lease, charter, and sell ships, and to form a corporation which may also operate ships; sections 14-28 define the board's regulatory powers; sections 29-35 specify fines and penalties; and section 36 authorizes the Secretary of the Treasury to refuse clearance to any merchant vessel which has refused to load cargo for which space was available.

These omissions were met in the Merchant Marine Act of 1920.[17] The act directed the board to determine as promptly as possible what steamship lines should be established to promote U.S. foreign and coastwise trade; to sell or charter the vessels necessary to maintain these services; or if no private citizen could be induced to provide the service on terms satisfactory to the board, to operate vessels itself until the business was developed so that the ships might be sold on satisfactory terms. In establishing sales prices, the board was directed to act "as a prudent, solvent businessman in the sale of similar vessels or property which he is not forced to sell."[18]

The intent of the 1920 act was simultaneously to pioneer new trade routes, to demonstrate that U.S. ships could be profitably operated in these trades, and, by engaging private businessmen as freight solicitors and managing agents for government-operated lines, to develop the private competence and familiarity with trade conditions necessary to a successful transition from public to private ownership. The program assumed that favorable business conditions would continue, so that the government lines could be operated at a profit and their sales negotiated on favorable terms.

In order to put the program on a sound, long-term basis, the 1920 act was prefaced by a declaration of purpose which reads as follows:

> It is hereby declared the policy of the United States to do whatever may be necessary to develop and encourage the maintenance of . . . a merchant marine . . . sufficient to carry the greater portion of its commerce and serve as a naval or military auxiliary in time of war or national emergency, ultimately to be owned and operated privately by citizens of the United States.[19]

This declaration of purpose is significant because, with minor amendments and some shifting of emphasis, it remains the basis for present-day maritime policy. It is noteworthy that the policy adopted in 1920, after more than fifty years of debate, was framed in an atmosphere of optimism that a strong merchant marine could be maintained under U.S. flag without direct government aid.[20] The Senate Commerce Committee

[17] 41 Stat. 988.

[18] 41 Stat. 990.

[19] 41 Stat. 988. Statutory statements of U.S. maritime objectives are compared in Appendix B.

[20] The 1920 act provided no overt, direct subsidies for private ship operations. However, it included three powerful indirect aids. First, the coastwise laws—tightened to eliminate temporary wartime access accorded foreign vessels—were extended to include distant island possessions. Second, upon a finding by the Shipping Board that adequate U.S. flag service was available, existing preferential rail rates on ship-

was probably justified in May 1920 to "take it for granted that every patriotic citizen now wishes to see a merchant marine under American flag large enough to carry the major part of our own foreign trade."[21] But as the costs of the project became apparent, this broad support dissolved.

Problems in Government Operations. Almost immediately following passage of the Merchant Marine Act of 1920, the shipping boom collapsed. By the end of the year, rates for time charters were approximately one-third the rate prevailing six months earlier; liner rates fell off somewhat more gradually but by 1922 had dropped to prewar levels. Almost 10 million tons (17 percent) of the world's shipping was idled.

The break in freight rates shattered the government's ship sales plans. Vessels which had been built at a cost of $200-$250 per ton and had sold for $150-$175 per ton in 1921 were offered the following year for only $30 per ton. Even at this price the market produced few takers. In November 1923 the board abandoned its efforts to sell individual ships and decided instead to concentrate on developing its liner services so that when the market recovered, proven organizations could be transferred to private operators.

The depression in the industry, however, also plunged Shipping Board operations into the red. A deficit of $52 million was recorded in 1922, $35 million in 1923, and $16 million in 1924. The effect of these continued losses was to put government under pressure to transfer its shipping lines to private ownership under whatever terms could be secured.

Problems in Private Operations. There were, however, few concerns in a position to assume responsibility for the operation of shipping lines. Most of the nation's ship operators had entered the business since World War I. Their experience was limited in most cases to acting as managing operators of the government-owned lines. They were generally undercapitalized. And, as managing operators with reasonably secure income, they were under no pressure to buy.

A second problem soon encountered by the board was that the terms of the 1920 act, combined with its plan to develop operating skills by

---

ments for export were restricted to shipments made via American vessels. Third, the President was instructed to abrogate all treaties which restricted the right of the United States to impose discriminatory duties or tonnage taxes. These latter two proposals were never implemented.

[21] *Report to Accompany H.R. 10378,* S. Rept. 573, 66 Cong. 2 sess. (1920), p. 1.

underwriting the development of U.S. flag foreign trade routes, invalidated the usual competitive bid procedures. The 1920 act established a statutory preference for sales to persons with local support or already engaged in steamship services in the general area. Their stake in the business and experience on the route gave these same persons a marked practical advantage in competitive bidding. Nevertheless, there were several instances in which a second company attempted to underbid, causing the Shipping Board to become entangled in fierce competitive rivalries within the industry.[22]

Third, no effective mechanism existed for assuring the long-term success of private operators, who acquired the government lines on minimum investment, or (until 1926) that they would even continue in the business. As time passed, American war-built ships were increasingly outperformed by more modern foreign-built ships, which the U.S. companies could not counter with additional investment. The gap between U.S. and foreign operating costs also widened. These developments clouded the outlook for the U.S. flag industry and discouraged further private investment.

Merchant Marine Act of 1928. The U.S. flag fleet's vulnerable position posed a serious dilemma. On the one hand, neither the Congress nor the Shipping Board was willing to risk the possibility that U.S. flag ships might be forced out of foreign trade. On the other, it appeared unlikely that congressional support could be obtained for direct subsidies to underwrite private ship construction or operation.

In 1928 the dilemma was resolved by enactment of legislation authorizing the Post Office to contract with U.S. flag lines for transportation of mail on such liberal terms that the industry would be able to meet its competition and accumulate capital for ship replacement. The mail contracts were intended to convey a hidden subsidy, but in sufficiently modest amounts and under sufficiently ambiguous conditions that congressional opposition to shipping subsidies would not be aroused.[23]

[22] The most damaging characteristic of the Shipping Board was its tendency to become embroiled in intra-industry disputes. Examples of apparently improper intervention by individual board members on behalf of one or another of the competing interests are reported in *Investigation of Air and Ocean Mail Contracts,* Hearings before a Senate select committee, 74 Cong. 1 sess. (1935). One of these battles, the sale of the United States Line, created such a furor that President Hoover had to appoint a special committee to review the matter.

[23] The legislation enacted as the Merchant Marine Act of 1928 (45 Stat. 689) was prepared in the House Merchant Marine and Fisheries Committee as an alternative to a Senate-passed bill authorizing renewal of a government construction program.

The legislation placed the Shipping Board in a most difficult position. Subsidy proponents had clearly won the day; however, the 1928 act did not provide either a clear mandate for subsidies or a sound structure for administering the desired aid. For example, the act lacked any useful standards, against which the proper amount of subsidy could be measured. Although the law called for competitive bidding for mail contracts, the statutory preference granted to established companies precluded any real competition in most trades. Finally, even though the principal purpose of the legislation was to generate funds for ship replacement, contractors were not required to pledge new construction or to reserve funds for this purpose.

The Shipping Board proved unable to administer the 1928 legislation successfully. At least initially, the board appears to have made little or no effort to develop regularized criteria or procedures. Contracts were awarded to all potentially eligible lines at the maximum rates authorized by law, without adequate safeguards and without investigation of the needs of U.S. shippers or even of the postal service. Sales of government-owned shipping lines, intended to be facilitated by the act, instead became bogged down in acrimonius controversy among competing applicants attracted by the subsidy. One of these controversies forced President Herbert Hoover to appoint a special investigatory commission whose review brought about some improvement in the board's procedures. For example, beginning in 1930 attempts were made to relate the subsidy component of the mail contract rate to estimated differentials between foreign and domestic operating costs and to the contractor's ship replacement plans. These improvements, however, came too late.

The New Deal in Merchant Shipping

By 1930 maritime subsidies had been a target of congressional and public criticism for over fifty years. The board's placement of mail contracts without competitive bidding and at maximum rates heightened the ire of its critics. With the onset of the Depression, the criticism increased, reaching a climax during the Hundred Days of 1933.[24]

The House bill was represented as including "the substance of the Senate bill." (*Report to Accompany* S. 744, H. Rept. 1279, 70 Cong. 1 sess. [1927].) The method proposed by the House for renewing the U.S. flag fleet—the primary purpose of both bills—was in fact, however, the opposite of that proposed in the Senate. The strategem accomplished its purpose. The bill passed the House with little debate and bipartisan support and was accepted by the Senate following only token opposition.

[24] During the boom years in the late twenties, criticism of the government mari-

During those turbulent sessions, three actions were taken to force revision of the 1928 program. First, a rider appended to the 1933 Independent Offices Appropriation Act authorized the President to modify or cancel any mail contract not found by him to be in the public interest. Second, again due to Appropriations Committee pressure, a select committee chaired by Senator Hugo Black was established to investigate air and ocean mail contracts. (The Post Office also had initiated an investigation in order to advise the President what contracts might be cancelled.) Third, the Shipping Board, in another economy measure authorized by the 1933 Independent Offices Appropriation, was stripped of its independent status, reduced in size, and reconstituted as a bureau within the Department of Commerce.[25] Upon acquiring this new responsibility the Commerce Department also initiated a study of maritime industry problems, assisted by an interdepartmental committee of staff level personnel.

Investigations and Findings. As the findings of the several investigatory groups were made public in the winter and spring of 1935, a pattern of opportunism, shoddy performance, and both public and private irresponsibility emerged. The most severe indictment, registered by Senator Black's group, charged that:

> Private ownership of merchant and aerial transportation with government subsidy has resulted in a saturnalia of waste, inefficiency, unearned and exorbitant salaries, and bonuses and other so-called "compensation," corrupting expense accounts, exploitation of the public by sale and manipulation of stocks, the "value" of which are largely based on the hope of profit from robbing the taxpayer, and a general transfer of energy and labor from operating the business to "operating on" the taxpayer. Measured by results, the subsidy system, as operated, has been a sad, miserable, and corrupting failure.[26]

The Black report called for outright repeal of the 1928 law and cancelation of any further aid to ship operations. Postmaster General

---

time program subsided. Beginning in 1929, however, criticism again became vocal. Allegations of improprieties in the 1929 sale of the United States Lines forced President Hoover to establish a special investigatory commission. A number of bills were introduced to curb alleged abuses. A Senate Appropriations Committee study, made in 1931, resulted in a strongly critical report and a more detailed study by the General Accounting Office. Thus, by the time the Democrats assumed office in 1933, there was a fairly well documented record of waste and mismanagement.

[25] Executive Order 6166, June 10, 1933. The order announced a dozen major administrative reorganizations which together were estimated to save $25 million.

[26] *Investigation of Air Mail and Ocean Mail Contracts*, S. Rept. 898, 74 Cong. 1 sess. (1935), pp. 39-40.

Farley shared Black's view that the 1928 act had led to major improprieties, but confined the recommendations in his report to tightening
up administration of existing law.[27] In contrast, an interdepartmental
committee, organized by the Commerce Department, stressed the importance of a merchant marine to the United States. While acknowledg-
ing that previous administration had been inadequate, the interdepartmental committee endorsed the principle that the United States should
support necessary tonnage through financial assistance to private firms.
The committee urged that aid be subject to proper supervision and
audit, and that payments be calculated to cover only the cost differentials between U.S. and foreign operations and construction. However,
it also recommended liberalizations in the 1928 program in order to
promote a more vigorous and effective U.S. flag merchant fleet.[28]

Proposals for Legislation. President Roosevelt transmitted the Post Office and Commerce reports to the Congress with a brief covering statement in which he presented to the Congress "the question of whether
or not the United States should have an adequate merchant marine."[29]
The President set down three reasons which led him to conclude a
national flag fleet was needed, and then noted:

> In many instances in our history, the Congress has provided for
> various kinds of disguised subsidies to American shipping. . . . I
> propose that we end this subterfuge. If the Congress decides that it
> will maintain a reasonably adequate merchant marine, I believe that
> it can well afford honestly to call a subsidy by its right name. . . .
>
> An American merchant marine is one of our most firmly established
> traditions. It was, during the first half of our national existence, a
> great and growing asset. Since then, it has declined in importance
> and value. The time has come to square this traditional ideal with
> effective performance.[30]

[27] The Postmaster General's summary report to the President was printed in H.
Doc. 118, 74 Cong. 1 sess. (1935). A complete report, detailing recommended actions
to be taken with respect to each mail contract, was not completed until the following
year.
[28] *Report of the Interdepartmental Committee on Shipping Policy,* H. Doc. 118.
[29] *Message from the President of the United States,* H. Doc. 118, p. 1.
[30] *Ibid.,* pp. 2-3. President Roosevelt's reasons for supporting a strong U.S. flag
merchant fleet were: to protect U.S. peacetime foreign commerce from restrictive or
rebating methods of foreign-dominated shipping combines, to permit the United
States to continue peaceful trade in the event of a major foreign war, and to provide
the Navy with auxiliary vessels in the event that the United States itself became
engaged in war.

In his message the President laid down some general specifications for a new, direct subsidy program. It should cover differentials in construction and operating costs and take into consideration the liberal subsidies which other nations provided to their shipping. It should not include indirect aids such as government loans for ship construction. It should be protected by adequate safeguards. And it should be accompanied by a reorganization of the present Shipping Board Bureau to separate administrative from quasi-judicial functions, which the President proposed be transferred to the Interstate Commerce Commission. The President also asked Congress to "provide for the termination of existing ocean mail contracts as rapidly as possible, and once its policy is determined, to back it up with annual appropriations in adequate amounts." The message did not deal directly with the question of how a government-assisted merchant marine should be owned or operated, nor specify the size and type of fleet that the President regarded reasonable and adequate. These questions the President left to the Congress to decide.

Merchant Marine Act, 1936. The President's message shifted the focus of activity from the executive branch to the Congress. Although his message, backed up by the interdepartmental committee report, established the general frame of reference, the legislation finally enacted was basically a congressional product. The debate on the subsidy bill, which ran through a total of thirty-five drafts, continued for fifteen months before enactment was at last achieved.

The debate illuminated a number of deep-seated conflicts among various blocs within the Congress and among the several parties at interest. The central issue debated in 1935 and 1936, as in the years before, was government versus private ownership and management of the merchant marine. A collateral question related to the extent to which government should intervene in the industry's management in order to secure public objectives and to protect public investment. Other questions concerned the organization of the program's administration, whether the outstanding mail pay contracts should be terminated, whether the government should continue to make loans for ship construction, whether minimum rates should be established by the government, and the extent to which discretion should be permitted to the administrative agency.

Because debate focused on techniques for maintaining an efficient foreign trade fleet under American flag, very little attention was directed to the objectives of the program. Most notably there was no attempt to probe the basic issues of whether the United States really needed a merchant marine, and if so, of what characteristics. Though both the House and Senate committees opened their hearings to all witnesses, there were none who commented on how the new law might be structured to secure maximum benefits for shippers or the defense establishment.[31] In fact, no official testimony at all was received from any of the military services.[32]

Finally, neither the administration nor the Congress was able to agree on quantitative objectives for development of the U.S. flag fleet. Colonel J. Monroe Johnson, Assistant Secretary of Commerce, asserted that the objective should be a fleet to carry 75 percent of U.S. commerce. But the department's most vocal witness on the bill, A H. Haag, chief of the Shipping Board Bureau's Research Division, urged that the objective not be to expand the fleet, but to improve it by replacing obsolete vessels on a one-for-one basis. The bill's congressional sponsors avoided identification with either camp and steadfastly refused to forecast how many ships would be constructed or to estimate the program's total cost.[33]

Lack of agreement on basic issues prevented the Senate from completing action on the bill during the 1935 session. In February 1936 the principals of the opposing camps were called in by President Roosevelt, who had thus far remained aloof, but not even his good offices could resolve differences. However, in order to accommodate the President's desire that legislation be brought to the Floor, the Commerce Committee in late March reported a compromise bill without recommendations.[34] Later in the spring the bill's proponents again attempted to reach agreement with Senator Black and others opposing the subsidy program. A compromise was finally reached only after the Senate Appropriations

[31] A number of shipper organizations testified on the proposed legislation, but their testimony was directed almost exclusively at a proposed minimum rate clause, which was struck prior to the bill's enactment.

[32] The Navy had participated in the interdepartmental committee study and later consulted informally with the Congress. However, the program's sponsors wished to avoid a military identification, and no official testimony was ever taken from any of the military services. Neither the Army nor Marines, who would be shipping's principal wartime users, appears to have participated at all in the program's formulation.

[33] Congressman Bland was reasonably specific with respect to the size of the operating differential which could be anticipated, noting that the approximately $10 million annual cost was a modest price to pay for an American merchant marine. He would not forecast the size of the annual construction program. *Congressional Record,* Vol. 79, Pt. 9, 74 Cong. 1 sess. (1935), p. 10087.

[34] S. Rept. 1721, 74 Cong. 2 sess. (1936). The Committee voted 12 to 7 to report the compromise bill. However, it split evenly 10 to 10 on its merits.

Committee threatened to withhold funds for mail contract payments. The Senate ratified this compromise proposal by voice vote on June 19, 1936, one day prior to its adjournment to attend the 1936 presidential conventions.

The bill approved by the Senate was rushed through the House without change. The final product was not entirely satisfactory to anyone. Thoroughly compromised, the 1936 act combined but failed to resolve differing points of view. On many key questions it is either silent or its intent is unclear. Thus its policies and objectives must be interpreted in the context of its legislative history.

Political Issues

The Merchant Marine Act, 1936, is a product of its times. Much of the political support for the program was based on a desire to provide useful employment to seamen, shipbuilders, and suppliers of the maritime industry. Economic recovery was in fact so dominant a theme that the Senate committee listed the opportunities for useful employment as the first and (by implication) most important reason for passing the legislation. Despite these depression influences, the policies expressed in the act were built upon the thinking and experience of the preceding thirty-five years. The men who framed the bill sensed it was to be a *Magna Charta* for the industry. Their work has proved durable in part because it represented the mainstream of political thought regarding the government's role in relation to the national flag merchant fleet.

Subsidy Policies. The 1936 act adopted a nationalistic and protectionist solution to the nation's shipping needs which built and expanded on the policies laid down in 1920. The new act accepted the premise that all the nation's domestic commerce and a "substantial portion" of its foreign commerce should be carried in American ships.[35] It proposed, furthermore, that as a matter of policy these ships should be constructed solely in American yards and manned exclusively by citizen personnel, although these policies were binding only on subsidy contracters.[36] Finally,

[35] The 1920 act had also specified that the "greater" portion of its commerce be carried in U.S.-registered ships. At that time the ships were available and the likelihood of meeting the objective even without subsidy appeared good. It was not reexamined during the preparation of the 1936 act. The implications of the shift in phraseology from "greater" to "substantial" portion are discussed in Chapter 3.

[36] Up to this time, citizenship requirements had applied only to watch officers. The 1936 act specified that all officers and crew should be citizens except a small

shipyards and operators were required by the act to use U.S. manufactured materials, supplies, and services to the maximum practical extent.[37]

In order to meet the higher costs of U.S. labor and supplies, the 1936 act provided for direct subsidies to qualified U.S. foreign trade firms to equalize ship operating and construction costs. This parity payment, or "tariff in reverse," had been urged by shipping interests more or less continuously since 1915, when advanced by the U.S. Chamber of Commerce, but had been doggedly opposed by congressional Democrats.[38] Nevertheless, in the Tariff Act of 1922, the Congress had adopted cost parity as the governing principle for fixing rates on dutiable articles.[39] In 1930 the Shipping Board had actually begun to apply this principle to its calculations of the subsidy component to be allowed within its ocean mail contracts.

In theory, parity is the negation of trade, for if all costs were truly equalized there would be no incentive for exchange. In fact, the Tariff Commission had found it virtually impossible to ascertain foreign costs with sufficient accuracy to implement the 1922 act. As a result, the point most energetically debated during consideration of the Merchant Marine

---

proportion of the unlicensed stewards, who were required to file a declaration of intent to become citizens. Companion legislation, approved June 25, 1936 (49 Stat. 1930), specified that 75 percent of the crews on all other U.S. flag ships must be citizens. These percentages still apply, although in practice the fleet is manned almost exclusively with citizen personnel.

The requirement for U.S. construction still applies only to subsidized vessels and ships for use in domestic trade. However, importation of ships for use in foreign trade was effectively barred by 1961 legislation (75 Stat. 565) excluding foreign-built ships from cargo preferences for three years following their U.S. registry.

[37] The act's "Buy America" clauses also extend to subcontractors.

[38] From the Civil War through the early months of Franklin Roosevelt's first administration, the Democratic party's aversion to direct subsidies had been one of its basic tenets. The party platform in 1932 had opposed as "illogical and unsound all efforts to overcome with subsidies the handicaps to American shipping." During the floor debate on the 1936 bill, William McAdoo, now senator from California, reminded his colleagues that twenty years earlier he had pledged that "no Democratic Congress will ever pass a ship subsidy bill and no Democratic President will ever approve one." (*Congressional Record*, Vol. 80, Pt. 10 [1936], p. 9905.)

[39] In Section 315(a) of the Tariff Act of 1922 (42 Stat. 941), the Congress had declared its intent that rates on dutiable articles should equalize U.S. and foreign costs of production and had authorized the President, upon a finding of the Tariff Commission, to proclaim appropriate increases and decreases in the duty. This procedure, known as the "flexible tariff," was continued with slight modification in the Smoot-Hawley Tariff of 1930 (46 Stat. 701). The Reciprocal Trade legislation, under which the Roosevelt Administration initiated its trade agreements program, voided the equalization requirement of the 1930 tariff only with respect to articles covered in a trade agreement. Therefore the "flexible tariff" technically still pertains today, although trade agreements in practice cover most articles in trade.

Act, 1936, was not whether cost equalization was sound, but whether parity could be determined with sufficient accuracy to make the system feasible and protect the government from undue pressure.

The best hope for keeping subsidies under control, in the opinion of President Roosevelt and his advisors, was to admit the necessity of direct financial assistance so that both the amount paid and the beneficiaries would be exposed to public view. This radical and daring innovation in public policy was unacceptable to many of the Democratic party's senior and more tradition-minded members. In fact, on the only representative, recorded vote, the Democrats split almost evenly on the bill, which was approved due to a small margin of Republicans who favored enactment.[40]

Shipowner Versus Shipper Interests. The 1916 Shipping Act treated the promotional and regulatory programs of the Shipping Board as alternative but complementary techniques for advancing U.S. shipping and shipper interests. With the onset of World War I, shipping regulation was all but eclipsed by the urgent tasks of building a wartime fleet. Following the war the government, as owner-operator of a number of shipping lines, gained a direct stake in the industry which it was supposed to regulate and gave the conference system its strong support. In fact, during the 1920's the Shipping Board became so completely identified with shipowner interests that many shippers lost hope of receiving a hearing for their interests.

The Shipping Board's promotional orientation not only rested on statutory sanction but also reflected the views of the congressional committees which supervised its regulatory activities.[41] Thus, when the Depression threatened to destroy the conference system, the board was sympathetic to proposals that it use its power to discipline carriers quoting less than the agreed upon rates. Later the board participated with the industry in drawing up a National Recovery Act code setting minimum rates in each trade. However, opposition from U.S. shippers,

[40] Tellers were taken in the House in its vote on the 1935 Bland-Copeland bill. Democrats split almost evenly with 138 favoring and 136 opposed, while the Republicans voted for the bill by a margin of 56 to 41. Democrats favoring enactment tended to be from coastal areas or the Great Lakes region. (For further analysis of the vote, see Harvard Business School, *The Use and Disposition of Ships and Shipyards at the End of World War II* [Government Printing Office, 1945], p. 306.)

[41] The 1920 act instructed the board even when exercising its regulatory powers to keep "always in view" that the development of an American merchant marine is "the primary objective to be obtained" (41 Stat. 988). Relationships between the board's regulatory and promotional responsibilities are further discussed in Chapter 9.

supported by the Department of State, prevented adoption of the code.

Proposals to empower the Shipping Board to set minimum rates were advanced again for incorporation in the 1936 act and were again defeated. However, in concentrating on beating back the restrictive practices being urged by the maritime industry, shipping interests failed to give any creative thought to how regulatory powers should be related to the new promotional program or the manner in which subsidies might best be employed to aid U.S. foreign commerce.[42]

The shippers also were unsuccessful in their effort to have responsibility for the regulatory aspects of the government's shipping program transferred to the Interstate Commerce Commission (ICC). Action to disentangle the board's promotional and regulatory functions was apparently supported by President Roosevelt, but was opposed by Shipping Board witnesses as well as by the shipping industry.[43]

The congressional committees handling the bill concurred with the Shipping Board Bureau's position that the conjunction of promotional and regulatory functions should not be disturbed, though in deference to the President they did provide that he might transfer the regulatory functions after two years if experience proved the statutory arrangement to be unsound.[44]

[42] Shippers testifying on the proposed legislation did not oppose the subsidy program, but gave it little positive support. In general they appeared unconcerned by their dependence on foreign flag lines. "The shippers of this country," testified one witness in 1935, "know that discriminatory legislation of our own making is to be feared far more than any remote predatory desire on the part of foreign steamship lines to exact unreasonable freight charges from transportation of foreign trade." (*Development of an American Merchant Marine,* Hearings before the House Merchant Marine and Fisheries Committee, 74 Cong. 1 sess. [1935], p. 490.)

[43] In his message to the Congress, Roosevelt had called for transfer of the quasi-judicial and quasi-legislative functions of the Shipping Board to the ICC. "Purely administrative functions, however, such as information and planning, ship inspections and the maintenance of aids to navigation should, of course, remain in the Department of Commerce." (H. Doc. 118, p. 2.) Roosevelt's statement was ambiguous as to how the Shipping Board Bureau's subsidy functions should be distributed between the Commerce Department and the ICC and his views were never spelled out by the Administration witnesses on the bill. A statement of the Shipping Board Bureau's position that the regulatory program was intended not merely for the "protection of shippers and users . . . but also the protection of the carriers, and of the tax payer, who in the last analysis pays the subsidy," is spelled out in *Development of an American Merchant Marine,* Hearings, p. 388.

[44] Sec. 204(b), Merchant Marine Act, 1936 (40 Stat. 1987). This authority was withdrawn by the Congress before it became effective (52 Stat. 955). Two years later, however, that portion of the Maritime Commission's regulatory jurisdiction bearing on coastwise and intercoastal traffic was shifted to ICC (54 Stat. 929).

Public Versus Private Ownership. The reports issued in 1935 by the Black Committee and the Postmaster General again raised the issue of government versus private ownership and operation of merchant ships. Senator Black's position, like that of most of the Democrats who had preceded him, was that unless substantial private capital could be drawn into the merchant marine and the business conducted without subsidy, government ownership and operation "best served the interest of the people."[45] Collaterally, Black and his associates argued that only direct government financing of ship construction and operations could assure that necessary ships and services would be maintained under U.S. flag.

Black's committee adopted the point of view that the government should not only retain title to ships it financed but also that complete control which accompanies legal ownership. The committee specifically inveighed against the various managing-operator contracts the Shipping Board had used to operate government-owned vessels since "the private operator took the profits and the government took the losses."[46] However, the committee recognized that some measure of private participation was inevitable.

Black failed to set out an alternative plan which would avoid the "inequities" of the past and provide incentives for more efficient and profitable operations in the future. Those sharing his point of view were thus limited to arguing over who should hold formal title to the ships and calling for specific protective clauses (discussed in Chapter 3) to regulate government-contractor relations.

The compromise finally enacted, although primarily directed to subsidizing private ship operations, contained many of the protective features urged by Senator Black and also a title which authorized and directed the government to build ships for sale or charter if necessary to fulfill the objectives of the act. This compromise tended to obscure and confuse the roles intended for the government vis-a-vis its private subsidy contractors in carrying out the promotional program and contained the seeds of many future difficulties.

[45] S. Rept. 898, p. 41. To dramatize the lines' dependence on government for capital, Black noted that data compiled by the Postmaster General showed that (exclusive of the United Fruit Company) the government had made a larger investment in the mail contract lines than their private owners. The comparison, however, failed to discriminate between mortgage capital, furnished by government, and equity capital, furnished privately.

[46] S. Rept. 1721, p. 40.

Program Administration. One matter on which almost all were agreed
was that arrangements for administering the subsidy program must be
completely reconstituted. The apparent inefficiency, liberality, and poor
judgment of Shipping Board officials had for years scandalized both
opponents and many supporters of its programs. Black and his associates were adamant that a "new, fearless and uncompromising" agency
be established, and that it "must not be compelled to take over the
entire personnel of the Shipping Board Bureau, shot through with the
destructive propaganda of the past."[47] Those friendly to the industry
were equally anxious that the administration of the new program would
be such as to gain public confidence and respect, and even agreed to
a clause barring appointment to any person who had had any financial
connection with the industry within three years prior to his nomination.

Many of the most acrimonious debates over the 1936 legislation
centered on the amount of discretion which should be given to the new
agency. Opponents of the subsidy program demanded strict limitations
on private profits, methods to assure conservation of funds for new construction, and controls to preclude diversion of public funds to private
ends. Furthermore, they insisted that protective clauses be mandatory.
The program's supporters were equally convinced that mandatory safeguards would frustrate completely the program's purpose. "Shipping
is a business of highly competitive and constantly changing nature,"
argued one committee report, "and its governmental contact must be
given the power of prompt decision dealing with situations as they
arise."[48] The issue was compromised by an understanding that two
"watchdog" members would be appointed to the new commission, which
was delegated considerable administrative latitude.

The administrative agency's relationships to the President and the
Congress were also at issue. In the 1933 economy drive the Shipping
Board had been reduced from seven to three members and brought
under the supervision of the Department of Commerce. In order to
strengthen its management, Secretary Roper's Interdepartmental Committee on Shipping Policy recommended that its administrative functions be transferred to a new Office of Maritime Affairs, headed by an
assistant secretary, and its policy functions to a Federal Maritime Authority, chaired by Commerce and including representation from other
interested departments and from private life. President Roosevelt gave
this proposal his general endorsement. The Congress, on the other

[47] S. Rept. 898, p. 42.
[48] *Report to Accompany* S. 2582, S. Rept. 713, 74 Cong. 1 sess. (1935), p. 4.

hand, lacked confidence in the Commerce Department and was virtually unanimous in the opinion that all maritime functions should be placed in a new, independent, bipartisan commission, titled the U.S. Maritime Commission.

The advantages anticipated from the commission arrangement were: freer access and greater responsiveness to the Congress; an ability to attract more highly qualified personnel and to act with greater discretion and vigor; and enhancement of the continuity, expertness, and coherence of the program's administration. The independent commission form, which was being widely used at the time, was not opposed by the Administration.

Influences on Policy Development

The Merchant Marine Act, 1936, is an acknowledged landmark because it provided the first systematic, peacetime formulation of the government's maritime program. The program itself was evolutionary in character, building upon the mail route system established after World War I. But its recognition that national interests demanded an outright subsidy to the U.S. merchant fleet was revolutionary. Prior to its enactment the Congress had steadfastly refused to face up to the issue of whether government aid to the maritime industry was justified.

The Congress approved subsidies in order to correct deficiencies in the mail pay program and to meet the industry's Depression problems. The acceptance of a long-term commitment to the U.S. foreign trade fleet, however, must be credited to other factors: particularly, the President's enthusiasm for the project; the prevailing isolationist attitudes in the country; the worldwide practice of economic nationalism; and the country's need to reestablish its self-esteem.

Given the particular circumstances existing in 1936, it was probably a foregone conclusion that the Congress and the country at large would concur in President Roosevelt's conviction that "the United States should have an adequate merchant marine . . . in keeping with [its] national pride and national needs."[49] Conversely, the controversial history of the government's maritime program made inevitable a wide divergence of opinion on how this objective should be secured. It was, therefore, in setting the specific terms and conditions of the 1936 program that the sway of normal interest group politics was most marked.

Over the thirty-five year period preceding the 1936 legislation there

[49] *Message of the President of the United States*, H. Doc. 118, p. 1.

was both an intensification and multiplication of special interests bearing on the government's maritime policies, as government participation in the industry increasingly defined the roles and interests of affected groups. Thus the debate which prior to World War I had been one of foreign trade policy between the two political parties had become by 1936 a multiplicity of specific issues between shipowners, builders, maritime labor, and shippers. The variety of interests shattered the consensus which had previously existed within each of the two parties.

To a considerable degree, government programs were responsible for these changes. For example, most of the companies operating U.S. flag ships in foreign trade in 1936 had been organized during or immediately after World War I as managing agents for the government lines. The government had encouraged and shared in their investment in war surplus ships. Without further aid, this investment was in 1935-36 believed likely to be lost. Hence the shipowners had to be (and were) effectively represented in the legislative process.

The shipbuilders had been powerful participants in the political process from the start, well organized and experienced in the business of obtaining naval as well as civilian contracts. The chairman of the House Merchant Marine and Fisheries Committee represented a shipbuilding district, and Senator Royal S. Copeland, chairman of the companion Senate group, a shipbuilding state. The industry skillfully prepared exhibits demonstrating that it drew on every one of the forty-eight states for supplies and equipment and would be able rapidly to put large numbers of persons to work. Despite the substantially higher costs of U.S. versus foreign yards, there was never any question that America's new subsidized merchant marine would be composed exclusively of subsidized, American-built ships.

The government's maritime policies during the nineteen twenties and thirties had alienated many of America's overseas shippers. Though several large organizations (such as the U.S. Chamber of Commerce, the National Foreign Trade Council, and the Mississippi Valley Association) supported the bill, all large shippers appearing individually confined their remarks to opposing any form of rate regulation as a device for building up an American merchant fleet. The farm organizations took a similar position, in addition expressing strict neutrality on the wisdom of extending subsidies to a second sector of the economy.

The maritime labor movement was badly disorganized during most of the period preceding passage of the 1936 act.[50] Prior to the Depres-

[50] Following a long period of gradual development, maritime labor organization

sion, American labor had flatly opposed shipping subsidies as an unwarranted largesse to management; in 1936, the older labor leaders continued to oppose subsidies. One or two younger men representing ship's officers and radiomen worked for the bill.

Nonetheless, there was within the Congress a strong desire to help the distressed working man and to alleviate the appalling conditions aboard ship.[51] The labor provisions of the proposed bill were second in priority only to expansion of employment opportunities. The desire to improve the seaman's lot appears to have been in part humanitarian, in part a spin-off of the general economic recovery program, and in part realization that no program to establish a fleet under U.S. flag could succeed without improvement in "the human side of the merchant marine."

The 1936 revision of the nation's maritime program was, in fact, permeated by a spirit of reform, liberality, and even do-goodism. The aim of all concerned was to make a fresh start at the vexing task of building a strong and healthy American merchant marine, based on a "scientific" subsidy system and a will to succeed. However, as the Congress proceeded with the development of a specific proposal, the impracticality of casting aside existing institutions became increasingly apparent. The legislation finally enacted did not make a clean break with the past. One of its principal results was simply to rationalize and legitimize the financial aid programs which had evolved in the years following World War I. Yet despite its limitations, even Senator Black appeared satisfied that the 1936 act provided "the nearest approximation of a subsidy which will protect the public."[52] Senator Copeland, for his part, achieved at least partial success in his objective "to perfect a bill which will be helpful and in no way harmful to the American merchant marine."[53]

---

was badly defeated in a 1922 strike and exercised little real leadership and almost no bargaining power until a new group of leaders gained control of the unions in late 1936 and 1937. A complete history of the maritime labor movement during this period is provided by Joseph Goldberg, *The Maritime Labor Story* (Harvard University Press, 1957).

[51] Wages on U.S. flag ships had fallen to $50 per month for able seamen; subsistence was estimated to be provided at less than $.35 per man per day; working conditions were appalling. Sixty percent of the seafaring workforce had no fixed address, 80 percent were unmarried. In Furuseth's words, "the average seaman looks upon himself as the last thing. There is nothing he can do outside that does not raise his self esteem." *The Merchant Marine Act, 1935*, Hearings, p. 404.

[52] *Congressional Record*, Vol. 280, Pt. 10 (1936), p. 10073.

[53] *The Merchant Marine Act, 1935*, Hearings, p. 29.

3

The Government Aid Program

THE 1935-36 DEBATE over U.S. shipping and subsidy policies resulted in a complete overhauling of the statutory framework for providing government aid to the U.S. flag industry and a thoroughgoing reorganization of the program's administration. The 1936 act and the institutions established pursuant to it have been the basis for all subsequent development of the government's maritime program. This chapter undertakes a detailed exposition of the terms and conditions of the statute and the arrangements provided for its administration. It includes also a brief synopsis of the new Maritime Commission's pre-World War II and wartime activities.

Statutory Framework

The Merchant Marine Act, 1936, was composed of eight substantive titles and a title of miscellaneous provisions and repeals. The act restated the policy of the 1920 and 1928 statutes but wiped away most of the substance of those laws. One of the most controversial portions of the 1936 act (Title IV) established guidelines for terminating outstanding ocean mail contracts, required to be canceled by June 30, 1937.

Although its declaration of purpose and one or two minor sections contain references to the domestic trades, the 1936 act was primarily directed to the U.S. flag, foreign trade merchant marine.[1] Within this

---

[1] Ships operating in the domestic trade had been protected since 1817 from all foreign competition. The domestic industry had prospered during the 1920's; during the Depression it shared in the nation's general economic distress. In the hearings preceding enactment of the 1936 act, tramp, Great Lakes, and coastwise carriers stated that they had no desire to participate in the subsidy programs. *Development of An American Merchant Marine,* Hearings before the House Merchant Marine and Fisheries Committee, 74 Cong. 1 sess. (1935), pp. 434, 482, and 616.

group, the act focused almost exclusively on dry cargo and passenger liners, the segment of the industry which had been supported under the mail pay program. The act provided for a study of the merits of aiding tramp shipping; it made no reference whatsoever to tankers. As a result it has come to be regarded as a liner statute only.

Development of a Plan. The 1936 act was based on the premise that a national flag fleet of some definite size and composition must be maintained in U.S. foreign trade. The act charged the new Maritime Commission with determining the proper size and composition and with developing a long-range plan for achieving its goals. The Congress required only that the plan provide for "an adequate and well balanced merchant fleet, including vessels of all types"; that the size and composition of the fleet be gauged to "provide shipping service on all routes essential for maintaining the flow of foreign commerce"; and that vessels in the fleet "be so designed as to be readily and quickly convertible into transport and supply vessels in time of national emergency."[2] In developing its plan the commission was instructed to work closely with the Navy Department in determining national defense needs, to encourage private ownership and operation 'insofar as may be practical," and to take all steps necessary to assure the new fleet's efficiency and safety.

The act failed to state what should be considered an "adequate and well balanced" U.S. flag fleet. Whereas the declaration of policy in the 1920 act called for a fleet capable of carrying the "greater portion" of U.S. foreign commerce, the 1936 act substituted the vaguer term "substantial portion." It appears this change was not made to signal any lowering of objectives, but simply to make the statute less rigid and to allay any fears abroad that the United States might try to ramrod an immediate expansion of its fleet in areas in which its present participation was weak.[3]

The Maritime Commission was armed with alternative procedures for implementing its plan. If private shipping firms were willing and able to participate, the commission was directed to use construction and operating differential subsidies to assist them in obtaining the ships and providing the services called for by the plan. Alternatively, the commission was authorized to construct ships for sale or charter to private

---

[2] 49 Stat. 2001.

[3] The debate on the 1936 legislation contains no information on the intent or meaning of the substitution of "the substantial portion" for "the greater portion." The interpretation reported here is that of John Mann, who served as Senator Copeland's aide in the preparation of the bill.

companies. Charters might be combined with operating differential subsidies at the commission's discretion. If no other arrangement could be made, the commission was authorized to negotiate charter agreements including lease-purchase provisions at very favorable terms.[4]

Essential Trade Routes. The procedures for designating the steamship routes and services essential to U.S. foreign trade, first written into the 1920 act to guide the Shipping Board in deploying its war-surplus fleet, were amplified and strengthened in the 1936 act. The Maritime Commission was to develop a route system as a part of its overall plan. Operating and construction aids were authorized only for ships serving the designated routes.

The act provided also that routes and services incorporated by the commission into its long-range plan be kept under continuous review to meet changing needs. Both in the initial plan and in its review the commission was directed to consider:

> . . . the cost of maintaining each of such steamship lines, the probability that any such line cannot be maintained except at a heavy loss disproportionate to the benefit accruing to foreign trade, the number of sailings and types of vessels that should be employed in such lines, and any other facts and conditions that a prudent businessman would consider when dealing with his own business, with the added consideration, however, of the intangible benefit that the maintenance of any such line may afford foreign commerce of the United States and the national defense.[5]

The emphasis upon securing benefits commensurate with the cost mirrored congressional apprehension that the commission might use its planning authority as a springboard for another expansive experiment, repeating the enormous losses experienced in the 1920's. But because the benefits of U.S. flag shipping to the nation's foreign commerce are so intangible and elusive, the criteria have lacked force.

Parity Concept. The second key concept of the 1936 act was that the subsidized U.S. foreign trade lines be on a parity with their foreign com-

[4] Sec. 714, Merchant Marine Act, 1936, authorizes the commission to place vessels on bareboat charter to the American flag operator established in a trade, without advertisement or competition, upon an annual charter hire of not less than 5 percent of their estimated foreign construction cost and to allow an option to purchase within five years with credit on the purchase price for all the charter hire paid. Operating subsidy might also be allowed the charterer. These provisions, included in the title chiefly sponsored by opponents of the subsidy portion of the bill, in actuality provide the more generous mode of assistance.

[5] 49 Stat. 1989.

petition. In order to achieve parity, both a construction and an operating subsidy were authorized—the former to offset the higher costs of U.S.-built ships, and the latter to compensate for differentials in operating costs.

Neither the statute nor its legislative history was precise as to the meaning of parity, the manner in which it was to be calculated, or whether the intent was to equalize costs, earnings, or opportunity. The act provides only that the payment shall not exceed the difference between the fair and reasonable costs of the same items of expense were the vessels operated under foreign flag or built in a representative foreign shipbuilding center.[6] An additional payment (or "countervailing subsidy") was authorized if needed to offset a subsidy paid to a foreign flag competitor.

The opponents of the 1936 bill had warned that the difficulty of calculating parity made the system unworkable and productive of fraud. In answer to these criticisms the bill's sponsors wrote elaborate precautions into the act. The most potent were provisions to recapture 50 percent of the subsidy payment to any line whose operating profits (averaged over a five-year period) exceeded 10 percent of capital necessarily employed in the business, and on subsidized construction to recover all profits exceeding 10 percent of the contract price.[7] The act also required annual redetermination of foreign-domestic cost differentials, separate calculations with respect to each foreign trade route and each item of expense, and detailed accounting for all domestic costs claimed by subsidized U.S. flag operators.[8] In addition it specified that the construction differential should not exceed 33⅓ percent of the domestic price unless four of the five members of the commission believed there was convincing evidence that the actual differential was greater, and that in any event the differential might not exceed 50 percent.

Construction and Operating Subsidies. The 1936 act extended eligibility for operating differential subsidies to any U.S. flag line whose pro-

[6] 49 Stat. 1996, 2002. The difficulties which the commission has encountered in implementing this ambiguous formula are recounted in Chapter 6.

[7] 49 Stat. 1998, 2004. The construction recapture has since been supplanted by renegotiation, applicable to the government's entire business with the shipyard. The recapture period for operating subsidy has been extended to ten years.

[8] These provisions were designed to refine the calculations so that the subsidy paid should equal as nearly as possible the actual difference between U.S. and foreign costs. The bill's legislative history favors a calculation based on actual cost rather than estimated cost, such as the incentive "lump sum" plan which the Shipping Board had used in contracts with some of its managing operators. Although attractive in concept, the "lump sum" contracts had been abused by certain operators.

posed service the commission found necessary to meet foreign flag competition and to promote the foreign commerce of the United States; who either owned or would acquire appropriate U.S.-built vessels, and possessed the ability, experience, financial resources, and other qualifications necessary to meet the competition; and who required a subsidy in order to operate on a parity with foreign flags. A specific protective provision barred payment of subsidy to a new U.S. flag service or either of two competing U.S. lines (if the effect would be to give one an undue advantage) unless the subsidy was deemed necessary to provide adequate service by U.S. flag vessels. Award of subsidy also required findings pertaining to the applicant's corporate structure; interests in foreign flag ship operations, and brokerage, nonshipping and related activities; and potential competition with domestic lines. Finally, the commission was required to make a general finding that the granting of aid was "reasonably calculated to carry out effectively the purpose and policy of this Act."[9]

Eligibility for construction subsidies was keyed to similar tests, including a finding that the ship was to be used in an essential service in U.S. foreign commerce.[10] In general the act anticipated that companies would receive both operating and construction subsidies. However, it was so designed that firms could draw one form of aid without assuming the obligations associated with the other.

The act offered little guidance on how its eligibility tests should be administered. Proponents of the program appear to have envisioned its embracing virtually all of the foreign trade liner fleet, while those who opposed it anticipated a rigorous examination of each applicant. The result was to pass on to the new commission the difficult tasks of developing some acceptable policy on the limits of the program and of evolving standards to guide its implementation.

Other Financial Aids. The purpose of the operating and construction differential subsidies was simply to neutralize disadvantages of the U.S. flag industry; parity alone was considered inadequate to build up an American merchant marine or to assure the introduction of more effi-

[9] Language specifying eligibility criteria is contained principally in sections 601-605, 804, and 805 of the Merchant Marine Act, 1936 (49 Stat. 1985).

[10] Sec. 501, Merchant Marine Act, 1936. The stipulation that ships acquired through the construction subsidy program must be used in an essential foreign trade service was withdrawn in 1952 (see Chapter 6). When a subsidized vessel is used in a service for which construction subsidies are not payable, the owner is required to make a pro-rata repayment to the government (49 Stat. 1995, 1999).

cient equipment. Government experts and many industry officials believed replacement of the largely obsolete, war-built vessels of the U.S. fleet to be a prerequisite to an efficient and competitive maritime industry.[11] Some even believed that with new ships, American companies would be able to compete without subsidy.[12]

One of the principal deterrents to acquiring new ships was the difficulty of obtaining private mortgage money on reasonable terms. In the volatile international shipping business, investment values have always been unstable. Regardless of the debenture form, ship mortgage loans inevitably have had many of the characteristics of equity investments—characteristics which were painfully evident in 1935 when one-third of all U.S. vessel mortgages were in default and the market value of the collateral of others was generally inadequate to secure the loan.

Because of the difficulties of obtaining private credit, the sponsors of the 1920 Merchant Marine Act established a construction fund through which the government could make construction and mortgage loans at modest interest rates. In 1928 the interest rate guideline was liberalized and during the next several years loans were extended at extremely low rates, dropping in 1930 to as little as one-eighth of 1 percent.[13] Because he believed that the loan program had been abused, President Roosevelt recommended that the Congress "terminate the practice of lending Government money for shipbuilding."[14] Congress chose to continue the construction revolving fund, but fixed a 3½ percent interest rate on all new loans.[15]

[11] A beginning had been made on the replacement of obsolete tonnage under the 1928 act; although only 29 ships had been built, these were relatively costly combination passenger-cargo vessels. Approximately 140 freighters—30 percent of the U.S. dry cargo fleet then operating in foreign trade—could have been built for the same expense.

[12] For example, see testimony of A. H. Haag, chief of the Shipping Board Bureau's research division, *The Merchant Marine Act, 1935*, Hearings before the Senate Commerce Committee, 74 Cong. 1 sess. (1935), p. 120.

[13] Sec. 301(a), Merchant Marine Act of 1928, keyed construction loan interest rates to "the lowest rate of yield . . . of any Government obligation . . . outstanding at the time the loan is made." Subsequent legislation allowed interest-free loans for certain purposes. The Shipping Board, faithful to the letter of the statute, reduced its rate to a nominal one-eighth of 1 percent. The total interest subsidy on construction loans under the 1928 act was later calculated by the Postmaster General at $34 million.

[14] *Message of the President of the United States*, H. Doc. 118, 74 Cong. 1 sess. (1935), p. 2.

[15] Neither the Postmaster General nor the Interdepartmental Committee on Shipping Policy had recommended to the President that the construction loan program be discontinued, nor were the merits of the President's proposal ever discussed in

The second nonparity aid included in the 1936 act was forgiveness of corporate income taxes on amounts set aside in capital reserves to finance ship construction. Since the maximum corporate tax rate in 1936 was only 15 percent, this benefit was of little immediate importance; but it gained great significance during and following World War II.

Government Construction and Operation. Sponsors of the 1936 statute were confident that private enterprise would respond to these incentives to rebuild the American merchant marine. The bill's opponents did not share this confidence. Thus the bill empowered and directed the government to take direct action to fulfill its long-range plan should the indirect incentives fail. The Maritime Commission was given authority to use its construction fund to build ships for government account, even if the vessels' sale could not be anticipated; to build vessels in naval shipyards in the event that no private yard submitted an acceptable bid; and to bareboat charter government-owned vessels to private firms. Curiously, in view of the broad mandate given the commission, the Congress repealed the portion of the 1916 Shipping Act which had authorized the government to operate ships with government personnel or through managing agents. The commission was given one year to sell the four government-owned lines still operated for government account or to convert to bareboat charter agreements.

Protective Devices. The disclosures of malpractice which had preceded passage of the 1936 act caused many protective provisions to be written into the new law to guard against their repetition. Their effect was to expose both subsidized and charter operators to such extensive government supervision as to make them in effect quasi-public corporations.

The 1936 act barred payment of salaries in excess of $25,000, restricted funds available for payment as dividends, and provided for recapture by the government of certain excess profits. Subsidized lines were prohibited from maintaining business relations with any persons or firms in which they held any pecuniary interest, except upon approval of the commission. Subsidized and charter operators were also barred from owning or operating foreign flag vessels, or acting as agents or brokers for foreign lines. Except for those previously in the trade,

---

the Congress. The questions discussed were whether government should retain title to ships whose construction it had largely financed and what down payment requirement it should impose. The 1936 act required a down payment amounting to 25 percent of the total construction cost. This stringent requirement was reduced two years later to 25 percent of the estimated cost to the operator after subsidy.

no subsidized line might carry domestic cargoes unless specifically authorized by the commission; in any event it was prohibited from diverting funds earned in overseas services to underwriting a domestic route. Finally, all contractors were admonished to operate in the most economical and efficient manner possible, and the commission was restricted to subsidizing only "fair and reasonable" costs.

In order to strengthen the finances of the U.S. flag industry, the act required that subsidized operators establish capital and special reserves. The operator was required to make an annual deposit to the capital reserve equaling the depreciation on his subsidized vessels, together with any funds realized from the ships' sale or other disposition. All earnings in excess of 10 percent of the capital necessarily employed in the business were to be paid into the special reserve fund, to be held until the government's recapture accounting was settled.[16] Special reserve fund balances in excess of 5 percent of capital necessarily employed might then be withdrawn for payment of dividends or other purposes.

Investment of the reserve funds was limited to approved interest bearing obligations, with the interest credited to the reserve. In general the management of the reserve funds was so closely supervised by the government that there was some initial confusion as to whether they should be considered government or private property. In 1938 a new statute made it clear that upon termination of a subsidy contract and settlement of all outstanding obligations, the remainder of the reserve would go to the operator.[17]

Labor Provisions. An entire title of the 1936 act was directed toward improving the position of American seamen serving aboard subsidized ships. Companion legislation, intended to advance safety at sea by improving the caliber of American seamen, was approved concurrently with the 1936 act.[18] Together, these statutes conferred important new

---

[16] The procedure for handling recapture accounting was administratively amended in 1949 in order to withhold from current subsidy payments the amount estimated each year to be likely eventually to be recaptured on account of that year's operations. Authority to make tax deferred deposits to the special reserves has, however, been continued.

[17] P.L. 75-705 (52 Stat. 953).

[18] P.L. 74-808 (49 Stat. 1930). This legislation established the three-watch system and eight-hour day on board all ocean-going U.S. flag ships, set out minimum standards for crew quarters, elaborated on qualifications and duties of able-bodied seamen and other ratings, and provided that the government should maintain a continuous record of each seaman's employment, an innovation which was bitterly opposed by most of the unions. These provisions are discussed by Joseph Goldberg in *The Maritime Labor Story* (Harvard University Press, 1958), pp. 182 ff.

responsibilities on the government to oversee wages and working conditions aboard U.S. flag ships. They also introduced new restrictions on employment of aliens on board U.S. flag ships.

More exacting standards were applied to subsidized than non-subsidized vessels. For example, the Merchant Marine Act required all officers and at least 90 percent of subsidized crews to be citizens; the companion legislation permitted 25 percent of the crews of non-subsidized ships to be non-citizens. The 1936 act also directed the Maritime Commission to incorporate minimum wage and manning scales into all its subsidy contracts, and to adjust the subsidy payments to cover any increases in vessel operating expenses occasioned by its standards.

Cargo Preferences. When the 1936 act was developed, it already was an established government policy to encourage U.S. shippers (and particularly government agencies) to patronize U.S. registered ships. A 1904 statute required that all military shipments be made in U.S. flag vessels, if available at reasonable rates.[19] When it was discovered in 1934 that certain foreign buyers were routing purchases financed by U.S. government loans via foreign flag, the Congress passed a resolution expressing its intent that all future government-financed exports be routed exclusively via U.S. flag vessels.[20] The 1936 act, in confirmation of these preferential policies, directed the commission to cooperate with shipowners in devising means to induce commercial importers and exporters to patronize U.S. flag vessels, and to work with other government agencies and independent trade organizations to secure preferences for American ships.

National Defense Features. Several sections of the 1936 act dealt specifically with the potential military role of a revived U.S. flag fleet. One provided that the commission check with the Navy on the plans and specifications for any vessels which it proposed to build or subsidize. A second provided that the commission pay the entire cost of "national defense features" recommended by the Navy and incorporated into the

[19] 33 Stat. 518.

[20] Public Resolution 17, 73 Cong. 2 sess. (1934). This resolution applies specifically to export shipments financed in whole or part by "any loans made by . . . any . . . instrumentality of the government." It may reasonably be assumed that the Congress would have taken an even stronger position on government-owned or government-subsidized cargoes. The Attorney General in 1935 interpreted the resolution as not binding upon the lending agency, but advised that the views of the Shipping Board as to the feasibility of U.S. flag routing should be obtained in each instance.

design. Vessels constructed with subsidy aid were made subject to re-purchase by the government at cost less depreciation. The commission was also given the power to requisition any privately owned merchant vessel during a national emergency declared by the President, subject to payment of "just compensation."[21]

Program Administration

The failure of the mail subsidy program was recognized in 1936 to have been the result of a malconceived statute compounded by extraor-dinarily maladroit administration. Thus reorganization of the adminis-tration of the subsidy program was agreed to be an essential concom-itant to revision of its statutory framework. The sponsors of the 1936 legislation also acknowledged that their bill was not perfect, for time had prevented adequate consideration of many important matters, and that the feasibility of the new plan would have to be tested by ex-perience and the program modified to meet new developments. For these tasks a creative, energetic administrative agency was considered indispensable.

Organization. The U.S. Maritime Commission was a five-member, bi-partisan, independent regulatory agency vested with a broad spectrum of promotional, quasi-judicial, administrative, and operating functions. Commissioners were appointed for staggered six-year terms and were removable only for neglect of duty or malfeasance in office. The Presi-dent designated the commission's chairman, who, until 1949, had no special statutory powers beyond those of presiding officer. Like the other members, the chairman received a salary (in 1937) of $12,000 per annum.

The commission's responsibilities under the statute were primarily to the Congress. Certain of its activities, such as the settlement of mail pay contracts, were subject to executive branch review, but in most of its work the commission was truly independent. The President's role was limited to appointments of commission members, preparation of the annual budget, and coordination under the Merchant Marine Act of 1920 of the activities of the commission and other maritime-related agencies.

The commission was vested with an extraordinarily wide range of functions. It was to perform economic and trade analyses to determine

[21] This power was liberalized in 1939 to permit requisition whenever the President shall proclaim the security of the national defense makes it advisable.

the type of fleet America needed and to plan how it could be obtained; to negotiate millions of dollars of subsidy, construction, and charter contracts and to adjudicate disputes among competing applicants for contracts; to carry forward the 1916 regulatory program; to investigate and reform working conditions in the U.S. maritime industry; to act as custodian for the remnant of the World War I fleet; and to oversee the operations of several government-owned shipping lines. The diversity and potentially incompatible nature of these activities did not appear to be of concern to either the Congress or the new commission. In fact, the concern was whether additional shipping functions, then administered by the Coast Guard, Bureau of Customs, and Steamboat Inspection Service, should not also be transferred to the new commission.

Special Assignments. The importance of the work of the new commission is suggested by the number and variety of special projects which the Congress delegated to it. Its most important task, of course, was to draw up a plan for reconstituting the maritime industry. In addition it was directed by the statute to:

Determine and keep up to date records on the relative costs of ship construction and operation in the United States and abroad.

Determine the extent and character of government aids granted to foreign flag fleets.

Advise the Congress regarding the adequacy and efficiency of the U.S. shipbuilding industry.

Investigate whether any provisions in the Merchant Marine Act should be made applicable to aircraft engaged in foreign commerce.

Investigate the advisability of establishing special export rates for farm and other bulk products.

Conduct an engineering research program in collaboration with industry.

Study new vessel designs and uses, including the construction of superliners convertible into troopships.

Investigate discrimination by foreign governments against U.S. commerce and shipping.

Investigate the desirability of the United States' sponsoring an ocean tramp fleet.

Investigate ways of improving intercoastal and inland water transportation systems.

Make annual reports to the Congress, including recommendations for new or amended legislation.

This long roster of tasks testifies to Congress' dependence on the administrative agency as well as Congress' inability to reach conclusions on these matters. It constituted an imposing agenda for a new agency charged with creating a viable industry out of near chaos.

Personnel Resources. To accomplish its mission the new commission was granted unusual latitude in selecting and establishing the conditions for employment of its personnel. Authority was given to recruit ninety employees plus an indeterminate number of field inspectors outside the usual civil service regulations and at salaries to be fixed by the commission. In addition the commission was authorized to employ former Shipping Board Bureau staff for a six-month probational period and then certify to the Civil Service Commission only those whom it found to be satisfactory.

For membership on the commission itself President Roosevelt nominated five distinguished and able men, whose qualifications were in sharp contrast to the indifferent and largely untrained personnel who had been members of the old Shipping Board since World War I. Joseph P. Kennedy, who had chaired the Securities and Exchange Commission during its initial year's operation, was the nominee for chairman. A senior vice admiral, H. A. Wiley, was vice chairman. Rear Admiral Emory Land brought solid experience in naval engineering to the commission. Thomas Woodward was a Shipping Board Bureau lawyer who had won the respect of both proponents and opponents of the new program. Former Congressman Edward Moran of Maine represented the group in Congress who profoundly distrusted the new enterprise.

Although Kennedy resigned after ten months to become U.S. Ambassador to Great Britain, the remaining membership on the commission was remarkably stable until World War II. Kennedy was succeeded as chairman by Admiral Land, who continued in this office through 1945.[22]

Financial Resources. The low esteem to which the Shipping Board had fallen had caused an erosion of its financial resources. In 1935 only 160 persons were employed by the board and its operating arm, the Merchant Fleet Corporation. In a major strengthening of the organization, the new commission was authorized in 1937 to employ 650 persons,

---

[22] Since World War II the commission and its successor agencies have not been able either to attract or to hold top personnel. Twelve individuals have served an average of only 1.7 years apiece as director or chairman of the maritime agency. In all, twenty-seven persons have served as members of the regulatory commission. See also Chapter 9 and Appendix D.

and succeeded by the end of the year in building its staff up to the authorized level.

To finance the new organization's programs, $108 million previously appropriated to the Shipping Board and Post Office for ship construction and mail payments was transferred to the commission. This fund was made available to the commission without limitation either as to time or as to the specific purpose for which it was to be used.

Legal Powers. Ample legal powers also were conferred upon the new commission. Specifically, the commission was authorized to adopt a seal, to keep an official record, to issue subpoenas as necessary in the discharge of its duties, to impose certain civil penalties, and to issue all necessary rules and regulations to carry out its duties under the act. In addition, because of the business nature of its operations, the commission was granted special authority to:

> make such disbursements as may, in its discretion, be necessary to carry on the activities authorized by this Act, or to protect, preserve, or improve the collateral held by the Commission to secure indebtedness, in the same manner that a private corporation may contract within the scope of authority granted by its charter.[23]

The Comptroller General was specifically instructed to approve any commission expenditures falling under this authority, notwithstanding any other provisions of law.

The Maritime Commission in Action

The machinery established by the Merchant Marine Act, 1936, was energetically activated as soon as Chairman Kennedy assumed office in April 1937. Mr. Kennedy brought to the shipping agency a fresh pragmatic approach and many new personnel who accepted their assignment to rebuild the U.S. maritime industry with enthusiasm, confidence, and relish.

Immediate Tasks. Three broad tasks faced the commission in 1937. The most urgent was to settle the expiring mail pay contracts, required by law to be terminated by June 30, 1937. The lines had filed claims under these contracts amounting to $166 million, while the Black Committee had filed extensive data with the Justice Department for possible prosecution of certain contractors. A few days before the June 30 dead-

[23] 49 Stat. 1988.

line, an agreement was reached by all parties to withdraw virtually all claims, and the mail contracts were terminated at a net cost to the government of less than $1 million.

The commission's second task was to draw up a plan for the American merchant marine. It soon concluded that a thorough survey of the current status and performance of the U.S. flag fleet was essential to establish a proper basis for long-range planning and made a major effort to achieve a definitive study, drawing upon the insights and expertise of industry and university personnel as well as government officials. In November 1937 the commission issued its *Economic Survey of the American Merchant Marine*, which remains one of the most penetrating and realistic documents in this field.[24]

The commission's third task was to make a beginning in rebuilding the U.S. foreign trade merchant fleet. The major areas of commission interest and responsibility in reconstructing the fleet were finance, subsidy administration, labor relations, and new ship construction.

Soon after taking office, Kennedy became convinced that sounder finances were a prerequisite to reconstruction of the U.S. flag fleet, and that this could be realized only by forcing mergers among the thirty-six corporate entities potentially eligible to receive subsidies. The commission estimated that the total net worth of these lines was only about $56 million; the majority of companies obviously were unable to finance any new construction or even to enjoy any flexibility in managing their business. Kennedy's objective was to reduce the number to about a dozen substantial companies, which would be capable of competing on equal terms with the largest of the European lines.

To complement company mergers, the number of separately delineated routes in U.S. foreign trade was drastically reduced by the commission and the trading area assigned to each subsidized operator expanded.[25] It was intended that only one subsidized operator would be maintained on each route.

The commission assumed that it could induce weak companies to merge with stronger lines, which it would certify to service the routes. Instead, many of the smaller lines chose to forego government aid. Of the thirty-two companies which had been receiving mail payments at the time of the enactment of the 1936 bill, only seventeen applied for

[24] U.S. Maritime Commission, *Economic Survey of the American Merchant Marine* (Government Printing Office, 1937).

[25] The Shipping Board had mail contracts with thirty-two lines operating over fifty-three routes. Government-owned lines operated in five other services. Kennedy's aim was to reduce the number of routes to approximately twelve.

subsidies which the commission offered on an interim basis in 1937 to any potentially qualified applicant. Only twelve still remained in the program by 1939, after qualifications had been more thoroughly examined.

Those lines which did apply for or participate in the subsidy program were subjected to rigorous supervision by the commission, whose field force was instructed to audit all facets of the companies' operations. The commission's involvement in the industry's management was further intensified when two of the largest U.S. flag lines (the Dollar and Munson Lines) went bankrupt. At the President's request, the commission took direct responsibility for organizing a new Good Neighbor service to South America. For several years it also continued to operate five older government-owned lines through charter arrangements with private firms.

Surveys to establish minimum wages and working conditions and related activities aimed at improving the industry's labor relations were another preoccupation of the new commission. During 1936 and 1937, union organization on board ship was in a state of flux, as new leaders attempted to unseat the old guard of the established unions. Unfortunately, even before Mr. Kennedy took office, temporary appointees to the new commission had become identified with management in its struggle against the insurgents.[26] During the first several months of his term, Mr. Kennedy attempted, with only partial success, to remain neutral in the struggle.[27] Later he became convinced that more stable, responsible labor relations were so critical to the industry's survival that additional government powers were needed; he recommended that a separate agency be established to mediate maritime labor disputes.[28]

[26] Temporary appointments were made to the newly established Maritime Commission on Oct. 1, 1936, in an effort to avert a threatened industry-wide strike. The temporary chairman, Henry Wiley, appointed another admiral to investigate labor-management disputes. The unions soon decided that the results of the commission's investigations would be at best only to delay their winning improved wages and working conditions. See Goldberg, *op. cit.*, pp. 155-57.

[27] Despite the commission's efforts to be impartial, its ultimate responsibility for operation of government-owned ships thrust it directly into the fray. The commission's dilemma was highlighted in the widely publicized strike aboard the S.S. "Algic," in which the commission ordered that sailors disobeying the captain's orders on board a government-owned ship in a foreign port be placed in irons. *Ibid.*, p. 188.

[28] The commission's recommendation was to apply arbitration procedures patterned on the Railway Labor Act to the maritime industry. This proposal was opposed by maritime labor, and Congress instead established a temporary Maritime Labor Board with conciliation and fact-finding functions only (52 Stat. 963). Authority for the board's operation was limited to three years. It concluded its activities in 1941.

The construction program announced by the commission upon completion of its *Economic Survey* was to build fifty ships per year to upgrade the existing fleet. The commission rejected any major expansion of U.S. capacity on the grounds that U.S. foreign commerce simply could not support a liner fleet significantly larger than the present operation. However, it placed a high priority on replacing the merchant marine's obsolete ships and proceeded with its plan under Title VII (construction for government account) when it became clear that the replacement program would or could not be privately financed.[29]

Proposed Legislation. As it gained experience under the 1936 act, the commission considered the revisions needed to put the program on a sounder long-term basis. After only one year the commission had begun to doubt that the structure of the 1936 act offered a reasonable likelihood that its objectives could be achieved. In fact, Chairman Kennedy stated flatly in November 1937 that the statute was "unworkable," that there was little chance that under it the commission could build an efficient merchant marine, and that he thought the act "about the worst piece of legislation" he had ever seen.[30]

The amendments suggested by the commission, however, were modest. Many were aimed at liberalizing what the commission concluded were unreasonable restrictions, others were simply clarifying amendments, and still others were designed to give additional options to the commission and its contractors. The proposal which in retrospect was perhaps the most significant—an option to build ships abroad in the event that the construction cost differential should exceed the maximum subsidy allowed by the 1936 act—was vehemently opposed by shipbuilding companies and their labor unions, and defeated. Most of the remainder of the commission's proposals were, however, approved.[31]

The commission's lack of confidence in the 1936 act grew out of the

[29] At the time the construction program was undertaken the commission estimated that it would be able to dispose of about 65 ships over a five-year period. By the end of 1939, of 127 ships contracted or launched under the construction program, only 38 had buyers.

[30] *Amending the Merchant Marine Act, 1936,* Hearings before the House Merchant Marine and Fisheries Committee, 75 Cong. 1 sess. (1937), p. 33.

[31] Among the more significant amendments approved in 1938 were: extension of the recapture period from five to ten years; provision for voluntary deposits to the tax-exempt reserves; authorization to subsidy contractors to void the contract and transfer their vessels to foreign flag in the event the government should default in its obligations or that it determines a reasonable profit cannot be earned on the route; reduction in the down payment requirements for ship purchase; and establishment of a ship mortgage guarantee program (52 Stat. 968).

compromise character of the legislation. The willingness of both opponents and supporters of the program to delegate unresolved issues to the new commission, amply equipped with both personnel and financial resources, accounted for the remarkable successes of the first year. But hardly had a year elapsed before apprehensions began to reappear. The real test lay in the future.

Wartime Activities. Germany invaded Poland on August 30, 1939—less than thirty months following the new Maritime Commission's activation. Neutrality legislation, barring American vessels from the war zone, was enacted in November. American rearmament was initiated with a $1 billion supplemental appropriation in May 1940; Lend-Lease was authorized the following January; 50 U.S. tankers were released to Britain in May. Although 175-200 American ships were able to carry goods to Britain by shifting to other flags, the bar to use of U.S. vessels in the war zone was not lifted until November 1941.

The Maritime Commission's program to construct 50 ships per year had not gotten underway until January 1939 when the first keel was laid. The commission had 127 dry cargo ships and 12 tankers (being built cooperatively with Standard Oil) under contract at the end of 1939. Its program was accelerated the following summer with the objective of contracting 200 freighters by December 1940. During December arrangements also were concluded to build 60 vessels to a simplified British design for sale to Great Britain. The first U.S. order for 200 of these "ugly ducklings," later designated Liberty ships, was placed in January 1941; before U.S. entry into the war, approximately 6 million deadweight tons had been contracted.

The magnificent contribution of U.S. shipping to the war effort is well known.[32] The scope of the undertaking was staggering. Five thousand ships were delivered from 1942 through 1945. Expenditure for merchant ship construction exceeded $12 billion. A work force of 4 million persons was directly engaged in the effort, including some 1.7 million in the ships' final fabrication. At their peak production U.S. shipyards were operating at a rate which would have reproduced the entire prewar tonnage of the U.S. merchant marine in only sixteen weeks and the entire world fleet in less than three years.[33]

[32] An official history of the Maritime Commission's wartime work is given by F. C. Lane *et al.*, *Ships For Victory* (Johns Hopkins Press, 1951).

[33] Statistics from Harvard Business School, *The Use and Disposition of Ships and Shipyards at the End of World War II* (Harvard University Press, 1945), p. 8. The figures assume that total yard capacity could be devoted to merchant ship construction.

The fact that a strong public institution had been organized and was in active contact with the shipping and shipbuilding industries at the outbreak of hostilities enormously facilitated meeting emergency needs. However, the wartime program failed to follow the pattern anticipated by the supporters of the 1936 legislation. Ironically, the long-standing prediction that the United States would lack the ships necessary to carry neutral trade was never realized (the immediate impact of neutrality legislation had been to idle about one-third of the fleet; even after the fall of France about 10 percent of America's ships were still in lay-up). More seriously, the assumption that a fleet adequate to carry the United States' peacetime commerce would also be adequate for wartime needs proved seriously in error.[34] Nonetheless, as one naval officer is reported to have phrased it, the foundations which had been laid by the prewar commission for its massive wartime program were "the best one could reasonably expect in a democracy in which private enterprise still flourishes."[35]

Concluding Remarks on Part I:
Underpinnings of the Government Program

The questions which Theodore Roosevelt put to the Congress in 1903—whether America's position warranted aid to its merchant marine and if so, the "exact costs and proper methods of carrying it on"—would appear on their face to be matters susceptible to logical analysis and ready disposition. They proved otherwise. To survey the development of U.S. maritime policy is to expose a welter of cross currents, conflicting objectives, and highly charged overtones. First the tariff issue, then the attempt to establish economic regulation, the problem of direct public assistance to private enterprise, the issues related to government versus private ownership, and the equities of shippers versus shipowners and

[34] The magnitude of miscalculation is forcibly expressed in the Harvard Business School study, cited above. Its conclusion is that the failure to have adequate ships and shipyards was due to the failure of government and private industry to play their correct roles. The report continues, "All the maritime legislation which was enacted in the 20th century and all the men who were Presidents during that time recognized the dual functions of the merchant marine as a transportation system in peace and a necessity in time of war. . . . All the merchant marine acts were designed both to promote trade and to provide an auxiliary fleet. None of them stated, however, that the national security demanded an adequate fleet even if there were no trade, even if there were no private enterprise. *None of them realized that the job which had to be done was a bigger job than private enterprise can ever do.* Thus the results were compromise attempts to build up private enterprise by artificial and nonprivate means to do a job which private enterprise as such could not do by itself." (*Op. cit.*, p. 23.)

[35] "Freedom of What Seas," *Fortune*, Vol. 20, No. 5 (Nov. 1939), p. 87.

of management versus labor all generated a high degree of political controversy. It required the unifying force of a world war and a major depression to achieve enactment of any legislation, and even these events failed really to resolve the ideological impasse among the various parties in interest.

The most enduring question in the debate over the government's policy toward an American merchant fleet in foreign trade was not the desirability of a fleet but the method of establishing it. The focus of this debate was the issue of public versus private ownership and control. At one pole were liberal Democrats like Senators William McAdoo and Joseph Guffey, who believed that government must play a dominating role in merchant shipping in order to assure that public objectives were achieved. Title VII of the 1936 act, which was the product of their point of view, assumed that the government should formulate a comprehensive plan for the development and utilization of a U.S. flag fleet and take whatever steps were necessary to execute its program. At the opposite extreme were men like Horace Greene, Schuyler Otis Bland, and Royal S. Copeland, who believed that the merchant marine, like any other business, should be allowed to operate unfettered by governmental controls. Their object was simply to establish a measure of protection which would permit a merchant fleet under U.S. flag to develop naturally in response to foreign trade opportunities. The parity provisions of the 1936 act reflected their point of view.

The Merchant Marine Act, 1936, combined but failed to reconcile these two divergent viewpoints. It treated the shipping industry as "an instrument of public policy"—neither wholly public nor wholly private— whose relationship to the government was so different from that of a normal public utility that it had to be defined through a special subsidy contract. These contracts neither granted the shipping companies exclusive franchises to their routes nor guaranteed a return on their investment, yet they established so significant a public stake in their operations that the government was inextricably committed to their welfare.

The compromises underlying the 1936 program make its real objectives difficult to identify. For example, it is not clear whether the various obligations imposed on recipients of parity payments (which in fact distort parity) are to be regarded as serious purposes of the government's program or as *quid pro quos* for government aid. Furthermore, the act lacked adequate standards to guide the commission in measuring the value of U.S. flag services and in assessing whether government construction and operation of merchant ships was warranted.

Emphasis on the methods rather than the objectives of the subsidy program also diverted attention from the basic question of whether America's position required that it be in the shipping business at all, and if so, for what purposes. "The most surprising fact of all," reported *Fortune's* editors, who devoted their September 1937 issue entirely to the problems of the U.S. maritime industry, was that "no scientific information whatsoever should be available as to its internal economics, its costs, its profits, or its value to the Navy, to the State Department, to agriculture or to industry. From the standpoint of intelligent statistics or analysis," continued *Fortune*, "the shipping business is a shambles."[36]

Neither in the 1936 statute nor in any of the supporting legislation or legislative history is there to be found even an attempt to articulate the proper relationship between the government's regulatory and promotional policies. During most of the 1920's and 1930's the regulatory program established by the Shipping Act was conceived as a supplementary technique for aiding U.S. flag lines rather than as a means of protecting U.S. shippers individually or the nation's export-import trade generally from discrimination. Similarly, promotion of a national flag fleet was considered desirable per se; no attempt was ever made to use the promotional and regulatory programs jointly in support of a defined foreign trade objective.

The relationship of the country's pre-World War II maritime policies to defense needs was also ambiguous. The dual functions of the merchant marine as an instrument of national policy in peace and war were widely recognized. However, none of the legislation or debate on merchant shipping indicated that these two functions were potentially incompatible or that ships might be needed for national security in greater numbers than could ever feasibly be maintained in commercial operation. Instead, the commercial orientation common to all the maritime legislation enacted from 1920 through 1938 inclusive was accepted as an inevitable and generally satisfactory compromise of defense and economic purposes.

Following World War I, U.S. shipping had increasingly become a business program managed for and by businessmen. In these years defense measures were unpopular, and domestic economic issues dominated national politics. Even the Navy had so little interest in the private maritime industry's defense potential that as late as 1939 planning the industry's defense role was the collateral assignment of a single junior officer.

[36] "Preface to Ships," *Fortune,* Vol. 16, No. 3 (Sept. 1937), p. 55. *Fortune* termed this lack of information and analysis "the rotten core of the shipping business." *Ibid.*

Furthermore, the shipping acts were constructed on the premise that the fleet's use as a naval auxiliary was a by-product of its basically commercial purpose. This order of priority became very clear as the commission set about its task of framing a long-range plan. Its proposal, seen in the context of the threatening war crisis, appeared totally inadequate to several interested congressmen. Mr. Kennedy responded to their criticism as follows:

> I am telling you what is necessary from a commercial point of view. If you decide you want to change the Act and build ships purely for defense, the responsibility then rests with the Government to have the ships built and tied up when we do not need them. *That is an entirely different matter.* But if the Commission's formula is to be to determine the essentiality of the trade routes and what ships are needed on those trade routes, then it is our obligation to tell you frankly that seventy-four additional ships is all that is needed by the present subsidized fleet.[37]

The program established by the 1936 act was unrealistic in certain other respects. The commission soon found a scientific determination of foreign domestic cost differentials to be impossible, and its parity payments consequently little more than informed guesses. "Even if an accurate measurement could be made," the commission reported in 1937, "changing conditions would make the figures out of date almost as rapidly as they could be assembled."[38]

Furthermore, the 1936 legislation gave the commission no real powers through which it might introduce greater efficiency into U.S. flag operations. Indeed, the parity system, by in effect both excusing and underwriting the higher costs of U.S. ship operation, tended to weaken incentives. In addition, the many protective features written into the 1936 act in reaction to past abuses were basically incompatible with imaginative and creative business enterprise.

The act gave the commission no effective powers to deal with increasingly difficult labor-management relations. By 1937 conditions had become critical. In the commission's view, "Unless something can be done to reduce inter-union friction, to increase the efficiency of our crews, and to restore order and discipline aboard our ships, all government efforts to develop a strong American fleet will be futile."[39]

Finally, the commission was hobbled by divided responsibility within

---

[37] *Amending the Merchant Marine Act, 1936,* Hearings, p. 47. Emphasis added.
[38] *Economic Survey of the American Merchant Marine,* p. 77.
[39] *Ibid.,* p. 86.

government for administering programs bearing on the U.S. merchant marine. Its difficulties in the field of labor relations, in which the commission found itself to be at odds with the Department of Labor, were a case in point. In an early report to the Congress the commission noted that no less than fifty federal agencies exercised some measure of authority over the industry.[40]

The statistic throws into bold relief both the intimacy of the government's involvement with this industry and the complexity of the relationships between the public and private participants in the maritime program. Although all forms of economic regulation are difficult, the environment in which the government's maritime program must be carried forward makes it especially so: first, because shipping is an international industry; second, because of the U.S. flag fleet's almost complete dependence on government policy; and third, because of the unique interdependence of the government's programs to regulate international shipping and to develop its own national flag merchant marine to participate in international trade.

Because the objectives of federal maritime policy have not been completely or clearly stated, the underpinnings for the government program have been insecure. From the turn of the century, this field of public endeavor has been dogged by controversy and imperfect results. The frustration of the Maritime Commission after only a year's experience suggested that, despite the improvements secured in the 1936 reforms, the fundamental problems of the maritime industry had not been solved.

[40] *Ibid.*, p. 60.

PART II

*Postwar Developments
and Public Policy*

The conclusion of World War II introduced new conditions for the conduct of the world's business. Changes in merchant shipping were particularly dramatic. At the outbreak of the war the United States had commanded only 14 percent of the world's merchant tonnage. It emerged with 60 percent. While U.S. tonnage quadrupled, the merchant tonnage of the remainder of the world was diminished by one-third. Roughly half of the great prewar British, French, Greek, Dutch, and Norwegian merchant fleets was lost in action. The fleets of Germany and Japan, which had both been important maritime powers prior to the war, were completely eliminated.

World War II ruptured former patterns of trade and upset international economic relationships. It also radically changed the structure, composition, and financial status of the U.S. maritime industry. Coastal and intercoastal dry cargo operations were drastically reduced, but in 1946 three times more U.S. shipping companies were engaged in overseas operations than in 1939. These companies had liquid capital sufficient to purchase some 7 million deadweight tons of shipping—approximately triple the 1939 U.S. flag foreign trade fleet. Seamen's gross wages doubled during the war. The seafarer's unions also benefited, emerging with sizable financial reserves.

The war and postwar reconstruction programs greatly increased the government's involvement in merchant shipping. For several years after the war a large percentage of America's exports continued to be shipped under government sponsorship. Furthermore, following World War II the military departments, which previously had operated only a small number of transport vessels, retained a significant number of ships to resupply the nation's new overseas bases and to provide a nucleus fleet in the event of future war.

World War II had a far-reaching impact on U.S. maritime policy.

It was not until the war demonstrated again how acutely the nation's security depended on its shipping that the merchant marine acquired its reputation as "America's fourth arm of defense." This wartime experience, coupled with America's new worldwide responsibilities, shifted official interest in U.S. merchant shipping away from its commercial role to an intense concern over the adequacy of the U.S. flag fleet for meeting defense requirements.

However, this new orientation was not accompanied by any major restructuring of the nation's maritime programs. In December 1946, the Maritime Commission announced resumption of operating subsidy payments which had been suspended during hostilities. The following June the commission completed a study, requested by the Senate Commerce Committee, to determine whether America's new position in world affairs necessitated any modifications to the prewar program; its report indicated that some modification might indeed be needed but made no positive proposals.†

Throughout the postwar years the Merchant Marine Act, 1936, has remained the keystone to the government's maritime program. Although frequently amended, modified, and amplified by administrative interpretations and rulings, and supplemented by new legislation, the basic thrust, importance, and structure of the statute have remained unchanged. It is this legislation which has provided the basic reference for each of the several agencies successively charged with its administration and which sets the level of expectation of interested industry groups.

The purpose of Part II is to assess how well the prewar program has been adapted to postwar needs. Chapters 4 and 5 report the major postwar developments which either have or should have influenced U.S. maritime policy. Chapter 6 describes how the 1936 act has been administered to meet these challenges. Efforts to extend the government program into new areas in order to fulfill national objectives more effectively are discussed in Chapter 7. Chapter 8 assesses the costs and achievements of the government's programs and the current status of the U.S. merchant marine and concludes with a brief appraisal of the impact of the government program and its adequacy in the light of changing needs.

† The commission's report is printed in *Proposed Amendments to the Ship Sales Act of 1946,* Hearings before the House Merchant Marine and Fisheries Committee, 80 Cong. 1 sess. (1947), pp. 809 ff. The Commission excused its failure to offer any positive proposals on the grounds that pressure of other business had not permitted it.

4

Changes in the Shipping Industry

INTERNATIONAL SHIPPING is a dynamic industry, highly sensitive to changing trade patterns, new technology, and the domestic policies of major maritime nations. To be effective, the government's subsidy program must be sufficiently flexible to adjust to these changes. This chapter identifies the principal postwar developments affecting U.S. foreign trade shipping and briefly notes their relevance to the 1936 program.

Because the conduct of the shipping business is so intertwined with government policies, it often is difficult to disentangle those changes in the industry's operations which have sprung naturally from economic and technological developments from those which have resulted (intentionally or unintentionally) from government policy. This chapter focuses on trends and events beyond the control of the government's maritime agencies in order to identify the challenges to which the program must respond.

The Postwar Market

At the conclusion of World War II, the U.S. flag fleet included approximately 4,500 vessels suitable for commercial use.[1] They were operated by some 130 private companies which had the experience, the funds, and in most cases the desire to continue in commercial operations. However, their future depended on a market for their services.

Even before the war's end, the United States had concluded that postwar reconstruction could be accomplished most effectively by

[1] The 1945 fleet included 2,500 Liberties, 527 Victories, 530 T-2 tankers, 282 coastal and special purpose ships, and 592 ocean-going dry cargo and passenger ships of superior types.

enabling its allies to rebuild their economies by participating fully in a sound system of international exchange. It was recognized that in implementing this general policy the United States should not use its overwhelmingly favorable position to dominate the international shipping industry. The 1946 Merchant Ship Sales Act, which guided disposition of the government's 4,000-ship merchant fleet, consequently was structured to facilitate ship purchases by America's allies as well as by U.S. citizens.[2]

Sale prices for dry cargo vessels were based on the estimated prewar cost of construction in foreign yards less normal depreciation (at 5 percent annually) and a 3 percent "wear and tear" factor for war service, adjusted for the individual vessel's special features and the cost of putting it in class. The basic sales price for Liberty ships was $545,000; for Victory ships, $879,000. Tankers were priced somewhat higher on the grounds that they would be used chiefly in domestic trade, where they would be shielded from competition with foreign-built ships. The pricing was attractive to U.S. buyers, who purchased 247 dry cargo vessels and 59 tankers during the first year of the act's operation. By December 1949, U.S. operators owned a total of 1,101 ocean-going vessels, 1,000 gross tons or over (644 dry cargo, 37 combination passenger and cargo, and 420 tankers) representing a tonnage 43 percent greater than the 1939 fleet. In addition, 111 government-owned ships were on charter to private companies under authority also provided by the 1946 act.

[2] The Merchant Ship Sales Act of 1946 (60 Stat. 41) established fixed prices for each class of government-owned vessel to be applicable to citizens and aliens alike, set a cut-off date for all sales, and provided that vessels not sold by that date be scrapped or placed in a National Defense Reserve Fleet for use only during a national emergency. Administration of the sales program was placed in the Maritime Commission. Ships were made available first to U.S. citizens for purchase. Then blocks of vessels were released by the commission for purchase and transfer abroad as appropriate.

The program was remarkably successful both in laying a basis for orderly demobilization of government ships and in restoring a reasonable balance among the world's merchant fleets. Prior to the 1948 expiration of its authority to make sales to aliens, the Maritime Commission sold more than 1,100 ships for foreign registry. (Authority to sell to U.S. citizens was extended until 1950, by which time 823 ships had been sold.) These sales reconstituted about half of the net wartime loss of the principal foreign flag fleets. Thus, by the end of 1948, U.S. registries (including the reserve fleet) had dropped to 36.4 percent of the world's tonnage; Great Britain's tonnage had been completely restored, although her share of the enlarged world fleet had dropped from 27 to 22 percent; Norway's fleet was within 10 percent of its former tonnage, as were the fleets of France and Denmark. For a complete tabulation, see S. G. Sturmey, *British Shipping and World Competition* (London: The Atholone Press, 1962), p. 139.

Deployment of U.S. Shipping. Over 80 percent of the dry cargo and passenger vessels purchased for U.S. registry through the 1946 ship sales program were placed in foreign trade. In contrast, approximately 60 percent of the fleet had been employed in protected domestic services before the war. Several factors contributed to this shift. The prewar domestic fleet had been sold to or requisitioned by the government early in the war and its business shifted to rails, trucks, and barges. In 1940 regulation of coastwise and intercoastal water carrier rates had been transferred to the Interstate Commerce Commission, a body which the shipping companies feared would not be sympathetic to their interests.[3] Climbing port and longshore charges had also reduced the economic margin which water carriers had previously enjoyed over their land competitors in handling nonpriority traffic.

Following the war the U.S. Maritime Commission tried to reestablish domestic services by operating government-owned ships in coastwise and intercoastal trade. But private companies hesitated to risk purchase of the government lines. By 1950, when the experiment was discontinued, there were only 150 privately owned dry cargo and passenger vessels in domestic service compared to approximately 440 before the war. If the roughly 50 ships engaged in services to Alaska, Hawaii, and Puerto Rico are excluded, the decline is even more precipitous—from about 400 freight and combination vessels in 1936 to roughly 100 in 1950 and only 50 ships in 1963.

The decline in coastwise and intercoastal dry cargo shipping has enormously increased the importance of overseas operations to the U.S. maritime industry. Although a large tanker fleet continues to ply America's coasts,[4] roughly 75-80 percent of the industry's total revenues and 70 percent of its deep sea employment now depend on foreign trade. With few dry cargo ships remaining in coastwise service and these mostly specialized to particular trades, the Department of Defense must depend upon ships in overseas operations to meet its emergency needs. These developments have increased the pressure on the United States to protect its national flag ships against competing foreign flags

[3] Regulation of coastal and intercoastal rates and services was shifted to the Interstate Commerce Commission by the Transportation Act of 1940 (54 Stat. 899) to achieve an integrated and balanced national transportation policy, administered by a single agency, and free of any built-in preferences for particular modes.

[4] Coastwise trade in petroleum products carried by U.S. flag tankers has grown, although the number of vessels has remained fairly static. In 1936, 267 tankers of 2.7 million deadweight tons were engaged in this business; in 1950, 266 ships of 4.0 million tons; in 1956, 263 ships of 4.4 million tons; in 1963, 240 ships of 5.3 million tons.

and to expand its subsidy program. They also have diminished the influence of domestic dry cargo operators and hence their effectiveness as a check on the subsidized sector of the industry.[5]

Foreign Trade Volume. Since World War II U.S. shipowners have enjoyed an expanding market for vessels employed in foreign trade. Although there have been normal year-to-year variations in business conditions, the trend in foreign trade has exceeded even optimistic predictions.[6] In 1960 the tonnage of world seaborne trade (including tanker cargoes) was more than double its peak prewar year (1929) and almost three times the Depression average. Dry cargo tonnage moving in U.S. foreign trade has been at least 50 percent over the 1930 to 1939 average every year since 1945 and since 1955 has averaged more than three times the average prewar lift.

Demand for U.S. flag ships has been further stimulated by a succession of unanticipated crises. Just as the postwar rehabilitation and relief programs were ending, new needs were created by the Korean crisis. After a brief dip following the 1953 Korean armistice, U.S. shipping received new stimulus from a step-up in government-sponsored agricultural exports. Prosperity was sustained through 1956-57 by the temporary closing of the Suez Canal. In 1958 there was a sharp reversal (dry cargoes in U.S. foreign trade fell off 17 percent) and since then the industry has intermittently complained of "overtonnaging." The proportion of world tonnage in lay-up, however, has been reduced from a peak of over 7 percent in 1959 to only 2 percent as of June 30, 1962. From mid-1962 to mid-1965 worldwide supply and demand for ships appears to have been remarkably well balanced.[7] The step-up of shipments to

[5] Domestic and overseas U.S. flag steamship companies have many overlapping interests. Among the most significant are the wages and working conditions to be offered seamen. Before the war, non-subsidized companies led in establishing the industry's wage pattern (the Maritime Commission's authority to fix the minimum wages to be paid seamen on subsidized ships was designed as a lever to encourage a more liberal attitude). Following the war, the subsidized companies took the lead; since then the check rein on wages expected to be exercised by non-subsidized companies has been relatively ineffective.

[6] For example, both the National Planning Association and the Commerce Department projections of postwar trade, made in 1945, anticipated an export-import merchandise business of only $12-$14 billion per year, expressed in 1942 prices. Actual export-import trade during the first decade after the war averaged $26 billion per year—substantially in excess of the estimates even when discounted for price inflation.

[7] Between 1923 and 1939 privately owned U.S. flag ships in lay-up fell beneath 10 percent in only three years. From 1931 to 1935 tonnage in lay-up averaged 27

Vietnam, beginning in the summer of 1965, has caused demand once again to outrun the supply of available U.S. flag ships. (Fifty-one ships had been taken out of reserve as of December 31, 1965.) This has caused charter rates to rise moderately, especially for older, slower ships which otherwise might have trouble finding a charter.

Foreign Trade Composition. While business conditions have been generally favorable throughout the international shipping industry, growth has been concentrated in certain sectors. In U.S. foreign trade, growth in irregular and bulk cargo movements has multiplied by six to eight times over prewar averages the amount of dry cargo tonnage carried in vessel lots by tramps, industrial carriers, and tankers, while increasing only modestly tonnage moved by liners (from 25-35 million tons per year before the war to 48-50 million tons today). In 1937-38, liners handled two-thirds of the dry cargoes in U.S. foreign trade; in 1961-62, they carried less than one-third.

This dramatic expansion in vessel lot shipments, predominately via foreign flags, has resulted chiefly from increased movements of cheap, nonperishable, bulk goods as compared to manufactured and finished products. A rough analysis of the tonnage of goods now typically loaded in bulk for shipment in U.S. export-import commerce indicates bulk shipments have quadrupled since 1937-38.[8]

Increased use of tramps and bulk carriers also reflects changing economies of ocean transportation. Prior to World War II, intense competition for cargoes and the concentration of government aid on berth services caused about one-third of the bulk cargoes in U.S. foreign trade to be shipped on liners. Since the war neither U.S. nor foreign flag berth operators have been compelled to consign so large a portion of their capacity to low-rated bulk goods.[9] Concurrently, new technology and

---

percent of the fleet. Against this perspective the fleet's postwar utilization has been extraordinarily favorable, even though some excess capacity appears still to exist in some services.

[8] "Bulk shipments" are defined as shipments which are loaded "without mark or count." The commodities now typically shipped in bulk are coal, fertilizer, grain, scrap iron, gypsum, bauxite, and other ores. The 1936-38 tonnage of bulk loaded commodities in U.S. foreign trade are estimated from *Annual Statistical Reports* of the U.S. Army Corps of Engineers. These tonnages were compared with 1961 data from vessel loading reports to the U.S. Maritime Administration. Bulk loadings have continued to increase relative to break-bulk shipments since 1961.

[9] In 1938 both U.S. and foreign lines appear to have devoted as much as 35-40 percent of their capacity to carrying cargoes now usually carried in bulk. Currently U.S. liners carry about 20 to 25 percent of their cargoes in bulk; foreign flag liners from 25 to 30 percent.

changing price relationships have placed tramps and bulk carriers in a relatively more favorable position to compete for cargoes which can be moved in bulk or large lots.[10]

Many of the large bulk cargo movements since the war have been crisis or government-created. Although the general trend has been sharply upward, year-to-year volumes have been erratic and the outlook often highly unpredictable. Liner operators, quite naturally, have been hesitant to expand their long-term commitments in order to move into an apparently short-term market.

Although liners have lost large tonnages to bulk carriers and tramps in the postwar period, they have lost only a modest part of the dollar value of their cargo traffic. In fact, the Commerce Department's Office of Business Economics estimates that on a value basis liners still carry 80 percent of the non-military dry cargoes moving in U.S. seaborne foreign commerce. Nonetheless, the development of the bulk cargo business, which was totally unforeseen by the authors of the 1936 act, has posed a major challenge to the government and the U.S. flag industry.

Government Shipments. Since U.S. companies are given preference in the movement of government-sponsored cargoes, the trends in this business are of particular significance to the U.S. merchant marine. Immediately after the war, relief and military goods constituted well over half of all dry cargoes shipped out of U.S. ports and probably in excess of 70 percent of the dry cargoes carried by U.S. vessels. As the European relief program phased out, vessels were shifted to carrying military cargoes to Korea and surplus grains to Pakistan and India. In the peak year, 1951, more than 1,300 U.S. flag dry cargo and combination vessels (including 675 government-owned ships from the reserve fleet) were engaged in overseas operations, principally on government account.

At the conclusion of the Korean war there was a sharp reduction in government shipments. From 1951 through 1953 these shipments had averaged just under 20 million tons per year, of which about 70 percent had been handled by privately owned U.S. flag carriers. In 1954 total government business dropped to less than 12 million tons and its composition shifted from military cargoes, required by law to be shipped

[10] The bulk carrier, specialized to the transportation of a single commodity over a fixed route with terminals equipped for rapid loading and discharge of cargoes, is essentially a postwar development and provides a highly efficient form of transportation. The economic position of the tramp has been improved by the increasing disparity in investment required for liner versus tramp operation.

exclusively by U.S. carriers, to predominately civilian goods, which may be shared equally with foreign flags. The roughly 8 million tons available to U.S. operators in 1954 provided employment for the equivalent of only 200-odd ships, rather than the 400-600 previously employed. Operators who had chartered vessels in 1950 and 1951 hastened to terminate their charter agreements, while those who had purchased obsolete tonnage to meet the temporary demand pressed for permission to transfer surplus vessels to foreign flag in anticipation that the government business had at last sunk to its "normal" peacetime level.

Since 1955, however, government shipments have persistently grown, principally because of the expansion of programs for disposal of surplus agricultural commodities under Public Law 83-480. All components of the U.S. flag industry have shared in the rising volume of business. However, owners of jumboized bulk carriers and those liner companies which operate in the trans-Atlantic and trans-Pacific trades have benefited most—the former because they have been able to underbid war-built tramps for contracts to move government-sponsored surplus grain exports and the latter because they have been favorably positioned to handle the steady flow of military cargo routed via commercial carrier.

Since the 1958 collapse of the world shipping market, U.S. flag liners have also bid for some surplus grain cargoes previously handled almost exclusively by tramps and tankers (treated so that they could safely stow grains). The liners have generally been able to secure as much of this business as they care to take. Between 1958 and 1963, the tonnage of Agriculture Department outbound cargoes carried by liners approximately doubled, providing a valued supplementary revenue whenever more highly rated cargoes were not readily available.

A recent development, of significance particularly to U.S. liner companies, has been curtailment of off-shore procurement by the Agency for International Development (AID) in response to balance of payments pressures. Many of the AID cargoes are highly-rated, break-bulk goods. Furthermore, an increasing proportion of these shipments (close to 100 percent by 1962) have been routed via American merchant ships. These actions have increased the volume of AID cargoes carried by U.S. flag ships from 2.4 million tons in 1960 to 6.2 million tons in 1963.

The importance of government-sponsored cargoes to U.S. flag merchant shipping has been increasing steadily (see Appendix A, Tables A7-A10). By 1962, overall tonnage (inbound and outbound) subject to government control was 20 percent over the 20 million ton 1951 to 1953 average. Twenty percent of all dry cargo shipments outbound from the United States fell within the cargo preference laws. Two-thirds of the tonnage carried by U.S. flag liners and approximately half their revenues were derived from government orders. These cargoes provided virtually the sole source of income for the U.S. flag tramp fleet. The development of this enormous government patronage of U.S. flag shipping was also totally unforeseen in 1936 and has provided an important vehicle for indirectly subsidizing the industry's operations.

Freight Rates. Wartime controls over ocean freight rates were discontinued early in 1946. Through 1948, charter rates on both U.S. and foreign tonnage stood at three to four times their depressed prewar levels. The war's impact on liner rates is more difficult to determine, but appears to have been more modest.[11]

Throughout the postwar period, liner rates in U.S. foreign trade have followed a generally upward trend, interrupted briefly in 1954 and more seriously in 1958. Rate stability has also occasionally been disrupted in specific trades, but these "rate wars" have been sporadic and short-lived. Overall, liner rates are reported to have risen roughly 40 percent from 1947 through 1957.[12] Reliable data on rate trends since 1957 are not available.

Tramp rates are more volatile. In mid-1948 the tramp charter market plunged to about half its postwar peak. At the outbreak of the Korean war tramp rates soared to almost triple their 1949 trough, to which they returned following activation of the U.S. reserve fleet vessels to handle America's cargoes. The Suez crisis caused tramp rates to sky-rocket once again, and again the activation of reserve ships operated as an important brake.

During periods of short supply, U.S. flag tramps have been able to operate profitably at the world market rate. However, when charter rates have dropped, American operators have been unable to meet foreign competition. As a result, U.S.-registered tramps have had to charge more than the going foreign rate. In 1963 this differential was approximately 2.2 to 1—a surcharge which only the government has been willing to pay.[13]

[11] Prewar and postwar liner rates are compared in *Merchant Marine Study and Investigation,* S. Rept. 2494, 81 Cong. 2 sess. (1950), pp. 252 ff.

[12] Allen Ferguson *et al., The Economic Value of the U.S. Merchant Marine* (The Transportation Center, Northwestern University, 1961), p. 365.

[13] A continuing comparison of U.S. and foreign flag charter rates is maintained by the Department of Agriculture. The 1963 figure reflects the ratio between actual U.S. and estimated foreign costs reported by Agriculture during the year.

Pressures on Costs

Both during World War II and throughout the postwar period, there have been severe pressures on the costs of U.S. flag shipping companies. These pressures, felt throughout the U.S. economy and abroad, have posed special problems for regulated and subsidized enterprises which cannot exercise plenary control over their economic destinies. The apparent inability of U.S. flag shipping companies to control costs has been the cause of much of the criticism of the U.S. maritime industry and the source of many of its problems.

Shipboard Labor. The most significant variable in shipping costs is shipboard labor. The wages of the officers and crew compose roughly one-third of the total cost (excluding cargo handling, but including depreciation and overhead) of operating a U.S.-registered dry cargo ship; they compose only 10-12 percent of costs of a comparable Italian dry cargo operation.[14]

It is impossible to make exact comparisons between U.S. and foreign wage data. The trends, however, are clear. An American able-bodied seaman, who in 1936 drew only $50-$60 per month, in 1964 earned about $825 monthly (including payroll taxes and "fringes") while at sea and working a 56- to 60-hour week. The seaman's purchasing power increased by a factor of seven during this period. His contract now typically grants five days vacation for each thirty days employed (up to sixty days per year). Working conditions, meals, and accommodations aboard ships have also enormously improved.

Prior to World War II U.S. seamen's wages were about 50 percent above those of the principal European maritime nations. Now they are three to five times greater. Seamen earned slightly less than the average production worker in U.S. industry in 1936; by 1947 their wages while at sea were about 50 percent greater. Seafaring wages have since advanced roughly 50 percent faster than wages in manufacturing generally, with the result that in 1964 an able-bodied seaman's gross earnings while at sea were approximately double the average manufacturing wage for a 40.7-hour week on shore.

About half the percentage increase in seamen's wages between 1939

[14] Repairs, insurance, and the crews' subsistence run about 10-15 percent of the costs (prior to subsidy) of operating under either U.S. or foreign flag. Other vessel operating expenses tend to be equal for both U.S. and foreign operators and therefore consume a larger proportion of the foreigner's total costs; depreciation, debt service, and overhead are too specialized to the operator's particular situation to generalize.

and 1964 and more than two-thirds of the increase in the differential between wages paid on U.S. and foreign ships occurred prior to 1948. Most of this increase was ordered by the government to compensate for war risks and the sharp rise in the cost of living in the immediate postwar period.[15] The War Shipping Administration introduced the 48-hour shipboard work week, with overtime and premium pay for additional duty. In 1951 the standard work week for pay purposes was reduced to 40 hours in an arbitration conducted by the government Wage Stabilization Board. In 1952 wage settlements reviewed by the board raised base wages for able-bodied seamen to about $300, which was almost 50 percent above the base rate paid five years earlier.

Sustained prosperity in the United States since World War II has increased the premium required to compensate for the isolation and discomforts of work at sea. Seamen on the average are also now older than the group which manned America's wartime fleet and have heavier family obligations. Over half are married. Finally, America's seamen are represented by well-disciplined and aggressive unions which have capitalized effectively on the industry's vulnerability to strikes and dependence on government aid.[16] The seafarers' unions furthermore have received substantial assistance from U.S. longshoremen's associations and the American Federation of Labor-Congress of Industrial Organizations (AFL-CIO), which since 1958 has been particularly interested in the maritime unions as a counter to the nonaffiliated International Brotherhood of Teamsters. Two seamen's union presidents, Joseph Curran of the National Maritime Union (NMU) and Paul Hall of the Seafarers Inter-

[15] General economic recovery together with aggressive union tactics and Maritime Commission minimum wage actions under Title III of the 1936 act had lifted base wages for able-bodied seamen from $50 to $70-plus between 1935 and 1939. Additional awards, granted before wage controls, to compensate for war hazards brought the able-bodied seaman's base wage to $100. During the war various bonuses ordered by the Maritime War Emergency Board increased seamen's gross earnings by about 100 percent. Upon termination of hostilities, a $45 increase in base wages was ordered by the War Labor Board in lieu of further bonuses. A series of other actions during 1946-47, either initiated or approved by the government, brought the able-bodied seaman's base wages to $204.

[16] Leonard Rapping in "The Subsidy and Labor Costs," included in Ferguson *et al.*, *op. cit.*, concludes that about 90 percent of the postwar increase in U.S. seafarers' wages can be ascribed to the industry's strong unions coupled with other, more general social and economic trends. However, Rapping acknowledges that "the impact of the total subsidy program, including the operating differential subsidy, substantially increases the demand for American seamen, and hence improves the union's bargaining position." The impact of subsidies on maritime labor rates and collective bargaining procedures is discussed further in Chapters 6 and 8.

national Union (SIU), are also vice presidents of the AFL-CIO and members of its governing board.

The success of American seamen in winning wage increases has not been duplicated abroad, although many of the same conditions apply. Postwar austerity policies caused a much sharper downturn from wartime wage levels abroad than in the United States. Foreign wages were not so sharply inflated during the Korean period. Since 1952 foreign and domestic seamen's wages have advanced roughly at the same *rate;* the *amount* of the U.S. increase has, of course, been much greater.

Capital Investment. Capital costs are the second most significant component of steamship operations. They may be measured in a variety of ways—for example, in terms of depreciation and interest expense, in terms of debt service requirements or amortization, or in terms of the reserve accumulations to meet future capital requirements. The three elements common to all these measures are the cost of equipment, the cost of money, and the timing of capital investment.

Both U.S. and foreign prices for new ship construction have more than doubled since World War II. However, although construction costs have moved steadily upward, prices have varied in relation to demand. Thus, standard medium-sized dry cargo vessels, which had been mass-produced during World War II for roughly $280 per deadweight ton, were priced at $1,000 per ton when the Suez crisis filled the orderbooks of America's shipyards. This was 25-30 percent above the amounts paid by the government for its Mariner class ships five years earlier and 20-25 percent above the prices which prevailed after the Suez boom had subsided. Since 1961, prices asked by U.S. yards have resumed an irregular upward trend.

Since U.S. and foreign yards serve different markets, the movements in their prices, although related, are only loosely linked. Prices have risen somewhat more rapidly in Great Britain, France, and Italy than in the United States and less rapidly in Japan. Because the U.S. ship construction subsidy is geared to prices in the lowest-cost major shipbuilding nation, the differential compensated by subsidy has risen to about 53-54 percent of the gross U.S. construction cost.[17] The differential is due chiefly to the higher labor costs of U.S. shipyards. Hence, for reconstruction

---

[17] Limits on the differential which may be allowed in computing construction subsidies, established in sec. 502(b) of the 1936 act (49 Stat. 1996) have been liberalized to accommodate differentials up to 55 percent for ship construction and 60 percent for reconstruction projects (76 Stat. 1200, 78 Stat. 313, and 79 Stat. 519).

projects, which are highly labor-intensive, U.S. costs are about 2.5 times those of low-cost foreign yards; but for tanker and bulk carrier construction, which depends also on the price of steel, U.S. costs are only about 1.5 times costs abroad.

In contrast to construction costs, the cost of capital has heavily favored U.S. investors since the end of the war. However, this factor is of little direct significance since most foreign operators receive credit aids from their government for ship construction and since American capital is available to U.S. companies (and certain foreign operators as well) on nearly as favorable terms for foreign-built ships as for domestic vessels. No attempt is made in the subsidy program to calculate interest differentials.

The timing of U.S. and foreign investments in new ships has had mixed effects. U.S. flag companies, which acquired the cream of the war-surplus ships in 1946-47, did not begin introducing new equipment into their dry cargo fleets on a large scale until 1958. Even net of construction subsidies, these vessels are five to seven times more costly than the ships which they replace and their acquisition has sharply increased the depreciation expenses of U.S. ship operators. The more substantial U.S. flag companies, anticipating increased replacement costs, have attempted throughout the postwar period to make payments to their capital reserves in excess of the amounts required to fund current depreciation. In contrast, most foreign flag lines have applied their capital resources directly to the business, introducing new vessels as rapidly as their finances and the trade permit. Their ships, although much more expensive than the war-built vessels of U.S. companies, have been obtained at lower prices than are likely to apply to future U.S. ship purchases.

Currency Exchange Rates. Changes in currency exchange rates have also contributed to the widening differential between U.S. and foreign wage, capital, and other costs. The most severe devaluation of foreign currencies occurred in 1949, when most European currencies were cut to about 70 percent of their prior value. These actions increased the gap between U.S. and foreign seafaring wages by 20-25 percent. Although official exchange rates have been maintained by most nations since 1949, rates applicable to foreign trade transactions have fluctuated.[18] Where

[18] Agreements with the International Monetary Fund require participating nations to revalue their currencies when market value deviates more than 10 percent from par. However, nations are not prevented from applying exchange controls or special exchange rates to special categories of international transactions. Special rates have been

foreign wages have not been increased to compensate for deterioration in actual currency values, further pressure is placed on the U.S.-foreign wage differential.

Currency valuations are of course related to the competitiveness of nationally produced goods and services in international trade. The fact that foreign devaluations have *increased* the gap between U.S. and foreign ship operating costs rather than correcting a trend developing in favor of U.S. companies is an indication that performance in this sector of the U.S. economy has not kept pace with other export industries.

Technological Change

The most compelling challenges to the U.S. flag fleet and to the government's postwar maritime policies have been posed by new technology. Even though shipping is a mature industry, there have been significant advances since 1946 in the design, construction, loading, and operation of ships. Fully exploited, these developments appear to have a potential for increasing productivity at a rate equaling or exceeding the rise in operating costs.

Marine Technology. To date, the advances in marine technology have been exploited principally in newly constructed vessels. The effects of these advances have consequently been gradually realized. As a practical matter, those nations which have been forced to build new tonnage to replace war losses have benefited most from technological advances.

Changes in the methods of building and operating ships since World War II have been numerous and diverse. Many new developments, such as high performance propulsion machinery, cargo containerization, automatic hatches and side-ports for faster loading, have been pioneered by the United States. Others, such as gas turbines and diesel power, have been more extensively used abroad. Improvements in many cases, such as welding techniques and hull configuration, have been so gradual as to be scarcely noticeable from year to year, although highly significant over the longer term. The sum effect of these improvements has been to increase the carrying capacity of general cargo vessels by about 25 percent over comparable ships built in 1946-47.

Out of the stream of evolutionary development, three innovations promise to have a decisive influence on the industry's operations. These

used as temporary expedients by many nations. A few, notably Brazil, Argentina, Korea, and (until the mid-fifties) Greece, also have frequently adjusted their official rate.

are the introduction of high capacity, specialized bulk carriers, the introduction of automated ship control equipment, and the increased use and standardization of cargo containers. None of these developments has as yet been fully assimilated into the industry's operations.

Prior to World War II, ocean-going dry cargo ships averaged about 9,000 deadweight tons; tankers had a somewhat larger carrying capacity but seldom in excess of 15,000 tons. The war-built Liberty ship was a 10,800-ton, 11-knot vessel; the T-2 tanker, 15,850 tons. Today, about three-quarters of all new dry and liquid bulk carriers under construction are rated at more than 30,000 deadweight tons and designed for operating speeds of 15 knots or more. Although only slightly over 1,000 of these "superships" are in operation, they provide more than 40 percent of the world's bulk cargo tonnage and at least half its bulk carrying capacity. These ships, the largest of which has a 150,000-deadweight-ton capacity, are operated by approximately the same crew as the war-built Liberties and T-2's.

At least one-quarter of the world's new bulk carrier tonnage (perhaps substantially more) is either owned or effectively controlled by U.S. citizens. However, all but 57 of these superships are registered under foreign flags. The government has offered some modest incentives to encourage tanker construction; but the ships built have in most instances been designed for use in coastwise trade, in which economies of scale are limited by relatively short hauls.[19] Interestingly the few really large tankers built for U.S. registry have found their principal market in carrying grains to India and Pakistan.[20]

Compared to the development of superships, ship automation has progressed slowly both in the United States and abroad. The reasons are numerous: the sophistication of the technology, the necessity of meeting or modifying numerous regulatory restrictions, labor resistance, and honest doubt whether savings in crew costs might not be offset by higher

[19] The government's bulk carrier construction aids were designed principally to protect against potential tanker shortages. The first effort to induce new tanker construction was made in 1954 through enactment of a "trade-in and build" plan (68 Stat. 680), which proved ineffective. In 1956 the Maritime Administration announced a liberalized "trade-out and build" program (21 *Federal Register* 8588), which generated a substantial amount of activity due to the extremely favorable chartering conditions following closure of the Suez Canal. Mortgage guarantees were also provided to facilitate financing for these ships.

[20] The Maritime Administration's incentives encouraged construction of 46,000-deadweight-ton vessels. Only four larger ships have been constructed for U.S. flag, including the "Manhattan" which at 108,000 tons was briefly the world's largest ship. Since it has not been economical to construct facilities to load these large tankers with Texas oil, they have been used entirely in foreign trade, largely to haul grains.

capital and maintenance expenses. Nonetheless, ship automation is being pressed forward even by low-wage nations such as Japan, and by Russia, Norway, and the United States. As of December 31, 1964, there were six U.S. flag liners with crews of 37 or less in operation; 40 semi-automated ships were under construction; and the President's 1966 budget proposed obligation of $10 million during 1965-66 to initiate a five-year program to retrofit the entire subsidized fleet with automatic control gear at a cost to the government of approximately $225,000 per ship.

Use of standardized cargo containers also has spread very slowly, although there is general agreement that containerization promises very significant economies if an entire transportation system can be adjusted to its use. Standard shipping containers have been used in some specialized trades since before World War II, but the first all-container ship was not placed in service until 1957. By 1964, there were sixteen container ships operating in the U.S. domestic trade and plans had been made by two American companies to place container ships in foreign operations. Container ships have also been placed in certain coastal trades abroad. Furthermore, several container leasing organizations have been organized, an international container-size standard promulgated, and various collapsible containers developed. However, most conferences still have not adjusted their tariff systems to make the use of containers attractive, insurance rates still do not fully reflect the pilferage savings which containers yield, premium pay is required by some longshore locals for loading containers, and many other regulatory and social problems remain to be solved before containers can be adopted for general international use.

Competing Transport Modes. From the beginning of history through World War II, the merchant ship enjoyed an unchallenged monopoly of ocean transportation. Since World War II new technology has introduced three types of competition: air transport, ocean-going barges, and transcontinental pipelines. In the future, merchant shipping may also be faced by competition from submarine pipelines and subsurface cargo craft.

Since 1949, air transport has reduced merchant shipping's share of the overseas passenger market inbound and outbound from the United States from 50 to 14 percent. The absolute number of sea passengers carried to or from foreign destinations reached a peak in 1956 and by 1964 had declined by almost 20 percent. This loss has been offset by the development of a lucrative cruise business, which now provides winter employment for a half-dozen U.S. passenger lines.[21]

[21] In 1961 legislation was enacted to permit subsidized passenger vessels to con-

Air transport has also begun to eat into liner freight revenues by skimming off premium cargoes. Although less than half of 1 percent of the tonnage has been diverted to air, over 10 percent of the dollar value of U.S. export trade is now handled air freight. These are mostly small-package cargoes which would draw top rates if shipped by sea.

Unfortunately, no data is available to assess the impact of barge operations on merchant shipping. However, barges are moving significant amounts of cargo in the Caribbean and have even been used for bulk movements to Hawaii.

Pipelines have significantly reduced tanker requirements throughout the world. The most severe impact on U.S. flag tankers has been from pipelines constructed to move oil from the Gulf of Mexico to the northeastern states. Commissioning of the Colonial Pipeline, connecting Houston, Texas and Linden, New Jersey is estimated to have displaced thirty T-2 tankers.

International Developments

Political changes have also had an important impact on the U.S. flag shipping industry and supporting public programs. The most tangible developments have been the proliferation of national flag fleets, the trend toward increased government involvement in shipping affairs, and the emergence of "flags of convenience." However, shipping has also been touched by the Cold War (in ways which will be discussed in Chapter 5) with many less direct effects.

Proliferation of National Flags. Since World War II a minor explosion has occurred in the number of national flag merchant marines. As of December 31, 1949, there were only 46 nations, including members of the British Commonwealth, which supported merchant fleets of five or more ocean-going vessels, 1,000 gross tons or over; fourteen years later this number had increased to 66. Eighty-five percent of the world's active tonnage in 1949 was concentrated under only a dozen flags, but by 1963 these nations controlled only 70 percent of total world tonnage, while the "developing" nations of Africa, Asia, and Latin America had increased their holdings from 3.9 to 10.8 million gross tons.[22]

---

tinue to receive subsidy during cruises as if operating on their assigned trade route, so long as service was provided on an essential trade route for at least eight months of the year (P.L. 87-45 [75 Stat. 89]).

[22] Figures cited exclude "flag of convenience" tonnage registered under the flags of Panama, Liberia, and Honduras, but include all other African, Asian, and Latin

The forces underlying this development have been varied. The principal motivation in many instances has been simply national pride. In other cases, developing nations have established national flag fleets in order to free their foreign trade from dependence on foreign-controlled steamship conferences or as a means of earning or conserving foreign exchange. In a few instances, the organization of a national flag fleet has been encouraged by United States foreign aid policies.[23]

The proliferation of national flag fleets has most seriously affected the established maritime nations of Western Europe, whose worldwide operations depend heavily on colonial and foreign-to-foreign trades. The growth of these fleets has also limited the development of U.S. flag services, particularly to South America, and secondarily has contributed to the spread of preferential and restrictive practices.

National Flag Preferences. One salutary result of World War II was the eradication of the network of preferential and anticompetitive practices which had beset the international shipping industry throughout the 1920's and 1930's. Furthermore, at the war's end, there was a strong sentiment among the leaders of the allied powers that steps should be taken to forestall revival of restrictive practices in international trade. In 1946 an international shipping code was developed within the framework of the proposed International Trade Organization (ITO). Although the ITO charter was never adopted, strong opposition to unnecessary obstructions to the free movement of trade has continued and has been partially successful in holding down their growth.

Massive governmental intervention was of course required to reestablish the war-ravaged fleets of the Western European nations, China, and Japan. U.S. government aid for this purpose is reported to have exceeded $225 million through 1951—an amount approximately equalling its subsidies to U.S. flag shipping over the same period.[24] Since 1951

American registries. Shifts in the flag composition of the world's merchant fleets are detailed in Appendix A, Table A1.

[23] Except for a grant of six ships to South Korea in 1954, the United States has not provided direct foreign aid to assist developing nations in establishing or expanding national flag merchant fleets. Special legislation authorized sale of war-surplus ships to China and Peru on favorable terms. In addition, the United States has provided technical assistance and trained foreign personnel, and has aided in port development.

[24] Data from U.S. Department of Commerce, *The American Merchant Marine and Federal Tax Policy* (the "Sawyer Report" [1952]), p. 81. The data includes all Economic Cooperation Act and counterpart funds used to build, purchase, or convert vessels. Additional amounts were provided through contributions of construction materials and heavy equipment and for reconstruction of damaged shipyards. The largest beneficiaries of the program were France, Germany, and Japan.

generally favorable business conditions have reduced the dependence of Western European and Japanese ship owners on direct government aid. At present, only the United States, France, and Italy provide substantial direct subsidy payments to their national flag fleets, although many other nations continue to grant aid in one form or another.[25]

Indirect subsidies through special credit and tax programs have slowly grown in number and extent during the postwar period. Among the most generous is the British Investment Allowance, established in 1954, which permits 140 percent of a ship's purchase cost to be expensed as depreciation. West Germany offers loans with 3 and 4 percent interest rates and has also underwritten the scrap market in order to encourage retirement of overage vessels. Japan permits deferred interest payments and has recently offered a five-year interest moratorium to companies joining one of its six quasi-governmental shipping trusts.

The number of state-owned fleets has also multiplied since the war, spurred both by the spread of socialist doctrine and by the difficulties which newly organized private companies have in breaking into established conference trades.[26] Of the 20 new national flag fleets organized since 1949, at least half were initially financed and continue to be largely controlled by governments. In such cases it is difficult, if not impossible, to determine the amount of "subsidy" extended to the fleet.

The conferences' reluctance to yield any portion of their trade to the new shipping lines has in some instances prompted preferential decrees. In many developing countries, foreign trade has been a government controlled activity, and cargo preferences a natural application of government power. On occasion, national flag preferences have been necessitated by a shortage of foreign exchange. These preferential practices, often established to meet temporary needs, tend to be perpetuated. Thus national flag discrimination has gradually increased even while foreign exchange difficulties have been easing throughout the world.

It is difficult to gauge the extent or impact of these discriminatory practices. Sturmey has calculated that discrimination has removed less than 5 percent of the world's total oceanborne commerce (including oil)

---

[25] Other nations granting subsidies include: Australia, Canada, India, Japan, Spain, and Yugoslavia. For a summary of aids, see Joint Economic Committee, "Subsidies to Shipping by Eleven Countries," *Economic Policies and Practices*, Committee Print, Paper No. 6, 88 Cong. 2 sess. (1964).

[26] The entry of new national flag fleets was sternly resisted by many of the established conference lines serving Africa, Asia, and South America. An attempt to force entry of a new service therefore involved risks which exceeded the resources of private corporations. Examples are cited by Sturmey, *op. cit.*, pp. 195 ff.

from competition.[27] This calculation would indicate that about 10 percent of the world's dry cargoes are subject to preferential routing. Since
preferential agreements are most widely used in the liner trades and between widely separated nations, even 10 percent is probably a low estimate of the proportion of freight revenues reserved to national flag ships
through discriminatory techniques.

The most common method of establishing national flag preferences
is through bilateral trade treaties containing restrictive shipping clauses.
These agreements are usually for a fixed term or apply only to specified
commodities so that their full extent is not precisely known.

A few nations have decreed that all or a stated portion of certain
categories of commercial import-export cargoes must be consigned to
the national flag line. Restrictions of this type have been successfully
maintained for prolonged periods only by the larger South American
countries and in colonial trades.[28] In these cases, the national flag lines
of the country's major trading partners have sometimes set up pooling
arrangements to divide cargoes and/or revenues with the country's own
national flag carrier.

International shipping has always been burdened by a plethora of
minor discriminatory practices relating to exchange controls, exchange
rates, port taxes, pilotage, and priorities in handling cargoes. For the
most part these practices are only minor irritants. It is not possible to
discern any trend in the volume of this type of discriminatory regulation.

Flags of Convenience. International competition in merchant shipping
has been further complicated during the postwar years by the emergence of "flags of convenience"—i.e., registries offered by nations with
few indigenous requirements for merchant shipping and willing to
enroll foreign ships subject to only minimum taxes and restrictions.
Foreign registries have been used by a few shipowners (chiefly American)
since the turn of the century. However, until Standard Oil decided in
1938 to transfer its German-registered tankers to Panamanian flags,
foreign registries had been used chiefly for commercial purposes and

[27] *Ibid.*, pp. 205-06. Sturmey's calculation is based on 1957 data, since which
time the volume of cargoes subject to some form of discrimination has probably
increased.

[28] Formal or informal national flag preference in routing of government cargoes is
widely practiced, even by some of Western Europe's advocates of unrestricted trade.
One of the most knotty issues, therefore, is to define what is properly a "government"
versus "commercial" cargo. This issue is discussed in Chapter 7.

were almost invariably those of established maritime nations.[29] Use of Panamanian and other foreign registries—literally for the convenience of the owner—increased under the stimulus of the U.S. neutrality statutes in 1939-40, reaching 800,000 gross tons by the end of 1940.

Following World War II, a number of Greek and Greek-American purchasers of U.S. war-surplus vessels selected Panamanian registry in order to avoid restrictive domestic regulation. Flag of convenience registries were swelled in late 1949 and early 1950 by transfer of about 50 U.S. flag tramps idled by cutbacks in reconstruction and relief shipments. Beginning in approximately 1950, new construction for Panamanian, Liberian, and Honduran (PANLIBHON) registries triggered a rapid expansion in their use. In fact, between 1950 and 1963 the deadweight tonnage of ships registered under those flags multiplied by four, growing from 6.1 to 24.2 million deadweight tons and from 5.7 to 12.8 percent of the active world fleet.

This prodigious growth, prompted by the extremely favorable terms of PANLIBHON registry, has led other nations such as Lebanon, Morocco, and Tunisia to enter the competition. The prize is not inconsequential, for registry fees, though comparatively low for the shipowner, yield substantial income to the registering state. The three Mediterranean flags, however, have not matched the success of the PANLIBHON nations. At the end of 1963 their combined fleets numbered only 193 ships of 1.4 million deadweight tons.

Historically, flags of convenience have been most attractive to American shipowners, for whom they provide a refuge from the world's highest seafaring wages, and to Greek owners, who were faced in the immediate postwar period by an unstable domestic political situation. Since 1953 the Greek government, through various tax incentives, is reported to have successfully repatriated about one-third of its foreign-registered fleet. Although definitive data on the beneficial ownership of the present PANLIBHON fleet does not exist, as of December 31, 1962, it was thought that 45-50 percent of the tonnage was owned by Americans, about 40 percent by Greeks, and 10-15 percent by others, chiefly European and South American owners seeking to escape national regulation.[30]

---

[29] Foreign-registered ships owned by U.S. citizens prior to the war were operated chiefly under British flag by British management. In those instances in which foreign flag operations were managed by Americans, as the United Fruit Company's Honduran-registered ships, there was usually alleged to be a trade or political reason for the foreign registry.

[30] Data from U.S. Maritime Administration and Sturmey, *op. cit.*, p. 214.

PANLIBHON ships also suffer certain disadvantages. The most important is a lack of national flag patronage and preferences. Flags of convenience have consequently been used almost exclusively for services (e.g., tramp, industrial, and cruise services) in which national flag allegiance is relatively unimportant.[31] They have an uncertain status in international law and lack any effective governmental protection, which can lead to inconvenience and embarrassment during periods of international tension.[32] They are bitterly opposed by organized labor and have been the target of picketing, litigation, and on one occasion a worldwide boycott; consequently the major owners of PANLIBHON vessels have had to offer wages and working conditions at least equal to most other foreign flags.

The effect of these disadvantages has been to check, at least temporarily, the trend toward flag of convenience registries. However, the volume of American-owned tonnage registered abroad has not diminished. Instead, there has been a slight shift from PANLIBHON registry to British, German, and other flags.[33] These registries now appear to some American shipowners to offer the best outlook for political stability, freedom from labor harassment, and favorable wage and tax costs.

Effect on Promotional Policies

The emergence of flags of convenience is dramatic evidence of the need to adjust U.S. maritime policies. These foreign registries have created an important source of competition for U.S. foreign trade cargoes and for U.S. investment capital. They also offer an alternative means for meeting U.S. maritime requirements, not available at the time the 1936 act was approved.

[31] The Maritime Administration reports PANLIBHON tonnage to be 59 percent tankers, 13 percent dry bulk carriers, 27 percent freighters (chiefly used as tramps), and 0.5 percent passenger vessels (chiefly used for cruises). U.S. Maritime Administration, *Merchant Fleets of the World* (June 30, 1963).

[32] Flags of convenience for example do not enjoy any effective consular services in foreign ports. Nor is there any government able to speak effectively on their behalf in order to meet a discriminatory or unfair practice, or in the event of military action. During the 1956 Suez crisis, the United States was successful in securing transit of U.S.-registered ships caught in the Suez Canal, but did not intervene to protect one American-owned vessel of Liberian registry which was in similar circumstances.

[33] Each year a trade journal lists the intended registries of ships under construction for American owners in foreign yards. Of 44 ships under construction December 31, 1962, 22 were designated for PANLIBHON registries, 10 for British registry, and 10 elsewhere. *Marine Engineering Log*, Vol. 48, No. 7 (June 1963), p. 108.

Developments in the international shipping industry during the postwar period have generally had the effect of increasing the expense and difficulty of sustaining a national flag fleet. Pressures on the costs of U.S. operation have made the flag of convenience alternative only appear more attractive. The U.S. has also been faced with block obsolescence of its war-built fleet, loss of its coastwise and intercoastal dry cargo business, an increasing number of national flag competitors in foreign trade, and a slow but apparently unremitting spread of cargo preferences. Other developments, such as the enormous postwar growth in bulk shipments, the introduction of superships and ship automation, and the increased government involvement in U.S. foreign trade, have not per se added to the costs of the subsidy program but have seriously challenged the adaptive capacities of the program's administration.

The pace of change is unlikely to slacken in the foreseeable future. For example, widespread adoption of containerization would probably be accompanied by marked changes in the industry's organization, its ties with domestic carriers, its rate structure, and perhaps even its susceptibility to national or international regulation. Nuclear energy, with its enormous power potential, may be used to move larger ships at higher speeds than any now conceived. In fact, the next twenty years may see the development of entirely new transportation techniques and governmental institutions. These possibilities simply emphasize the continuing need for flexibility in the government's maritime program, so that it will facilitate—not obstruct—desirable changes in U.S. maritime operations.

5

The U.S. Fleet's Changing Role

JUST AS THE CHARACTER of the international shipping industry has changed over the past fifteen years, the United States' stake in its national flag merchant marine has also changed. In part this shifting public interest is a product of developments within the industry itself; in part it reflects other developments—in military strategies, in this nation's world position, and in its economic and foreign policies.

National interest in the active commercial fleet during the postwar years has been influenced by the availability of large numbers of ships owned by U.S. citizens but registered under flags of convenience, mothballed in the government's reserve fleet, and assigned to the Navy's Military Sea Transport Service (MSTS). Estimates of the total number of ships owned or controlled by U.S. citizens, individually or corporately, or by their government, are presented in Appendix A, Table A4. Overall, the number is between 3,500 and 4,000 ships or about one-third of the world's total merchant tonnage. The enormous scope and variety of U.S. public and private maritime resources have modified, but by no means erased, the public interest in a privately owned national flag merchant fleet.

Defense Requirements

Because the national security rests on the competence and vitality of American industry as well as of the military establishment, defense requirements for merchant shipping have sometimes been equated with the broad national interest in maintaining a vigorous U.S. maritime industry. Actually the only official interest of the Department of Defense is to assure that its own MSTS, the reserve fleet, the shipping pool of the North Atlantic Treaty Organization (NATO), and private sources are capable of meeting the transportation needs of the military services in limited or general wars. Since 1947 the National Security Resources Planning Board and its successor agencies have been responsible for assessing the "sufficiency of the nation's productive resources" in relation to overall national security needs. The government's planning agency has also since 1954 had the specific duty of investigating and reporting to the President any instance in which foreign imports might have an effect on domestic industry which impairs or threatens to impair the national security. In 1962, the Department of Commerce was made responsible for assessing mobilization requirements for all forms of transportation to meet both military and civil needs.

The defense requirement for U.S. flag, privately owned merchant ships is further obscured by the lack of firm policies regarding use of foreign flag vessels in support of U.S. military operations and by the Navy's longstanding interest in promoting U.S. flag shipping as a means of strengthening U.S. seapower generally. Thus the Navy's attitude has typically run along the lines of the following 1947 requirements report:

> There is naturally no concern from a military view of the upper limit of the size of our active merchant marine. What is of vital concern, however, is the minimum to which that national asset should be allowed to fall before it becomes prejudicial to our Nation's security. While not susceptible of exact definition, it is a reasonable certainty that the lower limit of our active merchant marine should be sustained at or near the estimate of 11.4 million of deadweight tons which the Maritime Commission is understood to have presented as . . . economically justifiable.[1]

The effect of such statements has been to lend the weight of military necessity to almost any project which promised to enlarge the U.S. commercial fleet. Faced with the unanswerable questions as to where another war might come, when, on what scale, involving what weapons, and with what allies, responsible officials have tended to favor doing whatever seemed "economically justifiable" to reduce the risk of being caught short once again.

In the late 1950's the Department of Defense began to assess its commercial shipping requirements more cautiously. Concurrently, increased emphasis was placed on objective quantitative analyses of military logistics problems. In 1958 a departmental position paper on merchant shipping needs was rejected by the National Security Council on the grounds that it failed to deal adequately with the impact of nuclear

---

[1] *Report of the President's Advisory Committee on the Merchant Marine* (Government Printing Office, 1947), p. 52, citing testimony by the Navy Department.

weaponry. From that time through 1961, the Defense Department refused to publish any official estimate of its shipping requirements, although the Navy continued to issue its annual assessment of the general adequacy of the merchant fleet for meeting military needs and from time to time supported specific projects.[2]

In April 1962 the Defense Department broke its long silence. Secretary Robert S. McNamara agreed personally to report his conclusions on the question on merchant ship requirements to the House Merchant Marine and Fisheries Committee in an open hearing. The statement electrified his audience, for it conveyed a wholly new attitude toward the problem of military needs.

Actually, Secretary McNamara reaffirmed his Department's dependence upon the cargo and tanker capacity of the merchant marine. But he emphasized that it was *not* in the military's interest or in the nation's interest to imply that potential defense needs justified expansion of the subsidy program. "I do not wish to leave the impression that we have no requirement for merchant shipping," stated the Secretary. "Obviously we do. But rather I do not wish to overstate the military requirement, thereby providing an umbrella under which a huge ship construction program for the merchant marine can be justified."[3] Mr. McNamara stated flatly that:

> From a purely military point of view, because we are not qualified to survey other requirements . . . the reserve fleet, plus the vessels in service, plus the construction program that has previously been outlined, appear adequate to our needs.[4]

The Navy did not at first agree. Only a month previously Vice Ad-

[2] These annual statements, titled "Ocean Shipping to Support the Defense of the United States," were supplied by the Deputy Chief of Naval Operations (Logistics) to Senator John Marshall Butler, senior Republican member of the Senate Commerce Committee and for many years a staunch supporter of American merchant shipping and shipbuilding. Following Senator Butler's retirement, the statement was sent to the committee's chairman, Senator Warren Magnuson. Through 1962, the Navy's conclusions were typically expressed along the following lines: "Under the most optimistic assumptions, and on a quantitative basis only, the United States still possesses a marginal capability to carry out the sea transportation tasks of a general war. In situations of emergency and from the point of view of purely military requirements, the United States lacks sufficient active merchant shipping in the dry cargo category to meet our initial needs during certain periods of time. There are serious qualitative deficiencies. . . . Further aging of outmoded ships will aggravate this situation." (Excerpted from the 1962 statement, p. 22.)

[3] *Review of Merchant Marine Policy,* Hearings before the House Merchant Marine and Fisheries Committee, 87 Cong. 2 sess. (1962), p. 107.

[4] *Ibid.,* p. 92.

miral John Sylvester, in the annual Navy assessment of military requirements, had claimed a deficiency in both dry cargo and passenger capabilities.[5] A year later Secretary of the Navy Fred Korth delivered a strong speech reiterating Sylvester's position and claiming that American shipping was "faced with possible extinction."[6] Following Mr. Korth's retirement in October 1963, the Navy's position was modified to conform more nearly with Secretary McNamara's conclusions. But in November 1965, when shipping delays to Vietnam were proving troublesome, the Navy again questioned the adequacy of U.S. shipping and urged the merchant fleet's modernization.[7]

These differing assessments of the adequacy of the U.S. merchant marine for defense needs reflect different attitudes regarding the Defense Department's proper role in dealing with defense-related industries as well as different judgments regarding its sealift needs. Furthermore, these judgments have had to be based on incomplete and sometimes outdated information. Additional time has elapsed before the implications of new conditions have been fully reflected in requirements calculations. For example, adjustments in logistics studies to assume a nuclear response to a European war lagged several years behind Secretary Dulles' 1954 announcement of the doctrine of massive retaliation. Similarly, as late as 1965, requirements calculations still did not explicitly reflect the hazards to merchant shipping resulting from Russia's possession of long-range nuclear submarines.

The results of a nuclear exchange are so unpredictable and so terrible to contemplate that it is very difficult to plan against this contingency.[8]

[5] See note 2 *supra*. In his testimony Secretary McNamara acknowledged Sylvester's statement, indicating that reasonable men might differ in their assessment of the problem.

[6] Remarks of Secretary of the Navy Fred Korth before the New York Post of the American Ordinance Association, New York, May 23, 1963.

[7] Chief of Naval Operations, "Flag Officer's Newsletter," November 1965, indicated concern that some naval officers had "occasionally conveyed the impression that the present U.S. Merchant Marine is 'adequate' to meet major military requirements for certain wartime situations." The Newsletter noted that the term "adequacy" has many facets and admonished all naval personnel to support the "development and construction of a fleet of high performance characteristics." These statements were widely interpreted in the press to signal a reversal in Defense Department policy, an interpretation which was denied by Secretary McNamara in a January 28, 1966 press release.

[8] It is generally agreed that should the United States ever be subject to massive nuclear attack, its merchant shipping would emerge relatively unscathed. Because roughly half the active fleet is at sea at all times, ships would almost certainly be less damaged than the capability to fuel, load, or operate them. Merchant shipping could be of vital importance in reconstructing the domestic economy following a nu-

However, a great deal of thought and planning have been directed to maximizing the nation's preparedness for non-nuclear warfare. For the purposes of the discussion which follows, these conflicts are divided into two classes: limited and general wars, the first denoting situations handled by the nation's active and priority reserve forces, without necessitating general mobilization and frequently without involving any of this nation's allies, and the latter denoting any conflict which passes this threshold.

Planning for Limited War. The urgency of containing conflicts has caused the United States to place high priority on quick reaction with a balanced, integrated force. Since 1961 the sense of urgency in meeting this objective has sharply increased, and a large portion of the defense dollar has been devoted to improving the readiness, equipment, and mobility of the active forces. Concurrently, the reserves have been reorganized to identify six priority reserve divisions prepared to mobilize on forty-eight hours' notice.

Prior to the 1965 escalation of the Vietnam war, eight Army divisions were stationed in Hawaii, Alaska, and overseas. The remaining eight active divisions, together with the six priority reserve divisions and miscellaneous supporting units, made up the nation's strategic reserve—a force of about 350,000 men whose mission is to be prepared for anything anywhere. The equipment for this force weighs on the order of 780,000 short tons and requires approximately 3.8 million measurement tons (at 40 cubic feet per measurement ton) shipping space. Rapid deployment and support for these forces in a limited war situation is generally believed to be the Defense Department's most rigorous requirement for merchant shipping.

One measure of the military's requirement for merchant shipping in limited war is the number of ships required to deploy the strategic reserve. If the force were to be moved as a single unit and entirely by sea, an armada of 100 standard troopers and 300-350 Victory class cargo carriers would be required. Assuming a resupply requirement of 1-1.5 tons per division per day thereafter, an average of 3.5 ships daily would have to be dispatched simply to maintain a 6,000-mile trans-Pacific pipeline.

Of course, it is scarcely conceivable that fourteen divisions would be deployed in a single day but serious study is now being given to achieving

clear attack and in conducting post-attack military operations. It has been suggested that these possibilities justify steps to assure the survivability of the U.S. merchant fleet, chiefly by dispersing reserve fleet sites.

a deployment of this magnitude over thirty to sixty days, which would require approximately the same sealift since a ship once dispatched to Southeast Asia is not available for a second voyage for almost two months. Furthermore, the outbreak of war in one location is likely to be accompanied by troop deployments throughout the world to guard against additional enemy probes.

The shipping actually used during the Korean conflict provides a second measure of possible limited war requirements. About half of all MSTS shipments in 1952 and 1953 were consigned to the Far East. Shipments to Japan and Korea, where the United States was supporting a large indigenous force as well as its own 300,000 man complement (seven combat divisions plus supporting troops), totaled 8.8 million measurement tons per year. Approximately 38 percent of this lift was absorbed by the U.S. flag liners regularly operating across the Pacific, 12 percent by the MSTS-owned nucleus fleet, and the remainder by some 160-180 Victory-type vessels broken out from the reserve fleet and placed on charter to MSTS.[9]

Neither of these measures provides more than a rough cut at the military's limited war sealift requirement. Also, each assumes a logistics and deployment strategy along the conventional lines established in World War II and Korea. Defense's current war plans require a much more effective response and are based on a much more extensive and varied logistics capability than was available during the 1940's and 1950's. Several steps have been taken by the Defense Department to supplement conventional sealift in order to provide this capability.

First, the Department of Defense has equipped an increasing number of its general and special purpose forces with support and transport facilities. The multi-service Strike Command, Marine amphibious divisions, and many Air Force and Navy units are substantially self-sufficient within their theatre of operations. Thus the military's two transportation organizations—MSTS and MATS (the Military Air Transport Service)— are free to concentrate on long-range strategic deployment and resupply, chiefly of general purpose Army units.

Second, the Defense Department has acquired a very substantial troop and cargo airlift. Since 1963, it has invested approximately $700 million annually in new airlift aircraft—enough to purchase 150-200

[9] Data from MSTS statistical records and U.S. Maritime Administration *Annual Reports* for 1952 and 1953. A total of 778 ships were broken out of reserve during the Korean crisis. However, the great majority of these ships (about 600) were broken out to handle emergency shipments of coal to Europe in the winter of 1950-51 and to carry grain to India the following spring.

major aircraft per year. Department plans call for quintupling 1961 capacity by 1969. By the end of the decade, the overall capacity of the U.S. air transport fleet will be roughly the equivalent of 250-350 victory-type vessels.[10]

Defense's existing air fleet can handle most types of military equipment. By 1970 a still larger carrier (the C-5A) will be operational.[11] This aircraft has roughly four times the capacity of the best existing plane (the C-141) and on a 3,000-mile flight can deliver over 100 tons of military material on 4,400-foot forward-area landing strips. Even with this extraordinary aircraft, however, air deployment will continue to be expensive, potentially vulnerable to enemy action, and a prodigious consumer of fuel (slightly over one pound of fuel for each pound of cargo, including the return flight).

These limitations will be met in part by prepositioning men and material. Following the 1961 Berlin crisis, equipment sets for two divisions and their supporting units—totaling 150,000 short tons—were prepositioned in Europe. In the Far East, a three-ship floating depot has been established, providing permanent mobile storage for 25,000-30,000 measurement tons of combat gear. President Johnson, in his 1966 budget, announced plans to increase the number of depot ships to seventeen, which will provide facilities large enough to store heavy equipment for two armored divisions.

During the past several years, the Defense Department's investment

[10] The exact dimensions of existing and planned military airlift are not publicly available, but can be reasonably well deduced from public statements. Airlift resources available December 31, 1962, were reported in *Hearings before a Subcommittee on National Military Airlift*, House Armed Services Committee, Print No. 28, 88 Cong. 1 sess. (1963), p. 6077. This indicates an inventory of 885 four-engine planes (605 assigned to MATS). It excludes all special mission, reconnaissance, and administrative aircraft and all Air Force K-135 tankers which are readily convertible to cargo use. Only 287 C-130 planes are shown, although up to 700 of these craft were expected to be delivered to the military by early 1965. Some of these planes will be retired to reserve status before 1970. At the same time over 400 C-141's and 300-350 other four-engine planes will have been added to inventory. Additional capacity is available from the Civil Reserve Air Fleet. All told, on the order of 1,500-2,000 C-141 equivalents should therefore be available to the military by 1970. As a rule of thumb, about five to six C-141s can be taken to equal one Victory ship, assuming a 3,000 mile hop and cargoes having the size-weight relationships of an infantry division's standard equipment.

[11] The principal need for the C-5A is to provide means to move outsized items quickly to forward areas. Its 19-by-13-foot cargo doors and 34,735-cubic-foot capacity will accommodate 98 percent of all Army equipment items (the aging C-130 can handle 92 percent; the C-141 only 67 percent). The plane's special characteristics have caused Defense to limit initial procurement plans to only 58 aircraft, with an option to buy 57 more.

in transport aircraft and prepositioning facilities has exceeded its investment in sea transport by more than 35 to 1. President Johnson's 1966
budget, however, proposed to increase the MSTS cargo ship construction
program, previously held to less than one major ship per year, to provide
four rapid-deployment logistics vessels to be based in forward areas.[12]
Although this proposal signals renewed awareness of sealift's contribution to a balanced logistics program, enlargement of the MSTS fleet will
reduce dependence on commercial carriers for meeting limited war
emergencies.

The step-up of the military program in Vietnam during the summer
and fall of 1965 confirmed the need to maintain suitable sea transport
and dramatized limitations of both air and sealift in support of operations in distant underdeveloped areas. Although airlift successfully accomplished rapid deployment of 46,000 troops and 70,000 measurement
tons of military supply, it has proved far too expensive and limited a
resource to use for moving any but the most urgent items of resupply.
Thus, more than 98 percent of the dry cargoes shipped by Defense to
the Far East have been routed by sea.

The increased tempo of the Vietnam war has caused military dry
cargo shipments to the Far East to increase from about 235,000 measurement tons per month to 400,0000 in the late spring and 700,000 to
800,000 in the summer and fall of 1965. Although some minor difficulties
were encountered initially in arranging shipments (principally as a result of frictions arising out of the West Coast seamen's strike),[13] the
most severe limitation on sea supply has been the lack of port facilities
in Vietnam. This has caused delays in discharging needed cargoes averaging 25-30 days, discouraged private operators from providing liner
services, increased costs, and increased the need for charter ships.

At the end of the year, 120 privately owned U.S. vessels were under

[12] President Johnson's request was halved by the Congress; as late as December
1965 even the reduced amount had not been committed pending completion of
studies to assess how the military can best meet its logistics needs in the 1970's.
Alternatives under consideration include constructing up to forty rapid-deployment
ships to supplement military airlift. Although these procurements have not yet been
initiated, the MSTS has arranged to charter one rapid-deployment vessel which will
be constructed for the Isbrandtsen-Export Company specifically for MSTS use.

[13] The fact that a strike was in progress when MSTS needed ships to step up
shipments to Vietnam during August 1965 facilitated its locating vessels for charter,
since the striking unions agreed to man ships needed to move essential military supplies. Ships loaded with both commercial and military cargoes were not allowed to
sail. In these instances, foreign-owned flag ships chartered by MSTS to fill the gap
also were unable to sail due to their crews' refusal to carry cargoes into a war zone or
the neutrality regulations of the registering government.

MSTS charters, 51 government-owned ships had been commissioned and placed under general agents, an additional 25 reserve fleet ships were being activated, and most of the 22-ship MSTS nucleus dry cargo fleet was assigned to Southeast Asia operations. These MSTS, general agency, and chartered vessels handled over 60 percent of the dry cargo tonnage shipped to the combat theatre during July through September 1965. Almost all the remainder was shipped via U.S. flag liners, although three voyages were also made by foreign flags. (Additional foreign flag ships were chartered by MSTS during this period to assist it to meet requirements for shipments in other areas.) In contrast, petroleum was transported by private suppliers to Southeast Asia military depots chiefly in foreign flag vessels, many of which were manned with Chinese crews.

Planning for General War. Preparedness for general war presents a completely different military problem than planning for limited war. General war is presumed to require a general mobilization. Almost certainly it would involve (either directly or indirectly) conflict with one of this nation's major antagonists. In general war the full range of military weaponry can be expected to be used. Assuming that an apocalyptic nuclear climax can be avoided, the fighting may be continued to the point of national exhaustion.

Preparing for general war requires the military to gird itself for a broad range of contingencies. Since the course of the struggle can only dimly be anticipated, emphasis is on mobilization planning. However, it is impossible to be totally prepared. Needs change. Schedules are not met. Inevitably, critical shortages develop—shortages which impede the entire military effort. The object of planning for general war mobilization is simply to minimize difficulties by establishing stockpiles of those critical materials which are most difficult to produce and by developing plans to step up production of those materials which can be ordered later.

Ships fall in the category of materials difficult to produce; there is, however, strong opposition to stockpiling them.[14] As a result, the United

[14] Reserve fleets proved politically unpopular after both World Wars I and II, perhaps from fear they might undermine the privately owned fleet's defense justification or that the government might release them to check excess profits. The Navy has consistently taken the position that a ship in active service is more valuable to the national defense than a ship in reserve. One result has been enactment of legislation (74 Stat. 312) permitting U.S. shipowners to exchange obsolete vessels for more efficient ships held in reserve. In the three years following enactment, 48 ships were released under this authority.

States has twice within the past fifty years been embarrassed by lack of ships. There is naturally a fear that in any future general mobilization the military effort would again be hampered by an inadequate U.S. flag merchant marine.

The issue is a serious one. Although most persons would concede that a third world war will not repeat the pattern of the past, it can be persuasively argued that inability to maintain our supply lines could force a choice between nuclear escalation or defeat. Conversely, it can be argued that the omnipresence of the nuclear deterrent will force future wars to remain limited. In general, military planning, particularly in Europe, has been gauged to this latter assumption.[15]

There are important differences between the United States' situation today and its position in 1916 and 1941. In the first place, the United States now has a stockpile of some 1,600 rehabilitable vessels, roughly 50 percent more tonnage than the total of all merchant ships operating under U.S. flag in 1939.[16] Although these mothballed ships are slow, commercially obsolete, vulnerable to enemy attack, and in varying states of disrepair, they do still provide the United States a significant mobilization resource, whose value is being demonstrated once again in meeting requirements for the Vietnam war.[17]

Second, the United States now has access to a large number of ships registered under flags of convenience. Defense Department mobilization

[15] Officially, U.S. Army stock planning is premised on a war of unlimited duration. The National Strategic and Critical Materials Stockpile is premised on a three-year war. NATO war plans, although secret, appear to be officially geared to a three-month holding action. But none of the NATO allies other than the United States are stocked at a level which would sustain the conflict more than thirty days, according to press reports. (E.g., see *New York Times,* May 10, 1963, p. 1, and Department of Defense press release, May 10, 1963.)

[16] The Maritime Administration's mothballed fleet still includes over 400 reasonably up-to-date freighters (312 Victory-class ships and 100 coastal dry cargo vessels); an additional 111 ships, now configured for specialized military uses, could be readily converted to dry cargo carriers. Also in the fleet are 70 tankers, 57 passenger ships, 74 ocean tugs, 833 slow (10-knot) but still marginally serviceable Liberties, and 91 miscellaneous other types.

[17] The first order to activate reserve fleet vessels for Vietnam use was issued July 16, 1965. Commissioning of these ships required an average of $400,000 and 21 working days each. The last of the group was delivered for use on Aug. 17, 1965. Additional ships were ordered to be activated in August and September. Per ship costs for these activations were 25 percent lower, although commissioning required slightly more time. In total 51 merchantmen and 15 naval auxiliaries had been removed from the Maritime Administration reserve fleets as of Dec. 31, 1965, and 25 other ships were in process. The ships withdrawn from reserve had generally been in mothballs for at least eight years. Some difficulties were encountered with tubes and boilers following their commissioning, but their hulls were found to be sound.

planning anticipates shifting U.S.-owned ships registered in Panama, Liberia and Honduras (PANLIBHON) to U.S. registry and manning them, if necessary, with American crews.[18] Should still more capacity be required, U.S. shipyards, which are operating at several times their 1939 capacity, should be able to deliver new ships even more promptly than in World War II.

Third, the United States is now formally allied to all of the world's principal maritime powers and can call on their fleets. Although the stability of specific alliances is unpredictable and always controversial, all defense planning is predicated on the concept of mutual security and on the integrity of our alliances. The gross amount of shipping available to NATO nations is prodigious—approximating three-quarters of the merchant fleets of the world.[19] The shipping which would be available to the United States in a Pacific War not involving NATO is more limited, but still (including the U.S. reserve fleet) would approximate 30-40 percent of the world total.[20]

Finally, since World War II stockpiles of strategic and critical materials have been assembled which will support U.S. industrial production for a considerable period, even if the country is cut off from overseas sources of supply. This stockpile was initially intended to include a five-year supply of all nonperishable materials needed to support production

[18] The availability of PANLIBHON ships owned by U.S. citizens in the event of emergencies has been the subject of a long and inconclusive controversy. One group, most vocally represented by the maritime unions, points to the fact that many of these ships are legally subject to dual jurisdiction and argues that since they are manned by non-citizens and the governments of their country of registry may be overthrown, the ships cannot be regarded as a reliable defense resource. The government, on the other hand, notes that the owners of these ships have agreed to make the ships available, that the crews of the U.S.-owned portion of the flag of convenience fleet have been screened by their local national police prior to employment, and that the PANLIBHON governments have no means of exercising real jurisdiction over the vessels even if they should decide to do so. As a practical matter, while legal niceties might cause the U.S. government to refrain from pressing its claim to these ships in a limited emergency, in general war this tonnage would be forced to return to U.S. protection or to defect to the enemy or to escape to neutral harbors.

[19] The calculation includes both the U.S. reserve fleet and the fleets of the PANLIBHON nations, which are owned almost entirely by NATO nationals and which can reasonably be counted on to be available to NATO in any general war for mercenary if not for ideological reasons.

[20] The number of ships over which either the U.S. government or its citizens exercise control has been estimated at roughly one-third the world total (see Appendix A, Table A4). In addition, in a Pacific war the U.S. should be able at a minimum to count on assistance from Japan (10.8 million deadweight tons) and South Korea, Taiwan, Thailand, and the Philippines (1.4 million tons).

for general war. Although targets have since been lowered, 69 of the 87 stockpiles—including all of the dozen major materials—are sufficient to sustain U.S. production for three or more years.[21]

In sum, while general mobilization and general war would undoubtedly strain every aspect of national life, there is no compelling reason to anticipate that merchant shipping would impose a critical bottleneck on the war effort. Even if ship shortages could be foreseen, it is not at all clear that the best remedy would be expansion of the active U.S. flag merchant marine. The most likely effect of enlarging the U.S. commercial fleet would, after all, be to displace ships under other NATO flags, which would both reduce the number of friendly foreign flags available to the United States in a general emergency and increase strains already present within the alliance.

Role of Privately Owned Shipping. Military dependence on commercial sealift has been easing since the end of the Korean war. Commercial vessels, particularly general dry cargo ships and tankers, are still needed to maintain supply lines in limited wars and to contribute to the larger international effort in the event of general war. However, resupply missions require neither as rapid a response nor as many vessels as an initial deployment. Additional time permits greater use of reserve vessels to support U.S. forces in limited war.[22] It is only by holding ships

---

[21] For data on stockpile management, see *Inquiry in the Strategic and Critical Materials Stockpile,* Hearings before a subcommittee of the Senate Armed Services Committee, 87 Cong. 2 sess. (1962), Pt. 1, pp. 19 ff. A serious deficiency of U.S. maritime policy during the postwar period has been its almost total lack of correlation with stockpiling and other civil mobilization policies.

[22] Delays are inherent to mobilizing either active or reserve shipping. In the former case, ships must be returned to port and unloaded before they can be positioned for taking on military cargoes—a time delay which can vary from one to ninety days depending on the ship's location and whether it is permitted to complete its voyage. The median minimum time required to position a ship engaged in U.S. foreign trade approximates two and one-half weeks. Reserve fleet vessels can be placed in commission in as little as five days, if shipways are available and the ship is sound, or may require three to six months for repairs. During the Korean conflict, over 100 ships were activated within eight weeks of the decision to release ships from reserve. On the average, ships for Vietnam have been readied in 20-30 working days. The Maritime Administration is confident that it can improve on this record in future emergencies, and has prepared a plan calling for 94 ships to be ready for use in 30 days; 296 within two months; 430 within three months; and 580 within four months. The plans are based on the availability of dry-docking and other facilities to handle both the Navy's and Maritime Administration's priority tasks, and are premised on ships being activated on all three (i.e., Atlantic, Gulf, and Pacific) coasts.

in ready and standby reserves that overall tonnage of the allied fleets can be quickly expanded in a general war.

Post-Korea developments have enhanced the strategic importance of reserve ships and of vessels, such as the MSTS forward floating depots, which can be enlisted directly in military missions. Looking ahead, as the armed forces achieve still greater self-sufficiency, commercial shipping appears likely to make its principal contribution to defense readiness as a reservoir of trained personnel and a proving ground for new technology.

Many military missions can already be performed without recourse to commercial *ships* and in the future the number is likely to be enlarged. However, neither the military nor the nation at large can afford to abandon commercial *shipping* because only by engaging in the business can America sustain the organization, skills, interest, and up-to-date technology needed to back up naval operations and to make a reserve fleet viable. Conversely, only by maintaining additional tonnage in reserve can the values of a going organization be given the multiplier effect needed in a general mobilization. This argues for a combination of military, reserve, and commercial capabilities in planning a maritime strategy for the future.[23] But clearly there is no precise formula for determining the exact balance between them.

Support of Foreign Commerce

Even before World War II the importance of a national flag merchant marine to the conduct of U.S. foreign trade was questioned by some groups. Since the war various developments have attenuated U.S. dependence on national flag ships to carry its peacetime commerce, whereas the United States' new position in world affairs has virtually eliminated the possibility that it can ever again remain neutral in a major foreign war.

Maintenance of Service. One of the basic purposes of the government's

[23] Air carrier operations illustrate the mutually reinforcing relationship which can be achieved between the armed services, private industry, and a mobilization reserve. The military has underwritten most of the research and development for the air carrier industry, has trained a large portion of its flight and maintenance personnel, and has even furnished some aircraft for civil use. The private industry has served the government by providing facilities for certain specialized missions and as a mobilization base for general war. Both public and private aviation groups have benefited from the existence of a large and active reserve program, which has provided a use for equipment displaced by newer models and a source of supplemental income for the industry's personnel.

promotional programs (and the most frequently cited purpose of the essential trade route requirements of the 1936 act) has been to insure that ships will be available at all times and in the face of all contingencies to carry America's foreign commerce. The painful experience of the Boer War, World War I, and the 1926 British coal strike, when large numbers of foreign flag vessels were unexpectedly withdrawn from U.S. trade, had proven our exports could be left to accumulate on the docks. Protection against interruptions to commerce was listed in the Maritime Commission's 1937 *Economic Survey* as the principal advantage to foreign commerce of a national flag merchant marine.[24]

Developments since World War II have reduced the risk that the United States will ever be without ships to carry its peacetime trade. First, in the event of demonstrated need, government owned mothballed vessels may be commissioned for commercial operation.[25] Second, at least during peacetime, U.S. owned vessels registered under flags of convenience should be fully as responsive as U.S. registered ships to the needs of U.S. foreign trade. Third, in contrast to the early years of this century, U.S. goods are now carried by ships of many countries, so that the withdrawal of any one has only minor effects.[26] Finally, though the United States has long been a major factor in international trade, its position since the conclusion of World War II has been signifi-

[24] U.S. Maritime Commission, *Economic Survey of the American Merchant Marine* (Government Printing Office, 1937), p. 5.

[25] Sec. 11, Merchant Ship Sales Act of 1946, permits reserve fleet vessels to be used only during national emergencies declared by the President or at such other times as the President deems the national security to require it. However, legislation enacted early in the Korean conflict (P.L. 81-591 [64 Stat. 308]) authorized placing reserve fleet ships under bareboat charter for commercial use "in any service which, in the opinion of the Federal Maritime Board, is required in the public interest and is not adequately served, and for which privately-owned, American flag vessels are not available for charter by private operators on reasonable conditions and at reasonable rates for use in such service." The board's findings must be made on the basis of formal hearings.

[26] The Maritime Administration has recently published a country by country analysis of flag participation in major U.S. trade routes. Overall, U.S. companies secured 30 percent of the 1960 liner cargoes by weight, national flag ships of our trading partner 29 percent, and third flags 41 percent. U.S. flag ships now carry more than twice as much liner cargo as the ships of our closest competitors (Norway and Japan, both at 12.2 percent). More than 400 separate liner companies are now estimated to participate in U.S. foreign trade. See U.S. Department of Commerce, Maritime Administration, *An Analysis of the Participation of U.S. and Foreign Flag Ships in the Oceanborne Foreign Trade of the United States* (Government Printing Office, 1962).

cantly better than the prewar period.[27] "Our U.S. trade is the most luscious trade in the world," states one observer. "Foreigners just swoop down to serve those trades. . . . I do not think that anything could drive them out."[28]

The eagerness of foreign flag lines to share in U.S. foreign trade has enhanced the quality as well as the reliability of freight services available to U.S. exporters. In fact, a limited analysis suggests that foreign flags provide proportionately more service to smaller U.S. ports than do subsidized American operators.[29] Foreign companies also have developed more new services (for example, out of the Great Lakes) and offer a greater variety of services to more destinations than American lines.[30]

Improvements in the quality and reliability of shipping services in U.S. foreign trade have been in part simply a product of the increased volume of trade since World War II. Whereas before the war about a quarter of the major U.S. foreign trade routes supported less than one sailing per week, only one route in twenty-five failed to support at least a weekly service, according to a 1957 survey.[31] The survey group con-

[27] In 1961, over 30 percent of the world's trade (by value) moved either into or out of U.S. ports. Whereas in 1938 the United States had ranked second to Britain in the value of her exports, in 1961 the United States outranked her closest competitor by $8.3 billion. The share of the total tonnage of the world's seaborne trade generated by the United States has increased by 50 percent during the same time interval.

[28] J. J. O'Connor, attorney for the Isbrandtsen Company, in *Steamship Conference Study,* Hearings before a subcommittee of the House Merchant Marine and Fisheries Committee, 86 Cong. 1 sess. (1959), Pt. 2, p. 581.

[29] A sample survey of U.S. versus foreign flag services in 1960 to minor ports (those ranking 10th, 13th, 16th, . . . to the 30th in value of linear shipments handled in foreign trade) indicates that U.S. flag ships' share of cargoes shipped through minor ports was 20 percent below their participation in cargoes shipped through the nation's nine principal outlets.

[30] The Northwestern University group, under contract to the Committee of American Steamship Lines, conducted a survey of the trade development activities of the member lines in 1957. It found that American subsidized operators had established the first liner service on only three of the thirty-four essential trade routes designated by the Maritime Administration, and to only 49 of the 1,000-odd recognized foreign ports. Less than 7.5 percent of the voyages undertaken by subsidized operators touch ports not served by other foreign flag lines. This survey is reported in Allen Ferguson *et al., The Economic Value of the U.S. Merchant Marine* (The Transportation Center, Northwestern University, 1961), pp. 249 ff.

[31] Data from U.S. Department of Commerce, *Ocean Routes in U.S. Foreign Trade,* Trade Promotion Series No. 96 (Government Printing Office, 1930), pp. 8-14, and Ferguson *et al., op. cit.,* p. 334.

cluded that the growth in trade had been so substantial that "temporal monopolies"—i.e., monopoly conditions flowing from infrequency of competing services—were no longer a problem of practical importance in U.S. foreign commerce.[32]

If the market is large enough to support multiple competitive services, there is clearly less need for a system, such as the 1936 act provides, to guarantee that a regular sailing schedule is maintained by one or more U.S. flag operators. With more than four hundred liner companies now participating in U.S. foreign trade, it is reasonable to rely on normal market mechanics to balance supply and demand. Thus, while the minimum sailings and area of service specifications built into the essential trade route system may still be a useful device for managing the subsidy program, their relevance to the movement of U.S. foreign commerce has substantially diminished.

On specific trade routes, serious interruptions to commerce still can and do occur. However, their most frequent cause is not war or politics but labor disputes, and strikes have more often tied up U.S. flag vessels than their foreign competitors.

Protection Against Discrimination. During the postwar period concern regarding the reliability of U.S. foreign trade shipping services has been displaced by renewed fear of systematic discrimination by foreign dominated conferences, either in the form of higher rates on outbound vis-a-vis inbound goods or in rates on U.S. exports to third countries which make them uncompetitive with goods shipped from Europe or Japan.[33] Fear of such discrimination was one of the main motivations for the regulatory portions of the 1916 Shipping Act. Unfortunately, the extent of discrimination and the effectiveness of U.S. flag carriers in preventing it are extremely difficult to establish.[34] These questions are important,

[32] Ferguson *et al., op. cit.,* p. 339.

[33] For a brief period immediately following World War II, American operators were able to dominate steamship conferences in U.S. foreign trade. Now, U.S. lines are in the minority in all but seven of the 105 conferences currently active in U.S. foreign commerce. However, since the American companies are generally larger than their foreign competitors, they probably exercise a disproportionate influence to the votes which they command. Also, many conferences require unanimity to carry all important decisions. (A 1959 survey of 114 conferences in U.S. foreign trade indicates that to effect rate changes 44 required unanimity; 18 required the approval of three-quarters of their members; 37 required two-thirds; and 15 only a simple majority.) *Steamship Conference Study,* Hearings, Pt. 2, p. 611.

[34] Studies of rate disparities in U.S. foreign commerce were made by the Maritime Commission in 1937 and again during World War II. Neither report was able

since leverage effectively applied by U.S. shipping lines to improve rates and services for U.S. exporters and importers could have a significant economic value.[35]

The fact that export rates on the average are higher than rates on imports to the United States has been extensively documented and is generally acknowledged. The basis and significance of these differentials, however, are highly controversial. The ships generally sail fuller outbound and the cargoes, in the aggregate, are higher value, which tends to draw a higher rate. In some trades historical factors are believed to be important, since rates on many foreign-produced goods were set low after the war to encourage exports and are not easily adjusted. In other cases, U.S. cargo preferences, because they guarantee a nucleus cargo to the U.S. carriers, may reduce the carriers' incentive to set rates at a level gauged to promote additional trade. There are many situations which contradict these generalizations. Often rates appear simply to lack any logical pattern. Many rates appearing in the statistics also are not used.

The Federal Maritime Commission in its December 1965 decision on iron and steel rates asserted that the burden of proof must rest with the carrier to demonstrate the reasonableness of any rate which impairs the movement of U.S.-produced goods and is higher than the inbound rate on a similar commodity.[36] This doctrine has not yet been tested in court and many observers doubt that it will be sustained, or even if sustained, that equalization of rates can be enforced. Given the industry's international character, economic pressure probably will be more effective than litigation. This pressure can be exerted by government, by shippers, and by U.S. flag steamship companies following a conscious policy of U.S. trade promotion.

There are many disagreements as to the manner in which economic pressures can be most efficiently and practically applied, as well as to

---

to identify any evidence of systematic discrimination. (U.S. Maritime Commission, *Annual Report, 1937*, pp. 17 ff., and report of its Postwar Planning Committee, *The Postwar Outlook for American Shipping* [Government Printing Office, 1946], p. 84.) Since 1963, when the problems of rate disparities were again publicized by Senator Douglas, an enormous amount of attention has been directed to the problem.

[35] For example, the Federal Maritime Commission staff study of trade between U.S. North Atlantic ports and ports of the United Kingdom and Ireland (trade route 5) asserts that equalization of inbound and outbound rates would reduce rates on U.S. exports by 12 percent, yielding an annual savings of $2.6 billion on this route alone (Docket 65-45, Attachment A, p. 4).

[36] Federal Maritime Commission, Opinion and Order, *Iron and Steel Rates*, Docket 1114, Dec. 5, 1965.

the need for any action. However, if American shipping is to be used to influence conference rates, it will be necessary for the American lines to command a patronage which compels their competitors' respect. This is likely to be more important than whether the U.S. lines compete with or within the conference system, so long as they are not locked into either role.

Economic and Foreign Policy Roles

Due to its dependence on government protection and aid, the U.S. merchant marine must be uniquely sensitive to a wide range of government needs and policies. The industry is widely regarded as a quasi-public enterprise and considered to be "an instrument of public policy" —not simply in relation to defense and foreign commerce, but in all matters of public concern.

Domestic Economic Role. Certainly one of the most significant incentives to the enactment of the 1936 program was use of the merchant marine to provide employment and stimulate a lagging domestic economy. In the depressed conditions of the 1936 economy, the subsidy provided a simple and direct economic stimulus for accomplishing these objectives. In the more prosperous postwar period, government shipping subsidies can be justified on economic or employment grounds only if they are more effective than alternative uses of public funds.

Foreign Economic Role. Since ocean freight averages 12 percent of the dockside value of all American exports, policies regarding shipping are an important component of the United States' foreign trade program. Because U.S. shipping is heavily subsidized, its impact on the nation's shifting trade position and balance of payments has drawn special attention.

For almost a decade following the conclusion of World War II, many persons believed subsidies to American shipping to be inimical to the restoration of a healthy balance in world trade. Shipping, it was argued, was one of the few ways in which nations such as Norway, Greece, and even Britain and Japan could earn the foreign exchange necessary to rebuild their economies. Subsidies were consequently conceived as carrying a double cost, draining U.S. resources both directly as aid to American shipping companies and indirectly by enlarging our allies' need for aid.

As European recovery proceeded, the force of this argument diminished. By 1960 growing deficits in the U.S. balance of payments caused government officials to begin searching for ways to increase exports or otherwise deter the outflow of U.S. gold. This new interest was quickly detected by industry officials, who realized that U.S. shipping's foreign exchange earnings might now be used as a justification for increasing government aid.[37]

The need to earn or conserve foreign exchange is a strong incentive for small, poor nations to subsidize a national flag merchant marine. If the need for export earnings is acute and the subsidy kept small, a promotional policy can be economically sound. Since 1961 even the United States has been willing to pay a substantial premium in order to save dollars or secure additional foreign exchange.[38] But it has not as a general rule been willing to pay a premium great enough to justify subsidies to merchant shipping, an industry in which the U.S. economic disadvantage is so pronounced that on the average a dollar or more of subsidy is needed to generate a dollar of foreign exchange.[39]

There are also certain obstacles to using shipping to correct temporary maladjustments in the U.S. balance of payments. An industry which requires large fixed investments, such as shipping, cannot expand or contract rapidly enough to keep pace with America's changing foreign exchange position. Further, any attempt to achieve a rapid expan-

[37] Early in 1960 the Committee of American Steamship Lines (CASL) contracted for an economic study published later in the year by Frank M. Tamagna and W. Donald Bowles as *The Contribution of the American Maritime Industry to the United States Balance of Payments* (multilith). The study provided basic data extensively used by CASL in later publications and pronouncements.

[38] No hard and fast rule guides federal agencies in determining the additional cost which may properly be sustained in order to earn or save foreign exchange, and practices vary widely. For example, the Department of Defense will use foreign services in procurement for U.S. forces abroad only if domestic sources are unable to provide the product (including its transportation and handling) for within 150 percent of its foreign cost. The Agency for International Development on the other hand has attempted to tie all new grants and loans to procurement of U.S. goods and services unless simply unavailable at reasonable expense. Many other government departments have continued to follow a 1954 executive order which provides for only a 6 percent differential in evaluating bids by foreign versus domestic suppliers.

[39] An authoritative explanation of the contribution of the U.S. flag fleet to America's balance of payments is found in A. J. Clones and G. C. McKay, "Transportation Transactions in the U.S. Balance of Payments," *Survey of Current Business*, U.S. Department of Commerce, Vol. 43, No. 8 (Aug. 1963), pp. 23 ff. Clones and McKay estimate that only 42 percent of the gross costs of shipment affect the balance of payments, since so large a proportion of the shipping process is concerned with cargo booking and handling, which are local expenses.

sion through government aid would be likely to precipitate retaliatory actions, which might impair the nation's overall trade. The U.S. flag business cannot be expanded significantly without making serious inroads on the foreign exchange earnings of the British, Norwegian, Greek, and other nations with whom the United States maintains cordial relations.

The difficulty of trying to meet payments deficits through increased investment in the merchant marine has led the government to concentrate on achieving better utilization of existing U.S. flag ships. However, on the outbound leg, which provides about two-thirds of the freight revenues of American carriers, U.S. flag ships have for some time been sailing on most routes at close to their cubic capacity. And when word leaked that the Administration was considering steps to place even more export cargoes on American ships, there was a sharp reaction from our Western European allies, who carried the problem to the very highest levels of government.[40]

Impact of the Cold War. The difficulties experienced in this case illustrate the United States' dilemma in trying to reconcile strictly national interest objectives with the policies it wishes to pursue as leader of a great international coalition. In merchant shipping the fact that our political allies are also our most zealous competitors makes the dilemma especially prickly.

Maritime affairs have long been a turbulent area of international relations. International tensions during the past twenty years have simply brought into the open the conflicts which are inherent to the industry and heightened their importance to the public interest.

Since the late fifties, advocates of a strong U.S. flag merchant marine have emphasized the merchant fleet's importance in the Cold War. They note that the Soviet Union has placed a high priority on development of its merchant shipping,[41] and imply that if the United States does

[40] In April 1962, President Kennedy was reported to have instructed all government agencies to regard the fifty-fifty rule specified in cargo preference legislation as a floor rather than as a ceiling for U.S. flag participation in movement of government-sponsored cargoes and to use American ships "whenever practicable." This report, later found to be erroneous, caused the British House of Parliament to request that the Prime Minister call the deleterious effects of the U.S. action to President Kennedy's personal attention and press for its rescission.

[41] In 1962 the Soviets are believed to have depended on foreign shipping to transport 60-70 percent of their foreign commerce; their goal is to reduce this proportion to 25 percent by 1975. If the USSR fulfills its announced plan, tonnage under Russian flag will surpass that of privately owned U.S. registries by about 1970. The

not match its adversary's effort, it will become vulnerable to "Kremlin domination of the world charter market and . . . Soviet political intrigues."[42] Yet nations whose shipowners could potentially be hurt by the introduction of this large new fleet are also contributing substantially to its construction and are glad to get the business.[43] Although there is always a risk that state-supported enterprises may upset accepted commercial practices, there is no reason to suppose it is any greater in shipping than in other sectors of international trade or even that the Soviets will operate their fleet differently than other state-supported merchant marines. In any event, such risks as do exist cannot be diminished by trying to match the Soviet program ship for ship.

Other advocates of an enlarged U.S. flag fleet have suggested it be used by the United States to exert "positive economic pressures against the Sino-Soviet bloc."[44] They argue that it is important that the United States "show the flag" in the ports of underdeveloped and uncommitted nations and imply that the United States can somehow use its merchant marine to deny shipping services to unfriendly nations.

In the past, certain nations have established so decisive a grip over world shipping that they have been able to use that control to achieve important political goals. This strategy may again be possible at some future time. However, for the present, the international shipping industry's libertarian traditions and atomized institutional structure make it highly unlikely that any nation could successfully use its merchant fleet in this manner.

Soviets have projected a fleet of 22-26 million tons by 1980; this will probably place the Soviet Union among the world's top five or ten maritime nations. Assuming a growth in trade and shipping over the next twenty years commensurate with the last, its 1980 fleet would comprise 6.5-7 percent of the world's tonnage—about the position the U.S. flag fleet holds today.

[42] Remarks of Secretary of the Navy Fred Korth before the New York Post of the American Ordinance Association, May 23, 1963.

[43] In December 1962, the following noncommunist or non-aligned nations were participating in the Soviet ship construction program: Japan, 515,000 deadweight tons; Yugoslavia, 432,000; Italy, 288,000; Finland, 246,000; other noncommunist nations 65,000. Russia itself had only 304,000 tons under construction according to report (Poland, Russia, and East Germany, 752,000 tons). (Data from U.S. Department of Commerce, Maritime Administration, "New Ship Construction, Special Report." Source material for communist nations described as "limited and unreliable.") Since 1962 fewer orders have been placed in Western European yards.

[44] National Academy of Sciences-National Research Council, Panel on Wartime Uses of the Merchant Marine, *The Role of the U.S. Merchant Marine in National Security*, Publication 748 (Washington, D.C., 1959), p. 4. This panel, chaired by Admiral Arthur W. Radford, focused attention on the potential importance of shipping to Cold War strategies but failed to translate its general propositions into specific recommendations.

New Demands on the U.S. Merchant Fleet

Incidents such as the 1962 Cuban crisis and the abortive 1963-64 Russian wheat sales dramatically underscore the critical role which merchant shipping continues to occupy in world affairs. The tense atmosphere of the Cold War places a high premium on the United States' having an "adequate" maritime industry—but an industry whose adequacy is measured by quite different standards than those of 1936. In today's world it is less important that the U.S. flag maritime industry be any particular size than that it be vigorous, lean, imaginative, and efficient in order to measure up to the rigorous standards of performance required in the Cold War.

The present day importance of the competitive quality of the U.S. merchant fleet contrasts sharply with the values underlying the 1936 act. That legislation was based on the premises that an American merchant marine provided essential foreign trade services and that a certain number of ships (to be determined by the Maritime Commission) must therefore be maintained in service. It stipulated that subsidized ships be owned, operated, constructed, and manned by U.S. citizens but failed to establish any effective standards to assure the efficiency of the fleet's citizen personnel. The declarations of policy in the Merchant Marine Act of 1920 and subsequent legislation instead simply assert that "it is *necessary* . . . that the United States foster the development and encourage the maintenance of such a merchant marine."

In today's interdependent world this stress upon the necessity of the United States' maintaining a 100 percent American merchant marine has a somewhat remote, unreal cast. As a leading world power the United States is no longer "at the mercy" of foreign shipowners, as Woodrow Wilson argued half a century ago. Big business is now highly internationalized, and both American shippers and American shipowners control many large enterprises which are domiciled overseas. Furthermore, America's enormous investments in both productive and warmaking equipment over the past three decades have created reserves of ships and materials more than adequate to meet foreseeable emergency needs. With these resources the United States is unlikely to lack sufficient numbers of merchant vessels. However, America's wealth can also be its weakness if it diverts attention from the need to keep up skills, technology, and equipment.

Furthermore, America's international commitments require that she sustain the vigor and productivity of her economy. Insofar as possible, American industries must be able to stand on their own feet, even to meet stiff foreign competition, so that the nation may be as free as possible of the burdens and entanglements of subsidies, preferences, quotas, and price-fixing devices designed to protect domestic producers.

These new elements in America's world position are important both to the U.S. merchant fleet's commercial role and to its defense role. In the first instance America's most urgent present need is for an industry whose commercial operations are so excellent that they will induce a general improvement in the shipping services offered in U.S. foreign trade; in the second, for an advancing technology and skilled personnel who will be able to apply the most up-to-date techniques to military logistics problems.

America's economic and foreign policy objectives also demand a commercially aggressive, independent, self-reliant U.S. maritime industry. During full employment a national flag merchant marine is an economic asset only if it is operated at least as efficiently as other export industries. It contributes to national prestige only if its performance is admired. America's Cold War position makes it particularly important that neither the competitive situation, the traditions, nor the organization of the merchant fleet cause it to be obstructive or defensive in reacting to national needs.

In short, although America continues to need a merchant fleet, it is the industry's quality, not size, which counts most. Shipping's crucial position in world affairs vests the industry with unusual importance and unusual responsibilities. It is a sword which cuts two ways.

6

Postwar Administration of the 1936 Act

INTERNATIONAL DEVELOPMENTS and the changing public role of America's postwar merchant fleet create a continuing challenge to public policy and administration. The next two chapters describe how government has responded to these challenges. The first deals with the manner in which the Merchant Marine Act of 1936 has been administered, adapted, and amended to meet new conditions; the second reports on supplementary efforts to respond to the challenges of the postwar period outside the framework of that statute.

Between 1946 and 1964 five different agencies participated in the management of the government's promotional program. Through August 1949 the organizational arrangements were those specified in the 1936 act. Reorganization Plan Number 6 of 1949 strengthened the powers of the chairman of the U.S. Maritime Commission by designating him the agency's chief executive and administrative officer. However, in May 1950, Reorganization Plan Number 21 abolished the commission and divided responsibility for the maritime program's administration between two successor agencies, the Federal Maritime Board and Maritime Administration, both under the direction of a single head. This arrangement was modified by Reorganization Plan Number 7 of 1961, which abolished the Federal Maritime Board and transferred its promotional functions to the Secretary of Commerce. (Regulatory functions were transferred to a new independent regulatory agency, the Federal Maritime Commission.) However, the Secretary in turn delegated these tasks to the Maritime Administrator and to an administratively created Maritime Subsidy Board, subject to his review. In the text reference is to the agency which initiated the action under discussion.

128

Frequent reorganization of the maritime program is evidence of dissatisfaction with its administration. The program's implementation, in turn, has been complicated by the effort to meet postwar defense needs through a prewar statute, oriented principally to commercial and economic recovery objectives. Although virtually every official and unofficial study of maritime affairs between 1946 and 1964 has urged that the promotional program be aimed at developing a fleet sized to defense needs, no mechanism exists either in statute or practice for bringing defense judgments directly to bear on basic program decisions.

The 1936 act's commercial orientation is reflected in its stress upon essential trade routes, parity, and competitive safeguards. Most of the administrative issues discussed in this chapter have been fought out in reference to these criteria, which of course have no direct bearing on military needs. For this reason the official record often seems irrelevant to the program administrator's real and proper concern—that is, to assure operation of a merchant fleet adequate to the national defense.

Eligibility for Aid

As World War II drew to a close, intensive attention was given both by the U.S. Maritime Commission and various private groups to planning the transition to peacetime operations. One of many problems was whether operating subsidy payments, which had been suspended during the war, should be resumed and, if so, whether they should be granted only to a limited number of companies under contract to perform specified services or be available generally to any U.S. flag steamship company operating ships in foreign trade.

Although the problem was raised, the commission never seriously considered whether the vast changes wrought by the war in America's economic position removed the justification for a differential subsidy program. Cost differentials had existed in the past; it was assumed they would recur in the future. Authority to pay subsidies was available and had been used throughout the war to help defray the cost of ships constructed for private account.[1] Furthermore, the commission believed it had a moral if not legal obligation to resume payments to those companies which had entered into subsidy contracts prior to the war. Even though

[1] Although the bulk of the wartime construction program was of standard ships for government account, a total of 128 ships designed to private specifications were purchased between 1941 and 1945 both by companies holding operating subsidy contracts and companies not under contract.

aid was not immediately needed, both the commission and the subsidized operators regarded the reserve funds and tax advantages provided by the contracts as a useful means of husbanding resources against future emergencies. Finally, because the commission knew that it could recapture any subsidies resulting in excess earnings, it felt justified to take "a long-range viewpoint" toward the reactivation of subsidies "regardless of . . . the present high volume of cargo offerings and increased rates."[2]

Subsidy payments to the twelve companies which had held contracts before the war were resumed on January 1, 1947. Concurrently, the Maritime Commission encouraged resumption of non-subsidized operations by making war-surplus ships freely available to all U.S. citizens at attractive prices. For a time the coexistence of subsidized and non-subsidized American shipping companies posed few problems; there was business enough for all. However, in the latter part of 1948 rates once again declined to a level which made continued operations unprofitable for most non-subsidized U.S. flag ships. Once again it became apparent that the scale and character of U.S. flag foreign trade shipping operations depended on government subsidy policies. The future of important segments of the American maritime industry turned on the manner in which the Maritime Commission would interpret such statutory phrases as "substantial portion" and "adequate service," and on the willingness of the Congress to relax constraints or change the basis for awarding subsidies from economic to defense-related tests.

Targets for U.S. Flag Participation. Prior to the war, U.S. flag liners had carried 35-40 percent of the liner cargoes in U.S. foreign commerce (by weight), about 25 percent of the tanker business, and only a minimal share of non-liner, dry bulk products. The prewar commission had been generally satisfied with this participation, believing that American shipping companies could not and should not expect to share substantially in tramp trades. Rather than attempt to capture any arbitrary percentage of the business, the commission had early concluded that "a sound merchant marine policy should be predicated upon achieving [only] some measure

---

[2] U.S. Maritime Commission, *Annual Report, 1946,* p. 17. Curiously, because business currently was at so high a level, the immediate effect of the reactivation of subsidies was to *diminish* rather than to augment amounts payable to several of the lines. This occurred because inclusion of postwar profits in recapture accounting, calculated over a ten-year period, permitted recapture of some of the subsidies paid prior to 1942 as well as all of the differential accrued subsequent to the war. Thus, whereas subsidy accruals for the five prewar years had initially been estimated at $21.5 million, the amount actually charged against those years when the contracts were finally settled was only $12.1 million.

of representation in all important areas," which would protect American shippers against unfair treatment or possible withdrawal of foreign flags.[3] The twelve subsidy contracts which it awarded prior to the war covered only 35-40 percent of the U.S. flag dry cargo liners. Subsidized carriers handled only about 15 percent of the total liner business and less than 5 percent of the nation's total foreign trade. These carriers did, however, provide at least minimal service on all but four of the thirty-six principal U.S. foreign trade routes.

The U.S. merchant fleet's wartime expansion encouraged the postwar commission to adopt more ambitious objectives. In its 1945 *Annual Report* the commission announced that the American merchant fleet "can, and should, carry about 50 percent of the Nation's foreign trade, in addition to all water-borne domestic commerce."[4] The commission recognized that this policy would require U.S. flag carriers to obtain a very large share of the liner business in order to offset a much smaller participation in bulk operations. Its 1946 trade route report proposed U.S. flag liner services adequate to take 62 percent of the business. Since government policy also was to encourage revival of competing foreign shipping services, this target was not realistic. (Liner cargoes generally are shared both with the national flag lines of the trading partner and with third flags. Consequently, few nations carry even 50 percent of their foreign commerce.) The result was to diminish the usefulness of the commission's trade participation studies as a basis either for policy planning or for determining eligibility for subsidy.[5]

Subsidies to Competing Lines. The Maritime Commission's prewar essential service determinations had, with one exception, been predicated on the principle that subsidies would be paid to only one line on each route.[6] In order to achieve its more ambitious postwar objectives, the

---

[3] U.S. Maritime Commission, *Economic Survey of the American Merchant Marine* (Government Printing Office, 1937), p. 16.

[4] U.S. Maritime Commission, *Annual Report, 1945*, p. 3.

[5] More recent trade route studies have set more modest targets for U.S. flag participation. The 455-562 U.S. flag liners indicated in the 1960 Maritime Administration trade route report to be needed to "maintain essential services on U.S. foreign trade routes," for example, would have been sufficient to carry only 40-50 percent of the cargoes then being carried by liners in U.S. foreign trade. However, these targets were also 15-40 percent above the service actually being provided by American ships.

[6] The one exception made by the prewar commission to Mr. Kennedy's "chosen instrument" policy was the award of contracts to both the American-South African Steamship Company (now Farrell Lines) and Seas Shipping Company (now Robin Line, Moore-McCormack Co.) for service to South Africa. This decision of the commission was recognized to be an exception, based in part on understandings reached prior to the enactment of the 1936 act (see 3 U.S.M.C. 277 [1938]).

commission concluded, apparently with some reluctance, that it might have to relax this "chosen instrument" policy. Its statement as to the policies which would apply in reviewing postwar subsidy applications was expressed in its 1946 trade route report as follows:

> The Maritime Commission would prefer that private U.S. flag operations be conducted in the foreign trade without Government aid, but will enter into contracts for the payment of operating differential subsidies, in accordance with the provisions of the law, wherever this is necessary to maintain adequate United States flag service on essential trade routes. It is prepared to grant such a subsidy even though one or more U.S. flag lines are already in the trade, if it finds that is necessary to provide adequate services by vessels of U.S. registry.[7]

During the next three years the commission received nine requests from non-subsidized companies for subsidy on routes already covered by one of the twelve approved contractors. Most of these applicants argued that theirs was an "existing service" within the terms of the act, for which subsidy should be granted so long as it was not found to be "unduly prejudicial" to other U.S. flag lines—which in these cases were already receiving subsidies.[8] The commission, however, adopted the viewpoint that subsidy payments were made to obtain specific public purposes (i.e., to provide a minimum service on essential U.S. trade routes) and that the applicant must demonstrate that the existing subsidized service was somehow inadequate. Only one of the eight applicants surmounted this restrictive test. However, several of the commission's existing contracts were amended to permit subsidized lines to establish new services and extend existing services, even though in some instances partially competitive with another subsidized line.

The commission's policies appeared to favor the twelve companies (irreverently nicknamed "the Twelve Apostles") which had signed subsidy

---

[7] "Report of the U.S. Maritime Commission on Essential Foreign Trade Routes and Services Recommended for U.S. Flag Operation," printed in *Proposed Amendments to Ship Sales Act, 1946,* Hearings before the House Merchant Marine and Fisheries Committee, 80 Cong. 1 sess. (1947).

[8] Sec. 605(c) of the 1936 act, which controls grants of subsidy to competing U.S. flag carriers, distinguishes between applications to subsidize a new service and those to subsidize an existing service where there are already two or more U.S. lines operating in the trade. In the first instance the act requires the applicant to show that the existing service is "inadequate." In the second, a literal reading of the act requires inadequacy to be shown only if the grant of subsidy is found by the commission to "give undue advantage or be unduly prejudicial as between citizens of the United States." Presumably the chief purpose of these tests was to protect lines not applying for subsidy, although they have actually been used chiefly to protect subsidized operators.

contracts before the war. They were severely criticized by certain members of Congress and in particular by the House Appropriations Committee which wrote a limitation into the commission's 1951 appropriation barring payment of subsidy to any additional vessels unless the Director of the Bureau of the Budget certified with the concurrence of the Secretary of Defense that a larger program was required in support of the national defense. The following year the committee stipulated that 307 of the 1,522 authorized voyages should be reserved solely for lines which were not then participating in the program. In reporting its bill to the House the committee scored the new Federal Maritime Board for perpetuating the monopoly of subsidized lines and urged that the voyages authorized in outstanding contracts "be reduced so that other companies or individuals who have not enjoyed these benefits be permitted to do so."[9]

The board heeded the committee's advice. In its next case—a consolidated application by two companies to provide up to 82 subsidized voyages annually in the Pacific-Far East trade—it reversed the commission's "chosen instrument" policy and granted subsidy despite the fact that over 70 percent of the commercial business on this route and all military cargoes were already handled by U.S. flag ships.[10]

Since 1952 three additional companies have qualified for subsidy. (A fourth new line has been organized as a subsidiary of two previously subsidized operators, and two companies have withdrawn from the program.) In a half dozen other cases the presence of an existing subsidized carrier has been found to be no bar to subsidizing an additional line, although other obstacles have prevented subsidy awards. Service obligations specified in existing subsidy contracts also have been modified to increase the number of allowable ports of call and to authorize new or expanded services. As a result there are now two or more subsidized companies operating on fourteen of the thirty-three essential routes in U.S. foreign trade.[11]

[9] H. Rept. 753, 82 Cong. 1 sess. (1951), p. 12. When it became evident that the board would really have to restrict subsidized shipping operations in order to comply with the voyage limitation, the Congress relaxed the restriction.

[10] Pacific Far East and Pacific Transport Line Subsidy Applications, 4 FMB 136 (1952). This decision was challenged in the courts (112 F. Supp. 346) and later was the subject of a hearing, *Double and Triple Tracking on Subsidized Trade Routes,* before the House Merchant Marine and Fisheries Committee, 84 Cong. 2 sess. (1956). The Maritime Board was sustained in both cases.

[11] Since 1947 three new routes out of the Great Lakes have been designated as "essential U.S. foreign trade routes," but six routes have been consolidated with others in order to permit greater flexibility of service. Subsidized services are provided on thirty of the thirty-three routes. On sixteen of the thirty there is but one subsidized

Liberalization of the board's policy came too late to benefit most of the companies which had sought to establish subsidized services immediately following the war.[12] Instead, opportunities to acquire and develop new services have been seized chiefly by the stronger subsidized lines and have therefore tended to increase the concentration of economic power within the industry.[13]

The Federal Maritime Board's repudiation of the commission's "reasonable representation in the trade" theory cast the subsidy program loose from its moorings. The task of developing new criteria has so taxed the board's abilities that "section 605(c) cases," in which applicants for subsidy attempt to demonstrate the inadequacy of other existing services, have become one of the most troublesome facets of the government program. Uncertainty as to the intent of the law has been compounded by an even more basic uncertainty as to the contribution of U.S. flag services to American commerce. With no basic agreement regarding the merchant marine's commercial role and in the absence of a consistent, well-developed body of law, the board's decisions have often appeared arbitrary or to be based on irrelevant considerations.[14]

Generally since 1952, where U.S. flag ships have failed to secure at least 50 percent of the cargo tonnage moving via liners, the board has considered existing services to be, prima facie, inadequate. However, it has refused to be bound by any particular arithmetic percentage. Indeed,

---

line; on eight, two lines; on one, three; and on four, four. On one route (Pacific Coast to the Far East) five companies hold subsidy contracts. In nine cases still other companies have privilege of providing occasional services on the route.

[12] Of the nine companies applying between 1946 and 1949, five subsequently left the steamship business, two were purchased by lines which already held subsidy contracts, and two qualified for subsidy and are still in operation.

[13] As of June 30, 1964, there were twenty-three companies operating liners in foreign trade, of which fifteen were subsidized. However, these fifteen companies owned all of the American merchant marine's post-1946 built ships and three-quarters of its foreign trade liner tonnage. Within the subsidy program still further concentration has developed. Thus four of the fifteen subsidized lines are either owned by or under common control with other subsidized companies. Natomas owns the American President Lines and American Mail and exercises operating control over Pacific Far East; the Isbrandtsen Company owns American Export; Lykes and Grace jointly own Gulf and South American. These companies, together with U.S. Lines and Moore-McCormack, receive 84 percent of the government's operating subsidy payments and hold 84 percent of the industry's statutory reserves.

[14] For example, the board's decisions have sometimes appeared aimed at increasing the overall size of the U.S. flag fleet, at enhancing the profit opportunities of a lagging line, at demonstrating the potential of new operating methods, or at creating trade opportunities for an experimental ship—all of which may be useful and important reasons for providing subsidy but are irrelevant to the adequacy of the existing service.

in a recent decision, the Maritime Subsidy Board announced that it would "strive for the highest possible level of participation in all trade routes, and would not be content with 50 percent if a higher figure were obtainable."[15] In reviewing subsidy applications the maritime agencies have therefore tended to concentrate on whether additional subsidized sailings would tend to draw cargoes from an established U.S. flag line rather than whether the added service is needed by American shippers. In effect, the question before the board has thus become whether the trade is adequate to support additional U.S. flag service rather than whether the existing service is adequate to the trade.

Financial and Other Tests. As the importance of the "section 605(c)" test has diminished, other tests for admission to subsidy have become more critical. Before aid can be granted, corporate structure must be examined in detail, all non-shipping and foreign affiliations severed, financial resources found adequate, and the presence of low-cost foreign competition established. In recent years the Maritime Board has also examined the applicant's operating results and assessed his need (as well as entitlement) for government aid.

The board's financial requirements have posed the most important obstacle to subsidy. They specify that

> the applicant either own or can and will purchase, a vessel or vessels of the size, type, speed, and number . . . required to enable him to maintain the service . . . in such manner as may be necessary to meet competitive conditions, and to promote the foreign commerce.[16]

As a general rule the board has required that the applicant's net worth be sufficient to finance a 25 percent down payment on new vessels at such time as existing equipment becomes obsolete and to cover one-half the cost of making one typical voyage with each vessel in his fleet. However, these standards have been moderated from time to time to meet specific situations.[17]

[15] Maritime Subsidy Board, Reply to Petitions for Review and Reversal in Atlantic Express Lines' Application for Operating-Differential Subsidy, Docket S-124.

[16] Sec. 601, Merchant Marine Act, 1936.

[17] For example, the Prudential Steamship Company was permitted to post a $3 million bond to secure its pledge that it would float a security issue if necessary to meet ship replacement obligations specified in the contract. The Isbrandtsen Line met the board's financial qualifications through a complex transaction which involved purchase of a majority interest in the American Export Line, which in turn purchased Isbrandtsen's ships at prices which enhanced their book value. This transaction is described in *Review of Merchant Marine Policy*, Hearings before the House Merchant Marine and Fisheries Committee, 87 Cong. 2 sess. (1962), pp. 67 ff.

The net effect of the many obstacles to winning entrance to the subsidy program has been to make the prosecution of a subsidy application an agonizingly prolonged and expensive process. Of the six applications pending before the board in 1964, half had been on file since 1957 or earlier. One of this group even undertook a major internal reorganization in order to satisfy one of the board's requirements only to find that it failed to qualify under another. A second was reported to be on the threshold of receiving a subsidy contract when two competing carriers sought a court injunction against the board; by the time this issue was settled (in favor of the applicant), a financial obstacle had superceded it.

Each of the eight U.S. liner companies operating in foreign trade outside the subsidy program in 1964 was a substantial carrier of military cargoes. Freedom from trade route and other restrictions on subsidized operations has enabled these carriers to return a profit on current operations but not to build up sufficient reserves to permit replacement of their war-surplus equipment. The government has allowed these operators to exchange their least efficient ships for better vessels from the reserve fleet. However, it has failed to develop any long-term solution to the ship replacement and other problems facing this group.

Aid to Tramp and Industrial Carriers. The government's ambivalent postwar attitude toward U.S. tramp and industrial carriers is the result of its failure to restructure the 1936 act toward a defense objective. In 1946 the government-owned fleet included far more ships than could ever conceivably be employed in berth services. Their use as tramps, for which they were well suited, was supported by the Navy as desirable for national defense. Indeed, because not committed to any trade, tramps were believed to be more accessible and hence more useful for military missions than vessels in liner service. However, bulk shippers did not support the organization of a tramp fleet. Most of the great industrial corporations were content to depend for their raw materials on captive fleets operated under foreign flags; shippers of agricultural products, while not openly opposed to subsidies, appeared apprehensive that their extension to tramps would be accompanied by some form of rate regulation inimical to their interests.

Extension of subsidies to tramp and industrial carriers promised also to plunge government into a thicket of difficult administrative and legal problems. Most of the U.S. bulk carriers prior to the war had handled chiefly proprietary cargoes. Their owners included some of the largest and most solidly established American corporations, which neither wanted nor were politically suitable objects for subsidy. Furthermore, for the classic tramp-type operation, in which ships were sent throughout the world in search of cargoes, there was no apparent connection with U.S. foreign commerce, no ready gauge of foreign competition, and no basis for parity calculations or essential trade route determinations. The business was one in which Americans had had little or no prewar experience and was generally believed to be dominated by speculators and to be one in which U.S. flag companies would be at a severe disadvantage. A prewar Maritime Commission study of tramp shipping had described it as "the biggest gamble" in the industry. "There is no demand for the American government to subsidize tramp shipping," the report concluded, "and there is really no good reason why it should attempt to do so."[18]

Following World War II the military's interest in enlarging the active U.S. flag fleet coupled with the availability of ships led the commission to give lukewarm support to U.S. flag tramp operations. Operating subsidies were not authorized for tramps per se. But the commission did liberalize its prewar interpretation of "essential service" to include certain seasonal movements and the transport of ores from South America.[19] Construction subsidies were provided under the 1936 act to United Fruit, Alcoa, and Ore Steamship (a U.S. Steel subsidiary) to augment their proprietary fleets, and war-built vessels were both sold and chartered at favorable prices to newly-organized companies which had expressed an interest in experimenting in the tramp trades.

From 1949 through the mid-fifties numerous proposals were advanced to supplement the 1936 liner program with a subsidy for tramps or to do away entirely with the essential trade route system in favor of a subsidy payable to any qualified company operating U.S. flag ships in foreign trade. These proposals were all firmly opposed by the subsidized lines. Following an intensive study, the Senate Interstate and Foreign Commerce Committee recommended that tramps be aided, but only on terms and conditions which would assure they would not compete with U.S. flag liners.[20] The Maritime Commission also made a study, but was unable to

[18] U.S. Maritime Commission, *An Economic Survey of the American Merchant Marine*, p. 19. The commission made a special study of tramp shipping, as required by sec. 213 of the 1936 act, which was printed as H. Doc. 520, 75 Cong. 2 sess. (1938).

[19] "Report . . . on Essential Foreign Trade Routes and Services Recommended for U.S. Flag Operation," Hearings, pp. 827 ff. The commission anticipated that these bulk services might be an adjunct to regular liner operations and encouraged established companies to charter government-owned vessels to haul tramp-type Marshall Plan cargoes during 1947-48 (see U.S. Maritime Commission, *Annual Report, 1948*, p. 5).

[20] *Merchant Marine Study and Investigation*, S. Rept. 2494, 81 Cong. 2 sess. (1950), p. 91.

reach any position at all.[21] The Commerce Department expressed the view
in a 1949 report that some new system should probably be devised to increase the flexibility of American shipping operations and to place all U.S.
foreign steamship companies on an equal basis, but refrained from suggesting how this might be accomplished.[22] The following year the Department reported that, though it still had the matter under study, enactment
of tramp subsidy legislation

> would not be in accord with the program of the President, since it
> has not been established that under present circumstances there is a
> justification for the proposed departure from the basic principle of
> providing subsidies only to regularly scheduled services covering
> essential foreign trade routes.[23]

After extended hearings and negotiation the Congress in 1952 enacted
a Long Range Shipping Bill, which despite its title offered no solution to
the dilemma posed by the unequal treatment granted to subsidized and
non-subsidized shipping under the 1936 act.[24] The bill did clarify and
strengthen the board's authority to subsidize construction of tramp and
industrial carriers, and over the next six years applications for aid to construct a dozen vessels were filed by non-subsidized firms. None of these

---

[21] A staff committee recommended in a 1949 *Study of Tramp Shipping Under the
American Flag* (mimeograph, Maritime Administration library), that the commission
subsidize 200 tramps in order to meet defense requirements and assure that a substantial portion of U.S. trade could be carried in U.S. bottoms. The commission held
a hearing on the report but failed to reach a position.

[22] U.S. Department of Commerce, *Issues Involved in a Unified and Coordinated
Federal Program for Transportation,* Report to the President (Dec. 1, 1949), p. 14.

[23] Letter from Philip B. Fleming, Acting Secretary of Commerce, to Edward J.
Hart, Chairman, House Merchant Marine and Fisheries Committee, Aug. 20, 1950,
printed in *Encouragement of the Development and Expansion of Privately Owned
Tramp Shipping,* Hearings, 81 Cong. 2 sess. (1950), p. 8.

[24] The Long Range Shipping Bill liberalized the 1936 act by: (1) extending construction subsidy to vessels other than those operated on essential trade routes, (2)
authorizing non-recourse government loans for financing construction of large passenger
vessels, (3) reducing from 17 to 12 years the minimum age of vessels eligible for
trade-in to the government for the favorable allowances authorized by sec. 510 of the
1936 act, (4) extending the above trade-in provisions to vessels in domestic trade,
(5) authorizing use of construction reserves for vessel reconstruction and debt retirement and extending by one year the time limit within which they had to be committed
for expenditure, (6) authorizing recomputation, for depreciation purposes, of the life
expectancy of reconstructed vessels, and (7) removing the $25,000 limit on salaries
paid by subsidized operators. It may be noted that the majority of this legislation's
provisions, as finally enacted, favored the subsidized rather than tramp and industrial
carriers.

proposals, however, was accepted by the government. The conviction that none would be so long as there were any unsatisfied commitments of construction aid to subsidized lines was affirmed in 1962. In rejecting Bethlehem Steel's proposal to construct two ore carriers in its Quincy Yards, the Commerce Department announced, "We have come to the conclusion that our common carrier ship construction program should have first priority."[25]

Implementation of Parity

The prewar Maritime Commission recognized the parity principle as one of the cornerstones of the 1936 act and made heroic efforts to devise sound methods for calculating operating and construction cost differentials. It soon concluded, however, that the parity calculation was "not a scientific process, that the results are only approximately accurate at best, that some errors are likely to be made, and that only through periodic revision can subsidies be made to approximate the ideal . . . set forth in the 1936 Act."[26]

The commission's candid attitude, along with the fact that the program was just getting organized and subsidies were still small, caused the Congress to adopt a tolerant attitude which insulated the commission from controversy. Following the war, however, a much more critical atmosphere prevailed. Throughout the government, wartime and postwar contracts were being carefully re-examined. In shipping, enormous amounts were at issue, and a large audit program involving both Maritime Commission and General Accounting Office staff was underway.

Early Controversies. A special report filed by the Comptroller General with the Congress in July 1949 ignited the postwar controversy over the interpretation of parity.[27] The report alleged that the commission's allowance of construction subsidies for three passenger superliners had been "excessive due to various irregular procedures, inaccurate calculations, and

[25] Statement of Clarence D. Martin, Jr., Under Secretary of Commerce for Transportation, concerning S. J. Res. 160, printed in *Review of Merchant Marine Policy*, Hearings, p. 15.

[26] U.S. Maritime Commission, *An Economic Survey of the American Merchant Marine*, p. 77.

[27] "Construction-differential Subsidies and Related National Defense Allowances Granted by the United States Maritime Commission," Report of the Comptroller General to the Congress, July 11, 1949, printed in *Inquiry into the Operations of the Maritime Commission*, H. Rept. 1423, 81 Cong. 1 sess. (1949).

unjustifiably liberal interpretations of statutory language."[28] The commission rejoined that its conclusions were adequately supported, considering the unique character of the project, and more important, that a liberal interpretation of the act was necessary to getting the ships built. Superliner construction had been strongly urged by the new Department of Defense and was supported by the President.

The underlying issue in the superliner cases was whether the statutory parity formula was the proper vehicle for meeting stated defense needs.[29] However, the inept manner in which the commission handled the case diverted attention from this basic issue to a multitude of specific problems concerning the commission's computation of parity and its capacity for doing its job. Following extensive hearings, the House Committee on Expenditures in the Executive Departments reported:

> Subsidy determinations were in the instant cases [i.e., S.S. "United States," "Independence," and "Constitution"] based upon assumptions which were almost devoid of foundation, and calculations derived from their assumptions were replete with errors and inaccuracies. . . . The determinations of the Maritime Commission in connection with operating differential subsidies were inadequately supported and results were unreliable. . . . In the computation of subsidies better information on foreign cost could have been obtained than was obtained, and the information available could have been more effectively utilized.[30]

Under this barrage of criticism, a frustrated and tarnished Maritime Commission in 1950 finally retreated to the position that parity was essentially incalculable. An alternative suggested by the commission was to legislate a non-discretionary payment formula, but the Congress did not

---

[28] *Ibid.*, pp. 30 ff.

[29] The most celebrated of the three superliner cases concerned construction of the S.S. "United States." The United States Lines, the only U.S. flag company in a position to operate a high performance vessel of the sort desired by Defense, informed the Maritime Commission that it could not justify an investment of more than $25 million in the ship, which was substantially less than its share of the estimated cost required under Title V of the 1936 act. However, the proposed ship had no commercial counterpart and the statute permitted the commission to pay for the full cost of defense features. A liberal estimate of the cost effect of the ship's defense-oriented design coupled with a finding that there was "convincing evidence" that the construction cost differential exceeded 33⅓ percent was required to bring the government's contribution to a level which would permit the ship to be built. On the basis of these inescapable facts, but very weak documentation, the commission made the necessary findings, which it later was unable to support.

[30] H. Rept. 1423, p. 21, and *Further Inquiry into the Operations of the Maritime Commission*, H. Rept. 2104, 81 Cong. 2 sess. (1950), p. 29.

agree. As late as 1955, with the problem still unresolved, the House Merchant Marine Committee reported: "It is now conceded on all sides that unless some means is devised whereby companies desiring to build vessels under Title V are assured of valid and binding contracts, the object and purpose of this part of the statute are doomed to certain defeat."[31]

In 1955 compromise settlements were finally reached between the government and the steamship companies whose construction subsidy contracts for superliners the Comptroller General had challenged six years earlier. Two years later the Maritime Administration published a manual of procedure for construction subsidy calculations. Although for various reasons it is still impossible to establish precisely the magnitude of foreign-domestic construction cost differentials and though the system continues to have certain practical disadvantages, procedures are at least now well settled and provide a workable and mutually acceptable technique for getting aid to the industry.[32]

Calculation of Operating Differentials. During the mid-fifties progress also began to be made in fixing rates for operating subsidies—a task which had lagged seriously ever since the 1947 reactivation of operating subsidy contracts. In making these calculations the maritime agencies faced even more difficult problems than in construction determinations, although less controversy. Operating differentials required acquisition of cost data on all of the world's major merchant fleets, whereas construction estimates could be geared to a single representative (low-cost) foreign shipbuilding center. Furthermore, operating subsidy calculations required separate findings for each major item of expense—i.e., wages, subsistence, repairs, stores, and insurance—whereas the construction subsidy, though tied to estimates of component prices, applied only to the sales price of the ship.

The Maritime Aministration has worked diligently to acquire reliable foreign cost data and has been moderately successful in developing coop-

[31] *Vessel Replacement in the American Merchant Marine*, H. Rept. 843, 84 Cong. 1 sess. (1955), p. 7.

[32] The indeterminancy of construction subsidy calculations lies largely in the fact that the subsidy attempts to compensate for the difference in the *price* of obtaining a ship *built to U.S. standards* in a U.S. versus foreign yard. Although ship designs often appear similar, there are sufficient differences in the quality of construction and components to limit the usefulness of direct price comparisons. Other techniques, such as contracting with foreign yards to develop estimates of the costs of building to American design, have also been used, but cannot adequately reflect changing market conditions. The problems inherent to construction subsidy calculations are ably reviewed in a 1961 study prepared by the Arthur D. Little Co. under contract to the Maritime Administration, titled *Ship Construction Differential Subsidies*.

erative arrangements with foreign governments and others who share its interest in making the parity system work.[33] Official sources are supplemented from trade news and by an industry committee formed in 1950 to assist the government in establishing a firmer basis for subsidy determinations. Data limitations, however, continue to pose the greatest obstacle to precision.

A second problem relates to the indeterminancy of the parity concept itself. In theory parity is simple, in practice highly complex. For example, should the subsidy seek to equate U.S. and foreign costs or only to compensate the U.S. operator for the added costs imposed on him by the "buy America" features of the 1936 act? (The Maritime Administration follows the latter practice, except that wage subsidies are geared to equalizing wages to the crew as a whole rather than compensating for higher rates paid to crewmen individually.) If the "compensation" theory is adopted, should it be assumed that in the absence of restrictions the operator would make all his repairs, purchase his insurance, and so forth exclusively from foreign sources? (Generally it is.) If so, how are cases to be handled where domestic procurement would be less costly? (Initially these were calculated as offsets to the subsidy, but in 1955 this practice was dropped.)

A third problem is presented by aids given by other nations to their national flag fleets. Since these aids do not directly affect subsidizable costs, they do not enter into the parity calculation. But they can significantly affect the foreign line's profits and competitive strength. To meet these situations, the commission was authorized by both the 1920 and 1936 merchant marine acts to pay "countervailing subsidies" or to take other action as appropriate.[34] For diplomatic and other reasons, however, these powers are seldom used.[35] In fact, the government has not even received any application for "countervailing" aid.

[33] Most of the Western European governments recognize that if the parity system were to break down, some other, probably more objectionable, means of sustaining an American merchant marine would be erected in its place, and have therefore cooperated. However, even the registering government seldom has complete cost data. Data compiled especially to meet Marad's needs by cooperating lines is also suspect both in its authenticity and in the line's purpose in supplying it.

[34] Sec. 19, Merchant Marine Act of 1920, grants comprehensive authority to make whatever rules may be necessary to meet "general or special conditions unfavorable to shipping in the foreign trade, . . . which arise out of or from foreign laws, rules, or regulations or from competitive practices, employed . . . vessels of a foreign country." Sec. 604, Merchant Marine Act of 1936, authorized payment of "countervailing subsidies" to offset the effects of government aid paid to competitors.

[35] In most cases involving foreign discrimination, the maritime agencies have used a succession of devices to remove the offensive practice: first, through negotiation; second, by denying the ships of the offending national flag fleet access to export

Parity Liberalization. Over the years a large number of amendments have been made to the 1936 act, multiplying its non-parity features.[36] Without exception they have been designed to relax restrictions, make the terms and conditions of the differential subsidies more favorable to the subsidy contractors, or to supplement these subsidies with other related aids.

A desire to be sure that promotional and defense objectives are successfully achieved by the privately owned fleet has fueled the liberalization of maritime subsidies. Sometimes, as in fixing special sales prices for superliners, the promotional goal has come into direct conflict with parity principles;[37] sometimes the relationship has been obscure. In some instances the case for liberalization has been argued in equitable (parity) terms.

The most common specific concerns leading to liberalization have related to the U.S. flag fleet's physical condition—in particular, that "block obsolescence" of war-built ships be averted by beginning replacement before the end of their economic life. Most of the liberalizing legislation has consequently been directed at the terms and conditions of construction assistance, or has been justified as needed to assure that the industry could generate sufficient equity capital and mortgage financing for new ships.

The first important legislative amendment concerned the tax status of subsidized operators' deposits to their statutory reserves. The 1936 act, enacted when corporate income taxes progressed to a maximum of only 15 percent, exempted all mandatory deposits to the reserve funds from taxation. In 1938 tax exemptions were extended to voluntary deposits to encourage subsidized operators to strengthen their reserves. Subsequent increases in the normal tax rate, the addition of excess profits taxes, and large wartime and postwar earnings and capital gains combined to make

---

cargoes financed by Export-Import Bank credits; and only if other actions are not successful, by taking retaliatory action under section 19 of the 1920 act. For example, section 19 was invoked in 1960 to force Ecuador to repeal a 1-3½ percent ad valorem consular fee imposed on any goods imported on foreign ships. The fee was first imposed in 1946 and U.S. flag participation in the trade fell from more than 76 percent to less than 10 percent before retaliatory action finally was taken. A second "section 19" order to counteract a Uruguayan discriminatory practice was issued in 1964, but has been suspended to allow Uruguay time to take corrective action.

[36] Legislation liberalizing the 1936 act is included in Gilman G. Udall's *Laws Relating to Shipping and Merchant Marine* (Government Printing Office, 1960).

[37] Ten years after the 1949-50 superliner controversy the problem of arranging for the construction of superliners was raised once again. On this occasion the Congress authorized the ships to be sold for private operation at prices substantially lower than those which would have been applicable under the general statutory formula (P.L. 85-521 [72 Stat. 359]). The superliners have not been built.

these concessions enormously advantageous. In fact, the Treasury Department ment estimated that between 1938 and 1946 preferred tax treatment yielded the twelve subsidized operators $104.4 million—over eight times the total operating subsidy, net of recapture, paid during the same period.[38]

Treasury challenged the propriety of these preferences and in 1947 extracted "closing agreements" from the subsidized companies to claim only tax *deferments* on future reserve fund deposits in return for its withdrawal of most of its recovery claims.[39] Still further tightening of the subsidized operators' tax advantages was recommended by President Truman in a special 1951 message.[40] The Democratic 82nd Congress was more impressed by the industry's argument that its tax savings were needed to finance new construction and the reserve funds special tax status was preserved.[41]

Congressional concern for the shipping industry's financial position and ship replacement requirements also resulted in a number of minor liberalizations, packaged with the extension of construction subsidies to bulk carriers and tramps, in the 1952 Long Range Shipping legislation.

[38] *Scope and Effect of Tax Benefits Provided the Maritime Industry,* Supplementary Report (mimeograph, 1952), p. 13. The Treasury estimate was disputed by the Maritime Administration, the Senate Interstate and Foreign Commerce Committee, and the operators, who claimed that other avenues of tax relief could have been utilized under the law in the absence of the special provisions for the subsidized merchant marine.

[39] The liberality of the subsidized companies' wartime tax treatment was investigated in 1946 by the House Merchant Marine and Fisheries Committee and reported in *Tax Liability of Subsidized Operators on Wartime Earnings,* H. Rept. 3, 80 Cong. 1 sess. (1947). The position taken by the committee and used by Treasury in its subsequent negotiations with the operators was that the tax treatment authorized by the 1936 act became inoperative when the contracts were suspended in 1942. The closing agreements reached between Treasury and the operators provided that (1) taxes should be paid on all voluntary wartime deposits at the rates applicable to the year when earned; (2) all reserve fund deposits made subsequent to Jan. 1, 1947, would be considered tax-deferred rather than exempt from taxation (i.e., a contingent liability is established for payment on deposits not reinvested at such time as the subsidy contract is dissolved); (3) interest and other earnings on the reserve fund capital shall have the same tax status as the funds on which earned; and (4) any balances reverting to the operator on the termination of the subsidy contract shall be taxed at the rate then applicable. A complete exposition of the terms of the agreements is given in *Scope and Effect of Tax Benefits Provided in the Maritime Industry,* H. Doc. 213, 82 Cong. 1 sess. (1951), p. 7.

[40] Letter of President Harry S. Truman to the Honorable Sam Rayburn, July 31, 1951, printed in H. Doc. 213.

[41] Both House and Senate were willing to adopt at least a part of the President's proposed tax reform. However, their proposals differed, and no basis for compromise was found by the conference committee, which simply noted that the whole subject should be studied again the following session (it was not).

Two years later, broad new authority allowed government guarantees of up to 90 percent of privately negotiated construction loans and mortgages on all manner of ocean-going vessels, and in 1956, 100 percent guarantees were approved. A special "trade-in and build" program authorized the Secretary of Commerce to purchase war-built and prewar tankers on favorable terms if their owners would agree to construct equivalent new tonnage in U.S. yards. Other liberalizations reduced required deposits to capital reserves (by increasing the statutory life of vessels constructed subsequent to 1945 from twenty to twenty-five years); increased the maximum limit on construction subsidies from 50 to 55 percent (60 percent for reconstructions); allowed investment of reserve funds in approved common stocks; permitted a larger portion of the subsidy accrual due operators to be paid current; and relieved operators of charter hire payments on vessels to be traded in on new construction.

Several liberalizations resulted from hearings held in 1955 to consider administrative practices which the operators believed deterred ship replacement. At that time the Maritime Administration (Marad) announced that it would henceforth cover through subsidy the full differential calculated between foreign and domestic cost of subsidized items of expense (although this had long been its practice, Marad had occasionally threatened to adopt a more restrictive interpretation). The term of operating subsidy contracts was lengthened from ten to twenty years; charter rates on government-owned vessels were eased; and rules governing voluntary deposits to reserve funds were liberalized. A particularly significant administrative change was Marad's shift from a book to market value basis for appraising ships purchased from subsidized operators for entry to the reserve fleet.[42]

Effect of Liberalization. The cumulative effect of these and other concessions has been to alter significantly the scope and character of the government aid program. For example, capital gains allowed on vessel trade-ins —subject neither to current taxation or recapture—have amounted to ap-

[42] Sec. 507 of the 1936 act had provided for trade-ins at cost less depreciation as a part of the operating and construction subsidy scheme. Immediately after the outbreak of World War II, a new section 511 was added to permit the commission to purchase at market value any obsolete vessels (more than 17 years old and 3,500 gross tons) upon the condition that new tonnage of equivalent capacity would be purchased or built for U.S. registry. This program was directed at shipowners not participating in the subsidy program. Use of this authority in acquisitions of subsidized ships was, however, approved by the Comptroller General prior to the 1954 decision to shift from a book to market value basis in valuation of traded-in vessels.

proximately $500,000 per vessel. Tax deferments on reserve fund deposits, although not as significant as previously, have averaged $12.1 million annually over the past five years.

While many concessions have been made, the U.S. operator continues to carry some burdens not borne by his competitors. Perhaps the most important is the very weight of participating in the government aid program. In addition, U.S. companies carry substantially higher expenses for home office administration, though overhead as a percentage of operating costs is typically lower. Excess earnings are subject to recapture, and earnings opportunities are somewhat limited by trade route and other restrictions of the 1936 act.

Passage of time has multiplied the number of non-parity benefits and restrictions associated with the operating subsidy program.[43] The problem in relation to capital costs is even more complex.[44] The net effect of these

[43] Other government aids which supplement operating subsidies include free medical care and officers' training programs, availability of government cargoes on favorable terms, tax deferments on amounts deposited to reserve funds (and interest on the tax-deferred amounts), and war risk insurance on favorable terms. Government also helps publicize U.S. flag shipping services, arbitrates the industry's labor-management disputes, acts to remove foreign discrimination, and provides a variety of free health, safety, and consular services. In some trades, American vessels enjoy a small competitive edge on their foreign competition as a result of their qualification to carry cargoes between domestic ports (not available to foreign flag lines). On the other hand, American subsidized operators are subject to trade route restrictions and restrictions on affiliate companies and services, reserve fund investments, timing of capital investments, and arrangements for maintenance and repairs. Repairs accomplished and supplies purchased abroad are subject to tariffs. Excess profits are recaptured, and only certain specified items of expense are subsidized. (No subsidy is available to offset the U.S. companies' substantially higher overhead expenses or the larger amounts which must be earned in order to make a reasonable profit on their relatively larger investments.) Furthermore the subsidy program itself generates certain additional expenses and the government pays no interest on the very substantial amounts due subsidy contractors but not paid subject to audit.

[44] Non-parity features of the construction subsidy program have been examined by the Arthur D. Little Company and reported in *Ship Construction Differential Subsidies* (1961). The principal advantages which the construction subsidy conveys to U.S. subsidized operators are that the subsidy is measured against prices in the lowest cost shipbuilding center (rather than the costs actually incurred by their competition) and no attempt is made to assess interest expense differentials or the convenience (and monetary savings) of building domestically. U.S. operators also enjoy favorable trade-in arrangements, have generous credit aids, benefit from research and development assistance, and received the best ships out of the government's war-built fleet. On the other hand, they bear the extra costs (calculated at the foreign rate) of constructing their ships to American standards, are required to tailor their equipment plans to an industry-wide replacement program, and are limited by the statutory ceiling on the percentage of domestic costs which may be compensated by subsidy (55 percent) regardless of the computed differential.

many supplementary aids and penalties is difficult—probably impossible—
to assess. But their cumulative impact is of great importance.

The postwar trend in the subsidy program has caused Europeans to be
increasingly critical of U.S. policies. Subsidies designed only to permit national flag fleets to compete in international trade on an equal basis are
tolerated as a matter of international comity and agreement.[45] However,
foreign shipowners now claim, "U.S. liners are not given parity, but are
put at a great advantage over their competitors."[46] American shipowners
take strong exception to this allegation.

Supervision of Subsidized Fleet

Assistance to the U.S. flag fleet, although increasingly generous, continues to be hedged around by many administrative restraints, some resulting from the protective provisions of the 1936 act, others from the cautious stance of an administrative agency operating in what it has often
sensed to be a hostile climate.

The underlying restraint on the subsidy program, in which all parties
have a common interest, is the need to maintain the program's public and
political acceptability. The industry's sensitivity to this factor has generated what many believe to be an excess of caution. Any appearance of ir-
regularity or possibility of scandal is scrupulously avoided.[47] Investment
policy is extraordinarily conservative.[48] Executive salaries and dividend
distributions are generally modest.[49] The subsidized companies' com-

[45] The Convention establishing the Inter-Governmental Maritime Consultative Organization (IMCO) specifically provides that government aid to shipping per se is not
objectionable, but only if designed in a manner which restricts the freedom of all
nations to compete on a fair and equal basis (Article I[B]).

[46] Memorandum submitted to the Secretary of Commerce by the Norwegian government, November 1959, p. 14. See also the statement of the General Council of
British Shipping in *Survey of British Shipping* (London, 1960), p. 35.

[47] For example, in 1961 Lykes Brothers Steamship Company, one of the largest
of the subsidized lines, was cited by the Comptroller General for levying excessive
charges for movement of government-owned grains. Lykes stoutly maintained that its
charges, quoted on a bid basis, were perfectly proper even though almost double the
amounts charged for privately owned grains booked on the same vessels. Nonetheless,
Lykes promptly paid the government's claim rather than expose itself to the publicity
attendant to recovery proceedings.

[48] From 1936 through 1958 subsidized operators were required by statute to invest
their capital and special reserves only in U.S. government obligations. In 1958 this
extraordinarily restrictive requirement was relaxed to permit up to half of the reserves
to be transferred to a common stock fund administered by an approved trustee. As of
June 30, 1963, only five of the fifteen subsidized lines had established such trusts and
only 3.3 percent of the total capital and special reserve balances were invested in them.

[49] The $25,000 salary limitation contained in the 1936 act was replaced in 1952 by

plaints against the Maritime Administration's supervision of their activities have usually been muted in deference to the sensitivities of those dispensing aid and in order to avoid drawing undue attention to the program's controversial aspects. (In contrast, non-subsidized companies and maritime labor have often vehemently criticized the program's administration.)

Protective Policies. The conservative stance of the old-line companies now participating in the operating subsidy program is in marked contrast to the disorganized, free-wheeling enterprises to which the protective provisions of the Merchant Marine Act of 1936 were directed. The act's formal requirements for supervision of subsidy contractors nevertheless remain virtually intact and generate a workload which burdens both the industry and government.[50]

In ship operations and traffic matters, the government—though still requiring that appropriate notice be given—has generally approved any proposal not challenged by a third party. In these areas it has been felt that undue government interference could result only in blunting management initiative and in impairing the competitiveness of U.S. flag lines.

Restrictions associated with the essential trade route system have also been gradually eased, and the routes defined more and more broadly. For example, where there were once four routes from U.S. North Atlantic ports to destinations in northern Europe, there is now a single trading area. Ships may be diverted from their regular routes to pick up or discharge special cargoes for up to three days without loss of subsidy. Longer diversions and "privilege ports" are routinely authorized upon application to the Maritime Administration if no objection is entered. And since 1961, passenger vessels have been permitted to depart altogether from their normal service area for up to four months per year without loss of subsidy in order to participate in the lucrative cruise trade.

---

a rule providing that payments in excess of $25,000 could not be considered a legitimate expense for purposes of computing subsidy recapture. As of June 30, 1964, there were 109 officials in the subsidized industry who received gross remuneration of $25,000 or more (including retirement prepayments, fringe benefits, and bonuses, but excluding the value of stock options). The subsidized industry's most highly paid official, the president of the United States Lines, reported a gross remuneration of $97,000. The average salary of the subsidized lines' chief executive officers is under $60,000.

[50] For example, during its first three years' operation the Maritime Subsidy Board annually processed an average of twenty-three formal amendments to each of the fifteen subsidy contracts. These amendments ranged from approval of the renaming of a ship to authorization of a complex corporate reorganization.

The government has also been liberal in specifying the frequency of service to be provided on essential trade routes. Subsidy contracts fix only the maximum and minimum voyages to be made each year, typically allowing about a 20 percent spread. Temporary adjustments to the contract limitations have usually been easily obtained—particularly requests for reduction in service or shifting of vessels between existing services. One operator was permitted to suspend service on an unprofitable route even though its withdrawal left no other U.S. operator in the trade.[51]

One facet of subsidized operations on which the maritime agencies for many years maintained a strong, consistent position was that the subsidized lines should support the conference system and respect conference rates. This position, however, simply confirmed the operators' point of view. Thus neither the commission nor its successor agencies found it necessary to issue explicit directives on the subject until 1960 when the Isbrandtsen Line applied for subsidy. (Isbrandtsen had for years operated outside the conferences; the Federal Maritime Board wanted to be sure that it did not continue this practice after admission to subsidy.) The policy statement issued by the board to meet this situation did not impose binding restrictions; nonetheless it was severely criticized by a congressional committee which uncovered the board's circular letter two years thereafter, and was subsequently withdrawn.[52]

In contrast to the latitude allowed in operating matters, financial controls have been quite strictly administered by the maritime agencies. Minor liberalizations have permitted expenditure of capital reserves for approved company-sponsored research and development and for purchase of containers. However, the agencies have been reluctant to approve di-

[51] Grace Lines' operating subsidy contract was amended in 1958 to authorize an additional twenty-four voyages and require that at least this number (or a maximum of thirty-four voyages) be made from the Great Lakes to the Caribbean. Losses in developing the trade exceeded the company's estimate and it was relieved of any further obligation after only one season's operations in the Great Lakes under sec. 606(4) of the 1936 act, which provides that the commission shall modify or rescind a subsidy contract if it finds that the operator's claim that he cannot maintain a "service, route, or line" is proved.

[52] Prior to 1958 the Isbrandtsen Line had operated independently of any conferences and was competitive in several trades. The line's policy was modified after the death of its founder, and application filed for subsidy. The Federal Maritime Board stipulated that conformance to conference rates would be required as a condition precedent to approval for subsidy, and subsequently in Circular Letter No. 60-3 generalized this policy to apply to all subsidized lines. The circular letter was uncovered and attacked in June 1963 by Senator Paul Douglas, chairman of the Joint Economic Committee. The Maritime Administration reluctantly retreated to a policy of neutrality toward conference membership in August 1963.

versification plans which threatened the integrity of the reserve funds or to induce a steamship company to cut its investment in the industry.[53] Very conservative standards are applied in assessing the adequacy of reserves to finance ship replacements and in settling subsidy accounts.[54] Finally, unusually exhaustive financial reports are required and are subjected to intensive audit.

Efficiency of Operations. Subsidy contractors are admonished by the 1936 act to conduct their business in "the most economical and efficient manner." Only "fair and reasonable" costs are to be considered in computation of operating subsidies, and only "fair and reasonable" bids approved for subsidized construction. Finally, government agencies are required to consign 50 percent of their shipments to American vessels only if such vessels are available "at fair and reasonable rates for U.S. flag commercial vessels."

The repetition of the "fair and reasonable" qualification emphasizes Congress' concern that costs be kept in line and that the administrative agency be empowered to police the program effectively. Over the years

[53] For example, the Maritime Subsidy Board in April 1964 ruled that it could not approve a corporate reorganization and diversification plan submitted by the Moore-McCormack Line. In July 1964 the Secretary of Commerce issued an opinion and order in which he noted that "beyond fulfilling obligations set out in subsidy contracts, business decisions have generally been left to the management of these companies." The application was remanded to the board for approval subject to such conditions as might be required to protect the government's interest in an American merchant marine and assure compliance with any applicable law.

[54] The Maritime Administration assesses annually the adequacy of replacement reserves. The replacement schedules used for the computations are those specified in the subsidy contracts, which have not been amended to reflect the stretch-out in replacement dates tacitly allowed by mutual government-industry consent. The computation does assume continued funding of depreciation up to the construction date but assumes there will be no further voluntary set-asides of retained earnings (despite the government's policy to encourage such deposits by allowing tax deferments).

The conservatism of the government's financial procedures is also evident in the rules governing operating subsidy payments. The 1936 act permitted only 75 percent of the subsidy accrual to be paid on current account, an added 15 percent upon the completion of voyage audits, and the entire amount only after the year's operations had been completely audited and the books closed. In 1961 these percentages were amended to reduce the amount of subsidy withheld (on which no interest is paid) to 10 and 5 percent, respectively. However since the relationship between the government and the contractor is a continuing one, no real risk would appear to be present even in the amended procedure. Furthermore, the government has been both slow and unusually sticky in closing out its audits. As of June 30, 1963, there were still an estimated $20 million in unpaid back claims based on operations conducted in 1959 and prior years and an additional $27 million associated with 1960 and 1961 operations.

the merchant marine committees have re-emphasized this intent. Successive administrative officers have also pledged that high standards would be rigorously enforced, and that no unreasonable costs—even if required to be paid by the contractor because of a collective bargaining agreement —would be allowed in calculating subsidy.[55]

In practice, however, the difficulty of laying down standards of reasonableness has weakened these high resolves. For many years foreign-domestic cost differentials for most subsidizable items (the only significant exception being subsistence) were determined after the fact and without reference to any reliable objective criteria. The funds had been spent; it was difficult to prove the expenditure "unreasonable" and distasteful to imply that the operator had been irresponsible. Furthermore, the agencies' findings might be challenged in court. Hence, despite occasional threatening pronouncements, the U.S. Maritime Commission and its successor agencies from 1947 to 1964 made little effective use of their subsidy powers to enforce a lower cost standard or greater efficiency upon the industry. They did, however, intensively audit the subsidized companies' expense vouchers and contracting procedures in order to detect any unreasonable deviations from industry norms or charges which were not properly classified under one of the categories of subsidizable expense (wages, subsistence, maintenance and repairs, insurance, and, up to 1955, stores). Occasionally studies were made of such matters as industry practice in granting overtime and premium pay and the operators admonished to institute more effective controls. But these efforts were thinly staffed and geared in any event to industry practice. Disallowances also constituted only a tiny fraction of total subsidies paid and had no measurable impact on the lines.

Under Nicholas Johnson's leadership, the Maritime Subsidy Board has assumed a much more vigorous role. Its new attitude was climaxed by a series of decisions announced July 13, 1965, limiting the subsidizable portion of wage and fringe benefit increases provided in certain labor contracts negotiated two years earlier to an amount consistent with the President's 3.2 percent wage guideline and rejecting as unsound and unreasonable an unfunded pension plan which would have entitled marine engineers to a $300 per month retirement payment after twenty years service

[55] For example, see *Labor Management Problems of the American Merchant Marine*, H. Rept. 1658, 84 Cong. 2 sess. (1956). The principle was reiterated in 1960 in U.S. Maritime Administration Circular Letter No. 60-8 and even more emphatically in the Secretary of Commerce's July 23, 1965, Opinion and Order on Maritime Subsidy Board Dockets A-14, A-15, and A-16.

without limit of age.[56] These decisions were immediately reviewed by the Secretary of Commerce, who applauded the board's "courageous, intelligent" approach but who reversed most of its decisions. The Secretary agreed with the board that "approval of the specific collective bargaining agreements before me for subsidy purposes raises some very serious questions under the statutory test," but concluded that he had "also to take into account the fact that these wage contracts were signed by the employers about two years ago, without any prior notice that any new, stricter standard would be applied" and that the decision's "retroactive effect would work undue hardship" upon the parties.[57] The Secretary also noted that the President's 3.2 percent productivity guideline should not be the sole criterion against which to measure the reasonableness of wage settlements and that it also would be relevant to consider productivity data for the maritime industry (or better yet, for the carrier in question) and the comparative position of maritime versus other employees with comparable skills engaged in comparable shoreside jobs.

The Secretary then specified a procedure for more prompt and dispassionate review of future collective bargaining agreements. Each agreement is to be submitted to the Maritime Administration within ten days of its execution and forwarded by Marad within thirty days thereafter to a special wage review panel for preparation of recommendations to the Maritime Subsidy Board regarding the eligibility of any increased costs for subsidy. The Secretary's procedure offers hope of a more effective review of wage agreements but retains the basically ex post facto character of the present system, is largely silent as to the composition of the special

[56] Opinion and Orders of the Maritime Subsidy Board in Dockets A-14, A-15, and A-16, served July 23, 1965. These agreements had been filed with the board for its review between three and fifteen months earlier. The delay in their consideration was about par for subsidy rate-making matters, but the timing of the board's unprecedented decision was clearly influenced by the fact that a serious strike, involving the same unions and operators, was currently in process. The board also disapproved for subsidy certain training funds, payments to an automation fund (until its use could be determined), and paid vacations in excess of sixty days annually for mates, although masters were permitted to accrue up to twice that time.

[57] Opinion and Order of the Secretary of Commerce on Maritime Subsidy Board Dockets A-14, A-15, and A-16, July 23, 1965. The Secretary sustained the board on all of its technical disallowances resting on the definition of wage costs. His assertion that the board acted without giving the industry any prior notice is only partially true since statements by the board (and particularly its Circular Letter No. 60-8) can be interpreted as anticipating exactly the kind of action that was taken. (The difficulty was that these statements had never been validated by action.) It may also be noted that retroactivity is a built-in feature of a system in which all subsidy rates other than subsistence are fixed after the fact.

panel, and offers no firm guidelines for assessing the reasonableness of the privately negotiated wage agreement. Inasmuch as there are no shoreside jobs comparable to seafaring employment, because the wages of any possible candidates (i.e., construction work in remote locations, lumberjacking, military service) are extremely variant, and since reliable productivity data on the industry's operations is lacking, it appears likely that the "reasonableness" of wage determinations will continue to be troublesome.

An alternative approach, suggested from time to time in the past, would be to apply a formula to fix allowable wage payments in advance.[58] This approach, of course, can be conceived as unduly constraining free collective bargaining, as incompatible with the concept of parity, and as susceptible to abuse.[59] However, standards have been successfully used to predetermine crew feeding expenses. Since 1957, the Maritime Administration also has published guidelines in order to establish fair and reasonable tramp charter rates for U.S. flag ships carrying government preference cargoes, although the rates have usually been sufficiently high to attenuate their effectiveness.[60]

[58] Many possible approaches to wage subsidy determination have been suggested. Some would peg wage subsidies to differences in overall wage levels in nations abroad versus the United States (in order to compensate U.S. shipowners for the added costs of sustaining a U.S. standard of living among their crews); others, to wages in related U.S. shoreside occupations (in order to subsidize only a "fair and reasonable" wage); and still others, to the aid needed by the shipping industry to secure a reasonable rate of return. The 1963 Maritime Evaluation Committee proposal was for a lump-sum prepayment of the estimated "fair and reasonable" differential in maritime wage costs, to be redetermined after three years. The 1965 Interagency Task Force recommended that subsidy rates be calculated on the basis of overall maritime industry cost-parity experience in the trading area served and be paid in proportion to revenues earned on commercial cargoes (in order to maximize incentives to lower costs and increase productivity). These proposals have been rejected by the Maritime Advisory Committee and the Committee of American Steamship Lines in favor of continuing present methods.

[59] Various incentive subsidy systems, based on performance estimates, were tested during the early 1930's, but abandoned after experience demonstrated that (under conditions then prevailing) it was difficult if not impossible to withstand pressures to augment predetermined payments to lines threatened with losses. Although use of incentive systems is not anticipated by the 1936 act, they would be legal so long as payments did not exceed the difference between "fair and reasonable [U.S.] costs . . . over the estimated fair and reasonable cost of the same items of expense" abroad (49 Stat. 2002).

[60] Most of the Maritime Administration's guideline rates were computed in 1957-58. The computations were based on the costs of operating Liberty-type vessels, loaded to 92 percent capacity outbound and returning in ballast. The guideline rate was fixed at a level which generated sufficient cash flow to amortize investment and yield a reasonable (and taxable) rate of return. Few of these conditions apply to actual operations, which are conducted chiefly by jumboized Victories or large bulk carriers

Government Shipping Operations

The options given the government in the 1936 act to build and charter ships if necessary to accomplish the purposes of the statute provide an additional protection against misuse of subsidies. In the prewar period and early postwar years the government did not hesitate to use these options to implement its long-range programs.[61] Since 1953, however, no ships have been constructed under its Title VII authority and charters from the reserve fleet have been made only to meet short-term needs. Furthermore, although several routes lack any regular U.S. flag service, there has been no postwar use of Title VII authority to establish new U.S. flag services or as an alternative to subsidizing privately owned shipping in U.S. foreign trade.[62]

The reserve fleet has greatly expanded the potential for government shipping operations. Initially it was intended that these ships be available for use only in emergencies, but this restriction was relaxed in 1950 to permit use whenever the Federal Maritime Board found, after hearings, that adequate U.S. flag vessels were not available on reasonable terms. By the end of 1951 over 700 government-owned dry cargo and passenger vessels had been removed from mothballs to meet needs generated by the Korean conflict and the India-Pakistan wheat programs. Most of these ships were operated through general agents for government account with govern-

---

and which usually do not report taxable earnings. To meet this situation, Marad has recalculated guideline rates for some routes (e.g., East Coast to the Black Sea) and has applied a 20 percent discount for any shipments via large bulk carriers. Nonetheless, the guideline has been 20-25 percent above actual market for most of the 1957-64 period.

[61] For example, in addition to initiating a major construction program under Title VII and continuing operations of four government-owned lines, the commission launched a new service to Argentina and Brazil (the Good Neighbor Line) and, incident to bankruptcy settlements, acquired a stock interest in two of the nation's largest private carriers. It also assumed almost 30 percent of the cost of twelve tankers being built for Standard Oil in order to assure inclusion of certain national defense features. Following the war it sponsored several coastwise and intercoastal services in an unsuccessful attempt to re-establish commercial operations on these routes. Three government-owned vessels are still being used to service Alaska; all other charters have been terminated.

[62] Currently, three "essential" routes out of the Great Lakes have no regular U.S. flag service. There are several additional trade routes and other more narrowly defined services deemed essential by the Maritime Subsidy Board which are not covered by a subsidy contract. In these latter situations, however, at least occasional sailings are made by non-subsidized U.S. flag operators.

ment personnel.[63] During the same period tanker owners, faced with the alternative that their vessels might be requisitioned, formed a voluntary pool to provide tonnage to the Military Sea Transportation Service (MSTS) at rates well below the world market. It has been estimated that the availability of mothballed vessels during the Korean conflict saved the U.S. economy from $2.5 to $3 billion.[64]

In 1951 the government also moved rapidly to implement a controversial, defense-oriented, 35-ship construction program.[65] The Truman Administration authorized the outfitting of two experimental ships and initiated an $18 million program to upgrade vessels being returned to the reserve fleet. Government construction and development expenditures, other than for the N.S. "Savannah" project, were curtailed during the Eisenhower years.[66]

[63] General agency agreements are contracts for services under which the contractor mans and operates the government's ship for government account. Although furnished by the contractor, the captain and crew of a general agency ship are considered to be government employees by the Civil Service Commission.

The 1936 Merchant Marine Act had repealed authority for government to operate ships for its own account, but this authority was revived in the 1946 Ship Sales Act. Sec. 11 of the 1946 act, which authorized establishment of the reserve fleet, also authorized use of mothballed vessels "for the account of any department or agency of the United States" during emergencies declared by the President. Inasmuch as the Korean emergency has never been terminated, this authority has remained available since 1950 and provides the basis for the general agency agreements for operation of recommissioned vessels to support operations in Vietnam.

[64] "The Impact of the Reserve Fleet on Rates," in Allen Ferguson *et al.*, *The Economic Value of the U.S. Merchant Marine* (The Transportation Center, Northwestern University, 1961), Chap. 12. The author stresses that his estimates are approximate, noting *inter alia* that if the government did not maintain a reserve fleet, private interests would be more likely to maintain idle tonnage in lay-up against the possibility of a rise in rates making employment profitable. This, in fact, was the pattern during the prewar period, when time charter rates were remarkably stable for a period of over fifteen years. In contrast, charter rates have fluctuated violently during the postwar period.

[65] The Mariner construction program, initiated in 1951, was entirely a government project, private industry being virtually unanimous in its view that these ships, which have subsequently proved so successful, could not be employed in commercial service. Of the 35 Mariners built for the government, 29 were ultimately sold for private use, 5 assigned to the Navy, and 1 lost at sea. Maritime Administration studies clearly show that earnings on their operations have been significantly higher than on war-built C-type ships. In some services the Mariners have achieved an efficiency which would enable them to operate profitably without subsidy.

[66] "Getting government out of business" was one of the key precepts of the Republican Administration which assumed office in January 1953. MSTS operations were sharply scaled down and further regulated by an administrative agreement between the Defense and Commerce departments following the Korean war. An MSTS program

The 1956 Suez crisis impelled the government once again to activate a significant portion of its reserve fleet. In contrast to the Korean episode, this action was based on economic rather than defense considerations and the ships made available to operators on bareboat charters rather than being operated for government account. This additional tonnage was released to check spiralling tramp charter rates; it was welcomed by most U.S. flag shipowners as a means of participating more extensively in the profit opportunities created by the worldwide shortage of tramp and tank ships.

By June 1958, virtually all Suez charters had been terminated. Government operations continued at a very low ebb until the 1965 Vietnam build-up.[67] Approximately two-thirds of the MSTS augmentation to meet this requirement was accomplished through charters of privately owned ships and one-third through activation of government-owned vessels for general agency operations.

Postwar Significance of the 1936 Act

Throughout the postwar years the Merchant Marine Act of 1936 has remained the keystone of the government's promotional program. Although the statute has been frequently amended (sixty-two times between 1946 and 1964 inclusive), its basic thrust and structure remain undisturbed.

Several factors have contributed to the 1936 act's significance. It has provided the one reasonably comprehensive and coherent statement of the government's intentions, to which all may refer. Administrative reorganization and high personnel turnover have further increased dependence on the act as a guide to congressional intent and administrative action. Furthermore, much of its language setting out subsidy terms and conditions has been written directly into subsidy contracts. Since these contracts extend for up to twenty years, they lend weight to the statutory program. Perhaps most important, the program is one in which there has long been a high degree of congressional interest, with the result that matters which

---

to construct twenty tankers was also caught in the policy shift. After considerable wrangling, the project was scotched in favor of private construction with twenty-year leases to the Navy guaranteed.

[67] The only charters since 1958 have been to the Alaska Steamship Company and for operation of experimental, government-owned ships. After prolonged negotiations, the world's first nuclear ship, the N.S. "Savannah," was placed on charter at a promotional rate in early 1965.

in other circumstances might be accomplished administratively are often the subject of legislation.

The 1936 act's prewar origins have had important, often unintended, and sometimes unnoticed effects on the government's postwar maritime programs. The most important have resulted from the act's almost exclusive concern with liner services in foreign trade; this emphasis has been faithfully reflected in its administration, with the result that America's subsidized operators have displaced the once prosperous coastwise and intercoastal lines as the aristocrats of the U.S. merchant marine.

Essential Trade Routes. Government designation of essential trade routes was sanctioned in 1920 to facilitate organization of new shipping lines. The system was carried forward in the 1936 act in order to avoid disruption in existing operations, to provide a framework for orderly administration of the new subsidy program, and to permit specification of subsidized operators' service obligations. Subsidies were restricted to firms providing liner services on essential trade routes in part because they appeared more suitable objects for government aid than proprietary carriers, tankers, or tramps, and in part because they represented the segment of American shipping which then appeared most in need of aid. Whether liner services also were most important to U.S. foreign commerce and specifically whether the trade route system was necessary to their effective performance were never argued out.

The trade route system, however, has had several important effects. Most important, it has focused government aid exclusively on a single mode of ocean transportation. The companies franchised to essential trade routes for several years managed to block extension of subsidies to any competitors. Though this monopoly was broken, direct subsidies still are denied to tramps, bulk carriers, and contract operators catering to the military's transportation needs. Some of the companies excluded from subsidy maintain liner or quasi-liner operations; the remainder are engaged in fairly regular point-to-point services in U.S. foreign trade, though loaded chiefly with grains or military goods. In view of the eight-fold expansion of vessel-lot shipments in the U.S. foreign trade since 1936, it is difficult to argue that their operation is not equally as relevant as liner service to U.S. commercial needs.

Second, the trade route system has limited expansion and diversification opportunities for its beneficiaries. By challenging one another's applications to deviate from assigned trade routes, the subsidized lines have forfeited opportunities to attract special cargoes or participate in seasonal movements. More important, it seems likely that liner-type operations will in the years ahead face increasingly severe competition both from specialized bulk and charter ship operators and from air freight.

A third effect of the essential trade route system has been to force the government to act as mediator among the subsidized lines and between the subsidized and non-subsidized segments of the fleet. Clear principles to guide the government in this role have been lacking. In their absence the subsidy program may be used as a weapon in the industry's internal disputes and is vulnerable to various administrative and/or political pressures.[68]

Fourth, the system has inhibited competition for cargoes which by law or administrative order are required to be carried by U.S. flag lines. This has contributed to the adoption of shipping contract procedures which have probably increased military shipment costs.

Inasmuch as the trade route system is part of the fabric of the 1936 act, it has acquired certain functions (as in computation of parity) unrelated to its original, stated purposes. These make it impractical to abandon the system unless other changes are made concurrently. The system is therefore continued; its emphasis, however, has shifted away from meeting shipper needs to providing the government with a vehicle for monitoring and moderating competition among U.S. flag lines.

Conference Regulation. The trade route system has had an indirect effect of increasing both the industry's and government's commitment to the conference system. An operator who is limited to a trade route is unlikely to risk undercutting the conference rate, since failure to make good on the gamble would be tantamount to forcing himself out of business. Similarly, his long-range commitment to the trade is likely to make him intolerant of rate-cutting by others.

The subsidized operators' commitment to the conference system was

---

[68] In order to demonstrate the success of its program, the administrative agency is almost always under subtle pressure to protect its economically weak clients. Some evidence of this tendency in the maritime program has been noted earlier in this chapter.

Local political interest in trade route matters has been confined chiefly to applications for new subsidized services. Typically, these applications have been actively supported by local civic and commercial groups. However, there have been few instances of ports pressing for services not already proposed by an applicant line. When the Grace Line decided to terminate its Great Lakes service, there were no objections filed by the affected ports—suggesting that the ports' interest in the maritime subsidy program is typically a product of the interest of the affected line.

until 1963 paralleled by a firm belief within the government's maritime agencies that conference operation was a natural complement to the trade route system and that, together, they minimized the subsidy requirements of U.S. flag carriers. The agencies' reasoning was that this mode of operation minimized "destructive" competition among U.S. flag operators, permitted subsidy payments (calculated separately for each route) to be more accurately tailored to need, and increased the operators' earnings and thus the possibility that a portion of the subsidy might be recaptured. The fact that increased earnings were derived from quasi-monopoly rates was overlooked until the Joint Economic Committee investigations focused attention on this issue.

Labor Costs. The incentives built into the 1936 act to encourage adequate wages for U.S. seamen have also had a crucially important and continuing impact on the U.S. maritime industry. Despite the spectacular advances in seamen's wages, the 1936 procedures for handling wage costs in computing subsidy have been retained almost intact.[69]

The extent to which government subsidy and related programs have fueled the escalation of maritime wages is sharply debated. Persons defending present arrangements stress that although the operating differential subsidy covers 72 percent of wage costs, operators still have a stake in restraining wages; those attacking the system argue that the lines have only very indirect interests in holding down wages, since the subsidy covers the *entire* differential (excluding specific government disallowances). The system's proponents argue further that because labor contracts span both subsidized and non-subsidized lines, there is additional assurance of bona fide bargaining; their opponents contend that since the entire industry is shielded from foreign competition, this is not an effective check, and that in any event the smaller non-subsidized operators are too dependent upon current cash flow to resist independently union de-

[69] The adequacy of the government's procedures for reviewing wage costs in computing subsidy has gravely concerned top government officials who have realized, along with Secretary of Commerce Connor, that "Government simply cannot continue, in good conscience, to give routine and automatic approval to substantial wage and employee benefit increases after collective bargaining agreements have been signed." (Opinion and Order of the Secretary of Commerce on Maritime Subsidy Board Dockets A-14, A-15, and A-16, July 23, 1965.) In order to place the government in a better position to evaluate the reasonableness of these agreements and to give more timely and authoritative rulings regarding the eligibility of increased wage costs for subsidy, Connor promulgated the procedure requiring collective bargaining agreements to be referred to a wage review panel.

mands and play too minor a part in collective bargaining to influence substantially its outcome.

Other arguments are also advanced. According to the subsidized operators, the present wage scale is more the result of direct government intervention than the subsidy's indirect effects.[70] Another study sponsored by this group asserts that wage trends in the maritime industry have simply mirrored the general successes of highly unionized American industries and the greater premium which a more affluent society places on the discomforts of seafaring employment.[71] Data compiled by the unions indicate that the wages paid to American seamen tend, if anything, to be lower in relation to wage levels in other sectors of the domestic economy than is the pattern abroad.[72]

To some degree the subsidy system also has contributed to wage inflation. Indeed, since the system was designed to aid seamen in their fight for better wages and working conditions, it would be disturbing if it had not contributed in some measure to their spectacular success. But its effect cannot be delineated with any precision. Indeed, the most significant results of the subsidy system may be its indirect effects on the whole structure and atmosphere within which the industry's collective bargaining takes place. The disruption of normal bargaining processes associated with the operating subsidy affects the outcome of maritime wage negotiations in at least three ways: first, by artificially supporting the market for seamen's services; second, by whetting labor's appetite for more generous wages and diminishing industry's resistance to union demands; and third, by segmenting the industry and thus encouraging the unions to

[70] See Committee of American Steamship Lines, *Collective Bargaining in the Shipping Industry* (mimeograph, 1962). This study lists the principal conditions leading to settlement of each major contract renegotiation since 1939. It concludes that approximately 65 percent of the fivefold increase in base wages for able seamen gained since 1939 is attributable to settlements either arbitrated or reviewed by government or government-appointed boards of inquiry.

[71] Leonard Rapping, in a chapter titled "The Subsidy and Labor Costs," in Ferguson *et al.*, *op. cit.*, has developed a detailed and sophisticated argument that the escalation of maritime wages can be reasonably ascribed to causes independent of the operating differential subsidy—e.g., the increased inducement necessary to attract men away from normal homelife in the wealthier society now prevailing and the growth in union powers. Writing in 1959-60, Rapping concludes that there is no evidence that subsidy has been a major cause of wage increases, but acknowledges that "the impact of the total subsidy program . . . substantially increases the demand for American seamen, and hence improves the bargaining position of the unions." (*Ibid.*, p. 239.)

[72] Data compiled by the AFL-CIO Maritime Committee and reported to the author by Talmage E. Simpkins, Administrative Assistant, March 20, 1964.

use "whipsaw" tactics against uncoordinated management groups.

For many years the impact of operating subsidies on maritime wages was concealed by a more or less uniform wage pattern throughout the industry.[73] However, in 1961 the East and Gulf coast divisions of the Seafarers International Union (SIU), whose contracts are chiefly with non-subsidized companies, split with the National Maritime Union (NMU) on wage, job, and jurisdictional issues. As a consequence, the industry-wide wage pattern was displaced by a two-wage system with the NMU seamen, employed principally on subsidized vessels, enjoying a clear margin.[74] This negotiation, described more fully in the next chapter, provided a vivid demonstration that maritime wage negotiations are profoundly—and mischievously—affected by the anachronous structure of the government subsidy program, but produced no precise pattern of influence.

"Buy American" Rules. A fourth product of the depression origins of the 1936 program which has significantly affected its postwar effectiveness has been its strong "buy American" orientation. Rules requiring that subsidized operators build their ships exclusively in U.S. yards, man them with citizen crews, and supply them with "made-in-U.S.A." materials—all originally enacted to stimulate a badly depressed domestic economy—have been unswervingly applied in good times and bad, whether labor is plentiful or scarce, whether shipyards are operating at high capacity or slack, and whether the U.S. international payments balance is in a surplus or deficit position.

Inflexible application of a 100 percent "buy America" policy violates basic economic precepts, creates additional costs, and may frustrate U.S. foreign economic policy objectives. Furthermore, because "buy America" has been applied as a general all-embracing principle, there has until recently been no effort to relate its application to either defense or commercial needs. One result is that 15-20 percent of operating subsidies current-

[73] Minor differences in SIU and NMU contracts, particularly in manning, have existed for many years. These differences have been estimated by Rapping, *op. cit.*, p. 234, to have added 3-6 percent to the total wage costs on board subsidized ships.

[74] The disparity between East and Gulf coast base wages and overtime rates in SIU and NMU contracts was reported by the U.S. Maritime Administration in *Seafaring Premium Pay* (Government Printing Office, 1963) as 4-6 percent in June 1963. Differences in premium pay rules in SIU and NMU contracts are, however, so numerous that useful comparisons are exceedingly difficult. Overall (including differences in manning), it is estimated that total wage costs run 6-10 percent higher on board subsidized than unsubsidized ships.

ly support catering staffs on U.S. flag passenger liners—a group for which there is no defense requirement whatsoever. A second result may have been to accelerate unnecessarily the flight of U.S. shipping capital to flags of convenience. It is possible that if American shipowners were permitted to employ aliens to perform unskilled shipboard jobs, with U.S. citizens providing supervision, more searfaring jobs (or payroll) would be availble to citizens for any given subsidy expenditure than under the existing system.

During the postwar years, the act's "buy America" provisions have been gradually tightened. A little noticed but significant bill, enacted in 1961 ostensibly to "correct abuses" of the cargo preference system, has made it impractical to import foreign-built ships for any use under U.S. flag—thus nullifying the long and ultimately successful struggle of the pre-World War I shipping industry for "free ship" legislation.[75] Another statute has been enacted to prevent any possible circumvention of this protective principle by prohibiting even the welding of foreign-built midsections into U.S. registered vessels.

Credit Aids. A credit assistance program was included in the 1936 act, despite President Roosevelt's objections, because the Congress believed government financing would be necessary to get ships built in view of the extremely limited private credit then available. In contrast, since World War II investment funds have been relatively plentiful. In these circumstances the most likely effect of government loans and guarantees is not to stimulate investment but only to permit investment to be made more cheaply. Particularly as applied to the subsidized companies, government credit aids have become just another indirect subsidy. However, except for a brief experiment during the mid-fifties with partial government guarantees, the credit aids provided in 1936 have been retained and even expanded.[76]

[75] Prior to enactment of the 1961 legislation a number of American shipowners transferred tramp ships to PANLIBHON flags when world charter rates stood above the rate for U.S. flag vessels and returned to U.S. flag when the world rate fell below the more stable U.S. flag rates. Operators who remained under U.S. flag argued that they should not be exposed to an influx of redocumented ships whenever domestic conditions improved. The "abuse" was corrected by requiring that no vessel built or previously registered abroad would be eligible for cargo preference for three years following its documentation under U.S. flag.

[76] The 1936 act authorized government construction and sale to operators with 25 percent down payment and the remainder financed through a mortgage agreement bearing interest at 3½ percent. Title XI authority to guarantee private ship mortgages was enacted in 1938 and updated in 1953 and in 1955 to conform to postwar con-

Credit assistance, if not necessary to the promotional program, may have several undesirable effects. For example, in relieving U.S. ship operators of soliciting mortgage money on the open market, it has removed them from the market's normal disciplines. Credit aids also give the government a stake in the guaranteed venture, which tends to draw the government too intimately into private financial problems and may result in its favoring one operator over another.[77] Finally, because government has often hesitated to invest capital in merchant shipping, the long-term effect of its credit assistance program may actually be to stunt the expansion of the U.S. merchant fleet by preventing the development of an active and interested private capital market.

Government's Partnership with the Subsidized Lines

The 1936 act anticipated intensive government supervision of companies enrolled in the subsidy program, and for several years following its enactment, the commission attempted a detailed critical review of all phases of these firms' operations. The close working relationships of World War II generated a spirit of common purpose and mutual confidence, which continued after the war. At least up to 1961 there was an increasing sense of partnership between the government and its subsidized lines; this spirit, however, has not extended to the non-subsidized segments of the industry.

A sense of common purpose between regulated and regulating groups is a common characteristic of government programs. In the case of the government's maritime activities, natural tendencies have been reinforced by several unique factors. The extraordinarily scrupulous protective posture of the 1936 act, with its numerous requirements for government re-

---

ditions. In 1956 the guarantee was increased so that the government would bear 100 percent of the risk. Since 1955, credit assistance has been given exclusively through guarantees, in order to minimize the impact on the federal budget and to preserve the business for private sources. A third effect has been to increase the borrower's interest expense by 1-1½ percent above the 3½ percent which would be available through the direct government program.

[77] This difficulty has been most apparent in the administration of Title XI guarantees issued on tanker mortgages awarded during the 1956 Suez crisis. By the time the new construction had been completed, the charter market for the Title XI tankers had receded, and several operators experienced financial difficulties. In order to avert defaults the Maritime Administration negotiated payment moratoria with the mortgagors, advanced funds to shipowners in order to make payments to banks which would not grant moratoria, and assisted insolvent owners of Title XI ships in arranging income-producing fixtures with government agencies.

view and approval of contractor activities, has forced the Maritime Administration and the subsidized lines to work together. The industry's contribution to national defense provides a patriotic objective for the subsidy program which can be shared by both industry and government personnel. The knowledge that a high percentage of the industry's wage costs is paid by government, that most of the cash flow generated by the business must be paid into government-controlled reserves, and that 50 percent or more of the industry's free profits will in any event be turned over to the government in either taxes or recapture increases the sense of identity and common purpose. But economic regulation is only one of many ties binding the maritime industry and the government; in matters concerning consular services, customs, public health, marine safety, and navigation the maritime industry has probably been more closely regulated over a longer period of time than any other major U.S. industrial activity.

World War II shifted the political basis for the operating subsidy program from a commercial to defense justification. The government's commitment to achieve defense objectives through a privately owned merchant fleet has both provided fuel to pressures to expand its subsidy support and downgraded the usefulness of the foreign commerce criteria written into the 1936 program to control expenditure. The effect has been to transform the subsidy program from a limited aid, calculated to provide U.S. operators a fair opportunity but no guarantee of success, into a promotional instrument used to assist a privately owned, U.S. flag merchant marine to grow and prosper in U.S. foreign trade. Concurrently, the government's relationship with the subsidized lines has shifted from a contractual interest in specific performance to a generalized paternalistic interest in the industry's status and capacity to respond to defense needs.

This reorientation of the subsidy program has been accompanied by increased attention to the business problems of the industry. A principal object in administering the subsidy laws has been to permit the lines greater flexibility of operation, to improve their competitive position, enhance their profits, and, in sum, to do whatever is "fair and reasonable" to maintain their operations on a "sound business basis"—all to the ultimate end that the privately owned fleet may be a stronger instrument for national defense.

The same community of interest has never been established with non-subsidized companies, whether in tramp, industrial, domestic, or liner trades. Many of these companies have seemed only to have a speculative interest in the American merchant marine. Others are associated with foreign shipping interests, operate as subsidiaries of one of America's industrial giants, compete with land-based transportation, or are otherwise engaged in operations which it is either impractical or impolitic for the government to support directly.

The maritime agencies have found it difficult to articulate policies appropriate to this non-subsidized group. On the one hand there has been a strong desire to support the operation of this tonnage to provide jobs for American seamen and ships for national defense; yet these objectives have consistently been secondary to sustaining the direct subsidy program. Such aids as have been extended to the non-subsidized operators through the 1936 program have tended to be too little or too late. The problems of this segment of the industry (and certain problems of the subsidized segment as well) have therefore been met outside the framework of the 1936 act, causing a significant extension of the government's role.

The development of constructive solutions to postwar problems within the framework of the 1936 act has been hindered by semicontinuous and often unwarranted criticism of ship subsidies during the postwar years. Fear that the critics might undo the gains that had been made, apparently present both in the maritime agencies and the subsidized industry, has caused both groups to be defensive in their dealings with outsiders and warily conservative in advancing any proposals for change. These apprehensions have also added to the pressures to resort to indirect aids.

7

Extension of the Government Role

WHATEVER ITS LIMITATIONS, the Merchant Marine Act, 1936, had the great merit of providing a direct and clearly visible subsidy to accomplish promotional goals. The differential subsidy system facilitated development of orderly plans for strengthening American shipping, improved accountability, and minimized the U.S. maritime industry's conflicts with other sectors of the economy and with foreign carriers and governments.

Where the 1936 legislation has proved inadequate, the parties at interest have improvised new solutions. In some instances these solutions have contradicted existing principles and policies considered basic to U.S. maritime policy. In other cases they have precipitated conflicts with other groups. As a result, the extension of the government's activity outside the framework of the 1936 act has been a faltering, controversial, and erratic process. This chapter reports the most important of these developments and assesses their significance in relation to the government's underlying maritime objectives.

Preferential and Protective Practices

Although the central principle of the 1936 act was that American shipping, supported by "scientific" subsidies, should win its own way in fair and equal competition with foreign flags, the act also recognized that the government could and should assist the U.S. flag fleet in obtaining both government-sponsored and commercial cargoes and in meeting discriminatory practices which might be employed abroad.[1] These policies thrust

[1] Legislation requiring shipment of military cargoes in U.S. bottoms (1904) and Public Resolution 17 (1934), noting the sense of Congress that exports financed by the Reconstruction Finance Corporation or other government loans should be routed

166

the government into one of the most sensitive aspects of international shipping, since comity in giving fair access to cargoes is the cornerstone of much of the industry's operations and of the much acclaimed "freedom of the seas."

In international shipping no clear line divides "acceptable" from "unacceptable" preferential practices. The rule adopted in the Inter-Governmental Maritime Consultative Organization (IMCO) Convention is that government aid per se shall not be considered objectionable, but only assistance which is "designed in a manner which restricts the freedom of all flags to take part in world trade."[2] But since there is no agreement on the meaning of this formula, no useful international law on flag preference or other protective practices has evolved.

Controversies over Cargo Preferences. Government action to control the routing of cargo is the oldest, most powerful, most common, and most controversial of the discriminatory techniques practiced in merchant shipping. Generally it has been accepted that governments, when shipping cargoes for their own account, might favor their national flag fleets. Conversely, government interference to influence the routing of private commercial cargoes has been condemned as contrary to the interests of both shippers and the international shipping industry. The most persistent difficulty in framing U.S. preference policies has consequently been distinguishing the public and private spheres.

Three other factors have contributed to the controversy over U.S. cargo preferences. First, since 1949 the sharply higher labor costs on U.S. flag vessels have required that the government support its preference for U.S. flag vessels with charter payments substantially above the world market. Second, the United States' leading position in world trade and the importance of its patronage to Western Europe's merchant marines have focused attention on U.S. preference policies. Third, U.S. cargo preferences have been attacked domestically as inconsistent with U.S. foreign policy objectives and of marginal worth to U.S. defense.

For the first three years following the end of World War II, world shipping needs so far exceeded supply that U.S. and foreign vessels com-

---

U.S. flag, were undisturbed by the 1936 act. The 1936 legislation continued authority in the Merchant Marine Act of 1920 to make rules to counter foreign discrimination and contained a new mandate to the Maritime Commission to maintain liaison with other government agencies and private organizations in order to secure preference for American vessels.

[2] Article I(b), IMCO Convention.

manded equal rates and participated without serious friction in the movement of foreign aid cargoes. By 1948 sufficient competition had developed that a statutory preference for American vessels if available at "reasonable rates" was included in the annual Economic Cooperation Act authorization. This preference was strengthened the following year to specify that U.S. flag ships be used even if their rates were higher than competing foreign flags, so long as the rate was found to be "reasonable *for U.S. flag ships*."[3] Similar reservations were appended to six other specific foreign aid authorizations.[4]

This legislation at first drew only routine opposition from the Truman Administration. However, as the differential between foreign and U.S. flag rates increased, opposition to the system stiffened. In 1950 former Secretary of the Army Gordon Gray recommended to President Truman that merchant ships determined necessary for defense purposes be supported entirely through direct aids. His arguments were that:

> Cargo preference is, first of all, a concealed subsidy, and thus not subject to the scrutiny and supervision which is accorded to open subsidies. . . . Second, cargo preference is a blunt and capricious instrument for maintaining a fleet of security size. The volume of shipping kept in operation through cargo preference . . . is completely unrelated to estimated security requirements. . . . Finally, the cargo preference policy tends to relieve some of the pressure on ship operators to compete in service and rates, and it tends to encourage the adoption of similar flag discrimination policies by other maritime nations, thus impairing the efficiency with which world shipping resources are utilized.[5]

The impact of Gray's arguments was delayed by the onset of the Korean conflict, which quickly absorbed the small surplus capacity which had developed in 1949 and caused foreign flag charter rates to double. For the duration of the war, non-subsidized U.S. flag shipping was able to compete equally for government cargoes, and, despite higher costs, helped to restrain freight and charter rates in U.S. foreign trade. So long as these conditions prevailed, shipment of government cargoes via U.S. flag tramps cost no more, provided employment to American seamen, facilitated the movement of government goods, and could even be argued to be good economics.

[3] 63 Stat. 50. Emphasis added.
[4] Citations to the several statutory preferences can be found in *Administration of the Cargo Preference Act*, H. Rept. 80, 84 Cong. 1 sess. (1955), pp. 4-5.
[5] Gordon Gray, *Report to the President on Foreign Economic Policies* (Government Printing Office, 1950), p. 89.

Enactment of 1954 Preferential Statute. The negotiation of the Korean armistice was followed by a sharp reduction in U.S. tramp shipping requirements. By mid-1954, 43 percent of the privately owned U.S. tramp fleet was unemployed, with no prospect for employment in the foreseeable future. Concurrently, the newly elected Republican Administration was completing a general review of U.S. foreign economic policies, including the cargo preference problem. The Randall Commission, which filed its report early in 1954, reiterated Gray's call for a liberal foreign economic policy unobstructed by restrictive legislation in shipping or any other field.[6] Its main theses were adopted by the President. Specifically, the President urged that all aids required to ensure a merchant marine adequate to defense requirements be provided by *direct* means, and stated that recommendations to accomplish this aim would be transmitted to the next session of Congress.[7]

The Republican chairman of the Senate Merchant Marine Subcommittee, John Marshall Butler, saw the President's statement as a threat to the government's long-standing preferential policy. The day following the President's message, he introduced legislation requiring that *all* government cargoes, including *all* military shipments, be shipped via *privately owned* U.S. flag ships subject to waiver by the Secretary of Commerce only if sufficient vessels could not be obtained.

During the hearings which followed, the Departments of State, Defense, and Agriculture, the General Services Administration, and even the Federal Maritime Board—Maritime Administration testified in opposition to the bill.[8] Maritime interests and several key congressmen strongly sup-

[6] Commission on Foreign Economic Policy, *Report to the President and the Congress* (Government Printing Office, 1954).

[7] National Archives and Records Service, *Public Papers of the Presidents, Dwight D. Eisenhower, 1954*, p. 360. The recommendations were never forthcoming.

[8] Each of the executive agencies opposed Senator Butler's bill on different grounds. Defense feared that the proposed legislation, which required that privately owned vessels be given preference over those of the Military Sea Transport Service (MSTS), would tie its hands and in effect make the Navy-owned fleet an auxiliary to the privately owned merchant marine. Agriculture disliked the bill's proposed language stipulating that shipments generated under the recently enacted P.L. 83-480 program be accorded statutory preference. Private agricultural interests feared that the legislation would increase shipping costs, but more importantly that Europe would react to this protectionist measure by refusing to purchase P.L. 83-480 grains. The State Department also warned of retaliation, and of the harmful effects which "Balkanization of cargoes" would have on the shipping industry itself. Commerce limited its official comment on the bill to a statement that it was not in a position to support any alteration of existing law until certain studies, asked by the President, had been completed.

ported enactment. Only six shipper and other organizations appeared to testify, all in opposition to the bill.

The intensity of the Administration opposition forced supporters of the bill to compromise on several important points. First, to meet the Navy's strenuous objections the requirement that military cargoes be handled entirely by private industry was deleted from the bill. Second, the bill was amended to apply mandatory preferences only to half of the government's non-military shipments on the grounds that this was more consistent with the "substantial portion" objective of the 1936 act. Third, the Secretary of Commerce was relieved of direct responsibility for the program's administration. Finally, a proviso was added to make the preference operative only if ships were available at "fair and reasonable rates for U.S. flag commercial vessels"—a stipulation which was strongly emphasized during the Senate's brief debate on the bill.

As originally introduced, Senator Butler's bill directly challenged the President's liberal trade program. The committee's modifications, however, removed its most objectionable features. It appeared only fair that preferences be granted to American vessels if their rates were reasonable. Furthermore, it was widely believed that the legislation would affect only a relatively small amount of cargo and that its impact would diminish as U.S. foreign aid scaled off in years to come. The committee compromise encountered virtually no opposition in the Congress and was approved by the President on August 26, 1954.

Implementation of Statutory Preferences. The 1954 cargo preference statute has been marked by controversy since its enactment. Difficulties were first encountered by the Agriculture Department, whose new P.L. 83-480 program to facilitate sales of agricultural surpluses developed beyond expectations. This caused a sharp, unanticipated jump in demand for U.S. flag vessels. With only about one hundred suitable ships competing for the business and no guidelines as to what bids should be considered "fair and reasonable," rates for U.S. flag tramps soared. The effect was to provide profit windfalls for a few eligible shipowners at the expense of Agriculture Department appropriations and ultimately the American public generally. Furthermore, agricultural interests became convinced that shipping preferences had scuttled their chances of disposing of some $100 million of surplus farm products. Strong pressures began to build up for the legislation's repeal.

To head off these pressures, the House Merchant Marine and Fisheries Committee undertook an exhaustive hearing of shipper grievances.[9]

This action, which successfully fended off threats to the cargo preference program, had several other lasting results. One was to solidify the Commerce Department's support for the program, which it now described as absolutely essential to the maintenance of an adequate merchant marine. In a report which had been requested by the President two years earlier to explore methods of replacing indirect cargo preference subsidies with direct aids, the department announced its conclusion that preferences were not only necessary but provided a completely workable and "direct" technique for achieving the U.S. promotional objectives.[10] Testifying before the House committee, the Department's witness stated flatly, "There is simply no way for a feasible substitute to work."[11]

A second result of the review was to focus attention on arrangements for administering the preference program. In general, the committee believed that the program was weakened by dispersion of the government's traffic management activities. It recommended, for example, that the Agriculture Department's practice in its surplus grain sales agreements of having ocean freight bookings handled by the purchaser be changed and that all transportation functions associated with the program be centralized within the General Services Administration. The committee also instructed the Maritime Administration to publish "guideline" rates to help shipping agencies determine whether American vessels were available at a "fair and reasonable rate for U.S. flag commercial vessels" as required by the statute. Finally it also concluded that the Maritime Administration should "exercise general surveillance over the administration and operation of the Cargo Preference Act and report periodically to the Congress."[12]

The Maritime Administration (Marad) has attempted to respond to the committee's recommendations. Shipping arrangements, however, have

[9] *Administration of the Cargo Preference Act,* Hearings before the House Merchant Marine and Fisheries Committee, 84 Cong. 1 sess. (1955).

[10] U.S. Department of Commerce, *A Review of Direct and Indirect Types of Maritime Subsidies with Special Reference to Cargo Preference Aid* (multilith, 1956). The department's contention that cargo preferences should be classified as a direct aid was based on its conclusion that the intent of the statutes authorizing preference was unambiguously clear, the program applied directly to the purpose to which it was directed, and the amount of aid was directly susceptible to government control (through the 1954 act's "fair and reasonable" clause). *Ibid.,* pp. 30-32.

[11] The Honorable Clarence G. Morse, Chairman, Federal Maritime Board—Maritime Administrator, quoted in *Cargo Preference and its Relation to the Farm Surplus Disposal Program,* H. Rept. 1818, 84 Cong. 2 sess. (1956), pp. 12-13. The Department maintained this position through 1964.

[12] H. Rept. 80, p. 18.

continued to be the responsibility of the government's shipping agencies, and shipment costs—including even the incremental cost of shipping U.S. versus foreign flag—have continued to be assessed against their appropriations. The difficulty of coordinating anything as sensitive as cargo preferences without either an unequivocally clear mandate or financial control has prevented effective supervision by the Maritime Administration, with the result that there is little consistency among the shipping agencies even in such administrative matters as booking procedures, statistical reporting, and shipment terms.

Marad's only direct participation in cargo preference administration is to act on applications for waiver of the 1934 Public Resolution Number 17 requirement that all shipments financed through government loans should be carried by U.S. flag vessels. In examining these applications the Maritime Administration has followed a policy of allowing 50 percent of the shipment to be made in vessels registered by the purchasing nation, except in occasional cases when it has wished to chasten a nation which has discriminated against U.S. flag ships.

The most controversial problems associated with cargo preference administration have lain completely outside the Maritime Administration's jurisdiction. For example, the Maritime Administration was not even consulted during the early phase of the explosive Russian wheat transaction as to the applicability of the cargo preference statutes.[13] As the controversy over shipment terms intensified, the Maritime Administrator was only one of a sizeable group of government officials who tried to develop a compromise acceptable to the Russians, the private grain dealers, the longshore unions, and the Congress.[14]

---

[13] Technically, shipment of subsidized farm products through private channels does not fall within the scope of the cargo preference laws. However, in order to win support for the sales, maximize dollar earnings, and aid the U.S. merchant marine, President Kennedy (in October 1963) stipulated that government approval of wheat exports to Russia would be conditioned on their export in "available American ships, supplemented by ships of other countries as required."

[14] Efforts to temper and clarify the President's stipulation that wheat sold to Russia would be routed in U.S. ships began almost immediately. A system of guideline rates was established to determine whether ships could be considered "reasonably available"; efforts were made to locate ships which might be used in this trade relatively cheaply; and the open-end pledge to ship 100 percent of the business via U.S. flag was redefined to 50 percent. When the Soviets continued to resist any additional shipping expense, a deal was made by the Agriculture Department apparently calculated to allow the private U.S. exporter a cushion sufficient to absorb the extra expense of U.S. vessels. Despite these concessions the Continental and Cargill Grain Companies, which had negotiated the sale, applied for waivers on the basis that ships able to enter Black Sea ports were unavailable. When the govern-

One of the key issues in this negotiation, and a continuing problem in implementing the cargo preference statutes, has been to determine the availability of U.S. flag ships. "Reasonable availability" is a function of both price and time, since shipments frequently cannot wait until additional tonnage is broken out of reserve or diverted from other use. The problem has been particularly troublesome to the Agency for International Development (AID), which from time to time has been called upon to stage very large coal and grain shipments to avert shortages abroad, and to the Department of Defense, which often finds it difficult to meet its shipping requirements exclusively through U.S. flag ships. Both agencies have also had significant requirements for shipping service between foreign ports, which is not always readily available from U.S. firms.[15]

Determining the types of transactions to which cargo preferences will apply has created still another class of problems which has fallen chiefly on the government's shipping agencies. Since the 1954 enactment of the cargo preference laws, intense industry pressures have caused an extension of the preference principle to such marginal cases as contractor-owned materials for military use overseas and shipments financed by U.S. contributions to international organizations.[16] These organizations also are under

---

ment approved these applications for waiver, maritime labor charged that it had reneged on its commitments and announced it would refuse to handle the cargo. (See *Ocean Transportation of Grain to Russia,* Hearings before the House Merchant Marine and Fisheries Committee, 88 Cong. 2 sess. [1964].)

[15] Maritime groups have been particularly disturbed by AID's position that cargoes shipped foreign flag due to the non-availability of U.S. flag ships need not be considered in calculating its 50 percent U.S. flag obligation. Prior to 1961, 3-3½ million tons of foreign aid materials were procured abroad annually and waivers issued on 60-75 percent of this business. Since 1961, balance of payments pressures have caused offshore procurement to be reduced to a minimal level, although some foreign-to-foreign movements continue to be required by the Department of Defense.

[16] Cargo preferences now apply to all P.L. 83-480 programs, except shipments under Title IIIA by voluntary relief agencies and Title IIIB by private brokers exporting bartered stocks. (Prior to August 1963 sales under Title IV were also exempted.) Preferences also apply to all foreign aid, shipments financed from the Social Progress Trust Fund and the Inter American Development Bank, U.S. contributions to the World Food Program and to the Congo expedition, and all movements of personnel, household effects, automobiles, and equipment in support of U.S. overseas activities. Public Resolution 17, stating the sense of Congress that all cargoes financed by government loans should be routed via U.S. flag ship, has been construed to apply to the Export-Import Bank's long-term credits and project loans but not to its medium and short-term export credits, guarantees, insurance, and participations. Private shipments of subsidized agricultural commodities, whether from public or private stocks, also are outside the preference program as are shipments financed by the International Bank for Reconstruction and Development and its affiliate agencies. Voluntary agencies operating under P.L. 480, Title IIIA, although not subject to cargo preference, are under pressure to use U.S. ships and do so wherever possible.

pressure to apportion their shipments to the fleets of their sponsor nations roughly in proportion to the nations' financial contributions.

Continuing pressure has also been applied to increase routing of government-sponsored cargoes via U.S. flag beyond the 50 percent minimum prescribed in the statute. Agency practice has varied greatly, ranging from minimum compliance in the case of the Department of Agriculture to the use of American vessels whenever possible in post-1961 AID shipments out of the continental United States.[17]

Finally, the cargo preference laws have created problems for the industry itself. The most persistent difficulties have centered on the division of government cargoes among liners, tankers, and tramps.[18] In addition, operators who use only U.S. registry for their ships complained in the past of competition from other firms that transferred ships to flags of convenience when government cargoes were scarce, but returned to U.S. registry when the preference business picked up. In 1961 this "abuse" was eliminated by legislation barring vessels built or previously registered abroad from participating in the preference program for three years following their return to U.S. flag.

Contracting Arrangements. The procedures through which government shipments are arranged have also proved controversial since they

---

[17] Agriculture Department shipments are under the jurisdiction of the quasi-independent Commodity Credit Corporation whose board of directors has taken an official position that it would not be justified in using its appropriations to subsidize any more shipments via U.S. ships than are required by law. Although AID's policy is to use U.S. ships whenever possible, approximately 25 percent of its cargoes are consigned to foreign flags. Cargoes sent foreign flag are chiefly emergency famine relief; more highly valued break-bulk cargoes financed by AID grants and loans are shipped almost entirely via U.S. flag.

[18] Competition between liners, tramps, and tankers has been both political and economic. As noted in Chapter 4, the economic advantage lies with liners wishing to carry grains as "bottom cargo" and with the supertankers built with indirect government aid following the Suez crisis. The political advantage has also tended toward the liner and bulk carrier companies. As enacted, the 1954 preference statute had stipulated that "at least 50 percent of the gross tonnage of such [government-sponsored] equipment, materials, or commodities (computed separately for dry bulk carriers, dry cargo liners, and tankers), which may be transported on ocean vessels shall be transported on privately-owned U.S. flag commercial vessels. . . ." When U.S. flag liners became seriously interested in these cargoes in 1958 they found that the effect of the language was to cause a division of cargoes among the several categories of U.S. flag shipowners geared to the manner in which the non-U.S. flag share was moved on the open market, i.e. about 80-85 percent non-liner. The matter was taken up with the appropriate congressional committees, which adopted resolutions stating that the procedure then in use did not reflect the intent of Congress but that instead "available cargoes should be allocated among the various available privately-

significantly affect the rates paid on government cargoes and hence their attractiveness as compared to commercial business. These procedures vary from agency to agency and from case to case. In general, because a high degree of flexibility is required in arranging bookings, tramp shipping contracts are negotiated on the basis of informally solicited bids. Cargoes falling within published tariffs are shipped on regular government bills of lading and are handled by the lines in the same manner and at least ostensibly at the same rates as regular commercial business.[19]

Most military items have no commercial counterpart, so that there is no yardstick which can readily be applied to determine a proper rate. Furthermore, all military business is required by law to be routed via U.S. flag ships. By administrative ruling, the Department of Defense has narrowed competition even further by stipulating that all Defense cargoes not lifted by ships in the MSTS nucleus fleet shall be consigned to U.S. flag liners unless adequate space cannot be arranged.[20] In order to qualify as a berth line, a carrier must demonstrate that it has provided at least one sailing monthly on the route, including stops at specific ports, for three consecutive months preceding the application to carry defense cargoes.

In view of the specialized character of the military business and the limited number of companies eligible to handle it, shipment terms are generally negotiated. About 80 percent of Defense's peacetime shipments via commercial carriers (and 60-65 percent of the total military sealift, in-

---

owned U.S. flag commercial vessels on a fair and equitable basis, taking into account such features as types of cargoes, historical movement, availability of ships, freight rates, etc., without reference to the categories of foreign flag ships carrying the balance of the cargoes." (Letter from the Honorable Herbert C. Bonner and the Honorable Warren Magnuson to Secretary of Agriculture Benson, Sept. 22, 1959.)

[19] Prior to 1961 no regular system of tariff filing or publication was enforced in U.S. foreign trade, with the result that government agencies could have no real assurance that they were not being discriminated against through higher rates. Agencies may now check tariff rates (unless no rate exists for the item to be shipped) but still have to be on guard that cargoes shipped for government account are properly classified, not covered under a "paper rate" applicable only to this category of shipments, and otherwise receive equal terms and treatment as privately sponsored shipments.

[20] The MSTS liner preference was established by a 1954 agreement between Secretary of Defense Charles E. Wilson and Secretary of Commerce Sinclair Weeks as part of a broader compact designed to stabilize relations between MSTS and the privately owned merchant marine. Time and voyage charters are permitted only if it is not possible, with reasonable forethought and planning, to arrange shipment via a commercial line. Shipment on ships operated by general agents for government account or via foreign flag are permitted only if a private U.S. flag charter cannot be arranged. As of September 1965 the agreement still remained in effect despite a change of administration and supposed shift in government-industry roles. However, revisions were under consideration.

cluding shipments via government-owned ships) are made under contracts negotiated annually by the MSTS with associations representing the participating U.S. flag carriers.[21] (Other MSTS shipments are made on bills of lading, under individually negotiated rates, and on chartered vessels.[22]) The standard shipping contract classifies all military cargoes into about a dozen broad categories for rate purposes (the number varies for different routes), specifies rate and contract terms, and stipulates a procedure for allocating cargoes to the eligible liner companies roughly in proportion to their participation in the trade. Usually the same contract terms have applied to all MSTS liner cargoes moved in the applicable trade although neither the carriers nor MSTS is legally bound to operate exclusively through the carrier association. In 1965 the MSTS broke precedent by also shipping via an independent operator (the Sapphire Line) which offered the government a substantial discount below the association's terms.[23]

[21] Separate associations of the Atlantic and Gulf and the West Coast American Flag Berth Operators (AGAFBO and WCAFBO) have been formed to negotiate rate and service terms with MSTS under its open-end shipping contracts. These associations are treated as conferences by the Federal Maritime Commission and their operations subject to the Shipping Act of 1916. In May 1965 the commission initiated an investigation of the compatibility of their operation with the terms of the act, which in December 1965 had not been brought to a conclusion. However, in April 1966, MSTS announced plans to shift from negotiation to competitive bids.

A detailed description of the MSTS contracting system and of typical contract terms may be found in *Discriminatory Ocean Freight Rates and the Balance of Payments,* Hearings before the Joint Economic Committee, 88 Cong. 2 sess. (1964), Pt. 5, pp. 1228-1240.

[22] Bills of lading are used for through shipments to or from inland destinations or in the event that regular commercial tariffs may be below the rate specified in the shipping contract. (The government's right to ship outside the contract when more favorable terms can be secured commercially has been challenged but was sustained in *United States Lines v. U.S.,* 324 F. 2d 97 [2d Cir. 1963].) Special contracts are negotiated for outsized items and for cargoes requiring special handling. Government-owned or chartered vessels are used for shipments to remote bases not served by liners. In emergencies, ships may also be chartered to supplement liner service to major ports.

[23] The Sapphire Line commenced operations March 31, 1965, with five chartered vessels to provide a non-subsidized U.S. flag liner service between U.S. North Atlantic ports and Europe (from Hamburg to Bordeaux). To attract customers, Sapphire offered discounts ranging from 25 to 30 percent below conference rates. During the three months' operations required by MSTS regulations to qualify as a liner service, Sapphire lost approximately $500,000. As soon as the line officially qualified, MSTS assigned Sapphire as much cargo as its ships could carry, and the line shifted to handling MSTS business almost exclusively. Instead of using the standard MSTS contract, which would have required cargoes to be allocated in proportion to its sailings, Sapphire handled the MSTS business under its posted berth terms. By December 1965, the line's position had improved sufficiently to permit it to purchase three ships; one vessel was retained under charter.

The association subsequently adjusted its rates to meet the competition.

Surplus grain shipment rates are also negotiated, regardless of whether shipment is by tramp or liner. This conforms to general commercial practice, since rates for bulk cargoes are seldom if ever specified in published tariffs. Shipments made subject to Agriculture Department currency convertibility agreements (Title I, Public Law 83-480) are required by statute to be handled to the maximum possible extent through private channels of trade, and are arranged by foreign purchasing missions. Other grain shipments are negotiated by the voluntary service agencies, such as CARE (Title IIIA, P.L. 83-480). The only grains for which ocean transportation is booked by the Department of Agriculture are therefore those which are shipped for the government's account (emergency AID donations under Title II, P.L. 83-480, and shipments in exchange for stockpiled minerals under Title IIIB). Agriculture's practice is to book these shipments entirely through private brokers.

Although rates are negotiated, there is a potential for considerable competition among U.S. flag ships for the U.S. share of surplus grain cargoes. The hundred-odd ships in the U.S. flag tramp fleet are operated by some twenty to thirty independent or quasi-independent firms.[24] Where there is frequent berth service, U.S. flag liners may be able to handle a large proportion of the shipment as "bottom cargoes" without adding significantly to their costs. When rates are high or other business is slow, tankers may enter the grain trade to compete for shipments to Asia and Africa. And, so long as the government is satisfied that at least half of the total shipped under a specific sales agreement is routed U.S. flag, consignments may be given to foreign flag vessels if the shipper believes the U.S. offering is out of line.[25]

Despite these checks, rates paid for shipments via U.S. flag tramps

[24] The U.S. flag tramp fleet is operated through almost eighty separate corporations, many of which, however, have been created solely to limit the shipowner's liability. Furthermore, there are a large number of interlocking directorships and other evidences of common control which suggest that the large number of corporate entities may conceal a moderate degree of concentration in this industry, which is operated almost entirely out of New York by a relatively small number of entrepreneurs. Since the fleet is deployed throughout the world, competition for specific voyages may be extremely limited.

[25] Tramp shipowners and unions representing tramp seamen have frequently complained that the government and foreign purchasing missions use the threat of seeking foreign flag bids to force an owner who has offered a ship at less than the Maritime Administration's guideline to further reduce his price. See SIU Statement on Cargo Preference in *Maritime Labor Legislation,* Hearings before the House Merchant Marine and Fisheries Committee, 88 Cong. 1 sess. (1963), pp. 519-31.

have averaged more than twice those charged by foreign flags.[26] Furthermore, U.S. flag liners (both subsidized and non-subsidized) have been able to maintain their rates at approximately the level charged by U.S. flag tramps.[27] Rates for shipments (excluding cargo handling costs) via the few modern U.S. flag supertankers which have participated in the business appear typically to have been 20-25 percent below the tramp rates, although this difference may be partially a result of differences in the costs of loading and discharging cargoes.[28]

The extent to which cargo preferences and contracting procedures have inflated rates for other AID, Export-Import Bank, and Agriculture Department break-bulk shipments, if at all, is not so easily verified. Yet both logic and fragmentary empirical evidence suggest that certain of these cargoes and the cargoes shipped under MSTS contracts are shipped at rates substantially higher than would prevail in open competition on the world market. The indirect subsidy provided through these preferential rates and tramp charter payments is the lifeblood of the non-subsidized sectors of the U.S. flag merchant marine.[29] For the subsidized lines the in-

[26] The Department of Agriculture requires that countries purchasing P.L. 83-480, Title I grains repay the United States for the estimated world market cost of shipments sent U.S. flag due to cargo preference. These estimates are audited by the Department and the General Accounting Office and can therefore be regarded as a reliable index to foreign-domestic rate differentials. In 1963 the estimated expense of handling $147 million of U.S. flag shipments via foreign carriers was $67.5 million—54 percent below the U.S. rate.

[27] About $20 million of indirect subsidies is estimated to have been paid to U.S. flag liner companies through rates on government-sponsored bulk cargoes in excess of rates charged by foreign carriers for comparable service. This subsidy appears to have been shared about equally by subsidized and non-subsidized lines. Since the largest shipper of government bulk cargoes, the Department of Agriculture, does not maintain either payment or differential accounts by class of carrier, the estimates must be derived from shipment data and sample rates charged by U.S. and foreign liner, tramp, and tanker operators. The estimates have been reconciled to the total shipment costs and rate differentials reported by Agriculture.

[28] An adequate economic explanation is not available to support the apparent difference in tramp and supertanker rates for handling grains. (The difference is not statistically verified but was derived from examination of several hundred rate pairs developed by the Department of Agriculture.) The difference may reflect in part the attitudes of the government's contracting officers, who have applied a lower maximum guideline to shipments via large modern bulk carriers, and in part differences in operating costs. The offsetting cargo-handling costs flow from the need to use lighters to offload a portion of the deep-draft vessels' cargoes in certain ports and from the necessity for adequate facilities to warehouse their enormous cargoes

[29] It is impossible to quantify this indirect subsidy reliably. Nonetheless, a very rough estimate, presented in Chapter 8, indicates that the amounts paid by MSTS for its peacetime shipments may be as much as $50-$60 million above the amount for which foreign flag tramp and liner services hypothetically should be available. This

direct rate subsidy on government business provides an additional benefit on which some have come to depend heavily.

Dependence of U.S. Ships on Cargo Aids. U.S. companies tend to be attracted to government cargoes wherever they appear. The effect has been gradually to displace commercial business in both tramp and liner trades. By 1962, almost two-thirds of the total tonnage carried by U.S. flag ships (and more than 75 percent of their outbound business) was derived from government programs. Between 1956 and 1962, two years in which the total volume of U.S. export tonnage was almost exactly equal, the commercial business handled by U.S. flag liners dropped from 8.5 to 3.8 million tons; the commercial business handled by tramps dropped from 2.1 to 0.2 million tons.[30]

The tramps have more than offset their loss of commercial cargoes with increased government business. U.S. tramps once at least "topped off" with commercial shipments; their outbound business is now 98 percent government-sponsored. Inbound voyages are usually in ballast, or occasionally in ores for the government's strategic materials stockpile.

Among liner companies the dependence on government cargoes varies greatly. Several non-subsidized liner firms concentrate almost exclusively on MSTS cargoes, operating in effect as "captive carriers" to the military. In fact, with the exception of a few companies serving South America and Africa, *all* liner firms—subsidized and non-subsidized alike—depend heavily on government business. Overall the liners appear to receive a bit more than half of their gross freight revenues from government shipments. For some lines, including several subsidized companies, the proportion runs upwards of 70 percent.[31]

Whether the shift from commercial to government business has been a

---

differential, however, will vary in relation to changing demand for ships. There have been occasions when U.S. flag vessels were chartered for less than foreign flags, or at least for less than the foreign ships would have chartered in the absence of U.S. flag competition.

[30] Approximately 32 million tons were shipped out of U.S. ports on liners in both 1956 and 1962. In 1956 U.S. carriers took 13.7 million tons, 38 percent of which were sponsored by U.S. agencies; in 1962 they carried 11.2 million tons, of which two-thirds was government-sponsored. Outbound tramp shipments totaled approximately 66 million tons in both years; the proportion carried by U.S. flag vessels increased from 5.4 to 6.4 million tons, but the increase was due entirely to increased government shipments. A complete statistical analysis of the cargo preference program is presented in Appendix A, Tables A7-A10.

[31] Revenue estimates derived from government agency shipment reports, the Office of Business Economics, and other sources indicate that in 1963 about $400

matter of choice or of necessity is not clear. Favorable rates are available for only certain categories of liner cargoes. But for all government cargoes, booking expenses, credit risks, and insurance costs are lower than for commercial business, and the customer is probably less difficult to please. As a result, complaints are occasionally heard that American companies have become choosey about accepting commercial consignments, preferring to concentrate on the more lucrative government work. Some persons believe that the availability of preference cargoes, which are predominantly outbound, has been one of the primary reasons that rates are generally higher in export than in import trade. Probably nearly all would acknowledge that the shift to government business has hindered the U.S. flag merchant marine in achieving the commercial objectives of the 1936 act.

Trade Agreements and Pools. While the United States has jealously protected its national flag fleet's share of government shipments, it has also steadfastly refused since World War II to apply discriminatory tariffs, quotas, exchange controls, or any other coercive technique to its privately sponsored foreign commerce. The sharpness of the policy cleavage between shipments in the public and private sectors has heightened controversies over cargo preference in doubtful cases. The United States' approach is also in contrast to that of many other nations which are less doctrinaire in their attitudes toward government participation in commercial affairs.

Many shipping personnel believe the United States has been unduly timorous in responding to widespread formal and informal pressures to draw cargoes to national flag fleets. The 1936 statute instructed the commission to "cooperate with vessel owners in devising means through which the importers and exporters of the United States can be induced to give preference to vessels under United States registry,"[32] yet for many years nothing was done. In 1963 the Maritime Administrator sought to rectify this omission by appointing a former shipping line vice president as his special assistant for cargo promotion. This official has engaged in general promotional activity, has helped American carriers to obtain specific car-

---

million was paid by the government for U.S. flag liner services and about $350 million received by the lines on commercial shipments. Other data believed to be reliable are reported for the American Mail Line and United States Line in a Harvard Business School Case Study of the Moore-McCormack Company (1963), p. AM-P 174.

[32] 49 Stat. 1990.

goes, and has initiated a systematic study of factors influencing cargo routing.

The industry has also been critical of the State Department for failing to act aggressively in its interest.[33] Believing State to be unduly concerned with maintaining friendly relations with foreign governments and ineffective anyhow, the U.S. flag industry has taken its grievances instead to the maritime agencies, which have sometimes acted without even consulting State.

The weapon most frequently used by the maritime agencies to combat unfavorable trade practices has been denial of waivers on Export-Import Bank cargoes.[34] The Maritime Administration in 1960 threatened to invoke a countervailing tariff against Ecuador if it failed to remove a tariff discriminating against U.S.-transported goods (Ecuador complied). In another case the government is credited with taking a leading role in negotiating formation of a shipping pool to stem the shift of transpacific cargoes from U.S. to Japanese ships.[35]

Government approval of shipping pools, such as that proposed in the Japan-U.S. trade, has essentially the same effect as directly negotiated shipping clauses in bilateral trade agreements. The U.S. government's toleration of pools had by 1963 encouraged American operators to enter pooling agreements with Swedish, Yugoslav, Italian, Chilean, and Venezuelan lines covering general cargo movements in trade with those nations (or between particular coastal ranges) and with lines of various flags serving the Thailand-Malay rubber trade, the cotton trade to Japan, and the Great Lakes to Mediterranean trade route. Pooling proposals were on file with the Federal Maritime Commission to apportion coffee shipments from Brazil and general cargo shipments between the United States and Japan and on the principal U.S. to Europe North Atlantic trade route. However, this potentially significant extension of the preference principle

[33] The State Department has fairly consistently tried to maintain liberal trade principles and opposed the original enactment of cargo preferences. However, it has defended U.S. application of preferences to government cargoes in meetings with foreign governments. The Department has also effectively defended the U.S. position that Liberia and Panama should be recognized as legitimate registries and has cooperated with the Federal Maritime Commission's regulatory efforts.

[34] One action which received considerable publicity was the Federal Maritime Board's 1960 denial of a request by the Toyota Motor Co. for a waiver on a $12 million Export-Import Bank financed shipment. The action, taken to counter Japanese government pressures on Japanese shippers to make greater use of Japanese ships, came at a time when Japanese-American relations were particularly delicate (the Eisenhower visit to Japan had been cancelled just six months earlier) and outraged officials at the Department of State.

[35] See testimony of Joseph Klausner in *Discriminatory Ocean Freight Rates and the Balance of Payments,* Hearings, p. 228.

was nipped at the eleventh hour by a sharp shift in the Federal Maritime Commission's policies, placing the burden on the applicant to demonstrate that the proposed pool would be in the U.S. public interest.[36]

Support of Flags of Convenience

Since World War II the U.S. government has tacitly supported development of a U.S.-owned, foreign-registered fleet under U.S. effective control. This support has in part been passive, as in U.S. failure to take action to stem the flight of U.S. shipping capital to flags of convenience or to disapprove applications to transfer U.S.-registered vessels to foreign flag. However, impelled both by defense interests and the realities of international business practice, the government has also taken certain positive actions to strengthen the position of U.S.-owned shipping registered under flags of convenience (Panama, Liberia, Honduras [PANLIBHON]) and to secure its availability to the United States in the event of emergency. These actions have been vehemently opposed by organized American labor.

Elements of the Problem. Since World War II roughly a thousand merchant vessels (1,000 gross tons or over) are reported to have been constructed abroad for U.S. owners for registry under foreign flags.[37] An ad-

[36] The Federal Maritime Commission's changed attitude toward pools followed the appointment of a new chairman and managing director and sharply critical comment regarding the commission's earlier policies by the Joint Economic Committee of the Congress. The explosion of applications to pool revenues in important trades also caused a quickening of interest in the Department of Justice, which intervened in one case, and elsewhere in the executive branch. Since the commission shifted the burden of proof, one pooling application has been denied and four others withdrawn. The commission's pre-1965 reading of the statute was that the government should make a positive finding that the application was detrimental to U.S. foreign commerce.

[37] Data for 1947–52 from *Merchant Marine Studies,* Hearings before a subcommittee of the Senate Interstate and Foreign Commerce Committee, 83 Cong. 1 sess. (1953), p. 387; for 1950-62 from *Marine Engineering Log,* (June 15, 1963), p. 149. Orders for 239 ships totalling about 3 million gross tons were reported in the *Studies;* for 938 ships of 17.2 million gross tons in the *Log.* Obviously, the two reports overlap. Some vessels have undoubtedly been sold foreign since construction, and some orders may have been reported where U.S. interests have not actually held a majority of the capital stock. Neither source reveals how the data was compiled or the criteria used to distinguish U.S. from foreign ownership, but informed sources believe the lists to be reasonably reliable.

Unfortunately the 1,000-ship estimate cannot be verified from official records. The U.S. Maritime Administration's annual survey of foreign-registered ships owned by U.S. citizens identifies less than half of these ships and only 71 percent of the

ditional 700 ships constructed in the United States have been transferred to foreign registries by U.S. owners.[38] Less than half of this latter group, however, is still owned by American citizens.[39] Based on these data, only 40-45 percent of the American tonnage registered abroad appears to be enrolled under PANLIBHON registries. Yet, perhaps because they pose the issues most dramatically, public policy conflicts relating to the use of foreign registries have centered almost exclusively on the use of these convenience flags. Whereas American ownership of British, Dutch, or German shipping usually has some commercial justification, PANLIBHON registries can be justified only in economic terms. Furthermore, only this latter group is sufficiently free of national flag restrictions to be considered by the U.S. government to be under effective U.S. control.

The PANLIBHON group also includes a high proportion of large modern tankers and ore carriers, whose capacity is so great that they are able approximately to match the dry cargo foreign trade tonnage lifted by U.S. flag ships and to transport about one-third of America's oil imports as well.[40] Thus, U.S.-owned PANLIBHON shipping is a major factor in U.S. foreign trade; it permits U.S. industries to move a substantial por-

---

PANLIBHON ships believed to be U.S.-owned. The survey is limited to ships owned by foreign affiliates and subsidiaries of U.S. companies, incorporated under U.S. law. It does not detect ships owned by unlisted corporations, individuals, or corporations effectively controlled by U.S. citizens despite the absence of a majority interest.

[38] The 700 ships transferred foreign exclude ships sold to aliens under the Merchant Ship Sales Act of 1946, but include over 300 vessels (including virtually all the overage, privately owned ships built prior to World War II) which were approved for transfer under the highly permissive administrative policies applicable from 1946 to 1948. Following the Korean war (1954-55) an additional 100 freighters and 65 tankers were transferred foreign. The "trade-out and build" program, in effect for the following two years, caused an additional 71 freighters and 50 tankers to be released. Since 1958, U.S. flag transfers to foreign flags have been roughly balanced by redocumentations of foreign-registered ships in the United States.

[39] Up-to-date information on the ownership of ships transferred from U.S. to foreign registries is not available. Probably considerably less than half continue to be U.S.-owned. All U.S.-owned ships, regardless of registry, are nominally subject to requisition by the United States in an emergency, although the registering nation may prevent the necessary flag transfer. Most foreign-owned ships transferred from U.S. registry since the Korean war also are subject to title liens stating the United States' right to requisition the vessel in the event of an emergency. Some of these liens are secured by bonds.

[40] Data from U.S. Maritime Administration, Office of Statistics, "An Analysis of Ships under Effective Control and Their Employment in U.S. Foreign Trade During 1960" (Government Printing Office, 1962). The scale of "effective control" shipping's participation in dry cargo shipments in U.S. foreign trade is, of course, a result of the concentration of these ships in bulk cargo movements. Flags of convenience do almost no liner business in U.S. foreign trade.

tion of their cargoes in ships under their control but it also substantially reduces the cargoes available to a U.S. flag fleet.

The U.S.-owned PANLIBHON fleet is commensurately important from a defense viewpoint. In fact the Defense Department has stated that these vessels represent approximately half of the nation's total shipping capability for meeting national emergencies.[41] Not surprisingly, continued effective U.S. control of these ships has been deemed by Defense to be vital to U.S. military interests. Yet the controversial nature of flags of convenience causes uncertainty as to their long-term reliability.

Organized labor's interest in the "runaway flag" issue is partially measured by the number of billets which have been lost through transfers of U.S.-owned vessels to PANLIBHON flags (about 35,000) or the number which might be available for U.S. seamen were U.S.-owned vessels now under these registries brought under U.S. registry (19,000-20,000). However, organized labor also has a principle at stake, for the lack of effective labor regulations in the flag of convenience nations makes these registries havens from the international labor movement. The American unions' opposition to U.S. use of flags of convenience is consequently strongly supported by the International Labor Organization and the International Federation of Transport Workers, which in 1958 staged a four-day worldwide strike against runaway ships. The foreign flag issue was also a principal ingredient in the eighteen-day 1961 U.S. seamen's strike, and from time to time individual flag of convenience vessels continue to be picketed in ports around the world.

The use of flags of convenience is opposed on principle by most of the world's established maritime nations, which have insisted that a genuine link should exist between the ship and the nation of registry in order to enforce reasonable order and discipline at sea.[42] However, conditions of

[41] See U.S. Department of Justice, *Brief for the United States as Amicus Curiae, Incres Steamship Company v. International Maritime Workers Union* (Oct. 1962), p. 9. The validity of the Defense Department's assertion is somewhat questionable since the U.S.-owned PANLIBHON fleet includes few if any modern, general-purpose dry cargo vessels, for which Defense has the largest quantity requirements. However, the PANLIBHON fleet does have a larger tanker capacity than the U.S. flag merchant marine. As the military shifts to airlift, these tankers will become increasingly important to defense needs.

[42] The 1958 Geneva Conference on the High Seas, after much debate, incorporated the "genuine link" formula into Article V of its proposed Convention on the High Seas: "There must exist a genuine link between the state [of registry] and the ship; in particular, the State must effectively exercise its jurisdiction and control in administrative, technical, and social matters over ships flying its flag."

The Convention was ratified by the U.S. Senate in 1960 and proclaimed by the President following its adoption by the required number of signatory nations, on

registry vary so much among nations that the essential attributes of a "genuine link" have not yet been defined. Furthermore, even though PAN-LIBHON registries offer only a small cost advantage over most other flags, some use is made of them by citizens of many of the world's principal maritime nations. Consequently, opposition to flags of convenience has not been nearly so strong as opposition to cargo preferences.

The many divergent interests in flags of convenience plus uncertainties as to how effectively the United States could control ships pledged to its use in the event of emergency have combined to make the "flag of convenience issue" perhaps the most perplexing of the government's postwar maritime problems. American-owned PANLIBHON ships are in many respects fully as responsive to the ultimate purposes of public policy as are vessels registered domestically. Yet these ships lack many of the usual characteristics of national flag vessels. And they certainly lack the "all-American" attributes of the subsidized merchant marine.

Furthermore, there are practical limits on the influence which the United States can exercise over the use of convenience flags by American citizens. For example, the government has never directly barred U.S. investment abroad, except for specific national security reasons. On the other hand, it has reserved the power to disapprove applications to transfer U.S. flag vessels to foreign registries and can invoke both direct and indirect incentives to alter the relative attractiveness of U.S. versus foreign flags.[43]

Policies Toward Flags of Convenience. The usefulness of flags of convenience was evident even before the United States' entry into World War II, for these registries provided a means of circumventing the government's own neutrality statutes in order to carry American aid to the British Isles. Following the war, the commission and the Congress appear tac-

---

Nov. 9, 1962. However, the Senate declined to ratify a special protocol to the Convention, providing that disputes arising under it should be submitted to the World Court for arbitration. Furthermore, the State Department has made clear its view that no third party can rely upon the Convention to determine unilaterally whether a "genuine link" exists between a state and a ship. Its position, therefore, is that "the 'genuine link' requirement need not have any effect upon the practice of registering American built or owned vessels in such countries as Panama and Liberia [since] it is for each state to determine how it shall exercise [its] jurisdiction . . . over ships flying its flag." (See *Congressional Record*, Vol. 106, Pt. 6, May 26, 1960, p. 10382.)

[43] Government approval is required under the Shipping Act of 1916 to transfer vessels purchased from the board or during a national emergency declared by the President. Since the Korean emergency is legally still in effect, government approval is now required for all flag transfer proposals.

itly to have agreed that recourse to foreign flags was preferable to subsidizing the operation of a foreign trade tanker fleet for America's international oil companies.[44] Also, for as long as the 1946 Ship Sales Act permitted sale of U.S. war-surplus ships to foreign nationals (through 1948), the commission held that there was no basis for restricting transfers or foreign registration of citizen-owned ships.[45]

During the succeeding decade, ship transfer policies were the source of severe conflicts between maritime labor and shipowner interests. In general, the government took the position that it had no authority to interfere with the free exercise of the shipowners' property rights, including the right to transfer to foreign registries, in the absence of specific national interests. In reviewing transfer applications, the Maritime Administration considered defense and commercial requirements, the effect of transfer on U.S. foreign policy, and the effect on the competitive position of U.S. flag carriers, but not their effect on employment of American seamen.[46]

During the latter 1950's tonnage being built abroad by U.S. shipowners for PANLIBHON registry began to dwarf that which could potentially be transferred from U.S. flag, and the controversy shifted from ship transfer policies to the applicability of U.S. labor laws to U.S.-owned foreign-registered ships. The shipowners attempted to obtain injunctions against picketing of their ships, but their applications were rejected in a series of cases eventually reaching the U.S. Supreme Court.[47] The shipowners then

[44] The Maritime Commission's Postwar Planning Committee reviewed use of foreign-registered ships by U.S. companies and concluded in its report, *The Post-War Outlook for American Shipping*, p. 46, that there had been "strong reasons for the use of alien vessels in the past and these reasons presumably will apply with equal, if not greater force in the future." Also, the debate on the 1946 Ship Sales Act makes it clear that the Congress, in setting the sales price of tankers to be written into that act, was cognizant that the relatively higher price set for this class of ships (87½ percent prewar domestic construction cost versus 50 percent on freighters) was tantamount to a decision not to attempt to establish a U.S. flag tanker fleet in foreign trade. The increased revenue from this relatively higher price was estimated at $150 million (*Congressional Record*, Vol. 91, No. 7, Oct. 1, 1945, p. 9273).

[45] See U.S. Maritime Administration, Organization Methods Office, *Review of Vessel Transfer Activities* (mimeograph, 1954), for an official interpretation and justification of that agency's vessel transfer policies.

[46] Specific conditions considered have been summarized by the Maritime Administration in a statement titled "Transfer of U.S. privately owned vessels under Sections 9 and 37 of the Shipping Act of 1916, as amended" (mimeograph, 1962).

[47] The principal cases decided by the Supreme Court were *Benz v. Hidalgo, S. A.* (353 U.S. 138), and *Marine Cooks and Stewards v. Panama Steamship Company, Ltd.* (360 U.S. 365). The unions' rights to picket were conditioned by the Court on their being able to make a showing that there was a legitimate labor dispute meriting this interference with normal commerce.

sought to bar union organizers from boarding their ships and to prevent National Labor Relations Board (NLRB) certification of representation elections. These pleadings were also rejected by the NLRB, which asserted that it could claim jurisdiction in any labor dispute threatening to disrupt the flow of U.S. domestic or foreign commerce.[48]

The NLRB decisions were strongly supported by the Department of Labor but caused dismay elsewhere in government. The Commerce and Defense departments in particular were concerned that the NLRB doctrine would permit U.S. unions to influence wages and working conditions on U.S.-owned PANLIBHON ships which would cause their owners to transfer the vessels to other foreign flags, where their availability in national emergencies would be far less certain. The State Department believed NLRB's decisions asserted an unsupportable extraterritorial jurisdiction which would be interpreted by other nations as a precedent for further interference in their domestic affairs. The Bureau of the Budget was fearful that they would increase pressures on the government to subsidize the operation of "effective control" vessels under U.S. flag.

The issues at stake were deemed by President John F. Kennedy to merit thorough investigation by a cabinet-level committee, which was organized under the direction of the Secretary of Labor in February 1962. The President also instructed his Solicitor General to intervene as *amicus curiae* in actions challenging the NLRB rulings which had been brought before the Supreme Court by owners of PANLIBHON vessels. Because the Cabinet committee was unable to agree on a general policy toward use of "convenience" registries, the Solicitor argued only that NLRB's jurisdiction had been invalid in the particular cases before the Court, one of which involved a foreign-owned ship and the other a U.S.-owned ship under Honduran registry operated by a Honduran corporation and manned by a Honduran crew.[49] However, the Court announced a general doctrine that the National Labor Relations Act should not be interpreted in a manner which might cause embarrassment to U.S. foreign relations or jeopardize this nation's PANLIBHON defense resources.[50]

The Court did not rule that regulation of flag of convenience shipping was beyond the power of Congress. However, the Congress has shown little disposition to support the unions' effort to organize PANLIBHON

[48] For example, *Eastern Shipping Corp., McCormick Shipping Corp., employers, and Seafarers International Union, petitioner,* 132 NLRB 72 (1961).

[49] See U.S. Department of Justice, *Brief for the United States as Amicus Curiae in Empresa Hondurena* (Oct. 1962).

[50] *National Labor Relations Board v. Sociedad Nacional de Marineros de Honduras,* 372 U.S. 10 (1962).

ships and has made no effort to change the Court's ruling. Instead, litigation has been continued in an effort to trim back the broad language of its opinion to the situations which had been immediately at issue.

The Doctrine of Effective Control. Although anxious to insulate flag of convenience shipping from NLRB regulatory jurisdiction, the Defense, State, and Commerce departments have taken positive steps to assure effective control over these vessels in the event of a national emergency. For example, these departments have worked with the shipowners to weed out known communists and communist-sympathizers from their crews and to devise procedures to facilitate transfer of their ships to U.S. flag in an emergency. Transfer arrangements have also been discussed by the shipowners with the Panamanian, Liberian, and Honduran governments and understandings reached with them that the transfers will be permitted. In most cases the owners of effective-control ships have given the United States written assurance that their vessels will be made available for U.S. use in the event of emergency. In some cases, where the ship previously was under U.S. registry, the United States' emergency claim is written into the ship's title and secured by a $25,000 to $250,000 performance bond. In other cases the ships have been granted binders by the U.S. government to insure them against certain war risks not covered by commercial policies.[51]

The categories of shipping considered subject to effective U.S. control have shifted gradually over the years. At one time, all U.S.-owned foreign-registered ships were potentially eligible for inclusion in an effective-control list maintained by the Navy; however, in 1961 criteria were developed which limit the assertion of "effective U.S. control" to ships registered with one of the three PANLIBHON states.[52]

---

[51] War risk insurance was offered American shipowners during both world wars, but repealed upon the expiration of the emergency. Early in the Korean conflict, a third war risk program was enacted to expire in September 1960. This legislation has since been extended for two five-year periods and modified to provide a comprehensive and potentially very valuable coverage. In addition to U.S. flag and effective-control vessels, coverage has been extended to three or four other foreign flag vessels for which the Defense Department has stated a special requirement. If necessary to induce ships to serve U.S. foreign commerce, the Secretary of Commerce is authorized by the act to extend insurance coverage even to foreign-owned foreign flag vessels in U.S. foreign trade (64 Stat. 773).

[52] The criteria used in assessing whether effective control could be considered to apply were listed in a letter from Under Secretary of Defense Roswell L. Gilpatrick to Senator Warren Magnuson, Dec. 15, 1961. Gilpatrick conceded that he could not be absolutely sure of the availability of every vessel listed as under effective control, but that there was a high probability most would be in view of "(1) contracts, with

The Navy concept of effective control is geared to availability of foreign flag shipping during emergencies. However, for ordinary business purposes, American commercial interests obviously exercise effective control over whatever shipping they own or charter, regardless of registry. It is reasonable to assume that in most emergencies countries other than PANLIBHON will permit American-owned shipping registered under their laws to be enlisted in the American cause. Limitation of the effective-control list to PANLIBHON states does not, of course, deny this likelihood. It does, however, give evidence of U.S. concern that its effective-control doctrine not be unnecessarily extended so as to give undue affront.

Government Role in Collective Bargaining

The controversies over flags of convenience illustrate but one of the maritime labor problems in which government has become involved. Other pressures which, coupled with its general concern for the industry's stability and well-being, have drawn government increasingly deeply into maritime labor-management problems are its interest in the level of subsidizable wage scales, its responsibility under the Taft-Hartley Act to assure that labor disputes do not "imperil the national health, safety, or welfare," its interest in maintaining the flow of foreign commerce in order to earn foreign exchange, and requests from maritime management and labor themselves for assistance in resolving problems which seem almost irresolvable.

Elements of the Problem. Merchant shipping has long been noted for its turbulent and fractious labor relations. Indeed, there are a number of persons who believe that the industry's present difficulties are in large measure a product of animosities and suspicions bred during the twenties and thirties, when seamen were treated only a little better than criminals. The men who in the late thirties emerged as the seafarers' leaders were ener-

---

the Maritime Administration or assurances provided the U.S. Government by the shipowner, (2) the absence of operational control restrictions in the laws of Panama, Liberia, and Honduras, the limited shipping requirements on the part of these nations, and the probability that they will remain neutral in the time of war, (3) precedents established in World War II when all American-owned ships under Panamanian and Honduran flags were assimilated into the U.S. war effort, and (4) related considerations pertaining to protection of shipping, operational procedures, and ship maintenance." The American Committee for Flags of Necessity in *The Role of Flags of Necessity* (multilith, New York, 1962), p. 8, has estimated that the effective control designation has been applied to 85 percent of the PANLIBHON ships which are American-owned.

getic, strongminded, and independent individuals, who built their reputations on the effective use of sit-down and quickie strikes. Some of these men, and the management personnel who fought them, are still in key positions in the industry.

For a small industry, the U.S. merchant marine supports an unusually large number of independent, vocal, and effective unions. In all, there are thirteen affiliates of the AFL-CIO and fifteen independent unions competing for the roughly 50,000 seagoing berths available in the U.S. flag oceangoing merchant fleet. Both officers and crews are organized, so that four or more unions are represented on every ship. Negotiations are carried on with four major owners' associations representing over a hundred companies (about 90 percent of the entire fleet) operating out of Pacific, Gulf, and Atlantic ports. In most cases, the contracts developed in collective bargaining are not binding on participating companies; in virtually all cases, the standard industry contract must be amplified to specify manning practices and working conditions on particular ships. Until recently, there has not even been any congruity in the expiration dates of the industry's many labor contracts.

The postwar contraction in the U.S. flag fleet has heightened interunion competition for members and jobs and has intensified longstanding rivalries among union leaders. Rivalry has been most severe on the Atlantic and Gulf coasts, where the unions serving the dry cargo segments of the fleet have become polarized into two camps—one centering on Joseph Curran, president of the National Maritime Union (NMU), who has generally emphasized high wages within the framework of the present subsidy system; and the other on Paul Hall, Seafarers International Union (SIU) president, who has put his main emphasis on developing more jobs for U.S. seamen (through extension of cargo preferences and repatriation of U.S.-owned foreign-flag ships) and who has strongly attacked the present subsidy system.

The divisions within the maritime labor movement extend into the top councils of the AFL-CIO. Both Curran and Hall are vice presidents of this body. Curran is also chairman of the Maritime Committee, a CIO group which existed prior to the AFL-CIO merger and which coordinates the activities of several seafaring and shipbuilding unions. Hall heads the official AFL-CIO Maritime Trades Department, which has ties through its board of directors to the International Longshoremen's Association as well as the industry's largest licensed officer group. Efforts to merge these two AFL-CIO organizations have been unavailing.[53]

[53] The Maritime Committee is composed of the NMU, two seafaring officers'

Frictions among the several maritime unions have spawned an unusually large number of jurisdictional work stoppages on American ships. In addition, from 1947 through 1964 the U.S. foreign trade fleet experienced twelve major strikes (involving 2,000 or more workers) called on economic issues. In total, these work stoppages have extended over 245 days. One strike, called by the Sailor's Union of the Pacific in September 1948, lasted three months; however, West Coast unions since then have been involved in only two prolonged work stoppages—one in 1952, the other in 1962. On the East and Gulf coasts difficulties have been more frequent but less prolonged. Here there was an average of one major seamen's strike with an average duration of ten days roughly every other year from 1955 through 1964.[54]

Licensed officer associations have participated in some way in a high proportion of the seamen's postwar contract disputes. In recent years these associations have been particularly sensitive to issues touching on their members' pay and prerogatives. Indeed, the most difficult issues during the 1965 maritime strike, which extended over 74 days and is estimated to have caused some 490,000 lost workdays, arose from the licensed personnels' apprehensions regarding the impact of automation on manning.

Of the twenty-two injunctions ordered under the Taft-Hartley Act since its 1947 enactment three have been directed at seamen's strikes and five at longshore strikes. However, whereas the Taft-Hartley "cooling off" period has generally been successful in other industries, in the maritime industry it has tended to heat up emotions and prolong difficultlies. These difficulties have been particularly severe in longshore disputes (strikes were resumed after four of five Taft-Hartley injunctions), but have also undermined the usefulness of the Taft-Hartley procedure in seafarers' disputes which also have continued right up to (and in one case beyond) the expiration of the injunction.

---

unions, a Great Lakes seamen's group, and a major shipbuilders' union. The Maritime Trades Department embraces thirty unions, each having some connection with maritime transport, and claims to represent 400,000 workers. Both groups maintain small Washington staffs. In 1964 Thomas Gleason, president of the International Longshoremen's Association, organized a new Maritime Committee, which includes members from both of the older groups and which provides a vehicle for industry-wide cooperation on political issues in which all maritime labor unions have a common interest. This committee, however, lacks any institutional standing or staff support.

[54] In terms of workdays lost per worker, strike experience in the American merchant marine has been on a par with other unionized domestic industries. However, strike losses to the U.S. flag fleet appear to have been considerably in excess of losses to competing foreign flags. Furthermore, U.S. companies probably have felt the impact of the large number of longshore work stoppages somewhat more than their foreign competition.

Participation in Labor-Management Problems. Direct mandatory action in maritime labor-management matters, such as imposing a Taft-Hartley injunction, has been taken by government only as a last resort. Ordinarily during peacetime the government has attempted to avoid direct responsibility for the industry's contract negotiations. During wartime, of course, it has had to assume this responsibility, either directly as operator of government-owned vessels or indirectly through its wage stabilization boards.

The problem of devising effective mechanisms for collective bargaining was one of the most urgent and perplexing issues before the prewar Maritime Commission.[55] However, due to the intervention of two major wars, it was not seriously faced until 1955, when the House Merchant Marine and Fisheries Committee held extensive hearings to review the industry's collective bargaining procedures and to consider alternative ways in which government might assist in stabilizing its labor relations.[56]

Although yielding no legislative results, these hearings did provide a springboard to further study. The Maritime Administration was instructed in the committee's report to survey the industry's wage pattern, to conduct job analyses on board ship, and to compile comparative data on shipboard wages and wages in other industries.[57] The committee also emphasized the Maritime Administration's obligation to establish "fair and reasonable" criteria to guide maritime wage negotiations and undertook itself to coordinate the termination dates of the industry's labor contracts.[58]

[55] The commission recommended that maritime labor disputes be brought under the Railway Labor Act. This proposal was strongly opposed by organized labor, and the Congress established a special Maritime Labor Board to give the matter further study. The board's 1940 *Report to the President and the Congress* includes a perceptive history of the industry's labor relations from 1934 to 1939.

[56] *Labor Management Problems of the American Merchant Marine,* Hearings before the House Merchant Marine and Fisheries Committee, 84 Cong. 1 and 2 sess. (1955-56). Through a general investigation, the hearings also reviewed a bill introduced by the chairman which authorized the Federal Maritime Board to fix the *maximum* wage rates and manning scales that would be eligible for subsidy. The Committee took no legislative action, but did issue a thorough and thoughtful report (H. Rept. 1658, 84 Cong. 2 sess. [1956]) urging government, management, and labor to take a number of specific steps toward better informed, better coordinated, and more tolerant and responsible bargaining procedures.

[57] As a partial response to these recommendations, the Maritime Administration contracted with the Bureau of Labor Statistics for a statistical study, published as *The Earnings and Employment of Seamen on U.S. Flag Ships* (Labor Department Bulletin 1238, Nov. 1958). Subsequent statistical studies have been performed by the National Academy of Sciences' Maritime Cargo Transportation Conference and by the Maritime Administration's Office of Statistics.

[58] Uncoordinated contract termination dates were believed by the committee and by many in the industry to be due to the pressure on union leaders to achieve as much for their members as had been awarded other groups in previous negotiations,

Although slow getting underway, the factual studies and statistical work initiated following the hearings have been slowly expanded and now constitute one of the government's most important contributions to the conduct of more rational informed negotiations.

In 1963 the House Merchant Marine Subcommittee sponsored a second series of hearings on maritime labor problems, this time to consider proposed legislation to outlaw strikes in favor of a complex procedure culminating in compulsory arbitration.[59] The hearings coincided with intensive industry efforts to achieve acceptance for increased ship automation and were apparently aimed in part at impressing maritime labor leaders with the seriousness with which the problem was regarded by members of Congress and other influential persons and in part at exposing the industry's problems to public view. Although the hearings failed to produce acceptable proposals for improving the legal framework for maritime collective bargaining, the publicity which they generated may have contributed to a contract settlement between the American Merchant Marine Institute (AMMI) and the NMU, which was widely advertised at the time as a major step toward maritime labor peace and acceptance of automation.[60]

Since 1961 various executive branch officials have also been working in a sustained, undramatic manner to facilitate resolution of maritime labor issues. For example, in February 1963 the Federal Mediation and Conciliation Service sponsored a meeting of West Coast labor and management leaders, attended also by the Maritime Administrator. The meetings' purpose was to begin constructive exchanges among the parties in interest well before the 1965 expiration of the unlicensed union contracts.

---

and a little more. The committee chairman personally wrote to the presidents of each of the major unions to ask their cooperation in coordinating the timing of contract negotiations. Although there was no immediate response, there has been gradual improvement in both the span and phasing of maritime labor contracts. By 1965, all major unions were operating under four or more year contracts which extended through June 1969. However, many of these contracts include wage reopeners and/or provisions requiring that pay be maintained in a certain ratio to pay for other ratings or general economic indices.

[59] *Maritime Labor Legislation*, Hearings.

[60] The NMU-AMMI contract provided a four-year extension of existing contracts, negotiated in 1961, subject to improved vacation benefits, binding arbitration of wage and overtime questions, and establishment of an "automation fund," to which employers would be required to pay $0.25 per day per man on their rolls. (This contribution has been approved by the government as a subsidizable cost.) The new contract left specific manning issues to be worked out by each company and failed to designate the manner in which the new fund would be used to ease the transition to automated ships. Nevertheless, the contract has provided a framework for partially resolving what has become one of the industry's knottiest problems. The NMU was not among the unions directly involved in the 1965 strikes on automation issues.

Through this meeting and subsequent discussions, issues were defined, data needs identified, and fifteen specific questions relating to future government policies formulated for presentation to the Secretary of Labor.[61] Partially as a result of this work, work stoppages on the West Coast were avoided in 1965.

During the 1960's, government's role in maritime labor-management affairs has steadily intensified. Settlement of the 1965 East and Gulf coast strike was publicly first announced, not by the parties to the negotiation, but by President Johnson, who gave principal credit for the settlement to Secretary of Labor Willard Wirtz. Prior to the settlement, the Secretary had devoted more than a week of concentrated effort to finding grounds for a solution; by direction of the President he was to continue to discuss automation issues with the AFL-CIO to develop a basis for resolving outstanding issues.

Despite the clear trend toward more intensive involvement, the government has failed to establish any definite pattern of participation in labor-management discussions; significantly, all efforts to establish a more rational bargaining structure within the industry have also failed. As issues arise, interested federal agencies and private arbitrators work through whatever channels appear at the time to be most promising. This has sometimes caused confusion.[62] However, the issues at stake appear simply to be too sensitive for any single, explicit formula to be acceptable to all parties. In this industry as in others, the government consequently must feel its way from case to case, seeking to find the means, when necessary, to apply constructive pressures on the interested parties to develop their own solutions compatible with the general public good.

Regulation of Competition

The fourth area in which the government has enlarged upon the 1936

[61] The jointly formulated questions were listed as an attachment to a letter from J. Paul St. Sure, president of the Pacific Maritime Association, to Herbert Schmertz, assistant to the director of the Federal Mediation and Conciliation Service, dated Jan. 13, 1964. They were personally delivered by Mr. Schmertz to the Secretary of Labor shortly thereafter.

[62] At times it has been unclear in which agency the leadership lay, and the government's efforts have been impeded by lack of coordination. For example, a consultant to the Maritime Administration was reported in the 1965 strike to have interfered with negotiations being conducted by the Federal Mediation and Conciliation Service, which in turn was forced to yield to the Secretary of Labor. (See Helen Delich Bentley, "Mastermind Emerges as Hero or Wrecker of Ship Talks," *Baltimore Sun,* June 21, 1965.)

act is in regulation of competition within the industry and between the industry and the Military Sea Transport Service (MSTS at one time operated, directly or through general agency agreements, more ships than U.S. owners employed in foreign trade and even today operates a substantially larger fleet than the next largest U.S. flag carrier). As in each of the preceding cases, the maritime agencies' role has been chiefly to improve business opportunities for American shipowners and facilitate operation of privately owned American ships.

Government Competition with Business. Articulating a satisfactory relationship between public and private enterprise has been one of the most divisive issues in the development of America's maritime programs. One of the major achievements of the 1936 act was to enunciate a subsidy formula which fixed, at least in general terms, the limits to which the government should go to implement the preference for use of privately owned facilities (also expressed in the act) for achieving national objectives. The 1936 policy barring use of government vessels if privately owned ships were reasonably available did not, however, specifically prohibit government agencies from using ships under their own control to move government-sponsored cargoes.

Ever since the Spanish-American War, the military departments had operated a limited number of merchant type vessels to meet a portion of their transportation needs.[63] Late in 1940 the prospect that the United States would be drawn into the war triggered a sharp expansion of military operations, through ship purchases and charters and subsequently through requisitions for both use and title.[64] Virtually all new construction until the end of the war was held in government account. The military departments' attitude toward private operation of ships is revealed in a plan

[63] Following both the Spanish-American and First World War, both Army and Navy had briefly maintained substantial sea transportation facilities. In both instances obsolescence and economic pressures had led to progressive reductions. In 1939 the Army owned two freighters and six combination (freight and passenger) ships. The Navy Transportation Service was organizationally moribund, but retained paper assignments of two transports and seven other vessels.

[64] Ships had to be requisitioned for military use beginning in the summer of 1941. A large majority of the requisition agreements (79 percent of agreements with subsidized operators and 74 percent of the remainder) were, however, for use rather than title; these use agreements permitted the operators to exercise day-to-day control of their ships and receive an annual return on the estimated value of their investment. As the war continued it became apparent that this arrangement was far more favorable to the shipowner than the ship purchases which had been executed in the war's early stages.

worked out in May 1941 to operate all vessels regularly moving military cargoes with regular Navy personnel, regardless of whether publicly or privately owned.[65]

The Navy's plan, because of a dearth of personnel, never became fully effective, and most shipping in support of military operations remained in civilian hands throughout the war. Some merchant-type vessels, however, were operated as commissioned U.S. Navy vessels. This mixed pattern continued (on a reduced scale) after the war was over. Although the Army began to look to the private merchant marine for a majority of its postwar shipping needs, the Navy concentrated on making full use of its fleet vessels and routed only 15 percent of its cargoes via the commercial merchant marine.

The organization of the Military Sea Transport Service in 1949—just two months following the establishment of a Department of Defense—did not therefore represent any innovation in military shipping policy. However, consolidation of the military's shipping functions within Navy did appear to presage greater emphasis on government versus privately owned facilities. Furthermore, the volume of military shipping requirements was contracting rapidly during 1949. If no reductions were made in the government fleet and if Navy insisted on using this fleet to capacity, many private operators feared that they would be forced out of the defense business altogether.

The private industry reacted sharply to the apparent threat, and attacked the organization of a single government-owned shipping agency to handle all military business as a contravention of established policy, unfair to business, and a step toward socialism. Most shipping men were convinced that it was wasteful for the military to use government-owned facilities. But perhaps most nettling of all, maintenance of a large in-house merchant fleet, scaled to support the needs of a large peacetime army, threatened to undermine industry's role as a military auxiliary and invalidate its claim on public support as "the fourth arm of defense."[66]

The incipient struggle between private industry and the MSTS was

[65] Use of Navy personnel on all vessels controlled by the War or Navy Department was formally agreed by the two departments in May 1941. The principal motive for the arrangement was the Army's fear that it would be unable to cope with the unionized crews then operating its ships. (See U.S. Navy, Bureau of Personnel, *Military Sea Transportation and Shipping Control* [Manual 10829-A, 1954], p. 64.)

[66] The Navy responded to commercial attacks on the MSTS by stressing its requirement for a completely reliable, responsive transport arm, immediately available to the military for any mission and free of the labor difficulties which confronted the private industry. For example, see *Military Sea Transport Service*, Hearings before a subcommittee of the Senate Interstate and Foreign Commerce Committee, 83 Cong. 1 sess. (1953), p. 53.

averted by the outbreak of the Korean war in June 1950. Chastened by its experience during the preceding months, the newly organized MSTS determined to meet the Army's rapidly expanding shipping requirements through private charters and general agency agreements in lieu of expanding its own fleet. In 1952 some $475 million (75 percent of the MSTS operating budget) was paid directly to commercial shipping interests. A large percentage of the remainder of the MSTS budget passed indirectly to the industry through the regular Navy procurement activities. "These figures," stated an MSTS report, "go far to account for industry's change of attitude toward the MSTS."[67]

Since the end of the Korean war, the private shipping industry has continued to absorb 75–80 percent of the MSTS budget. By 1964, the MSTS passenger ship complement had been reduced to only 16 ships from 65 vessels in 1954. Its fleet of nucleus dry cargo ships had also been gradually curtailed until it included only 24 oceangoing freighters, mostly engaged in activities such as Arctic and Antarctic supply which are not attractive to commercial operators. Present policy, stated in numerous official documents, is that "the Department of Defense does not try to duplicate the general cargo and POL capabilities in the merchant marine under U.S. control."[68]

Tensions between MSTS and the commercial shipping industry have not, however, been eradicated. In 1960 their uneasy equilibrium was again disturbed by a Defense Department order curtailing military travel on commercial passenger vessels in order to utilize the sixteen MSTS troop ships more efficiently. Its effect was to deny U.S. carriers about 15 percent of their passenger business, and also to place the Department in the embarrassing position of opposing a congressional policy which had been justified entirely on defense grounds.[69] The Department was severely criticized in the Congress; its 1962 appropriation, and that of each subse-

[67] U.S. Navy, *Military Sea Transportation and Shipping Control*, p. 206.

[68] For example, see *Military Posture*, Hearings before the House Committee on Armed Services, 88 Cong. 1 sess. (1963), p. 459. Since the conclusion of the Korean conflict no new conventional dry cargo tonnage has been acquired by MSTS. Twenty new tankers have been constructed for the MSTS fleet under long-term lease agreements and two new "roll on, roll off" carriers acquired.

[69] Only two months before the Defense Department order was issued, the House Appropriations Committee, in its report on the *Department of Defense Appropriation Bill, 1961*, H. Rept. 11998, 86 Cong. 2 sess. (1960), had noted that "major movements of military troops and hardware cannot be accomplished now or in the foreseeable future without basic reliance on sealift capacity" and urged that U.S. flag passenger ships be used by the Department "to the fullest possible extent." The episode noted in the text is fully described in *Refusal of Government Agencies to Support Established National Maritime Policies*, H. Rept. 2205, 86 Cong. 2 sess. (1960).

quent year, made $7.5 million available only for passenger movements via commercial sealift. Nonetheless, Defense was able to secure certain concessions from the carriers before rescinding its controversial order.

Competition Between Conference and Non-conference Lines. Government's entanglement in controversies over its competition with business is an unavoidable consequence of a mixed economy. Its involvement in regulating competition among private U.S. and foreign flag carriers, and in particular between conference and non-conference lines, is a product of several less direct, conflicting objectives.

A federal responsibility to monitor competitive conditions in the international ocean freight industry was first stipulated in the Shipping Act of 1916. This legislation, designed to promote fair competitive practices among carriers as well as shippers in U.S. foreign trade, was framed at a time when there was no significant U.S. flag participation in international shipping. Its prohibitions against fighting ships, deferred rebates, and other anti-competitive practices appear to have been principally geared to protecting American shippers by assuring that the conferences would not be able through unfair tactics to monopolize their trades. Although the 1916 act was concerned chiefly with direct government supervision of conference agreements, it buttressed the Shipping Board's regulatory powers with language aimed at preserving at least the opportunity for non-conference operators to offer competitive services.

The introduction of large numbers of U.S. flag ships into U.S. foreign trade following World War I added yet another dimension to the government's regulatory program. Although the language of the 1916 act (aimed at maintaining fair and equal competitive opportunities for all ocean carriers regardless of flag) remained unchanged, the Merchant Marine Act of 1920 was prefaced by a statement that even in exercising its regulatory functions the Shipping Board should keep the promotion of U.S. flag shipping "always in view . . . as the primary objective to be obtained."[70]

The Shipping Board and its successor agencies have guarded against any overt use of their regulatory powers to advance the position of any one group of carriers, but have usually made no secret of their support for a strong conference system as the most favorable means for developing an American foreign trade fleet. For example, during the 1930's when competitive pressures threatened to destroy the conference system, the board was sympathetic to proposals that it discipline carriers quoting less than the agreed upon rates. Later, it participated with the industry in drawing

[70]41 Stat. 988.

up a National Recovery Act code which required minimum rates in each trade. Opposition from U.S. shippers, supported by the Department of State, prevented the code from being placed in effect.

Following the war, improved business conditions restored the conferences' ability to contain the independent ambitions of their members. As a result, their interest shifted to halting government interference in their own efforts to maintain the integrity of their tariffs and ward off competition by non-conference lines. Postwar regulatory controversies have consequently centered on the propriety of specific competitive tactics and in particular on the use of contracts designed to win the exclusive patronage of important customers.

Use of exclusive patronage (or dual rate) contracts had been contested even before World War II on the grounds that they unfairly discriminated among shippers and were indistinguishable in their effect from deferred rebate contracts specifically barred by the 1916 act.[71] The commission rejected these arguments on the grounds that dual rates were an essential attribute of the conference system and therefore implicitly sanctioned through its approval of conference agreements. The agency's opinions, however, were appealed to the courts. In 1958 the leading case, involving a dual rate contract used to meet Isbrandtsen competition in the Japan-Atlantic trade, was brought before the Supreme Court. The Court found that the specific contract at issue was unjustly discriminatory. However, its decision was interpreted by the conference carriers as invalidating any meaningful exclusive patronage agreement and hence as a challenge to the very basis of the conference system.[72]

The Isbrandtsen decision triggered a major congressional investigation of the conference system and, incidentally, of the relation of promotional to regulatory programs.[73] Legislation to correct deficiencies uncovered by

[71] In its first case involving exclusive patronage contracts (adjudicated in 1922), the Shipping Board had held that contracts conferring preferential rates were discriminatory and in violation of the 1916 act. However, in its second dual rate case, adjudicated in 1933, the board reversed its earlier decision and found dual rates, when used simply as a device to reinforce the conference system, to be a legitimate maritime practice. (These and other cases are summarized in *The Ocean Freight Industry*, H. Rept. 1419, 87 Cong. 2 sess. [1962], pp. 210 ff.)

[72] *Federal Maritime Board v. Isbrandtsen*, 356 U.S. 481 (1958). Justice Brennan, writing for the majority, stated that the Shipping Act barred dual rate systems "only where they are employed as predatory devices." Justice Frankfurter's dissent, however, claimed that the distinction was meaningless, and that the effect of the majority decision was to "outlaw a practice . . . that is employed by at least half of the 100-odd conferences subject to the Board's jurisdiction." The industry adopted Frankfurter's interpretation of the case.

[73] The investigation was conducted by a staff reporting to the Anti-trust Sub-

the Judiciary Committee's anti-trust investigatory group was prepared by the House Merchant Marine and Fisheries Committee. In attempting to devise a bill acceptable to the U.S. maritime industry, the shipping public, and the Judiciary Committee (supported by the Department of Justice), Merchant Marine and Fisheries sanctioned dual rates, but only subject to conditions designed to prevent their abuse.[74] The legislation proposed by the committee and approved by the House also made a number of other important improvements in the regulatory program.[75]

However, the Senate Commerce Committee rejected the key safeguards in this bill. In doing so, the committee made clear that its support for the conference system and unrestricted use of dual rates rested on the conviction that American carriers, even though subsidized, needed the shelter of a strong conference system to survive.[76]

committee of the House Judiciary Committee, chaired by Emanuel Celler. Its report, *The Ocean Freight Industry*, H. Rept. 1419, was the product of over three years' study and provides a comprehensive description of industry competitive practices and regulatory problems. The Celler Committee investigation was supplemented by a general investigation of steamship conference practices, sponsored by the Merchant Marine and Fisheries Committee preliminary to its preparation of a specific legislative proposal. These hearings are published under the title *Steamship Conference Study* (3 vols.), 86 Cong. 1 sess. (1959).

[74] The House bill initially stipulated ten specific clauses which must be written into all dual rate contracts in order to protect shippers (most of these clauses, though somewhat relaxed, were retained by the Senate). However, it also provided that each steamship conference must agree to provide the government with needed information and be legally accessible as a condition to approval of the conference agreement, and that its dual rate contracts not be "intended . . . or be reasonably likely, to cause the exclusion of any other carrier from the trade." These latter two sections were stricken in their entirety by the Senate.

[75] The House bill proposed a general strengthening of the regulatory program—the first since its initiation in the Shipping Act of 1916. In addition to the provisions regulating use of dual rate contracts, the bill prohibited agreements between conferences in naturally competitive trades unless each party reserved the right of independent action; codified the board's administrative policy of requiring conference agreements to allow members to join, rejoin, and withdraw from the conference under reasonable conditions; required conferences to adequately police their activities and maintain reasonable procedures for hearing shipper complaints; instituted a comprehensive tariff filing system and required reasonable notice of proposed rate changes; and stated that the "commission shall disapprove any rate or charge filed by a common carrier by water in the foreign commerce of the United States or conference of carriers, which, after hearing, it finds to be so unreasonably high or low as to be detrimental to the commerce of the United States." These provisions were adopted by the Senate and included in the statute (P.L. 87-346 [75 Stat. 762]).

[76] The House and Senate reports and pertinent floor debate on the dual rate bill are printed in *Index to the Legislative History of P.L. 87-346*, S. Doc. 100, 87 Cong. 2 sess. (1962). Senator Clair Engle, who managed the presentation of the Commerce Committee's bill on the floor, for example, argued that "in an international ocean rate war our American lines, even if subsidized, could not survive for long. This is so

The committee's arguments were strongly challenged by Senator Kefauver in floor debate. To counter its assertion that the conference umbrella was necessary to the survival of American shipping, he introduced evidence to show that a dozen major U.S. flag liner companies operated non-conference in one or more of their services and that the legislation was opposed by certain U.S. operators of foreign flag ships.[77] In answer to the argument that the legislation was needed to protect U.S. subsidized lines, he quoted the chairman of the Federal Maritime Board: "Operating subsidy is intended to enable the American operator to take care of himself in any situation that develops in foreign trade."[78] His principal argument, however, was that the benefits of an "administered price system" would accrue largely to foreign flag lines, while its costs would be borne largely by the American exporter—i.e., that it would be a hidden, but very costly, subsidy to the American flag fleet.[79]

The issue was clearly drawn. The Senate decided in favor of rate stabilization and quasi-monopoly. By a 45 to 33 vote, it rejected Kefauver's efforts to restore the protective language which had been adopted in the House as a check on conference powers. Then the House, despite the fact that two of its committees had spent an aggregate of six years developing a record in support of its position, abandoned its own bill in favor of the Senate version.[80]

The Congress' endorsement of dual rates was evidence of its willingness to shape regulatory policies to promotional objectives. The action reaffirmed the somewhat unusual doctrine of the 1920 act that, even in regulation, the development of the U.S. flag fleet was the principal objec-

---

because operating subsidy does not cover all items of operating costs. . . . And so it is, that our American lines, including all our subsidized lines, have the most to lose if . . . conferences are forced to dissolve." (*Ibid.*, p. 251.)

[77] *Ibid.*, p. 343.

[78] *Ibid.*, p. 353.

[79] *Ibid.*, pp. 343-344. The deleterious effects on American exports likely to result from permitting foreign-dominated conferences to dominate ocean commerce were thoroughly aired during the debate, and much of the material later used by Senator Douglas to dramatize the Federal Maritime Commission's alleged dereliction was inserted in the record by Senator Kefauver during the 1961 debate.

[80] The House Merchant Marine and Fisheries Committee had initally prepared its bill in consultation with the several interested groups and under strong pressure from the Judiciary Committee members and staff to include meaningful curbs against conference powers. However, Chairman Bonner of the Merchant Marine Committee was also under pressure from friends in the industry and from the ranking minority members of his committee to accept legislation along the lines enacted by the Senate. With his own committee split, the Senate position clearly expressed, and Judiciary pressure somewhat relieved, Mr. Bonner apparently did not feel in a position to urge retention of the safeguards adopted by the House.

tive. In effect, it appeared that the government's conference policy was to be treated as an extension of the promotional program.

It was this apparent congressional intent which was initially followed by the new Federal Maritime Commission, established concurrently with the bill's enactment in 1961. However, within two years the assumption that the regulatory program should be conducted for the benefit of one of the regulated parties was successfully attacked by Senator Paul H. Douglas, causing a major reorientation of the commission's operations and the appointment of new personnel to its key positions. Although the commission's investigatory program and decisions have since then more nearly conformed to the original 1916 statute, there remains uncertainty as to its appropriate posture toward the interests of American vis-à-vis foreign carriers.

Impact of Indirect Aids

Subsidy programs, once initiated, appear to create a suction which draws government ever deeper into the affairs of the subsidized industry. In merchant shipping, government has come to exercise a determining role in every major facet of the industry's activity. Government is the industry's major customer; it monitors its competitive practices, supplies its credit, underwrites its costs, trains its officer personnel, develops its technology, arbitrates its labor disputes, is responsible for its safety, and even provides a complete program of free medical care for its workers.

The forces which have led to this enlargement of the government's role have been varied. Clearly, the need for a U.S. merchant fleet in the interests of national defense has been an important incentive to congressional action. However, the need for additional government assistance has been pressed most vigorously by the industry itself—not by the Department of Defense—and government's present entanglement in the industry's affairs may therefore be regarded as principally the product of the industry's own desire.

The proliferation of *indirect* aids to the foreign trade fleet is partially the result of the restricted eligibility for *direct* aids. The operating and construction differential subsidies were *limited* subsidies, meant to support only *minimum* U.S. flag services on essential trade routes. This restrictive interpretation of the 1936 program was incompatible with the inherently *unlimited* character of the industry's postwar defense role.

Restrictions on eligibility for direct subsidies have been supported by those in the program. But whereas the subsidized lines have successfully prevented the extension of direct aids to tramp operators, they have worked with the non-subsidized group in energetically supporting cargo preferences, restrictions on use of government-owned ships, and a strong conference system. In these cases the industry has achieved near unanimity and, despite vigorous opposition, has been able to win additional protection from the Congress.

Enactment of indirect aids has been facilitated by the fact that their costs and impact are concealed. Congressmen who would be reluctant to recommend additional direct subsidy appear to have no difficulty in recommending potentially far more burdensome indirect aids. And legislation instructing administrative agencies to give only such assistance as is "fair and reasonable" is virtually impossible to oppose.

The layering of direct and indirect aids which has resulted has had several unfortunate results. One is the great variance it produces both in the amount of assistance available to competing companies and in the conditions under which aid may be received. Because neither the Congress nor the executive branch has been willing to acknowledge the full extent of the indirect financial aid granted through cargo preference, virtually none of the protective features built into the 1936 act apply to this program. Companies handling preference cargoes are not required to establish reserves for ship replacement and are not limited as to salaries or as to the uses of their profits. They may have collateral interests in foreign flag fleets (several do) or be partially controlled by foreign interests (some are). Others are engaged in substantial non-shipping enterprises. Nearly all have been organized by entrepreneurs who have no continuing commitment to the shipping industry. Yet these companies, which receive significant amounts of indirect subsidy aid, are not even subject to audit by the Maritime Administration.

A second result of the proliferation of indirect aids has been to fragment administration of the program. Only about 40 percent of the total operating aid to U.S. flag ship operators is directly controlled by the Maritime Administration. Other agencies required to contribute to the support of the merchant marine are able to give little attention to this responsibility and in some cases have had little sympathy for the program and inadequate resources to insure its proper execution.[81] In other cases, a mandate to promote U.S. shipping has been essentially incompatible with the agen-

---

[81] Payment of over $75 million in cargo preference subsidies incident to P.L. 83-480, Title I shipments is in effect delegated to foreign nationals employed by the purchasing missions of the recipient nations, subject to Department of Agriculture and General Accounting Office audit. The P.L. 83-480, Title II program, which involves freight charges of about $25 million per year on grains shipped for government account, is handled by three Agriculture Department professionals working through private ship brokers.

cy's primary mission. In every situation, administrative fragmentation has multiplied the difficulty of establishing proper standards and sound objectives for governing subsidy grants.

Third, the rules and conditions of the multiple aid programs have operated to segment the American merchant marine, artificially isolating domestic from foreign trades, liners from tramps, and subsidized from unsubsidized lines and from any foreign flag affiliations. This segmentation has seriously biased the development of American steamship companies, preventing some from diversifying, balancing, or rounding out their services and causing others to resort to foreign registry of their ships. It has also led to factionalism within both maritime management and labor organizations and to dissipation of the energies of the U.S. flag industry on intra-industry disputes.

Fourth, indirect methods of assisting the merchant marine have caused inordinate international and domestic controversy. Preferences to American shipping have hurt American exporters as well as the foreign flags excluded from the business. Efforts to solve U.S. carriers' competitive problems through cargo allocations and other quasi-monopolistic practices have similarly precipitated a host of practical and political problems.

Fifth, indirect aids, once set in motion, are extremely difficult either to control or eliminate. Preferences tend to be met with counter discriminations. The combined measures are likely to so tie up the trade as to compel the national flag lines to relinquish exclusive rights in favor of a pool which will at least balance in and out loadings. The pool in turn reduces competition which requires that the government, now operating in a regulatory role, rule whether the advantage to the national flag lines justifies the risk that the consortium may monopolize the trade and somehow abuse its economic power.

Sixth, none of the direct or indirect aids adopted by the government is directly targeted on the ultimate purpose of the program, maintenance of the necessary marine skills and equipment to prime the nation to meet defense emergencies. The government has instead become immersed in the immediate problems of the industry itself. Its preoccupation with the emergencies of the moment has militated against development of any longer range plans for achieving its more basic objective.

Finally, resort to indirect aids and the new promotional orientation of the direct subsidy program have increased substantially the cost of maintaining the U.S. merchant fleet. The increase in costs reflects a worsening in the basic economic position of U.S. flag shipping and is the subject of the next chapter.

8

Accomplishments of the Promotional Program

THE GOVERNMENT'S MARITIME PROGRAMS have been a center of controversy since their inception. But though they have evoked a storm of criticism, they have proved extraordinarily durable. This chapter, by probing the costs and accomplishments of the government's promotional program, is directed to establishing whether the program has proved durable because it is effective, or whether an ineffective program has been maintained simply because the political system lacked the resilience to change it.

Subsidy Costs

Each of the government's maritime subsidy programs since its first pre-Civil War promotional mail packet contracts has, once initiated, tended to grow both in scope and expense until changed circumstances or public reaction have forced its curtailment.[1] The Merchant Marine Act of 1936 has been no exception. In fact every conventional measure of the direct cost of the 1936 program has shown persistent and pronounced inflation. By 1964 subsidies defrayed roughly half the direct operating expenses of

[1] The history of federal aid to shipping has been meticulously documented by J. E. Saugstad in *Shipping and Shipbuilding Subsidies* (U.S. Department of Commerce, Trade Promotion Series No. 129, 1932). The government's first contract to subsidize a mail packet service was let in 1845 and provided payment of $200,000 per year. Total pre-Civil War payments, spread among six lines, were $14.4 million. Two subsidized mail services were reestablished following the war, but terminated following the Pacific Mail Scandal. A third experiment was initiated in 1891; payments increased from $454,000 to $1.3 million annually by 1906. The fourth mail subsidy program, established by the Merchant Marine Act of 1928, increased from an initial annual cost of $7.6 million to $24.6 million at the time of the program's termination in 1936.

subsidized vessels, ranging from an average of $2.1 million for each of thirty-two passenger and combination liners to $495,000 for each of 285 dry cargo ships—an overall average of almost $658,000 per ship as compared to only $117,000 in 1949.[2] Operating subsidy cost indices for selected years are compared in Table 2.

TABLE 2. *Operating Subsidy Cost Indices*

Item	1938[a]	1949	1956	1964
Net subsidy accrual, after recapture (millions)	$ 3.6	$ 29.7	$106.2	$208.6
Number of ships under subsidy contracts	119	254	305	317
Average subsidy paid per ship (thousands)	$ 30	$117	$348	$658
Average subsidy in constant dollars (thousands)[b]	$ 70	$140	$362	$655
Subsidy as percent of freight and passenger revenues	—[c]	—[c]	18%	27%
Percent of wage costs met through subsidy	40%	61%	72%	71%
Percent of gross subsidy recaptured	70%	33%	17%	1%

Source: Maritime Administration data.
[a] Estimated.
[b] Subsidy payments adjusted for changes in wholesale price index, 1957-59 base.
[c] Not available.

The 15 percent increase annually in per ship subsidy costs between 1949 and 1956 was partially caused by factors outside the industry's control, such as devaluations in foreign currencies and reduction in recapture due to less favorable business conditions. In part it resulted from increases in U.S. wage rates, which during this period substantially outpaced those abroad. In the eight years following 1956, the 7 percent average annual increase in subsidy payments was the result both of lower profits (and recapture) and higher costs across the board.

The pronounced growth in direct operating subsidy is, however, only a portion of the total inflation in the costs of the government's promotional programs. Cargo preference, tax, and other aids have added significantly to the program's direct public expense. Further, both the direct and indirect subsidies have created hidden costs whose magnitude can be only roughly estimated. Finally, tariffs, price supports, price administration,

[2] Forty percent of the subsidized lines' ships in 1964 were of postwar construction and were significantly larger, faster, and more efficient than the war-built ships in use in 1949. If the new vessels were 50 percent more productive than those they replaced, the average productivity would have increased by roughly 20 percent; concurrently the purchasing power of the dollar declined by 25 percent. Adjusting for these two factors and for the fact that the 1964 subsidized fleet includes a higher percentage of passenger vessels it would appear that 1964 subsidies per freighter were about 2.5-3.0 times the 1949 level.

and protection have become common enough in both U.S. and foreign economies to make it necessary to look behind the direct and indirect costs of the government aid program in order to determine the industry's real economic position.

Cargo Preferences. Assessment of the extent and direct governmental costs of indirect aids to shipping presents such a variety of conceptual and factual problems that no official estimates of these costs or the benefits they provide have ever been compiled. The most significant source of indirect aid is through payment of charter and shipping contract rates on government cargoes which are substantially above the world market.

The size of the rate differential can be readily quantified for bulk shipments and vessel charters. A complete accounting of estimated foreign-domestic rate differentials is maintained on certain of the Agriculture Department's programs under Public Law 83-480 (P.L.480), from which reasonably reliable estimates can be calculated for all other bulk shipments.[3] In fiscal year 1963, the total indirect subsidy incident to bulk shipments is estimated to have exceeded $100 million, as compared to roughly $30 million in 1958 and $10 million in 1954. These amounts exclude losses incurred due to a requirement which applied from 1954 through 1964 that the United States pay in dollars for the entire cost of P.L. 480 shipments on U.S. flag ships, subject to reimbursement of their estimated world market cost in foreign currencies, which often were of no value to the United States. (In 1963, dollar outlays for P.L.480 shipments reimbursed with currencies which had been officially declared to be excess to foreseeable U.S. needs totaled almost $50 million.) The practice of accepting nonconvertible currencies to defray the estimated world market cost of P.L.480 shipments was, however, stopped by a 1964 amendment to that legislation.[4]

[3] The contract and partial repayment procedure from which P.L. 480, Titles I and IV foreign-domestic rate differentials are calculated is described in Chapter 7. A differential is estimated by the purchasing mission for each shipment gauged to the particular manner in which the shipment was handled (i.e., by vessel or partial lot, liner versus tramp). These estimates are verified by the Department of Agriculture. For Title II shipments, tonnage, destination and cost of shipments via U.S. flag carriers are recorded, so that the foreign-domestic rate differential can be easily estimated. For Title III barter programs, only tonnage, commodity, and destination data are available, so that the indirect subsidy can at best be only approximated.

[4] P.L. 88-638 (78 Stat. 1035). U.S. shipping companies opposed enactment of this legislation. Together with certain Administration officials, they feared that imposition of a requirement that the U.S. be reimbursed in dollars for the estimated world market cost of shipments via U.S. flag ship would either deter sales or would build up pressure to remove cargo preference or both. These fears appear to have been groundless since surplus grain sales have continued to increase since the new legislation's enactment.

There is no reliable method for calculating the indirect subsidy that results from military shipments. Many persons argue that the rules requiring use of U.S. flag ships in this case do not convey any subsidy at all, since the rules simply confirm what would be militarily necessary anyway. Others note that in wartime, American vessels have frequently been chartered at less cost than foreign flags. In peacetime, however, requiring all military cargoes to be shipped exclusively on U.S. flag ships clearly increases the government's costs and benefits (i.e., subsidizes) the U.S. shipping industry.

Since military cargoes are unique and not open to free international competition, there is no direct way to calculate the amount by which costs are increased by cargo preference rules. Estimates can be made in four ways, each of which is conceptually vulnerable, and can yield only gross approximations. One is to make an item-for-item comparison of individual civil and military rate classifications, adjusted for differences in the way the cargo is handled. A second is to compute the cost to the Military Sea Transport Service (MSTS) of chartering enough foreign flag ships to service its Far East and European routes (to be added to present contract costs of servicing routes on which the volume of military business could not justify shipping in vessel lots). A third method is to compare the average measurement ton revenue received by U.S. flag lines from their military business with the average received from nongovernment sources (adjusted to exclude cargo handling costs) on the same trade route. Finally, there are several U.S. flag liner companies which specialize in MSTS business and carry little commercial cargo; a comparison of their costs with those of typical foreign flags also may suggest a rough measure of the difference in the revenues they must obtain to make a profit. Calculations of sample data by each of these methods indicate that military shipping contract rates in peacetime are somewhere in the order of 40-50 percent above the level which would obtain in open international competition and can therefore be considered to convey an indirect subsidy on the order of $50 million per annum. This amount appears to have remained about constant from 1954 through 1964.

Tax Benefits. A second source of indirect assistance, available only to subsidized operators, is deferment of taxation on deposits to capital and special reserves. During World War II and the Korean conflict this deferment sheltered large amounts from excess profits taxes and substantially contributed to the subsidized companies' financial growth. At present the special rules applicable to reserve fund deposits reduce subsidized operators' current tax payments by about $12 million per year.[5] Since the deferred tax will ultimately be paid when reserve funds are withdrawn or the subsidy contract is discontinued, this is simply a temporary tax reduction. However, the cumulative tax deferment, which now totals in excess of $150 million, does operate as an interest-free loan to the subsidized lines, providing an "interest subsidy" of approximately $9 million per year.

Credit Aids. Government assistance in financing new ship construction provides a third source of indirect subsidy aid to U.S. flag companies. Like tax deferments, the importance of credit aids has diminished over the past decade, but credits granted in past years continue to reduce operators' current costs by roughly $8 million per year. The capitalized value of a $5 million 100 percent 25-year government mortgage guarantee, if assumed to reduce the interest rate by 7 percent, would be $450,000. About $50 million of guarantees are currently issued each year.[6]

Other Indirect Aids. A host of other indirect aids and services are provided to U.S. flag shipping, some of which are subject to quantification and some not. Two fairly important, measurable programs which cost approximately $12 million in 1962, are free medical care for merchant seamen and subsidized training programs for seagoing officer personnel. In most jurisdictions, seamen are also the beneficiaries of a variety of local welfare programs and are eligible to receive unemployment compensation on favorable terms.[7]

Terms of the construction subsidy, research and development, and ves-

[5] The text estimate applies a 52 percent tax rate to the following tax privileged transactions reported by the lines during the five-year 1958-62 period: net deposits to special reserves, $18 million; voluntary deposits to capital reserves, $30 million; estimated interest earned on reserve balances, $47 million; capital gains (at 26 percent tax savings), $41 million. The average annual tax benefit during the first 14-year interval following enactment of the 1936 act was $11.1 million.

[6] Through 1953 the government wrote 3½ percent first mortgage loans on most of the vessels purchased from it under the Ship Sales Act of 1946 or through the construction subsidy program authorized by the 1936 Merchant Marine Act. Outstanding loan balances as of June 30, 1964, were $126 million. Since 1954 government credit assistance has been confined to mortgage guarantees. As of June 30, 1964, $454 million of guarantees were outstanding. To calculate the indirect subsidy granted through credit aids, it was assumed that direct commercial loans would be 2½ percent above the government's interest rates and that government guarantees reduced interest costs by 1 percent.

[7] The particularly favorable terms applicable to seamen's unemployment compensation in the most populous states is probably more a result of the peculiarities of the seaman's conditions of employment than any desire to favor seamen. However, payments to seamen in New York (the one state tested) appear to average three to four times those paid in other industries.

sel trade-in programs also probably permit subsidized firms to obtain better ships at relatively less cost than on the open market. However, construction aids are beyond the scope of this study. These programs are therefore excluded from the summary in Table 3 of estimated government subsidies in support of U.S. vessel operations.

TABLE 3. *Estimated Operating Subsidies to U.S. Vessels in Foreign Trade, 1962*

Item	Total	Subsidized		Non-subsidized		
		Combi-nation[a]	Freight	Liner	Tramp	Tanker[b]
		(millions of dollars)				
Net direct subsidy	$188	$60	$128	....	....	....
Indirect subsidies						
P.L. 480 and other bulk cargo	102	....	10	$10	$62	$20
MSTS shipping contracts	50	—[c]	30	20	....	....
MSTS time and voyage charters	8	....	....	2	6	....
Interest saving through credit aids	8	3	4	....	....	—[c]
Interest saving through tax deferred reserves	9	2	7	....	....	....
Medical care and training	12	3	5	2	2	—[c]
Total	$377	$68	$184	$34	$70	$20
Number of ships	560	30	285	110–130	90–110	20–30
		(thousands of dollars)				
Cost per ship	$675	$2,265	$645	$310	$700	$800

[a] Includes passenger vessels; excludes subsidy conveyed through government passenger patronage.
[b] Reports assistance to tankers carrying dry bulk cargoes.
[c] Less than $1 million.

Distribution of Costs Among Carriers. Data gaps make any distribution of subsidy costs by type of carrier particularly tenuous.[8] The distribution shown in Table 3 is largely based on a qualitative assessment of sample rate and shipment data. The estimated amounts, however, conform to reasonable expectations. The large crews aboard passenger and combination

[8] Since the Agriculture Department keeps no accounting of cargo preference costs by category of carrier, estimates of its contribution to the several segments of the U.S. flag fleet must be based entirely on inspection of tonnage, destination, and rate statistics. AID segregates expenditures for shipments made via liner, tanker, and tramp, but does not maintain a regular account of the differential between U.S. and foreign flag rates.

vessels make them much the most costly to support. Tramps require substantial government aid because the vessels are old, expensive to operate, and earn almost no backhaul revenue. Many tankers engaged in hauling P.L. 480 grains are modern, efficient ships, but are burdened by heavy debt service charges, having all been built without subsidy in U.S. yards.[9] The tankers also earn no backhaul revenues.

The cost per ship to support the subsidized group is almost the same as that for non-subsidized tramps. However, about 30 percent of the direct subsidy to these operators is either returned to the government through taxes or dedicated to future construction projects by deposit to reserves. The subsidized ships are also larger, faster, and more productive than other general cargo freighters. If adjustments are made for these factors, the cost per ship within the subsidized group appears to be competitive even with non-subsidized liners and to be substantially less than that of the relatively inefficient U.S. flag tramps.

Costs to the Economy

The cost data reported thus far represent direct and indirect charges on the government's budgetary accounts. Such data provide a convenient reference to the approximate burden (or cost) which shipping subsidies place on the public sector. However, they are inadequate guides to the burden which the program imposes on the economy as a whole.

Considerable attention has been given by economists to the sundry economic effects and values of the maritime subsidy program. Various induced costs have been identified, and qualitative analyses made of the effects of subsidies on resource allocations, operating efficiency, and prices.[10] Other studies have analyzed the economic benefits of subsidy.[11] A

---

[9] Rates charged by U.S. flag tankers appear often to be substantially lower than those charged by American tramps for comparable services. In some cases tankers have secured rates equal to tramp rates. The lack of any clear pattern and the variability in types and number of ships participating in the trade make estimates of indirect subsidies to tankers particularly vulnerable.

[10] Induced costs are comprehensively treated by Allen Ferguson *et al.*, *The Economic Value of the U.S. Merchant Marine* (Northwestern University, The Transportation Center, 1961). The most comprehensive economic analysis of the effects of shipping conferences on ocean shipping rates and operating practices is Daniel Marx, *International Shipping Cartels* (Princeton University Press, 1953). For an interesting theoretical analysis of the economic effects of shipping subsidies, see also F. Evershiem, *Effects of Shipping Subsidization* (Bremen, 1958).

[11] The classic study of the merchant marine's economic value is the 1937 Maritime Commission report, *Economic Survey of the American Merchant Marine*. Two recent

third group of investigations, potentially relevant to analysis of subsidy costs, is concerned with disparities between the prices of goods produced for domestic consumption and of goods placed in international trade.

Costs Created by the Subsidy Program. All subsidies, because designed to divert economic activity from its natural state, create certain costs, or diseconomies, which provide no benefit to either the donor or the beneficiary of the subsidy grant. The most obvious example is administrative overhead—a cost which for the maritime subsidy program runs about $15 million annually to the government and industry combined.[12] Other induced costs are both more significant and more controversial, for they have developed as unwanted and indirect side-effects of the subsidy program.

The subsidy's impact on maritime collective bargaining provides an example. Neither the unusually sharp increase in maritime wage rates nor the frequency and duration of the industry's strikes can be directly and unequivocally linked to the subsidy program; yet there is ample evidence that availability of subsidies has disrupted normal processes of collective bargaining. This has added to the inflationary forces in the industry, escalating wages in the subsidized sector to a level estimated in Chapter 6 to be 6-10 percent above those of non-subsidized lines and an undetermined amount above what might have prevailed in the absence of subsidy. In Chapter 6 certain economic penalties were also found to be associated with the essential trade route system, but it was impossible to estimate their magnitude.

Two features of the operating subsidy program which tend to distort management decisions and create diseconomies are: (1) the practice of gearing the amount of aid to the disparity between foreign and domestic costs, and (2) the uneven application of subsidies to wages, capital, and other expenses. Their effect is to suppress characteristics of U.S. economic

---

studies of the economic value of the U.S. merchant marine are the Northwestern University study (Allen Ferguson *et al., op. cit.*) and a monograph prepared by the Committee of American Steamship Lines, *The Economic Contributions of the American Merchant Marine* (mimeograph, 1963), designed as a rebuttal to the Northwestern study. The premise of each of these analyses is that the subsidy is indeed a cost to the economy. The opposite conclusions which they reach are therefore for the most part the product of basically different evaluations of the "worth" of a U.S. flag fleet rather than of different economic methodology or data.

[12] Subsidy administration costs to the Department of Commerce total $9.5 million; costs to other government agencies of administering cargo preference and other indirect subsidies are estimated at $2 million. Costs to the industry of winning and accounting for subsidy aid appear to run from $2 to $5 million.

strength (i.e., superior service, high capital investment in labor-saving equipment and procedures, and a high degree of skill and technological sophistication) in favor of European modes of operation.[13] The system offers little reward for technological innovation, for any savings achieved by reduced manning are realized by the government, which pays 100 percent of the incremental wage costs of U.S. citizen crews. In fact, because of differences in calculating construction and operating subsidies, an operator who constructs a more expensive ship in order to achieve wage savings is actually penalized.[14]

Subsidies affect ship design and operations in a number of other less dramatic, but nevertheless important, ways. For example, the fact that wages are subsidized but fuel is not should cause subsidized U.S. operators to make more port calls and operate at lower speeds than would otherwise be the case (actually government pressure for higher speeds and express services has offset these economic biases).[15] However, research and development work has concentrated on improving the efficiency of propulsion machinery to reduce fuel costs rather than on the potentially more rewarding but contentious field of automation. Several marine architects, concerned by the increasing cost of U.S. merchant ship designs, have called attention to the subsidy system's premium on low maintenance costs and the resulting tendency of subsidized companies to specify unduly high quality material in initial construction.[16] Ships may also have

[13] This point of view was first publicized by a National Academy of Sciences panel which had been requested by the government to develop recommendations for a maritime research and development program. (See National Academy of Sciences-National Research Council, *Proposed Program for Maritime Administration Research,* Vol. 1 [Washington, 1960].) More recently, the theme has been taken up by the Northwestern study (Ferguson *et al., op. cit.*), in the 1963 report of the Secretary of Commerce's Maritime Evaluation Committee, and in various assessments of ship automation and related issues performed by the Arthur D. Little and Norton companies under contract to the Maritime Administration.

[14] Construction subsidies are based on the estimated difference in the U.S. and foreign cost of building a ship to U.S. design. Operators are therefore required to pay the estimated foreign cost of equipment installed to reduce manning, even though wage savings accrue entirely to the government.

[15] The Northwestern University study includes an elaborate estimate of the impact on costs of the 18- and 20-knot speeds required by the Maritime Administration in ships constructed with subsidy aid. Its conclusion is that the speeds slightly exceed the economic optimum and would create an economic cost of roughly $18 million annually if maintained in all subsidized services (Ferguson *et al., op. cit.,* p. 179).

[16] Many detailed examples of uneconomic overspecification have been alleged in papers dealing with this problem. See Paul E. Atkinson, "Shipbuilding Costs as Seen by the Shipbuilder," paper presented to the New York section of the Society of Naval Architects and Marine Engineers (SNAME) in 1961, J. J. Henry, "Shipbuilding Costs, American and Foreign," *Marine News* (April 1960), pp. 16 ff., and George

been built to more different designs, in smaller lots, and in more yards than would have been the case in an unsubsidized industry.[17]

The maritime industry's subsidized environment also affects the quality of its management. Concern has been expressed since the beginning of the subsidy program that it would divert shipping management from operating ships to "operating on the government." This concern seems to have heightened in recent years. Even counsel to the usually sympathetic Merchant Marine and Fisheries Committee has publicly noted "an attitude among the subsidized lines that they enjoy an exclusive and preferred status—that 'Uncle' can be depended upon to solve all their problems—and on their terms."[18] Paul Hall, President of the Seafarers International Union, goes further and charges that the effect of the subsidy has been to "literally rob this industry of 100 percent competent management."[19]

Hall's charge can be neither refuted nor substantiated. Nonetheless, it expresses a widely held opinion. Traditionalism permeates the industry, both in the United States and abroad. The roots for this conservatism lie in the character of the industry itself—its complexity, international involvement, and instability. Its fruits, however, tend to become identified with the subsidy system, which provides little or no reward for labor-saving innovations and substantially reduces opportunities for management discretion. Furthermore, an important portion of the time and energies of the top management of the subsidized companies necessarily is diverted from running the business to getting, protecting, and accounting for government aid.[20]

Costs Created by Preferential Policies. Even more difficult to assess are the induced costs which the government's cargo preference, pooling, and

---

Kurfehs, "The Cost of Ships," paper presented to the New York section of SNAME. The Maritime Administration has also concerned itself with this subject.

[17] See U.S. Maritime Administration, *Reduction of Construction Costs in Government Subsidized Ships* (mimeograph, May 1961).

[18] Remarks of John H. Drewry, Chief Counsel, Committee on Merchant Marine and Fisheries, at Panel Session on Maritime Legislation at the National Convention of the Propeller Club of the United States, Jacksonville, Fla., Oct. 11, 1961.

[19] *Maritime Labor Legislation,* Hearings before the House Merchant Marine and Fisheries Committee, 88 Cong. 1 sess. (1963), p. 497.

[20] An extremely interesting report on the operating problems of one subsidized line—the Moore-McCormack Lines, Inc.—and management's response to them is contained in a case study prepared under the direction of Dr. John R. Yeager for use in the Harvard Business School Advanced Management curriculum. The case study is limited to factual materials and interviews.

conference policies may have imposed upon the economy. Yet it is clear that such costs are present, perhaps in significant amounts. For example, a readily demonstrable result of cargo preferences is restriction of the free movement of trade. The U.S. cargo preference system, which is heavily biased to outbound shipments, has accentuated the imbalance between inbound and outbound business on U.S. carriers and may thereby have contributed to the disparity in inbound and outbound liner rates.

Bilateral agreements and national flag pools overcome some of the inefficiencies of unilateral cargo preferences, but create other costs in their stead. Where pooling creates monopolies, it permits higher rate structures than could otherwise be maintained. Pooling arrangements which have been used to meet foreign discrimination have sometimes been disadvantageous to American carriers. For example, the revenue apportionment formula used by the Grace-Chilean Pool caused Grace to pay over $6 million of its freight revenues to its Chilean partner between 1950 and 1960 inclusive.

The stabilizing influence of the conference system permits liner companies to plan their operations with greater confidence and thus to achieve certain economies which might not otherwise be available. The diminished competition which is necessary to a successful conference also permits rates to be held at a level which protects its relatively inefficient members while rewarding its front-runners. Many economists believe that the promise of profit from administered rates draws excess tonnage into conferences and leads to inefficient utilization of the conference's ships. To the extent that the U.S. government, in promoting the interests of U.S. flag carriers, has strengthened the conferences' quasi-monopoly position, it also has reinforced their tendency to overtonnage and thus created an avoidable cost to the U.S. economy.[21]

Prices and Costs in International and Domestic Trade. The induced costs created by subsidies to U.S. foreign trade shipping are for the most part tolerated in domestic deep water trade. This can be regarded as imposing a further economic burden upon the economy. Conversely the fact that these costs are marginally tolerated even where there are competing modes of land transportation may indicate that the cost structure of the U.S. foreign trade merchant marine is not atypical of the domestic economy as a whole.

It is generally agreed that the prices of goods moving in international

[21] The relationship between conference cohesiveness, costs, rates, and efficiency is developed by Marx, *op. cit.*, in Chap. 12, "The Economics of Shipping Conferences."

trade are lower than prices of goods produced for domestic consumption. A 1963 study by Robert Lipsey finds the differential to have averaged about 37 percent of the lower, export price between 1955 and 1960.[22] Other studies have found differences between domestic U.S. product prices and their production or selling prices abroad to have been on the order of 30–35 percent during the mid-fifties.[23] These differentials create obstacles for U.S. exporting industries which in a significant number of cases are overcome only because of special circumstances or with U.S. government aid.[24]

The differential between U.S. domestic and international prices is the product of an indistinguishable mixture of natural and artificial factors. It is impossible to quantify an average subsidy granted U.S. export firms which can be compared with the assistance granted the U.S. merchant marine. However, it is clear that shipping subsidies are not the only deviation from a pure economy and hence not wholly to be condemned.

Shipping differs from other U.S. export industries in many respects. Clearly, it is no longer an enterprise in which America, because of its particular resources, technology, or skills, uniquely excels. However, the foreign trade merchant fleet is the only important segment of U.S. industry which sells virtually its entire product in the international market, and

[22] Robert E. Lipsey, *Price and Quantity Trends in the Foreign Trade of the United States* (Princeton University Press, 1963), pp. 32 ff.

[23] Leading studies of U.S. and foreign price and productivity differentials are Milton Gilbert and associates, *Comparative National Products and Price Levels* (Paris: Organization for European Economic Cooperation [OEEC], 1958); National Industrial Conference Board (NICB), *Costs and Competition: American Experience Abroad* (New York, 1961); and D. Paige and G. Bombach, *A Comparison of National Output and Productivity of the United Kingdom and the United States* (Paris: OEEC, 1959). Subject to many limitations and stipulations, the Gilbert and Paige studies identified about a 30–35 percent differential using 1950 and 1955 data. The NICB study of production costs in manufacturing plants operated by U.S. corporations at home and abroad found U.S. costs to be equal to or lower than costs in most Asian, South American, or African nations but substantially higher than costs in the Common Market and England—the countries which offer the principal competition to the U.S. merchant marine.

[24] Of $20.6 billion of 1962 merchandise exports, about $2.7 billion was financed through military and economic assistance grants; loans and credits (gross) were issued covering sale of $3.2 billion (including P.L. 480 sales); approximately $2.5 billion was realized from private sales of subsidized agricultural products; and probably an additional $2-$4 billion for items for which the U.S. is sole source (such as replacement parts) or whose distribution is controlled by internationally integrated producers (e.g., oil and chemicals). For a large share of total U.S. exports, production costs are therefore a secondary factor in the U.S. competitive position. In some other cases, the exporting firm arranges export sales at prices substantially below prevailing domestic prices (e.g., drug sales in South America).

under a price system which makes it difficult for American operators to secure higher rates for superior services. Furthermore, the steamship business presents an unusually fluid market. Not even the best established company can ever safely consider its customers to be its "captives." Therefore, in contrast to most exporting industries, a competitive merchant marine must be able to sell its services at all times at prices at or below the world price, and to maintain production costs at a level which permits a profit to be made on this business.[25]

The U.S. maritime industry's present dependence on government aid results from factors both external and internal to the industry. The studies of domestic and international price differentials provide a rough measure for determining the portion of the subsidy attributable to the industry's unique economic environment. If an overall differential of 25 percent is posited, the burden which the generally higher price level imposes on subsidized shipping companies would approximate $120–$130 million, or about half the direct and indirect costs of the subsidy program reflected in the government's accounts.[26] The remaining cost of government aid can be taken to be the result of the subsidy program's various induced costs and of factors within the industry itself.

The subsidy's long-term tendency to create costs contradicts the hopeful expectations of those who devised the subsidy program. Rather than restoring the industry's economic viability, the subsidy has further undermined its position. The effect of the program, as the National Academy of Sciences committee described it, has been "to hide the symptoms while allowing further deterioration of the basic difficulty."[27] This is a high price to pay.

Achievements of the Promotional Program

Because the objectives of the government's programs to promote the U.S. merchant marine have never been clearly articulated, there is considerable disagreement over their achievements. A few of the industry's ad-

[25] An adequately financed merchant shipping company having a long-term stake in the business may, of course, choose to set rates at a level which creates short-term losses in expectation of a long-term gain, just as any other enterprise. However, in contrast to most manufacturing concerns, a shipping company cannot support its export "price leaders" from profits secured through a continuing domestic trade.

[26] The 1962 operating expenses of the subsidized lines were roughly $500 million, excluding costs incurred for longshore and port services, fuel, brokerage, and agency fees—all of which are substantially unaffected by the flag affiliation of the carrier. The percentage cited in the text is applied to this net cost figure.

[27] National Academy of Sciences-National Research Council, *op. cit.*, Vol. 1, p. 34.

vocates argue bravely that the operating differential subsidy system, at least, has been a resounding success, and that America's subsidized liner firms meet the high expectations of those who established and have since supported the 1936 program.[28] Most industry personnel, however, qualify their evaluations. Spokesmen for the industry's non-subsidized sector describe the 1936 program as completely inadequate; they are candid enough to acknowledge that cargo preferences, though providing their bread and butter, have failed to develop an efficient U.S. flag tramp industry.[29]

Analysis of the program's achievements requires examination of its effectiveness as an instrument for supporting an efficient, enterprising, and expanding private industry and for meeting specific defense and other national needs. There is, to be sure, considerable overlap between the subsidy program's immediate industry-oriented objectives and its broader national purposes. However, there are also sufficient inconsistencies between industry and national objectives to merit their separate treatment.

Strength of Postwar Fleet. Superficially there are striking analogies between the position of America's merchant fleet in 1963, eighteen years after the victory over Japan, and in 1936, eighteen years after the World War I armistice. Both wars required the United States to build up the world's largest merchant marine. Following both, the tonnage of the active fleet dropped to about half its postwar peak, the amount of new construction was modest, the fleet became relatively aged, and the contraction created a widespread impression of failure. In both 1936 and 1963, U.S. registries represented roughly the same share of the world's merchant tonnage (about 13 percent in 1936, 10 percent in 1963), excluding the U.S. reserve fleet and the quasi-stateless tonnage under flags of convenience.

However, closer examination shows America's 1963 maritime position in several respects to have improved significantly over 1936. For example, the U.S. flag share of the world's dry cargo tonnage in foreign trade (excluding the reserve and convenience flags) almost doubled during this period.[30] The gross tonnage of U.S. combination and dry cargo shipping is

---

[28] E.g., see Frank A. Nemec, "Our Four Merchant Marines—Challenge of the Sixties," a speech delivered March 12, 1964, before the Federal Government Accounts Association and distributed by the Committee of American Steamship Lines. The argument adopted by Nemec in this speech has since been elaborated in a series of publications by the Committee of American Steamship Lines.

[29] E.g., see Statement of Marvin J. Coles, counsel for the Tramp Shipowners Association, in H. C. Reese (ed.), *Merchant Marine Policy* (Cambridge, Maryland: Cornell Maritime Press, 1963), pp. 47 ff.

[30] Data are not available on employment of foreign flag vessels, so that the U.S.

now surpassed by only one other nation (Great Britain) and closely rivaled by only three (Japan, Greece, and Norway). If the U.S. effective control and reserve merchant ships are included, the United States outstrips even Great Britain by a substantial margin and can claim the world's largest tonnage in the tank ship as well as dry cargo and passenger categories.

Furthermore, the foreign trade dry cargo fleet now being operated under U.S. flag is substantially larger than the fleet which the Maritime Commission anticipated in 1945 could be supported by our postwar export-import commerce.[31] It handles roughly 30–35 percent of the non-bulk cargoes (including military cargoes) shipped in or out of the U.S., despite its meager participation in bulk movements (only 6 percent in 1963), and receives an estimated 30 percent of all freight revenues earned moving dry cargoes (including bulk) in the U.S. foreign trade.[32] Although on the basis of cargo tonnage U.S. liners have lost ground as compared to 1936, the U.S. share of freight revenues (because of new military business) is substantially higher than before the war.

Since World War II the United States' dominance in merchant shipping has been slowly eroded—at first intentionally in order to build up the economies of friendly foreign nations and more recently as a result of both industry's and government's reluctance to expand costly subsidy pro-

---

share of total tonnage engaged in foreign trade cannot be calculated with precision. The assumption used is that 10 percent of foreign dry cargo shipping, excluding PANLIBHON registries, was employed in domestic coastal commerce both in 1936 and 1963. This compares with a U.S. ratio of 55–60 percent in the 1930's and 15 percent in 1963, but there is of course no other nation which even approaches the United States' opportunities for coastal, intercoastal, and non-contiguous domestic trades.

[31] Estimates of the size fleet which could reasonably be supported following the war were prepared by the Maritime Commission, the Commerce Department, the Harvard Business School, and various industry groups. These estimates all projected a total fleet of 850-1,300 vessels and approximately 8.5 to 13 million deadweight tons, but anticipated that only about 5 to 6 million tons could be profitably employed in overseas commerce. The present foreign trade fleet is 7.3 million tons; the total active U.S. commercial fleet totaled 13.8 million tons as of March 30, 1963.

[32] This apparent contradiction results from the fact that U.S. flag carriers not only carry a higher proportion of packaged versus bulk cargoes than their foreign competitors but also obtain more valuable cargoes billed at higher rates. Thus the Committee of American Steamship Lines in its report, *Progress of the U.S. Liner Fleet under the Merchant Marine Act, 1936* (December 1964), estimates that the $45 average revenue per weight ton earned by U.S. flag liners was 50 percent above the average earned by their competitors. Data compiled by the Commerce Department's Office of Business Economics shows total U.S. flag dry cargo freight revenues to have increased from $121 million in 1938 to over $700 million in 1962. Adding the roughly $200 million paid U.S. operators by MSTS, their share of total revenues from dry cargo shipping services appears to have risen from 26 to over 30 percent during this period. (See *Survey of Current Business*, Vol. 43, No. 8, August 1963, p. 23 for additional data.)

grams. Since the mid-fifties, however, U.S. flag companies have maintained their share of the slowly growing overseas liner trades. This has been accomplished chiefly by the introduction of larger and more efficient vessels, rather than through an increase in the number of U.S. liners.[33] In the non-liner dry cargo trades the capacity of a roughly constant number of tramp ships has also been significantly increased since 1955 by "jumboizing" war-built hulls but not at a rate equal to the rapid expansion of vessel-lot shipments in U.S. foreign trade.[34]

Since the conclusion of the Korean conflict there has been continued attrition in domestic dry cargo and tanker trades. Over 160 ships were retired from these services (about one-third the 1955 total) during the eight-year span from 1955 through 1963. However, the sixty-odd tankers built during this period (including twenty-three ships built under the post-Suez "trade out and build" program and now being used principally in overseas trade) have offset most of the tonnage lost to the U.S. domestic fleet. On an overall basis, between 1955 and 1963 the *number* of privately owned merchant vessels shrunk by 100. The fleet's gross tonnage increased 10 percent. World merchant tonnage during the same period increased 41 percent.

Financial Position of U.S. Lines. The postwar erosion in the position of U.S. flag shipping cannot be attributed to a lack of capital within the industry, although financial resources have been unevenly distributed. Earnings have also been unevenly distributed and somewhat unstable from year to year. However, even where profits have been relatively generous (i.e., in the subsidized sector), they have failed to attract new equity investment into the industry or to provide a springboard for substantial expansion.

Net Worth of Subsidized and Non-subsidized Lines. Restoration of a

---

[33] Dry cargo liners constructed in the 1950's and 1960's have averaged about 25 percent faster and 25 percent greater cargo capacity than the ships they have replaced. Cargo handling equipment has also been improved to reduce turnaround time commensurately. The introduction of some 115 of these improved vessels into the U.S. flag foreign trade liner fleet between 1955 and 1965 has increased its capacity by 15–20 percent. During the same period, dry cargoes carried by liners have increased 10–15 percent.

[34] The tramp fleet has been upgraded both by jumboizing warbuilt dry cargo ships and by converting jumboized T2 tankers to dry cargo use. During the 1955-65 period, about 40 percent of the ships engaged in tramp operations were jumboized and/or converted, increasing their cargo capacity by 138,000 deadweight tons or 10 percent (net of attrition from the fleet). During the same period, dry cargoes carried by tramps have increased by more than 50 percent.

sound financial base for the U.S. maritime industry was one of the chief objectives of the Maritime Commission's prewar program. During the war the financial problems which had dogged U.S. shipping throughout the Depression disappeared. As of December 31, 1944, the net worth of all U.S. dry cargo shipping companies was estimated by the Maritime Commission's Postwar Planning Committee to be $587 million—more than double the $273 million figure estimated for 1939—and to include liquid assets of some $366 million.

All segments of the industry profited from the war, but the subsidized lines most strikingly. Due to its favorable tax position and highly leveraged capital structure, this group was able to multiply its 1937 net worth by five between 1937 and 1946; non-subsidized operators only doubled their equity. Whereas before the war the subsidized operators had commanded slightly less wealth than the remaining U.S. flag operators in foreign trade, after the war they enjoyed a margin of roughly three to one. In fact, the assets of the subsidized lines in 1948 probably exceeded the total available to all other U.S. flag dry cargo shipping.

Since 1948 the margin between the "haves" and "have-nots" of the industry has widened. The net worth of the subsidized companies has again more than doubled. The assets of the remainder of the dry cargo sector of the industry in contrast have probably declined.[35] The number of freighters enrolled in the subsidy program, however, has increased only slightly, from 250 in 1948 to 287 in 1963. During the same period, non-subsidized companies have suffered a net loss of roughly 250 ships through transfers, scrapping, and loss at sea. From 1949 through 1963 inclusive a few less than 30 non-subsidized ships were purchased by subsidized operators and thus brought within the subsidy program; a few more than 30 have been directly qualified for government aid.

Earnings of Subsidized and Non-subsidized Lines. The shift in the financial strength of the subsidized group mirrors a substantial and apparently growing disparity in their earning power. From 1946 through the midpoint of the Korean war (1952) subsidized operators earned (after recapture and taxes) an average of 12.6 percent on net worth; non-subsidized lines reporting to the Maritime Administration earned 6 percent. During

[35] Complete financial reports are available to and published in summary form by the Maritime Administration for only 29 of the 122 separate corporate entities which own dry cargo vessels not covered by the subsidy program. From an extrapolation of this information and knowledge of the vessel types owned by the remaining companies, it would appear that the net worth of the non-subsidized component of the fleet might be in the range of $180-$220 million. See Appendix A, Tables A11 and A12 for financial data pertaining to both subsidized and non-subsidized lines.

the next five years, earnings for both groups were lower but still reasonably adequate. However, the 1958 break in the shipping market plunged most non-subsidized lines into a loss position, while the subsidized group, although also seriously affected, continued to show some return on net worth, averaging 4.6 percent (after recapture and taxes) from 1958 through 1962 inclusive.

The current financial position of U.S. flag vessels operating outside the direct subsidy program cannot be assessed with any confidence. Public reports are filed only by carriers holding government-financed ship mortgages or operating in a regulated domestic trade. On the highly volatile and speculative tramp industry, there is no reliable or comprehensive information available. Although the tramp group claims heavy losses on a current income and expense basis, the frequent transfers in corporate ownership of their ships suggest that the business has been geared to maximizing tax-free cash flow from depreciation and to taking capital gains on ship sales.[36]

Profit data pertaining to the subsidized lines is also affected by factors unique to their operation. For example, taxes paid by subsidized steamship companies have averaged only 25 percent of pre-tax profit over the past few years, as compared to 46 percent for other corporations. Second, the subsidized firms' large statutory reserves, invested largely in government bonds, have significantly reduced these companies' return on invested capital, while also reducing investment risks. Thus, the 1958-62 rate of return from subsidized vessel operations, if one excludes reserve fund investments and the income derived thereon, was 33 percent above the 4.6 percent figure previously cited, or 6.1 percent. This is also the approximate profit calculated by the Maritime Administration to have been returned on the subsidized industry's "capital necessarily employed"—a base roughly analogous to the "rate base" used to calculate profits in other regulated industries.[37]

[36] In order to limit liability, independent shipowners have often organized separate corporations for each ship. As of Oct. 31, 1962, 130 ships were owned by 79 companies classified by the Maritime Administration as irregular or tramp operators (about 30 ships owned by this group chartered to MSTS or liner operators not considered part of the tramp fleet). The extent to which the ownership and control of these companies interlock is not fully known. Ownership and corporate organization in tramping are also extremely fluid. Less than half of the 79 companies identified by Marad had been in business over three years. (See U.S. Maritime Administration, "A Statistical Analysis of Tramp Ships Operating Under U.S. Flag" [multilith, Jan. 1963].)

[37] Capital necessarily employed (c.n.e.) is intended to embrace all of the owner's equity which is required for the production of income through subsidized ship operations. It includes the unencumbered valuation of ships and other assets, necessary

A "proper" rate of return for the steamship industry which takes into consideration the risks involved, opportunity for capital gains, debt versus equity capital, and the like, has never been determined. The industry continues to pass through widely fluctuating cycles, and individual companies have in a number of instances performed erratically. Among tramp companies, bankruptcies have been fairly frequent, although their real effect is hard to determine. Only one subsidized firm, operating one ship, has failed. The subsidy program was of course aimed at diminishing the industry's feast-and-famine characteristics and in this has been successful—perhaps to the point of unduly sheltering its participants from the stimulus of risk.

Earnings of U.S. Versus Foreign Flags. The financial success of the subsidized segment of the U.S. merchant marine appears to be confirmed by comparison of its earnings with the earnings of a representative sample of its foreign flag competitors.[38] Such comparisons are at best hazardous, and in the absence of complete disclosure may be misleading. Generally, European lines have newer, and therefore more costly, equipment which is also amortized more rapidly than is American practice. Different accounting practices are employed, and the incidence of taxation varies. Differing results are also obtained depending on the measure which is applied.

The measures least affected by differing capital structures and accounting techniques are cash flow and dividend distributions achieved per ship. For the period 1958-61 inclusive, the fifteen U.S. subsidized lines reported an average net cash flow (after subsidy, recapture, interest, and taxes, but excluding depreciation) of $79.6 million annually or $230,000 per ship per year. After-tax earnings were $125,000 per ship, and dividends $50,000 per ship. During the same period, eight major European

---

working capital, depreciation paid into the capital reserve, and special reserve deposits up to 5 percent of previously computed c.n.e. The rate of return on c.n.e. is calculated annually by the Maritime Administration in order to estimate the amount of the subsidy accrual which is likely to be recaptured. This recapture calculation is confined to subsidized operations. It includes income derived from investment of the portion of the reserves included in c.n.e., but excludes capital gains along with profits from any non-subsidized activities of the subsidy contractor.

[38] Comparative data on U.S. subsidized companies and eight major foreign lines, abstracted from *Moody's Industrials,* are summarized in Appendix A, Table A14. So far as is known, no studies of comparative earnings of U.S. and foreign flag lines have ever been attempted by any U.S. agency. The Europeans through the Maritime Transport Committee of the Organization for Economic Cooperation and Development have, however, given a great deal of attention to the problem. These studies have not been published or exposed to challenge by the U.S. companies.

lines reported in *Moody's Industrials* and owning 780 vessels averaged cash flow of only $127,000, earnings of $21,000, and dividends of $13,400 per ship.

The more generous return achieved by the U.S. flag lines is, of course, completely dependent upon subsidy aid. Stripped of subsidies, the fifteen subsidized companies would show substantial losses even if their ships were donated. But with this aid, and backed by substantial reserves, their competitive position and their capacity therefore to withstand rate wars or develop new trades appear to be very strong indeed.

New Capital Investment. Despite the excellent results achieved by subsidized shipping, the subsidy program has attracted virtually no new equity capital from outside sources since the end of World War II.[39] This apparent paradox springs from several related sources. The industry's inflating costs have caused subsidy expenditure to increase so rapidly that both the government and subsidized industry hesitate to increase outlays still further by adding to the subsidized fleet. On the other hand, the 1936 act was structured to encourage accumulation of capital reserves. The generous earnings during and immediately after the war were voluntarily deposited in reserve funds where tax deferments were allowed; these funds now dramatically exceed the industry's investment opportunities. In fact, reserve funds were calculated in 1961 by the Maritime Administration (using a very conservative procedure) to be some $300 million more than needed to meet contractual ship replacement commitments.[40]

Solicitation of new private capital is further discouraged by the industry's poor investment status. Most companies are very closely held. Shares of only six of the fifteen subsidized companies are traded on public exchanges. Furthermore, all six are traded at substantial discounts from book value, and at price-earnings ratios which have historically stood at about half the New York Stock Exchange average. In 1958 American Export actually hit a low at which it could be purchased at less than twice the year's after-tax earnings. Under such conditions it would of course be foolhardy to attempt a public subscription.

In contrast to the subsidized companies, non-subsidized shipping has attracted a significant amount of risk capital, much of it frankly specula-

[39] From 1936 through 1962 subscriptions of capital stock brought a total of only $16 million of new equity capital into subsidized companies, excluding $12 million of stock issued in exchange for vessels. All but $4 million of the cash subscriptions occurred prior to World War II. (Data from Maritime Administration records.)

[40] See Joseph Klausner, "Prepared Statement," in *Discriminatory Ocean Freight Rates,* Hearings before the Joint Economic Committee, 88 Cong. 1 sess. (1963), p. 267. Data are as of Dec. 31, 1961.

tive. Nonetheless, it is ironic that this sector of the industry should have attracted more investor attention than the companies participating in a program intended, among other things, to enhance their investment status.

Physical Plant. The physical condition of the American merchant marine reflects the uneven effects of the government's promotional program. A strong financial position coupled with construction subsidies and mortgage guarantees has permitted the subsidized companies to acquire some of the world's finest dry cargo liners and to undertake a systematic program for replacement of their fleets. In contrast, there is no program at all for replacement of the war-built freighters operated outside the subsidy program and no likelihood within the framework of the present subsidy program that one can be arranged. Since World War II only five new dry cargo vessels have been built for non-subsidized service (four to provide experimental roll-on and container services in the domestic trade and one to haul P.L. 480 cargoes under contract to the Israeli government). Furthermore, two of these ships, plus two expensively converted passenger vessels designed for use in the domestic trades, proved economically infeasible and were taken as collateral by the government.

The dismal position of the non-subsidized companies is in part their own fault, for most of them supported enactment of the 1961 legislation barring foreign-built ships from cargo preferences until documented for three years under U.S. flag. The effect has been to cut off completely imports of foreign-built ships. Under the circumstances, non-subsidized firms in foreign trade must either break the precedent barring them from construction subsidies, restore their access to foreign yards, or phase out their operations when it is no longer possible to make do with their own aging equipment or war-built ships no longer wanted by the government or by the subsidized fleet.[41]

In contrast to the position of the non-subsidized, foreign trade dry cargo companies, the equipment situation and outlook for all other groups is relatively good. Forty-three percent of the ships operated by subsidized companies as of December 31, 1964, had been constructed since World War II. American oil companies and other tanker operators had replaced approximately half their war-built tonnage with modern ships. Even the domestic dry cargo carriers had introduced about a dozen new or exten-

---

[41] Ship exchange legislation, authorizing vessels to be traded out of the reserve fleet, was enacted in 1960 (74 Stat. 312). Although there is no legal bar to subsidized operators selling ships directly to non-subsidized operators, the practice has been to sell to the government, which resells to the non-subsidized company, usually at a small loss.

sively renovated vessels into their fleets, which in total comprise less than 100 vessels, and had shown a lively interest in capitalizing further on opportunities for technical innovation.

Although the subsidized companies' replacement programs now are well underway, they were slow to get started and have been extended to the point that some war-built ships will be retained until 1975. The delays were caused partly by the operators' reluctance to commit themselves to new construction until they had exhausted their war-built vessels' economic life, partly by indecision regarding the financial terms under which the program would be undertaken, and partly by delays in construction subsidy appropriations. The operators were also slow fully to appreciate the potentialities of new marine technology. However, the higher speeds and improved cargo handling and other equipment pioneered by the goverment in its Mariner program have now been enthusiastically embraced by the subsidized lines, which operate five times as many 20-knot ships as the rest of the world combined and 25 percent of all cargo liners rated at 17 knots or over.

Labor Relations. The subsidy programs' uneven effects have caused difficulties also in the industry's labor-management relations. The impact of these difficulties on the industry's operations can hardly be overstated. They have alienated customers, pushed up costs, retarded introduction of new technology, undermined public confidence, discouraged investment, and contributed to the contraction of the U.S. flag fleet. Although the causes of the industry's turbulent and often embittered labor relations are many and complex, they are intimately related to the workings of the government's promotional programs.

Paradoxically, maritime labor's very success in achieving the social welfare objectives of the 1936 act appear to be a principal source of unrest today. Abetted by the stimulus of subsidies, shipboard wages have risen to a level well above the wages for such jobs as are otherwise available to seamen. Job rationing has been practiced by certain maritime unions for many years. Formal rotational systems, fairly common in the industry, accommodate the many seamen who have decided that the maritime wage level justifies their remaining in the industry, even though they can secure only part-time employment. Overall (excluding seasonal workers on Great Lakes ships), unlicensed personnel average only 181 days per year under articles. The average ship-time for officers is slightly higher, but still only about six and a half months of the year.[42]

[42] National Academy of Sciences, Maritime Cargo Transportation Conference, "Study of Age and Employment Characteristics of Deepsea and Great Lakes Seamen

Many of the men undoubtedly take other jobs while not at sea. However, job rotation schemes almost inevitably result in dissipation of the high wages earned at sea in periods of enforced idleness or underemployment. It is a system which heightens pressures all around: on seamen to get in as much seatime as possible to guard against the possibility that a shoreside job may not turn up; on shipowners to pay wages which include a factor against this contingency; and on unions both to keep wages up and to increase the number of jobs which can be shared by their members.

The postwar rise in wages has therefore been accompanied by a concomitant preoccupation with jobs. This concern has intensified the jurisdictional jealousies of the several maritime unions and fueled their efforts to organize U.S.-owned foreign flag ships. By 1961 these rivalries had become so intense they precipitated what is probably a unique occurrence in American labor history—a strike called in part to *prevent* introduction of higher wages.

This episode nicely illustrates the manner in which the maritime industry's collective bargaining has been conditioned by the subsidy system. A major factor in the strike appears to have been an attempt by the Seafarers International Union (SIU, which on the East and Gulf coasts represents chiefly seamen on non-subsidized ships) to capture leadership of maritime unionism by "exposing" the failure of the National Maritime Union (NMU) and subsidized operators to engage in tough, honest-to-goodness collective bargaining. The SIU also wanted to force a re-examination and broadening of subsidies by highlighting the deficiencies of the 1936 program. When the managements of subsidized companies reached a settlement with the NMU the SIU group accused them of yielding to inflationary wage demands in anticipation that their application throughout the industry would force certain tramp operations out of business. When the engineers' union, which was allied with the SIU in this episode, struck the NMU ships, it was accused of trying to wreck the subsidized industry.[43]

---

under Articles During the Period April 1, 1962, Through March 31, 1963" (unpublished report). In addition to time spent under articles, the typical seaman remains in pay status during about 5-10 days port time and earns about 30 days paid vacation per year.

[43] Related issues in the 1961 negotiations involved the unions' rights to organize foreign flag vessels owned by companies also operating U.S. flag vessels and a proposed joint labor-management committee to work for enlargement of government aid programs. The engineers' strike was terminated after 18 days by a Taft-Hartley injunction. Later, the SIU group accepted a compromise settlement which granted it a limited opportunity to organize foreign flag ships and set up the labor-management committee (later declared illegal and reorganized as the American Maritime Association) and

The opportunities for secret alliances, the frequency of strikes on jurisdictional issues, together with the scars remaining from the prewar period have combined to create in the maritime industry an atmosphere of unusual bitterness, intrigue, and distrust. In such a situation, cooperation between management and labor in considering mutual problems has been extremely difficult. On the most pressing and explosive issue of all—shipboard automation—there had not even been any serious discussion as late as June 1962. With prodding from the government, an agreement was nonetheless reached between the American Merchant Marine Institute (AMMI) and the NMU in August 1963 to establish automation funds and to submit any specific manning proposals on which agreement could not be reached voluntarily to binding arbitration. On the strength of this agreement, and without any assurance of cooperation from the licensed officer groups, the Maritime Administration ordered that certain automated features be included in all future subsidized ship construction and planned a program to retrofit subsidized vessels already in operation. Some halting progress was made during the next twenty-two months, despite disputes over manning several new and retrofitted ships.[44] However, in June 1965 the automation issue broke out in a prolonged and widespread strike (ironically called by the Maritime Engineers Beneficial Association only against AMMI, the shipowner group which had attempted to resolve automation problems with the NMU). The contracts signed on the conclusion of this strike failed to resolve basic automation issues, which the President asked be studied further by the Secretary of Labor and George Meany, president of the AFL-CIO. Settlements on specific manning issues raised during the 1965 negotiations and previously have, when combined with automation fund payments, so narrowed the savings which can be achieved through automation that the Maritime Administration has temporarily suspended its retrofit program.

Effectiveness of Subsidized Shipping

The frustrations, irritations, and high costs associated with maritime subsidy programs have definitely diminished the U.S. flag fleet's effectiveness for meeting national needs. Yet some frustrations are inevitable in

---

liberalized fringe benefits somewhat. The agreement failed, however, to include any increase in base wages, such as had earlier been obtained by the NMU.

[44] By December 1964—sixteen months after the NMU-AMMI agreement was announced—six U.S. flag vessels were operating with crews of less than 38 men and forty more semi-automated vessels were under construction. The introduction of the first two semi-automated ships (and several follow-on vessels) was marred by brief work stoppages called on minor issues.

even the best conceived and managed public program and, for that matter, even in industries which operate without government aid. A fair assessment of the program's effectiveness must therefore consider whether the frustrations, irritations, and costs have been *unduly* burdensome in relation to the program's achievements; whether certain attributes of the program obstruct specific national aims; and whether it has helped to build the lean, imaginative, and competitive shipping industry argued in Chapter 5 to be the nation's highest priority present need in relation to its merchant marine.

Role as Military Auxiliary. In his message to accompany his 1961 budget, President Eisenhower declared that the U.S. flag industry's high operating costs "seriously hampered . . . efforts to maintain a U.S. merchant fleet adequate, along with the ships of our allies, to meet national defense requirements." This concern was shortly thereafter echoed by Secretary McNamara, who stressed the importance of efficient use of the nation's resources to its economic and military strength. "We do not use them efficiently," continued McNamara, "when we apply them to a field in which we have a handicap of 100 percent in construction and 50 percent in operating costs, unless such application is [seriously] required from a military point of view. It is for that reason that I have been very careful in stating the military requirement."[45]

Over the past fifteen years literally hundreds of industries (including manufacturers of dental burrs, wool felts, and clinical thermometers) have sought to prove that their operations were vital to the national security. Few, if any, have established the case so firmly in both the public and official mind as the U.S. merchant marine. It is a case which is supported both by the authority of history and the courage of U.S. seamen during World War II. Yet, the startling fact is that even though the postwar period has been punctuated by emergencies of all kinds short of general war, only two privately-owned U.S. flag vessels have actually had to be requisitioned for military use.[46] This is a tribute both to the U.S. flag industry's ability to absorb military requirements in its routine operations and to the Defense Department and Maritime Administration's flexibility in acquiring additional shipping from other sources.

[45] *Review of Merchant Marine Policy, 1962,* Hearings before the House Merchant Marine and Fisheries Committee, 87 Cong. 2 sess. (1962), p. 107.

[46] The two requisitions since 1946 occurred during the 1958 Lebanese crisis, when two dry cargo vessels were ordered to Beirut. Because additional U.S. vessels could not be readily obtained, a number of foreign flag ships were chartered to support the Marines which had been sent into Lebanon.

Conflicts of Military and Commercial Roles. There are several good reasons for the Defense Department's reluctance to call up privately owned merchant shipping in military emergencies. The most important is that ships cannot simultaneously serve both commercial and military needs. For both practical and political reasons the military have tried to minimize disruption to normal commerce during limited emergencies.

The subsidized lines, of course, are explicitly charged with maintaining services essential to the foreign commerce of the United States despite international tensions. In any situation short of general mobilization, their contribution to the nation's military program is likely to be incident to their normal services. In this manner U.S. flag liners contributed materially to such tasks as theatre supply during the Korean conflict and support of the United Nation's Congo operations in 1963. In theory, the non-subsidized lines and tramp ships should be able to respond more flexibly to special defense needs than the subsidized lines. But because these ships have become almost exclusively government carriers, their deployment to meet urgent military requirements necessitates deferring or making alternate arrangements for other government shipments.

Second, the trend toward use of more special-purpose ships to perform both civil and military missions diminishes the effectiveness of the commercial merchant fleet in responding to military needs. The trend toward giant supertankers in the privately owned merchant fleet has already posed a serious problem for the military, which must have smaller drafts in order to supply forward depots. Concurrently, the military has developed requirements for specially designed or equipped vessels to participate in its forward floating depot, to permit rapid deployment of armored equipment, and to support amphibious warfare, inter-island missions, and Arctic operations. By and large these requirements cannot be met by privately owned merchant ships.

In contrast to the years before World War II, when over half the U.S. dry cargo fleet was employed in coastwise and intercoastal services, there is now only a remnant of this tonnage operating in readily accessible trades. Typically, about 25 percent of the foreign trade fleet is at any one time berthed in U.S. ports; and to return the remainder to domestic waters could require up to three months, assuming that ships already at sea are permitted to complete their voyages. These delays and other factors make the use of government-owned mothballed vessels an attractive and realistic alternative to withdrawing ships from commercial service.[47]

[47] Delays incident to mobilizing commercially employed and reserve ships are compared in Chapter 5.

Reserve Fleet and Personnel Policies. During the Korean mobilization, a large proportion of the additional shipping required by the the MSTS to supplement established liner services to the Far East was obtained from the reserve fleet. A similar pattern appears to be developing to support U.S. operations in South Vietnam. Providing suitable ships are available, the reserve fleet will undoubtedly also be the military's principal resource for meeting future limited emergencies. However, there is no assurance that such ships will be available, for lack of attention has permitted a serious deterioration in the quality and mobilization readiness of the mothballed fleet. In fact, the government's modest and faltering support to this defense facility stands in sharp contrast to its unqualified support of the active, commercial industry.

The key role of the reserve fleet was noted in several postwar studies.[48] In order to assure that it would be supported at a level commensurate to its importance, a group convened by President Truman to examine postwar needs recommended that the fleet be transferred from the Maritime Commission to the Department of Defense. This recommendation, however, was never seriously studied; and with responsibilities blurred, neither the Navy nor the Maritime Administration has given high priority to maintaining the efficiency of the National Defense Reserve Fleet. Vessels are purchased for the reserve only when commercial operators are unable to find a more lucrative sale. Ship maintenance has been reduced to less than $6,000 per year per vessel. Furthermore, both the Navy and the Maritime Administration supported legislation allowing exchange of worn out vessels from commercial service for better reserve fleet ships (forty-eight were exchanged during the first three years under this authority).

Even less attention has been given to maintaining the skills of reserve personnel, despite the fact that during the Korean war manpower shortages significantly delayed the activation of needed vessels.[49] Only a tiny percentage of the 600,000 to 700,000 Americans who have served on

[48] For example, see the *Report of the President's Advisory Committee on the Merchant Marine* (Nov. 1947), pp. 51-53, and U.S. Department of Commerce, Under Secretary for Transportation, *Maritime Subsidy Policy* (the "Murray Report" [multilith, April 1954]), pp. 4-23.

[49] See U.S. Maritime Administration, *Annual Report,* 1951 and 1952. The most severe shortage was in experienced radio operators. The Maritime Administration canvassed more than 5,000 men who had received training during World War II, but identified only 67 willing to return to sea. To augment this number the FCC relaxed its standards for granting operators' licenses, the Coast Guard permitted employment of aliens, and the Army released draftees willing to serve on board ship.

Shortages of certain seafaring skills have also developed due to the Vietnam expansion of U.S. flag operations.

American merchant ships are now enrolled in reserve programs. In fact, in 1952 the special Merchant Marine Reserve Corps, established some 27 years previously, was disbanded due to lack of interest. Training programs in such matters as convoying and communications, although occasionally available by correspondence and through the Maritime Administration's district offices, have generally been neglected.

Defense Features. The Navy has also paid little attention to the design of defense features for commercial merchant ships. Until recently, two knots reserve speed capacity was built into new subsidized vessels, which were also fitted out with special cargo handling and fire control equipment. However, no concentrated effort to design a defense-capable commercial merchant ship has been made by the government since the Mariner project in the early 1950's. Proposals by private naval architects intended to enhance the defense capabilities of merchant ships have been given only slight attention, and in 1963 even the reserve speed feature was dropped.[50]

Impact of Subsidies on Military Strength. The relative neglect of specific defense-support shipping programs, such as the reserve fleet and training programs, incorporation of defense features in commercial construction, and almost complete suspension of construction for the MSTS, suggests that U.S. military readiness may have suffered from the government's general preoccupation with subsidy programs, which have been consistently regarded as the primary vehicle for meeting military needs. The subsidized industry has, of course, supported this viewpoint, and has rightly believed its defense role was important as well as the key to its public and political

---

[50] The average investment by the government in defense features placed aboard 38 dry cargo and combination vessels contracted between 1955 and 1960 was $115,000 each. The government reimburses only for additional features ruled to have minimal commercial value. The operators have contended that the government's procedures have required them to bear capital costs which are not really commercially justified and to cover maintenance expenses for equipment which is acknowledged to be required only for defense purposes. The operators' distaste for carrying any unnecessary equipment aboard their vessels, even if initially financed by the government, has probably contributed to the de-emphasis of defense features in recent construction contracts.

Over the years a number of proposals for special ship types to serve both military and commercial needs have been advanced by private operators and ship design firms. These proposals have contributed to the Navy's own thinking and have led to some projects. However, both the Mariner project in the early 1950's and the fast deployment logistics (FDL) project planned for the late 1960's have been principally government conceived and sponsored activities. The government plans to enlist industry in a "complete systems" competition for design and construction of the FDL ship, thus departing from traditional contracting methods.

support. The industry also has worked to restrict the scope of MSTS operations, to obtain ship exchange legislation, and to free itself of what have occasionally appeared to be unnecessary training or maintenance burdens associated with its defense role.

These ancillary effects of the subsidy program emphasize the importance of preventing the privately owned fleet's becoming excessively subsidy dependent, since the necessary balance between public and private, active and reserve shipping facilities can easily be upset if either the military or the private industry loses confidence in the capabilities or fairness of the other. Strains have in the past existed between the military and the shipping industry. Thus in the immediate postwar period the private industry may have legitimately felt that its contributions were not adequately recognized. Conversely, from the mid-fifties through at least 1962, direct defense-support programs were clearly neglected; by 1965, there were some indications that this neglect might be corrected.

The subsidy program also has affected the U.S. merchant fleet's resilience and inventiveness in devising new and better operating methods and technology. These are among the most important contributions of any defense related industry to the nation's mobilization potential. Recognition that an unduly protective attitude quashes these qualities has contributed to the executive branch's hesitance to use subsidies, quotas, and the like to assist defense-related civilian industries. For example, though a national security clause has been included in each extension of the trade agreements legislation since 1954, this authority has been sparingly used.[51] In the absence of absolutely conclusive evidence, the risk of manufacture of particular defense-related products being discontinued has been preferred to that of an overprotected industry relaxing its standards or becoming frozen into obsolete technology.

Commercial Performance of the Fleet. The statutory objective of the government's subsidy program is a safe, suitable, well-equipped, and

---

[51] Sec. 232, P.L. 87-794. The Director of the Office of Emergency Planning is to investigate any application by a domestic firm or industry claiming that foreign imports may have an effect on U.S. industry which will impair the national security and report his findings to the President. The President (unless he is unable to concur in the findings) is directed to take such corrective action as he deems necessary.

Of nineteen petitions which had been filed through June 1963, only one (a joint application by the Departments of State and Defense relating to crude oil and its byproducts) was favorably acted on by the President. Among the applications rejected was an argument that maintenance of adequate tanker capacity demanded that 50 percent of all U.S. petroleum imports be carried in U.S. flag ships. However, the status of the U.S. flag tanker fleet continues to be of active concern to the Office of Emergency Planning.

efficiently operated merchant marine able to carry all domestic water-borne commerce and a substantial portion of the nation's export-import trade. The act's qualitative objectives clearly are interrelated, since it is unlikely that any amount of subsidy could create commercial success if the recipient's services proved inadequate. Conversely, highly effective service should be able to win a "substantial portion" of the trade, granted subsidy assistance.

Participation in Foreign Commerce. At no time since 1947 has the U.S. flag merchant marine carried as much as 50 percent of the total dry cargo tonnage moved in U.S. foreign trade, the implied objective of the 1936 act. The government has not even attempted to win a substantial segment of the private bulk cargo or tramp cargoes for U.S. flag ships, but has instead tacitly accepted use of foreign flags, including U.S.-owned flags of convenience, to handle non-liner commercial business. In the liner trades, on which the subsidy program has been focused, U.S. flag ships have achieved a substantial participation. If military and other preference cargoes are included, its share of the liner market ranges from 35 to 40 percent (revenue basis). So long as a significant portion of the world's shipping continues to be carried by third flags, 35-40 percent can probably be considered a fair share for a national flag merchant fleet. It compares favorably with the shares of the German, Italian, Dutch, and Danish merchant fleets, although the British, Japanese, and French shares in their dry cargo foreign trade appear to be somewhat higher.[52]

If military and other preference cargoes are removed from the statistics, the U.S. flag position is less impressive; in fact, in recent years U.S. flag liners appear to have secured only about 20 percent of the commercial business, down from over 30 percent in 1955. The opportunity to earn higher profits on government business probably contributed to this precipitous decline. Yet on its face, the loss of almost 45 percent of their 1955 commercial business would appear to be dramatic proof that even though U.S. liners have retained a "substantial portion" of the total lift, they have failed to satisfy legitimate commercial needs.

Shipping Rates and Services. The disappointing performance of U.S. flag lines is probably traceable more than anything else to the number of strikes within the U.S. flag industry. In contrast to the typical shoreside industry, shipments are frequently not postponed during a seamen's strike but lost forever to competing foreign carriers.[53] And if the U.S. flag ser-

[52] Estimates of the participation of various national flag fleets in their national foreign trade are presented in Appendix A, Table A5.

[53] Only fragmentary data on strike effects is available, the most complete published

vice comes to be regarded as unreliable or if the foreign operator extracts a promise of continued patronage as its price for temporarily handling the business, the customer may be lost as well.[54]

Special studies of the impact of work stoppages on the U.S. flag liner industry provide some basis for assessing their effect on patronage. As indicated in Chapter 5, limited efforts have also been made to identify the number of U.S. and foreign ports served by U.S. and foreign flag lines, the extent to which each group has pioneered new services, and the scale of their trade development activities. However, the apparently inferior position of the U.S. flag companies in these respects is statistically insignificant. Similarly, there is no real way to assess the relative vulnerability of cargoes shippped U.S. versus foreign flag to pilferage, the adequacy of claims service, or any of the myriad factors which help to attract customers to a superior line.

With one or two exceptions, U.S. flag lines have generally supported the conference system—not at all times and in all trades, but at least as fully as the typical foreign flag. Within the conferences, U.S. companies are generally thought to have stood for higher rates, although there is little objective evidence to demonstrate that they have actually influenced rates either one way or the other.[55]

Prior to Senator Paul H. Douglas' "exposure" of the apparently discriminatory pattern of conference rates in U.S. foreign trade, the U.S. government (in contrast to common practice abroad) had refrained with few exceptions from even discussing rate matters with its subsidy contractors. Under pressure from Douglas' Joint Economic Committee, the government during the past two years has made strong efforts to make the U.S. merchant marine more responsive to American commerce. Although ship-

---

analysis being a study compiled by the U.S. Maritime Administration on the 1962 West Coast strike and published in *Maritime Labor Legislation,* Hearings, pp. 446 ff. This study indicates that only about 50-60 percent of the regular shippers via U.S. flag ships diverted any of their cargoes to foreign flags during the strike, which lasted for 26 days prior to being halted by a Taft-Hartley injunction.

[54] In the Maritime Administration study cited above all but 29 of 161 respondents indicated that they had reverted following the strike to their pre-strike pattern of patronage. However, Marad concluded on the basis of shipper comments that the "negative psychological effects of the strike" would make it increasingly difficult for U.S. flag lines to enlarge or maintain their commercial business. (*Ibid.,* p. 451.)

[55] Sample reports of what shippers believe to be the impact of U.S. flag companies on rates may be found in Milton Goldfogle, *A Report of Interviews with Maritime Industry Users, and Related Activities* (unpublished report to the U.S. Department of Commerce, Dec. 1959), particularly at pp. 123-25. Empirical evidence bearing on the relationship of the presence of the U.S. flag fleet to the rates charged by conferences in U.S. foreign trade is assessed by Ferguson *et al., op. cit.,* p. 373.

per interest has been disappointingly weak, several of the U.S. flag lines and conferences have shown their sensitivity to public opinion and shipper requirements by voluntarily eliminating certain offensive rate differentials.[56]

Role in Cold War. The Cold War has created new and greater demands on U.S. merchant shipping and shipping policy. In quasi-military situations, such as the 1962 Cuban crisis, the U.S. flag industry has responded rapidly and well. However, in other instances problems encountered in arranging shipping terms and policies have obstructed U.S. policy objectives. The most serious of these incidents have been outgrowths of the cargo preference program. However, the government's regulatory program, its support for flags of convenience, its labor policies, and its direct subsidy payments have each generated frictions which have contributed to the strains within the western alliance.

These frictions, coupled with the inherent difficulty of the problem, have also prevented the nations of the North Atlantic Treaty Organization developing a common strategy to use their overwhelming strength at sea as an effective Cold War weapon. The United States' efforts unilaterally to embargo shipping to Cuba and Communist China have failed to win international support and have been generally ineffective. Results in these cases have been so unsatisfactory that through December 1965 the government had not even attempted to curtail shipments into North Vietnam. Also, the western nations have not only been unable to check the development of a Soviet merchant marine, but are actually constructing most of its new tonnage.

The Cold War costs of obstructive or irresponsible actions in the international shipping industry are potentially far more serious than the economic costs of the subsidy program, which the nation is rich enough to bear. However, it should be noted that the two costs are related. The occasionally defensive attitude of America's merchant shipping industry is a product of the industry's economic vulnerability. Subsidization which is

[56] For example, in the general investigation of export-import rates on iron and steel products (FMC Docket 1114) only one American steel exporter appeared to testify that demonstrated rate differentials were detrimental to U.S. foreign commerce. Despite this lack of interest, however, the conferences have made some symbolic gestures toward rate equalization. For example, the United States to United Kingdom outbound conference in 1964 lowered its rate on bourbon whiskey so that the United States might export bourbon on the same terms that it imported scotch. In press statements, Lykes and Bloomfield lines also announced that their resignations from the Gulf to United Kingdom conference were prompted by the desire to service U.S. foreign trade more effectively.

grudging, inadequate, and indirect produces a captious response. Sound operations, confident of customer and public support, on the other hand, can afford to demonstrate their statesmanship in international affairs.

Current Status of U.S. Fleet

Considering the crosscurrents and contradictions within America's postwar merchant marine, it is not surprising that the industry has both supporters and detractors. There are strong elements, including both a nucleus of well-established and stable companies operating with citizen seamen under U.S. flag and a large number of fine, efficiently managed ships under PANLIBHON (Panama, Liberia, and Honduras) registries. There are also many disappointing aspects. The persistent decline from their wartime peaks in the number of U.S. registered ships and in jobs for U.S. seamen is one which has affected the whole industry. The apparent disorganization of the U.S. tramp fleet is another. Slow physical deterioration of the reserve fleet is a third. The coastwise and intercoastal trades have almost completely collapsed. And, because of escalating costs, service to non-contiguous states and territories has become so expensive as to be considered (at least in Alaska and Puerto Rico) an important drag on the developing economies of these areas.

Operating from a favored position, the subsidized lines, together with one or two of the lines in the non-contiguous trades, have become the aristocrats of the U.S. flag sector of the industry. They operate the best and most expensive ships; they enjoy ample reserves and earnings; for the most part, they have long served their present trades, are well established in the business, and are protected from destructive competition both through membership in conferences and through the Maritime Administration's surveillance of essential U.S. trade routes. In contrast, most of the industry's non-subsidized foreign trade companies operate aging warbuilt equipment on narrow margins. Their future, tied to the unpredictable shipping requirements of the government's foreign aid agencies, is highly insecure, and no provision has been made to assist them to replace their obsolete equipment.

The contrasts in the subsidized and non-subsidized companies are coming to be mirrored in the bifurcation of the industry's labor movement. Like its employers, the National Maritime Union has prospered and tends to support the status quo. It is sufficiently confident of its position that it has accepted a modification and extension of its 1961 contracts through 1967, subject to clauses which assign potentially sensitive wage and manning issues to binding arbitration. Other unions have been much more guarded and even refractory in approaching automation issues.

All this has had its effect upon the remainder of the fleet. Rivalries have developed on both sides of the bargaining table between the subsidized and non-subsidized sectors. Some companies which have not been able to pass on premium wages have been forced to pass out of existence. Non-subsidized firms have found that during dips in the liner market subsidized companies are able to carry away a larger share of the government business, on which the non-subsidized group totally depends for its livelihood.

The disparity between America's subsidized and non-subsidized shipping companies and the internal conflicts which this disparity begets contribute to the U.S. merchant marine's image as a sick and troubled industry. The successes of the industry's leading companies have attracted as much or more criticism than the difficulties of its laggards. Partly, this has simply reflected an envy of good fortune or suspicion that it may have been unfairly won. However, the very successes of the subsidy program have created problems. For example, the emphasis on restoring sound finances within the industry has led to accumulation of reserves by the most successful companies which far exceed foreseeable investment opportunities in shipping operations. Because invested chiefly in government bonds, the reserves have been vulnerable to the eroding effects of inflation and have limited the lines' opportunities for maximizing their rate of return. Furthermore, one subsidized company has been liquidated in order to gain access to its reserve assets.[57]

The cargo preference program also has been successful in producing an expanding business for U.S. flag operators. This "success" has, however, created severe problems—one being that it has deflected U.S. flag carriers from one of their principal statutory purposes—i.e., service to U.S. foreign and domestic commerce.

Both the direct and indirect subsidy systems have operated to reduce the flexibility of U.S. flag ship operations and have contributed to inflation of the industry's costs, including the costs of subsidy. This has increased the program's vulnerability and has deterred its supporters from acting completely directly or adequately to meet industry problems.[58] It has also

---

[57] The circumstances under which this liquidation occurred are reported by Joseph Klausner in *Discriminatory Ocean Freight Rates and the Balance of Payments,* Hearings, p. 226.

[58] For example, see the statement of Thor Tollefson, senior minority member of the House Merchant Marine and Fisheries Committee, *Maritime Labor Legislation,* Hearings, p. 421: "When it comes to extending the subsidy program, all of us are pretty

increased the industry's dependence on subsidies and added to the pressure to liberalize and supplement the basic subsidy and preference aids.

Increased dependence on government assistance has forced the industry to become intensely conscious of its subsidy aids. Though reactions to the government's programs are as diverse as the individuals engaged in the industry's management, the fact of subsidy is an inescapable element of every business calculation. The industry's abnormal economic environment has discouraged private investment; biased labor relations; discouraged innovation; influenced management decisions; probably deterred young management talent from entering the industry; and subjected the industry's operations to political caprice, with the attendant demoralizing suspicions that success may be the product of favoritism rather than merit.

Finally, mounting costs and increased foreign competition have made the industry so vulnerable as to undermine shipping men's self-confidence. Apprehensive of its future, the industry has demanded and obtained statutory guarantees of a substantial portion of government cargoes for its national flag ships, 100 percent guarantees of its ship mortgage money, virtual insulation from the rigors of the investment market, and the right to police its own competitive practices through "neutral bodies." Most recently, the subsidized portion of the industry has even expressed the desire that the government assume a larger, more systematic role in its labor relations so that it can be assured that settlements are "fair and reasonable" and are achieved except in the most extreme situations without recourse to strikes.

The insecurity in certain segments of America's merchant marine is evidence that the partnership of government and industry has failed to resolve certain basic problems arising from changing postwar conditions and has created new ones. The industry's descent from its leading postion immediately following World War II to its present situation has been described by Secretary of Commerce Hodges in the following terms:

> There were, in the face of severe foreign competition, several choices. One choice was to backwater in the face of it—in effect, to give up the game. For those who made this choice, the important thing became to get what they could out of the industry while it lasted. They ignored long-range problems and opportunities, and concentrated almost completely on obtaining the greatest amount of subsidy—a concentration which hindered the development of other lines of income.

---

practical on this committee and we have a feeling I am sure that if we come before the House with a proposal which is going to cost some more money, we are not sure we are going to get very far with it."

Risk-taking for long-term benefits was discouraged. The attitude of "what's in it for me here and now" caused further deterioration in labor management relations. And gradually we lost more and more cargoes.[59]

The Secretary's judgment, even though aimed only at a portion of the industry, is a harsh one. Many of the industry's personnel have been very much concerned about long-range problems and opportunities and, within the bounds of the government's programs, have done what they could to solve them. But government, as well as portions of the industry, has hesitated to take risks in order to win long-term benefits. Its choice—and it was one which almost no one seriously challenged—was to build the entire postwar program around a safe and conservative prewar act, which was not gauged either to the industry's current situation or to the nation's long-term needs.

Concluding Remarks on Part II: Adequacy of the Postwar Promotional Program

In 1946, as the U.S. Maritime Commission prepared for the conversion of America's huge wartime merchant fleet to peacetime purposes, it assessed its postwar prospects in the following terms:

> The American merchant marine is today in a better position than it has been in for many years. We have at this time most of the ingredients required for success at sea. We have a great shipbuilding industry. We have trained workers, both in the yards and aboard ship. We have experienced managements. We have a modern fleet. We have the support of the public. Yet there is no cause for complacency.
>
> We must endeavor at all costs to avoid a repetition of our experience between World War I and World War II. We started then, as we are starting off now, with high hopes for the future. We failed before to produce a sound competitive merchant marine. Will we do better in the future? We must do better. The stakes are high. And we might not get another chance.[60]

The postwar program falls conspicuously short of these high expectations. Despite massive aid to subsidized companies, the 1936 program has clearly failed to reach its objectives. The gloomy conclusion of the National Academy of Sciences committee which reviewed the situation in 1960 is

[59] Address of Secretary of Commerce Luther H. Hodges before the Port of Washington Propeller Club, May 22, 1962.

[60] U.S. Maritime Commission, Postwar Planning Committee, *The Post-War Outlook for American Shipping* (Government Printing Office, 1946), p. 105.

that "the subsidy system as it now stands is actually hindering U.S. maritime progress,"[61] while the Secretary of Commerce has described his department's efforts as "in general . . . disappointing."[62]

It is agreed by all that the government's shipping program has not developed in the manner anticipated by the authors of the 1936 act. That legislation was designed to put the subsidy on a scientific basis, to make it direct and visible, and to establish explicit conditions to control its award. But in fact, the subsidy formula has proved unstable, eligibility criteria have been restricted, and supplementary indirect aids have come to overshadow the direct subsidy program.

What has gone wrong? Where has the program gone astray? Obviously there are no simple answers. Some of the seeds of future difficulties lay in the 1936 act itself. The statute was a compromise which failed to reconcile the divergent views of those who believed that private shipping was entitled to a differential subsidy as a matter of equity and those who believed that public funds should be expended only insofar as necessary to meet distinct and definite public needs. It failed to establish useful standards to guide the commission in determining what was "fair and reasonable" in its dealings with the industry or to aid it in unraveling the conceptual mysteries of parity. Most important, it failed to define clearly government and industry's respective roles, relying instead on the faith that a joint cooperative effort could mold American shipping into an effective instrument of public policy.

Difficulties inherent in the act were exacerbated by the commission's failure following World War II to recognize that its commercial orientation was unsuited to the merchant marine's new defense role. In fact, neither the commission nor its successors really tried to distinguish between commerce and defense, long regarded as "twin objectives of U.S. maritime policy." The prevalent attitude was that since every ship added to the nation's military strength, as many U.S. flag ships as possible should be encouraged to operate in U.S. foreign and domestic trade. Commercial and defense objectives thus became virtually identical. "We have to have merchant marine, Period," stated Sinclair Weeks in 1953; "I do not think you can draw a sharp line between private operation and defense."[63]

[61] National Academy of Sciences-National Research Council, *Proposed Program of Maritime Administration Research*, Vol. 1, p. 37.

[62] Address of Secretary of Commerce Luther H. Hodges before the Port of Washington Propeller Club, May 22, 1962.

[63] *Military Sea Transportation Service*, Hearings before the House Merchant Marine and Fisheries Committee, 83 Cong. 2 sess. (1953), p. 143. Weeks' comment was in

This attitude toward the maritime problem nullified any effort to discriminate between the program's multiple objectives and to develop specific plans through which they might be attained. If private operation *has* to be supported in order to meet defense objectives, neither cost nor efficiency can be a controlling consideration. The job must be done. Even competition must be sacrificed, since competition implies risk and military resources must be secure.

These realities, however, have never been admitted by either government or industry. The aim has always been both security and efficiency, and the possibility that these objectives might be basically incompatible has been simply turned aside. In general, problems facing the industry have been considered with little regard for the long-term effects of the solutions chosen. In the guise of strengthening private enterprise, government funds and regulations have been permitted to penetrate into almost every cranny of the industry's operations. The effect has been to erode the industry's long-term strength.

The postwar period has also been marked by a pernicious tendency to maintain U.S. shipping "on the cheap." The lure of somehow getting something for nothing has contributed to the adoption and spread of cargo preference and other indirect aids. An undue amount of administrative energy has also been spent on making essentially meaningless adjustments to subsidy payments, which has created unnecessary friction and diverted attention from more significant trends.

The costs of niggardly and restrictive attitudes have run high. For example, the government's insistence that vessel depreciation be fully funded and invested in U.S. government bonds has deprived the industry of opportunities for equity investments which would have yielded millions in capital gains. Perpetuation of the practice of fixing subsidy rates on the basis of a post-audit of the contractors' accounts has seriously diminished incentives for improving cost controls.

The principal penalty of the government's unwillingness to provide sufficient direct subsidies to satisfy its needs has been the greater cost of maintaining U.S. flag ships through indirect aids. Cargo preference, the Maritime Adminstration now admits, "has been a miserable failure."[64] It

---

response to a question whether President Eisenhower's appeal for a subsidized fleet sized to defense requirements might not imply a departure from the 1936 statute and the prevailing philosophy regarding the identity of commercial and defense requirements.

[64] Remarks of Nicholas Johnson, Maritime Administrator, before the Mid-Gulf Conference on Transportation and Industrial Modernization, New Orleans, Feb. 9, 1965.

has failed to induce any new construction; it has escalated subsidy costs, precipitated both domestic and international conflicts, and reopened the possibility of malpractice and scandal. Administered grudgingly by agencies which have no real interest in U.S. merchant shipping, it has encouraged the industry to assume a hostile and defensive posture, which has made it more difficult to resolve the problems which have arisen.

The administration of the government's maritime program has been subjected to persistent criticism ever since the conclusion of World War II. The administrative agencies have been charged with being too lax, too stringent, too liberal, and too inconsistent. As the industry sees it, the problem is not that the government is doing the wrong things, but that it is doing them without sufficient vigor and dedication. Thus one industry spokesman asserts that the government's vascillation in administering the promotional program has frustrated achievement of "a genuine national maritime program."[65] Another scores the "general apathy of the United States toward a merchant marine,"[66] while Admiral Arleigh Burke has warned that continuation of present trends will cause "one of the greatest assets of the American economic structure to die of neglect."[67]

This study has argued the opposite point of view. The government program has been inadequate to the challenge of building a vigorous, lean, efficient, imaginative, and expanding American shipping industry because the government has yielded too often to the industry's importunings for additional aid. In some instances, expediency has been substituted for prudent judgment in determining ways to meet alleged defense needs. In other cases, administrators of the maritime program have appeared to lose sight of its ultimate public purposes in their effort to be reasonably responsive to what the industry conceived to be its immediate need.

Perceptions of the causes of the present unsatisfactory situation vary from person to person. On one point, however, almost all are agreed. The implementation of U.S. shipping programs has not been adequate to postwar needs; in this area, government has failed to adjust and up-date its policies to the challenges of the nation's new frontiers.

[65] John M. Will, "By Ship—the Salt of the Sea Notwithstanding," *Annals of the American Academy of Political and Social Science,* Vol. 345 (Jan. 1963), p. 84.

[66] Wilfred J. McNeil as quoted by C. R. Wilhide, "Our Merchant Marine Is Dying," *U.S. Naval Institute Proceedings,* Vol. 89, No. 6 (June 1963), p. 32.

[67] Adm. Arleigh Burke's preface to C. R. Wilhide, *op. cit.*

PART III

The Politics of the Government's Shipping Program

The government's apparent inability to up-date its maritime programs to meet the changing needs and conditions of the postwar period raises serious questions regarding the adequacy of its processes for policy re-examination and reform. Some of the main sources of difficulty, arising from the structure of the subsidy program itself, have already been discussed. For example, the concept of partnership between the industry and the maritime agency which has suffused administration of the direct subsidy program has created many problems, while easing others. Indirect aids have created even more difficulties inasmuch as their administration has been decentralized to several government departments and because in each case they are linked with other public programs or areas of private economic activity.

These features of the government's maritime activities give emphasis to the need for effective political and administrative processes to guide and spur the development of public policy in this area and to ensure its constructive application to specific cases. The formulation of shipping policy must be properly integrated into a broader political framework in order that it may harmonize with other national policies and changing national needs. The policy formulation machinery needs to include mechanisms for the early identification of emerging problems, for the consideration of all relevant information, and for hearing all legitimate interests. It must assure a measure of stability and continuity in pursuit of long-term objectives. Yet it must also be capable of timely action, of finding grounds for compromise where necessary, and of finessing deadlocks between competing interests.

Part III is aimed at identifying characteristics of the political-administrative setting of the government's shipping program which may have contributed to the difficulties in this field. The first of its three chapters describes the government's formal machinery for maritime policy development and administration. The next chapter is concerned with the groups interested in the industry and the manner in which their actions supplement the formal administrative structure. The third chapter describes the operation of the political system in overseeing and up-dating administrative activity and the system's principal effects upon the maritime program. Part III concludes with a discussion of the manner in which the politics of the government's shipping program have retarded innovation.

9

Machinery for Policy Development and Administration

DEVELOPMENT OF SUITABLE MACHINERY to carry forward an activity as complex and far reaching as the government's shipping programs is both enormously difficult and enormously important to their success. Merchant shipping is the direct responsibility of many federal officials, agencies, and congressional committees; the resources of still other organizations are utilized in the extension of indirect aids. Somehow the contributions of these diverse instrumentalities must be correlated if there is to be a reasonably coherent, viable program.

The sustained attention given to organizational arrangements and administrative procedures attests to the difficulty of the task. From the end of World War II through 1950 there were four important changes in the structure and/or operations of the government's maritime agencies, two of which were accomplished through formal reorganization plans. In 1961 the maritime agencies were reorganized once again in an effort to correct deficiencies in shipping regulation and to strengthen Executive direction of the promotional program.

Improved organization has not overcome the necessity for extensive arrangements to supervise and coordinate the government's many maritime activities. Furthermore, the effectiveness of these activities continues to depend principally on the expertness and dedication of the persons responsible for their management and the resources available to them. The internal organization, staffing, financing, and direction of the administrative agencies therefore are critical to the successes and failures of the government program.

Official Participants

The number of federal instrumentalities associated in some manner with regulation or promotion of merchant shipping is very large—on the order of fifty to one hundred if congressional committees are included. The long-standing public interest in maritime affairs and their intrinsic fascination have stimulated unusually active congressional participation. A large number of Executive departments and agencies have significant responsibilities or an institutional interest in the conduct of the government's shipping programs. However, in most cases, this interest is secondary to the agency's principal mission, with the result that worries and concerns felt at staff level only occasionally percolate to the top.

Congressional Committees. In the House, congressional interest in maritime affairs is centered in the Merchant Marine and Fisheries Committee and its subcommittee on the merchant marine. Maritime affairs in the Senate are handled by a subcommittee of the Senate Commerce Committee, which has usually been chaired by the chairman of the full committee and been one of his primary interests. Both the House and Senate groups have developed unique characteristics as a product of their membership, background, staffing arrangements, and interests.

The House Committee on Merchant Marine and Fisheries was organized as a permanent standing committee in 1887 as successor to a Select Committee on American Shipbuilding and Shipowning Interests. It was the House committee that prepared the initial drafts of the Merchant Marine Act of 1936. Judge Schuyler Otis Bland, principal author of that legislation, served as chairman until 1947. One of his successors, Congressman Herbert Bonner of North Carolina, served twenty-four years with the committee, including ten as chairman (of both the merchant marine subcommittee and the full committee) before his death in 1965. The chairmanship of both groups is now held by Edward Garmatz of Baltimore, Maryland.

The House committee draws most of its members from seaboard states.[1] It does not follow, however, that the members necessarily have

[1] Statistically, the Merchant Marine and Fisheries Committee has for many years drawn about twice as many members from coastal districts as would result from a random selection. Over-representation of seaboard districts on the committee has increased somewhat over the past three decades. From 1890 to 1920, between 40 and 50 percent of the committee members came from coastal towns and cities. The percentage increased to 57 percent in 1930, 65 percent in 1940, and 72 percent in both

had any strong interest in or even contact with the U. S. merchant marine. Judge Bland's Newport News constituency, for example, was more involved in ship construction than operation. Mr. Bonner's interests when he joined the committee were chiefly in Coast Guard affairs. Although membership of the Senate's Commerce Committee is more broadly based, assignment to the merchant marine subcommittee is usually based on a member's particular interest. During most of the postwar period the Senate unit has often proved a more zealous advocate for an American merchant marine than the more conservative, tradition-minded House.

Although completely committed to the maintenance of the U. S. flag fleet, the congressional maritime committees have not acted simply as a rubber stamp to industry desires. In the first place, the industry as a whole is seldom of a single mind on issues before the committees. Second, the personal philosophies of the chairmen and senior members leave a distinctive mark on the work of the committees.[2] The committees do, however, provide friendly forums where industry problems can be aired before a knowledgeable and sympathetic audience, and provide the industry a channel of communication both to the Congress at large and to the executive branch.

The merchant marine subcommittees do not hold a monopoly over congressional interests in maritime affairs. Over the years the appropriations committees have demonstrated a continuing interest in both the scope and content of the subsidy program. The House Government Operations and Judiciary committees and the Joint Economic Committee have each conducted major investigations of special facets of the government's program. Legislative matters affecting the U. S. merchant marine are occasionally processed by the Armed Services, Ways and Means, and Agriculture committees.

Congress is assisted in its watchdog function by the General Accounting Office (GAO), which has been particularly attentive to ship subsidies since World War II. The GAO's conservative standards have oper-

---

1950 and 1960. About half of the committee's members are typically in their first or second congressional term. Assignment to the committee can usually be gained by any member who desires it. Freshman members frequently receive Merchant Marine and Fisheries as a second or third choice and move on to more prestigious and influential committees as soon as their seniority permits.

[2] Mr. Bonner's ties were to the industry's management, particularly the management of the subsidized lines. Senator Magnuson, chairman of the Senate committee, is strongly supported by labor organizations in his home state and emphasizes labor interests in a U.S. flag fleet.

ated as a powerful restraint on the maritime agencies and have significantly influenced the development of the government's program.[3] GAO's reports have also been a source of information for members of Congress who are basically opposed to the subsidy program, such as Senators John J. Williams of Delaware and Frank Lausche of Ohio.

Executive Officials. Presidential and Cabinet interest in U.S. maritime problems has been intermittent and not channeled through any set structure. Prior to 1950 the President had few official responsibilities for maritime affairs other than those exercised as Commander in Chief or as a consequence of his budget and appointment powers.[4] The 1949 Hoover Commission reports, however, urged that the President assume a more active role in transportation policy development. In 1950 the reorganization plan which established the Maritime Administration within the Department of Commerce authorized an Under Secretary of Commerce for Transportation "to assist the Secretary in supervising the varied and complex transportation programs of the Department and providing central leadership in transportation matters."[5]

Although both transportation policy and administrative responsibility for maritime affairs are now lodged in the Commerce Department, maritime policy problems probably come to the President nearly as frequently through his secretaries of Labor, Treasury, State, Agriculture, and Defense as from the Secretary of Commerce. Other maritime problems are brought to the President through the Office of Emergency Planning, the

[3] The GAO itself has been criticized for the conservative, essentially negative, influence which it bears on Maritime Administration programs. An Arthur D. Little report to the Maritime Administration, dealing with techniques for foreign-domestic cost determinations, for example, asserts that the effect of the GAO's reports in this area has been to "spread a cloud of skepticism." Somewhat whimsically, the report then comments, "The Government really ought not to make so much trouble for itself." Arthur D. Little, Inc., *Ship Construction Differential Subsidies* (September 1961), pp. 136 ff.

[4] The President was specifically charged with certain powers by the Merchant Marine Act of 1920 (e.g., to consider the compatibility of executive agency regulations pertaining to shipping to the program of the U.S. Shipping Board [sec. 19] and to require that U.S. flag shipping be used in trade with American Samoa and the Philippines [sec. 21]). In 1956 additional legislation was enacted requiring the President to approve proposed ship construction contract allocations to assure an adequate mobilization base for national defense (P.L. 84-805 [70 Stat. 657]).

[5] *Message from the President Transmitting Reorganization Plan Number 21 of 1950,* Doc. 526, 81 Cong. 2 sess. (1950). Under the Reorganization Act, the President's transmittal message is to be considered a part of the plan. The language cited in the text is the principal authority for the Under Secretary's government-wide transportation leadership.

National Security Council, Bureau of the Budget, and directly from the industry itself.

The avenues through which the President has sought advice and assistance on these matters have been as varied as the sources of the problems themselves. During most of President Truman's tenure, the White House staff included a member interested and knowledgeable in maritime affairs. However, during the Eisenhower and Kennedy terms, presidential interests in routine matters were usually met through the institutional facilities of his Executive Offices, while more urgent problems required *ad hoc* arrangements.[6]

Administrative Agencies. All but one of the government's departments and several major independent agencies make some contribution to American merchant shipping. Six departments have a significant interest in the course of U.S. shipping policy.

Technical services, which tend to be relatively free of policy implications, are provided to U.S. merchant shipping by the Public Health Service (vessel inspections and medical care), the Department of State (consular services), the Corps of Engineers (port development), the Census Bureau (statistics), the Coast and Geodetic Survey (nautical charts), the Customs Bureau (ship documentation and recording of vessel liens and mortgages), the Coast Guard (safety and licensing activities), and the Federal Mediation and Conciliation Service. All of these services involve responsibilities which can have an important bearing on the government's promotional program. The Coast Guard's marine inspection activities, for example, require it to certify the seaworthiness of each new vessel type and to pass on the adequacy of proposed manning tables for automated and other ships. The Customs Bureau's admeasurement rules influence vessel design. Customs also must examine citizenship prior to granting American registry and advises the Congress on the propriety of proposed exceptions to established documentation rules.

A second group of agencies participates in maritime programs princi-

---

[6] Several units in the Executive Office of the President have played significant roles in assisting the President in merchant marine matters. The most active on a continuing basis is the Bureau of the Budget. In past years, the Office of Defense Mobilization also had a major interest in the industry. Other participants include the Council of Economic Advisers, the Office of Science and Technology, and the staff of the National Security Council. However, none of these units devotes substantial time to maritime problems (their combined investment probably does not exceed four or five man-years). Only the Budget Bureau is staffed with as much as one man full-time in this area.

pally as shippers of government-owned or financed goods. This group includes the Agriculture Department, Agency for International Development, Defense Department (the Military Sea Transport Service [MSTS]),
General Services Administration, State Department, Post Office, and Export-Import Bank. The contracting procedures used by these agencies
have an important influence on the overall scale of government aid. The
agencies, in turn, have an important interest in assuring that the cargo
preference program is administered in a manner which minimizes the im-
pediments to their primary missions.

A third group of agencies are interested or participate in regulation of
maritime rates and services. The Federal Maritime Commission and Interstate Commerce Commission share primary jurisdiction in this field. Other
agencies with at least a marginal role include the Commerce Department
(export promotion and control), the Civil Aeronautics Board, the Department of Justice (which has participated as *amicus curiae* in regulatory
cases), the Department of State, the Saint Lawrence Seaway Development Corporation, the Panama Canal Company, and the Office of Emergency Planning, which administers the national security clause of the
Trade Expansion Act.

The fourth and smallest group is composed of agencies with a promotional interest in the U.S. merchant fleet. This group includes the Commerce, Defense, and Labor departments and the Atomic Energy Commission (for nuclear ships). Within both Commerce and Defense there are
multiple units with different interests in merchant shipping. The Bureau
of International Commerce, for example, has a strong interest in trade
promotion and for many years maintained a transportation staff to advise
U.S. exporters on shipping problems and to assist in resolving their complaints. Within the Department of Defense, maritime specialists are at-
tached to the Office of the Assistant Secretary for Installations and Logistics, the Joint Chiefs of Staff, the Chief of Naval Operations, and in the
MSTS and in naval intelligence.

Despite the large number of units with some stake in merchant shipping matters, the executive branch has very limited resources for maritime
policy formulation and evaluation. Within the Maritime Administration,
for example, there are only thirteen positions classified at general schedule
grade sixteen (with a salary of roughly $20,000) or above; within the Fed-
eral Maritime Commission there are eighteen jobs at this level. Throughout government the total number of career executives and senior military
officers principally concerned with shipping is in the range of fifty to sev-

enty-five persons. The number of administrative personnel under their direction appears to be 1,500 to 2,000 people.[7]

Administrative Organization and Coordination

The inventory of agencies participating in the maritime program dramatizes the variety and span of governmental activity in this field. Sheer numbers increase the difficulty of achieving effective administrative organization and coordination. However, the most challenging administrative problem is the interrelation and overlapping of their activities and responsibilities.

In a system of divided powers, responsibility is also necessarily divided. Furthermore, the division of responsibility is seldom clearly delineated. Power in Washington, as many have observed, is not really divided, but dispersed, diffused, and shared. The complexity of the government's maritime program multiplies the difficulty of developing coherent, viable policies within the federal structure.

The fact that each of the organizational structures devised for the government's maritime program has in some respect been found wanting is proof that the difficulties are deep-rooted. They are probably imbedded in such basic characteristics of the program itself as its intermixture of promotional and regulatory objectives (and of the programs supporting each goal), the need for both executive and quasi-judicial powers in both programs, the ties of both to the missions of other agencies, and the dependence on the contributions of other agencies for their success.

Promotional and Regulatory Duties. It is probably pure happenstance that both promotional and regulatory programs were initially lumped together in the Shipping Act of 1916. The two programs had been developed separately, for different purposes, in part by different people, and within a different environment. Regulation was concerned with peacetime commerce; promotion with building up the U.S. flag fleet to meet a wartime emergency.

Regulation and promotion are clearly related; their relationship, how-

[7] The Maritime Administration is the largest of the government's maritime agencies with administrative staff of approximately 1,250, most of whom are engaged in some facet of the subsidy program. The Federal Maritime Commission reported an employment of 239 in 1964. The MSTS has a 350-man complement in its Washington headquarters, most of whom are concerned with ship operations. In contrast, the Agriculture Department has only eight professionals in its Foreign Agricultural Service Ocean Transportation Branch to oversee the expenditure of some $150 million.

ever, has never been clearly articulated in either theory or practice. In theory, the success of the promotional program and the guarantee of fair practice in the industry are mutually interdependent.[8] In practice, application of the lofty maxim that self-interest is best served through self-discipline has often proved painful.

The realities of the international shipping business prevent any neat distinction between regulatory and promotional activities. Consider, for example, some of the problems posed by pooling proposals. Review of the effect of a proposed pool on other carriers, shippers, ports, and on U.S. foreign commerce generally is explicitly required by one of the regulatory sections of the 1916 act. However, pools also present problems for the promotional agency, since their effect is to compromise the separate identity of the American carrier and to remove the U.S. flag line as a separate competitor in the trade.[9] Furthermore, the underlying justification for pooling has often been to overcome foreign discriminatory practices—a problem which necessarily concerns the Presidency (through the Department of State) as well as both the promotional and regulatory components of the government's maritime agencies.

Distinctions between regulatory and promotional functions have been further obscured by the tendency to identify regulation with adjudicatory procedures and promotion with the maritime agencies' executive and administrative activities. Actually both programs, as defined in this study,

[8] Supporters of the 1916 bill argued that open competition was a prerequisite to establishing the proposed new U.S. flag lines in foreign trade (see *Hearings on the Regulatory Features of the Shipping Act of 1916*, Hearings before the House Merchant Marine and Fisheries Committee, 64 Cong. 1 sess. (1916), pp. 4-20). In 1935 President Roosevelt argued that "the maintenance of fair competition alone calls for American ships of sufficient tonnage to carry a reasonable proportion of our foreign commerce." *Message from the President of the United States,* H. Doc. 118, 74 Cong. 1 sess. (1935), p. 1.

[9] The background and structure of the 1936 act shows maintenance of competition to have been one of the objectives of the subsidy program. Sec. 601 of the act explicitly provides that subsidies shall be granted only to meet foreign competition. This competition should be bona fide in order to give meaning to essential trade route determinations and parity calculations. In addition, the act specifically prohibits subsidized carriers from acting as brokers or agents for foreign carriers, unless specifically exempted by the commission upon a showing of good cause and for a limited period of time. The Maritime Administration (Marad) has consequently required subsidized contractors to submit all pooling proposals for its review. However, reasoning that any pool which has been approved by the regulatory agency as meeting the standards of the 1916 act meets the competitive standards of the 1936 statute, Marad has typically confined its evaluation of pools to their likely impact on the contractor's business position rather than upon the trade. The criteria used by Marad in evaluating pools are listed in *Discriminatory Ocean Freight Rates and the Balance of Payments,* Hearings before the Joint Economic Committee, 88 Cong. 1 sess., Pt. 4, p. 642.

draw upon both quasi-judicial and administrative/executive processes. Here the term "regulation" denotes activities designed to resolve competing claims between all shippers, ports, conferences, and carriers, whether operating under U.S. or foreign flag, and to curb unjust discriminatory use of monopoly power. The term "promotion" embraces the whole complex of activities, including adjudication of competitive problems associated with applications for subsidies.

Integration of Programs. The merits of assigning both promotional and regulatory functions to a single agency were not seriously debated prior to the organization of the U.S. Shipping Board in 1916. Sponsors of the 1916 legislation were primarily concerned that the administrative agency should have sufficiently broad powers to be able to deal with the full range of the United States' problems in ocean shipping. However, after the 1922 collapse of the ocean freight market, the board came under strong pressures to use its regulatory powers to buttress the U.S. flag lines against excessive competition, and its ambiguous position soon became evident to all concerned. Convinced that they could win no satisfaction from an agency wedded to the industry it was assigned to regulate, shippers began to agitate for transfer of the board's regulatory jurisdiction to the Interstate Commerce Commission (ICC). They were answered with arguments stressing the interdependence of the board's functions and the need to protect the government's investment in the U.S. flag merchant marine by reposing its regulation in an agency fully conversant with its operations and problems.[10]

President Roosevelt's recommendation in 1935 was to separate the Shipping Board Bureau's administrative and quasi-judicial functions, the former to remain with the Department of Commerce and the latter to be transferred to the ICC. However, the Congress rejected this recommendation in favor of a new commission vested with plenary powers to promote and regulate the industry. The commission's operations appeared to sustain Congress' conviction that the two programs could be successfully colocated;[11] hence in 1938 a proviso to the 1936 act authorizing the Presi-

[10] The debate between those favoring transfer of the Shipping Board's regulatory functions to the ICC and those opposed was essentially a debate over the purpose of maritime regulation. If its purpose was to protect and promote American shipping, its separation from the subsidy program made no sense. If aimed at maintaining competition and protecting shippers against discrimination, the ICC clearly was more likely to deal evenly with U.S. and foreign lines than the maritime agency.

[11] Appointment of a new, energetic, and independent commission caused a brief step-up in the pace of shipping regulation during the latter portion of the 1930's. From 1936 through 1940, some 325 regulatory cases were concluded—approximately five times the volume in the preceding five years.

dent to transfer the regulatory program if the commission arrangement proved unworkable was repealed.

Disassociation of Programs. President Roosevelt's proposal to shift regulation to the ICC sprang in part from his desire to achieve greater consistency in the regulation of competing modes of transportation. Although the congressional merchant marine committees prevented implementation of his plan, a first step tward rationalizing transportation regulation was authorized in the Transportation Act of 1940 which vested regulation of the rates and practices of coastwise and intercoastal carriers (whose operations were directly competitive with rails and trucks) with the ICC.

Following World War II renewed attention was given to the organization and management of the maritime programs, first by the President's Advisory Committee on the Merchant Marine, then by a congressionally sponsored management survey team, next by the House Committee on Expenditures in the course of its examination of construction subsidy allowances for the S.S. "United States," "Independence," and "Constitution," and finally by the Hoover Commission and its supporting task forces.[12] All attacked the diffuse organization of the U.S. Maritime Commission and its commingling of regulatory, quasi-judicial, business, and executive functions.

The first real attempt to meet these objections by disassociating regulatory and administrative functions was made in 1950. The reorganization plan submitted by President Truman identified three groups of functions. The first group was concerned with *regulating* rates, services, practices, and agreements among ocean carriers; investigating discriminatory practices; and devising rules and regulations to meet conditions unfavorable to U.S. foreign trade shipping. The second group of functions was concerned with *quasi-judicial* problems associated with executing, amending, and terminating operating and construction subsidy contracts; investigating U.S. and foreign cost differentials; and determining adequacy of service and potential discrimination among U.S. flag carriers. The third was

[12] See *Report of the President's Advisory Committee on the Merchant Marine* (Government Printing Office, 1947), pp. 7-8; U.S. Senate Committee on Expenditures in the Executive Departments, *Management Survey of the U.S. Maritime Commission,* 1948; House Committee on Expenditures in the Executive Branch, *Inquiry into the Operations of the Maritime Commission,* H. Rept. 1423, 81 Cong. 1 sess. (1949), p. 26; and Commission on Organization of the Executive Branch of the Government, *Department of Commerce,* Rept. 10 (1949), and *Regulatory Commissions,* Rept. 12 (1949; a task force study on the *United States Maritime Commission,* by James McG. Burns, was published as Rept. 12H). It is interesting to note that Joseph P. Kennedy served as a member of the Commission on Reorganization of the Executive Branch.

concerned with routine *administration* of subsidy contracts; specification of essential trade routes; supervision of ship construction; maintenance of the reserve fleet; consideration of applications to transfer vessels to foreign flag; and all other miscellaneous activities required in the administration of the maritime laws. To succeed the completely independent Maritime Commission, President Truman proposed establishment of a three-man Federal Maritime Board, within the Department of Commerce, and a Maritime Administration, to be directed by the chairman of the board acting ex officio. Under the plan, regulatory and quasi-judicial functions were assigned to the three-man board, administrative to the Secretary of Commerce (in anticipation they would be delegated to the Maritime Administrator to be executed under the Secretary's supervision). In discharging its regulatory functions the Federal Maritime Board was to be independent of the Secretary of Commerce and in its quasi-judicial work associated with the subsidy program to be "guided by the general policies of the Secretary."[13] In the interests of economy, the chairman/administrator was authorized to employ a single staff for both agencies, which came to be known under the hyphenated designation, Federal Maritime Board–Maritime Administration.

This plan was adopted over strong opposition and only because it appeared to promise freedom from the discredited stewardship of the old commission. Even its supporters had reservations about the distinctions between regulatory, quasi-judicial, and administrative functions. However, these difficulties were glossed over in the congressional debate on the plan.

The absence of clear legislative history, the dual role of the chairman/administrator, and the employment of a joint staff all tended to obscure the distinctions between the new agencies' several functions. The work soon blended into a single continuum of activity. By 1959 the situation had become so confused that the chairman/administrator, Clarence G. Morse, acknowledged that he signed all correspondence and orders in both capacities in order to be sure that his action could not be challenged on the grounds that it was based on the wrong authority.[14]

Several difficulties soon became apparent. First, because functions were confused, the proper role and responsibilities of the chairman/ad-

[13] Reorganization Plan Number 21 of 1950, sec. 106. The language of the plan placed the burden for conforming with the Secretary's general policies on the board, rather than giving the Secretary directive authority or even directing that he should establish policies for the board's guidance.

[14] See *Reorganization Plan Number 7*, Hearings before a subcommittee of the House Government Operations Committee, 87 Cong. 1 sess. (1961), p. 80.

ministrator were uncertain. Second, because there was no precedent as to how the Secretary of Commerce might guide the board, the restriction on the board's freedom of action in quasi-judicial matters was a source of potential friction which tended to inhibit communication and cooperation between the maritime agencies and the Commerce Department.[15] Although the board and the Secretary usually were able to avoid overt conflict, it was often perfectly apparent that basic disagreements existed between them. The "two hats" arrangement provided a convenient refuge to the chairman/administrator to speak his mind and operate on his own initiative with other agencies and the Congress. Thus, while the 1950 reorganization nominally brought the promotional program under the cognizance of the Executive, it was a partial and sometimes irritating relationship which ensued.

The long-standing dilemma of the degree to which the board's promotional objectives should be reflected in its regulatory decisions also remained unresolved. However, this problem was obviated by the board's minimal attention to its regulatory responsibilities. Regulation had long been only a secondary activity of the Maritime Commission; within the more action-oriented atmosphere of an executive department it was almost totally eclipsed.[16]

A conviction that the greater glamour of promotional work would inevitably cause neglect of the regulatory program was the principal basis of the 1961 reorganization, developed at the initiative of persons who were dissatisfied by the Federal Maritime Board's handling of its regulatory responsibilities.[17] This reorganization completely severed regulatory

[15] See testimony of Thomas E. Stakem, Chairman, Federal Maritime Board–Maritime Administrator, *ibid.*, p. 38. Mr. Stakem reports that during his period of service with the board (1956-1961) there had been only one direct confrontation between the Secretary of Commerce and the board on a matter of official policy, and that in this instance the Secretary withdrew his objection to the board proposal. Mr. Stakem also notes a number of instances in which the board cooperated with the Secretary's wishes in matters bearing on the administration of the subsidy program, including particularly the overall size of the government's subsidy investment.

[16] In 1961, two years after the Celler Committee had first exposed the weakness of the board's regulatory program, only 54 of the maritime agencies' 2,765 employees were assigned full-time to regulatory work. Commenting on this situation, Congressman Celler noted, "It is thus obvious that rather than face the unpleasant task of attempting to perform inconsistent functions, the Board simply chose to turn its back on one and devote its energies to the other." (See *The Ocean Freight Industry*, H. Rept. 1419, 88 Cong. 1 sess. [1963], p. 379. The decline of the board's regulatory program is copiously documented in this comprehensive investigatory report. See particularly, Chap. 9, "The Federal Maritime Board—A Study in Desultory Regulation.")

[17] The 1961 reorganization was primarily the product of the antitrust subcommittee

from promotional activities. The former were placed in a new independent, five-member regulatory agency; the latter, including responsibility for quasi-judicial decisions required in connection with the subsidy program, were vested in the Secretary of Commerce. This last feature of the plan was opposed by the subsidized lines, who argued that placing the power to grant or withhold subsidy in a single political officer would expose the program to improper political influence and destroy its continuity. In order to meet these objections the Secretary agreed to establish an administrative board, chaired by the Maritime Administrator, which would hear and reach a finding on the record on all quasi-judicial questions previously the responsibility of the Federal Maritime Board, subject to the Secretary's review.[18]

Effectiveness of Current Arrangements. Reorganization Plan Number 7 has been operative for too brief a period to arrive at any conclusions regarding its effectiveness. So far, there has been little evidence of the dire results forecast by its opponents. There have been no accusations of political favoritism or serious charges that the administration of the subsidy program has been capricious. However, there has been concern on the one hand that the Secretary's staff resources and procedural safeguards may not afford an adequate review of appealed cases,[19] and on the other that

of the House Judiciary Committee, whose staff prepared the initial draft of the proposed plan. However, the incompatibility of the Federal Maritime Board–Maritime Administration's diverse assignments, and their effect on the agencies' work, had also been noted by James Landis (President Kennedy's Advisor on Transportation), by the House Merchant Marine and Fisheries Committee, and by staff in the Bureau of the Budget. (See James M. Landis, *Report on Regulatory Agencies to the President-elect,* Committee Print, Senate Judiciary Committee, 86 Cong. 2 sess. [1960] and Congressman Herbert Bonner's letter to President-elect John F. Kennedy, dated Dec. 15, 1960, printed in *Reorganization Plan Number 7 of 1961,* Hearings before the House Merchant Marine and Fisheries Committee, 87 Cong. 1 sess. [1961], p. 10.)

[18] The arrangement adopted by the Secretary following consultation with the Committee of American Steamship Lines, representing the subsidized operators, provided for delegation of the secretary's quasi-judicial authority to the Maritime Subsidy Board and executive authority to the Maritime Administrator. The Subsidy Board was initially composed of the Maritime Administrator, who acted ex officio as chairman of the board, the deputy administrator, and comptroller, whose seat was later shifted to the agency's general counsel. (Department of Commerce, Order 117, Aug. 11, 1961.)

[19] The Maritime Subsidy Board has been overruled by the Secretary in several key cases. In one case (the application of States Steamship Company to call at Hawaiian ports [Docket S-124]) the Secretary was later constrained to ask the District Court, to which an appeal had been taken, to remand the case for further consideration because of discovery that improper ex parte presentations had been made to his staff. The Commerce Department's general counsel and the Maritime Administrative Bar Association are now jointly reviewing the department's procedures to protect against such incidents in the future.

the considerable personal attention given by the Secretary to maritime problems may be undermining the Maritime Administrator's effectiveness in dealing with the industry.

Reorganization alone was an insufficient stimulus to revitalize the government's regulatory program. The chairman and the nucleus of the professional staff of the new agency were drawn from the Federal Maritime Board and brought their established policies and ways of doing business to the new organization. By the spring of 1963 the agency had proved to several of its original supporters, both by its handling of domestic rate cases and its acceptance of international freight pools, that it was too sympathetic to the industry's problems to regulate it effectively. When in May 1963 Senator Paul H. Douglas was able to dramatize how an unfavorable rate structure could affect America's ability to sell its goods abroad, criticism of the new agency grew to a crescendo.[20]

Senator Douglas' recommended reforms were supported by the White House and the Secretary of Commerce. Within three months both the commission's chairman and its executive director were removed from their posts in an effort to inject into the commission the full measure of regulatory vitality and rigor intended by the sponsors of Reorganization Plan Number 7. The new personnel in the agency's key positions have reoriented the commission's objectives toward stricter regulation and have intensified and expanded its activities.

Although the new commission's work has drawn upon and had to be coordinated with other federal agencies (notably Commerce and State), it is apparent that its activities have been facilitated by its independent status. Thus, despite the lack of any immediate impact, Reorganization Plan Number 7 has set the stage for sharpening both promotional and regulatory objectives. This is a clear gain, which is generally agreed to more than offset the drawbacks of further fragmentation of responsibility for administering government maritime activities.

---

[20] In May 1963, the Joint Economic Committee, chaired by Senator Douglas, received testimony from the Commerce Department's Office of Business Economics suggesting that unfavorable freight rates might be deterring expansion of U.S. sales abroad and thus harmful to the U.S. balance of payments position. Specifically, it was brought out that rates on many steel products were higher outbound than inbound. After a further hearing at which Maritime Commission witnesses generally confirmed the analysis, Senator Douglas, on the floor of the Senate, described the situation as "shocking" and excoriated the commission as "grossly negligent and gravely derelict in its duty to protect American industry, the public interest, and the U.S. national interest." (*Congressional Record,* Vol. 109, No. 69, May 9, 1963, pp. 7742-43.) Douglas followed up with letters to the President and the commission asking, in effect, what they proposed to do in response to the committee's findings.

So far, there have been no direct policy conflicts between the two maritime agencies. Indeed, despite their long association, the two agencies have shown little interest in each other's work. Though they have worked cooperatively to develop factual materials on conference rates and economic trends and have coordinated policy statements in areas of obvious mutual interest, neither agency has either asked or given active support to the objectives of the other, although opportunities for collaboration do exist.[21] Instead, both the commission and the administration appear to have avoided becoming closely identified with each other, perhaps partly for bureaucratic reasons but also partly to avoid criticisms that either program might be contaminated by the other's objectives.

Executive and Quasi-judicial Responsibilities. The accepted government practice of assigning regulatory functions to independent, bipartisan, quasi-judicial boards is intended to assure a fair hearing of individual cases, promote continuity of policy, and strengthen the regulated industry's confidence in the government program. Conversely, programs requiring a high degree of management skills or adaptability to changing situations are generally believed to be more suitably placed under the direction of a single executive. In many situations, however, both quasi-judicial and executive qualities are needed. To meet such cases, a variety of intermediate arrangements have been tried, nearly all of which can be illustrated in the development of the government's maritime program.

The history of the maritime program demonstrates that organizational form does not necessarily determine the manner in which an organization operates. The personalities of the chairman and other members of the board, the conditions under which they work, and their relationships to the President and the Congress have often been determining.

In wartime, requirements for executive leadership and rapid, responsible decision-making have been overriding. Although legally coequal with his associate commissioners, the maritime agency's chairman in both World Wars I and II (and in the Korean conflict) operated in much the

[21] Operating subsidy payments are a potent weapon which might be used by the government to enlist the benefiting lines in a joint effort to control conference actions. Conversely, effective regulation is essential to assuring that the development of new U.S. flag services is not blocked by entrenched cartels. Existing law also requires that the Maritime Administrator withhold subsidy from any U.S. flag line which engages in discriminatory practices against other U.S. carriers (sec. 810, Merchant Marine Act, 1936). Interestingly, this section was never invoked against the U.S. flag carriers participating in the Atlantic/Gulf to Japan conference, whose dual rates were specifically found by the Supreme Court to have discriminated against another U.S. flag line, the Isbrandtsen Company.

same manner as the head of an executive department, working closely with the President and enjoying wide scope in the internal management of his agency. Both wars were followed by a reaction against a strong chairman in favor of more deliberative procedures in which all commissioners participated equally. The results, particularly during the period 1946 through 1948, were extremely unsatisfactory and caused the commission to be without effective leadership during the most critical periods in its history.[22]

Structure of the Maritime Agencies. The government's first maritime agency, the U.S. Shipping Board, was headed by five members each of whom had equal legal status. Recognizing that the acquisition and operation of a government-owned fleet would probably require a more decisive and flexible instrument, the 1916 act authorized the government to organize an operating corporation and even to sell up to 50 percent of its stock to the public. The Emergency Fleet Corporation, established under this authority, functioned as the board's operating arm from 1917 through 1936. Similar organizations were established in World War II and during the Korean conflict.[23] Both of the latter organizations were headed by the chairman of the maritime agency, but operated semiautonomously.

Organizational arrangements in peacetime have been more variant. Following World War I the membership of the Shipping Board was increased and its operating duties reduced to permit it to give more attention to its regulatory, quasi-judicial, and policy development roles. Most operating functions were continued in the Emergency Fleet Corporation under the direction of a manager who was under the "general supervision" of the board. When conflicts between the corporation and the board caused this arrangement to become untenable, the board (against President Coolidge's wishes) assumed direct control of the corporation's oper-

[22] The vacuum of leadership immediately following both wars was the result of a combination of factors. Organizational relations and internal procedures were adjusted following both wars to give coequal status and full participation to each member of the commission in all facets of the agency's business. However, in both 1918 and 1946, the commission was handicapped by loss of experienced personnel at all levels. Between 1918 and 1921, the U.S. Shipping Board was headed by four different chairmen. In 1946 the entire commission that had served with Admiral Land during World War II resigned. Following both wars there was of course also a crisis of presidential leadership, the effects of which reached even to the management of the government's shipping agency.

[23] Executive Order 9054, Feb. 7, 1942, established the War Shipping Administration as an independent agency responsible to the President and directed by the chairman of the U.S. Maritime Commission, acting ex officio, to manage wartime ship operations and priority allocations. Executive Order 10219, Feb. 28, 1951, created the National Shipping Authority, patterned on the War Shipping Administration, to conduct operations during the Korean conflict.

ating functions. The Shipping Board's effectiveness, however, was dissipated in factional disputes among its members and between the board and officials of the corporation.

Executive authority was partially restored in 1933 when the board's membership was reduced from seven to three and its operations transferred to the Department of Commerce. Effective leadership was not achieved, however, until the government's shipping policy had been clarified by the 1936 act. The momentum established by this enactment, which gave the government's maritime programs their most vigorous direction since World War I, lasted through the Second World War.

The authority and prestige associated with the chairmanship of the U.S. Maritime Commission from 1937 through 1946 rested on its chairmen's personal qualities, their relationships with the President, and the necessities of the situation rather than on special statutory powers. Legally each of the commisioners had an equal say in the commission's business. Upon the wartime chairman's 1946 retirement, the commissioners determined to exercise their full legal role and to pass collegially on every item of commission business. This decision had a profound impact on its operations. From 1946 through 1948 the commission totally lacked executive authority or leadership.

Effective delegation to the commission's staff became impossible. Given the range of the commission's responsibilities, the new system soon created a major administrative crisis.[24] The commission was agonizingly slow in arranging sales of tankers to alleviate Europe's critical fuel needs, it proved powerless to quell the industry's serious labor problems, it failed in an abortive attempt to re-establish coastwise and intercoastal freight and passenger services, and gave little or no effective support to efforts in the industry and by its own staff to plan the U.S. flag fleet's peacetime role. Instead, the commission allowed itself to become hopelessly bogged down in sorting out claims for and against the government arising out of its wartime operations and later became embroiled in disputes over subsidies for new ship construction. In 1947 the respected Comptroller General, Lindsey Warren, informed the Congress that he had "just about lost patience" with the commission.[25] The year following, the House Committee on Executive Expenditures reported that disagreements within the commission had led to such "constant and uncompromising frictions" that the agency was unable to carry out its duties properly.[26]

[24] An excellent account of the difficulties encountered during this period and analysis of their causes is found in Burns, *op. cit.*

[25] *Ibid.*, p. III-16.

[26] *Inquiry into the Operations of the Maritime Commission,* H. Rept. 1423, p. 24.

The commission itself soon realized the need for corrective action. An internal study led in 1948 to a thoroughgoing restructuring of the agency's internal organization, appointment of a general manager, enlargement of the commission's delegations to its staff, and a partial return to the earlier practice of assigning specific areas of the agency's activity to each of the commission's members. These reforms were followed in 1949 by Reorganization Plan Number 6, which implemented a Hoover Commission recommendation that presidentially appointed chairmen should direct the internal management of multi-headed agencies. This action, however, was not enough. Belief that the commission structure was simply unsuited to the many new administrative responsibilities of the maritime agency was a principal factor leading to the 1950 reorganization (plan number 21), establishing the Federal Maritime Board–Maritime Administration within the Department of Commerce.

The Korean war broke out hardly a month later. Admiral E. L. Cochrane, President Truman's selection to head the new board, attacked his duties as chairman/administrator with vigor and authority. The two associate members of the board were drawn into this effort and later were given formal ex officio appointments to the Maritime Administration as special assistants to the administrator so that they might participate freely in nonregulatory work. Administrative and operating activities progressively consumed more and more of the board's time and energies and regulation less and less. By the late fifties the dearth of agenda items caused the board to meet an average of less than four hours per week. At that, most of the business brought before it related to the promotional program.

The internal operations of the Maritime Administration were therefore little affected by Reorganization Plan Number 7 of 1961, except to bring the agency's activities more effectively under the supervision of the Secretary of Commerce. The agency's quasi-judicial functions are now conducted by an administrative rather than a statutory board, and its members have other regular administrative assignments. However, this administrative board (the Maritime Subsidy Board) has been more active than its predecessor and brings more expertness to its decisions.[27]

[27] In its first three years of operation, the Maritime Subsidy Board held 264 meetings and decided 1,155 cases ranging from approving a new name for a subsidized ship to cases vitally affecting the well-being of specific U.S. shipping concerns. Although only a small portion of the board's work is subject to the Administrative Procedures Act, it keeps an official record of its proceedings and in major matters publishes a reasoned defense of its decisions.

The Maritime Administration has convened other administrative boards to handle specialized matters falling outside the purview of the Maritime Subsidy Board but appropriate for collegial consideration. One of these boards handles all ship valuations

Appeal Procedures. The procedures devised to guide consideration of cases within the maritime agencies and for appeal to other authorities complement the maritime agencies' internal structure. By and large, matters arising out of the Shipping Act of 1916 fall under the Administrative Procedures Act and can be appealed directly to the Circuit Court. The Administrative Procedures Act also applies to those promotional decisions which, under law, can be reached only following hearings (these include such matters as assessing whether subsidy grants may prejudice the position of a competing U.S. flag operator or whether adjustments in subsidy payments are warranted by changed conditions on an essential trade route). However, the appeal in these cases is to the District Court, which usually supports any reasonable action by an administrative agency which respects due process of law.

Since 1961 all substantive decisions of the Maritime Subsidy Board also have been subject to review by the Secretary of Commerce, on his own motion or in response to an appeal from one of the parties to the proceeding.[28] During the first three years of the board's operation, appeals were infrequent (only 25 out of 1,155 official decisions) but were filed on the board's most important cases. Ten petitions for review have been granted and three cases docketed by the Secretary on his own motion. The board was upheld in seven cases; it was reversed or the case remanded in six.

Matters considered by the Maritime Administration or Maritime Subsidy Board which are outside the purview of the Administrative Procedures Act can also be brought before the District Court on equitable grounds after exhaustion of administrative remedies. However, in two cases in which competing lines sought injunctions against the award of subsidy contracts, the court ruled that it would be premature to consider the matter before contracts had been signed and damages, if any, assessed.[29] Even if this rule were not applied, the delays associated with bringing cases to court and prosecuting further appeals within the judicial system

---

for trade-in or sales. Another inspects records of ship trials and accepts completed ships on behalf of the government.

[28] Departmental Order 117, Aug. 11, 1961, establishing the Maritime Subsidy Board, specified that appeals to board actions based on hearing must be filed within 25 days and in all other cases within 15 days of the board's decision, which will then become final if the Secretary (within these same time limits) has not announced an intent to review.

[29] *American President Line* v. *Federal Maritime Board,* Civil Action 1327-60, U.S. District Court for D.C.; and *U.S. Line* v. *Waterman Steamship Co. and FMB,* Civil Action 1951-60, U.S. District Court for D.C.

make it unlikely that in cases of this type the courts can provide a useful remedy.

For this reason, and because the beneficiaries of the subsidy program have perhaps been reluctant to challenge the decisions of the program's sponsor, judicial review has been of little importance in the development of the promotional program. This is in contrast to the regulatory program, in which issues have frequently been appealed to the courts, often with the effect of overturning the administrative decision. A somewhat more effective review of the administrative agencies' promotional work (for example, by permitting decisions based on statutory hearings to be appealed directly to the Circuit Court) might well have provided a more efficacious and less troublesome check upon arbitrary administrative action than the procedures requiring collegial decision-making within the agencies themselves.

Maritime and Other Agencies' Missions. Another organizational problem arises from the need to relate the Maritime Administration's programs to those of other agencies. These problems have stirred numerous organizational issues over the course of the maritime program's fifty-year history.

Commerce–Defense Relationships. The dominance of the defense justification for shipping subsidies and the difficulty of obtaining timely and responsible estimates of the military's shipping requirements have caused many observers to conclude that the Department of Defense should assume a greater responsibility for the administration of the subsidy program than was provided in the 1936 act.[30] Although the possibility is occasionally discussed, no group has seriously proposed that the entire promotional program be shifted from Commerce to Defense. There have, however, been recommendations to transfer certain discrete activities and a continuing effort to clarify responsibility and procedures for obtaining estimates of the military requirements for merchant shipping to meet defense needs.

The reserve fleet, as originally conceived, was intended solely as a de-

[30] The only responsibilities vested by the 1936 act in any of the military departments were to cooperate with the commission in developing its ship construction programs and to review specific proposed vessel designs in order to recommend to the commission changes which would be desirable in the interests of national defense (49 Stat. 1989, 1995). Subsequently, the act was amended to provide that the Secretary of the Navy cooperate with the Secretary of Commerce in periodically surveying the adequacy of U.S. privately owned shipyards as a mobilization base for national defense (52 Stat. 957) and supplemented to require defense concurrence in vessels to be retained in the reserve fleet (60 Stat. 44) or released from mothballs (74 Stat. 312).

fense facility.[31] The 1947 President's Advisory Committee on the Merchant Marine consequently recommended that responsibility for maintaining the reserve fleet be transferred from the Maritime Commission to the Navy, but no action was taken.[32] Subsequently, various actions have broadened the allowable uses of mothballed shipping (i.e., for vessel exchanges, for non-military emergencies, and to handle unusual foreign aid needs) and therefore somewhat complicated the organization issue. Nonetheless, transferring the reserve fleet to Defense would give the agency with primary interest in its use the responsibility for its upkeep, and might help also to correct the apparent disparity in attention to active and reserve facilities.

Similar reasoning has recently been applied to financing the defense features requested by the Navy for vessels constructed in the replacement program. The President's 1965 budget proposed that the costs of these features be assessed against the Department of Defense, but the proposal was rejected by the Congress on technical grounds. Substantive legislation has since been submitted to authorize the proposed shift of funding responsibility, but no congressional action taken.

Delineation of defense requirements for merchant shipping has been complicated by the fact that in wartime both military and industrial needs must be met.[33] Defense Department statements have not always been precise in indicating their coverage. On other occasions, the utility of the Defense requirements statements has been diminished by security limitations, ambiguous phraseology, and the absence of any objective measures against which to assess priorities. The latter concern has been at least temporarily relieved by Secretary McNamara's thorough and dispassionate analytic methods, but replaced by fears that if merchant shipping experts do not participate in drawing up and evaluating Defense cost/benefit studies, this mode of meeting the military's logistics needs will receive short shrift.

Cargo Preference Administration. A substantial segment of the U.S. flag merchant marine now depends upon government preference cargoes for its survival; the cargo preference statutes in turn cause the government's principal shipping agencies to be dependent upon American vessels to

---

[31] The Ship Sales Act of 1946 titled the fleet a National Defense Reserve Fleet and imposed strict limits on its use in order to protect against government use of reserve ships to depress the commercial market.

[32] *Report of the President's Advisory Committee on the Merchant Marine*, p. 54.

[33] The division of responsibility for estimating direct military and other defense-related shipping requirements is outlined in Chapter 5.

fulfill their shipping commitments. This latter fact has led the Congress to specify that the cargo preference program should be administered by the shipping agencies, under the general coordination of the Maritime Administration. This arrangement, however, is not wholly satisfactory to anyone.

The decentralized and often hostile manner in which cargo preferences are administered has been of particular concern to tramp shipping interests, who believe that they could win a better deal if responsibility for the program were centralized in the Maritime Administration. This proposal is appealing to the Department of Agriculture, which regards cargo preferences as an irritating burden. But it is opposed by the Department of Commerce, which is reluctant to assume the costs or to become the target for the tramp owners' pressures to expand the program, and by the subsidized lines, which fear that additional attention to cargo preferences might weaken support for the operating subsidy program.

To abandon existing arrangements would also create serious operating problems and administrative complications. The shipping agencies should presumably still bear the world market costs of shipment and would have to maintain overall control over the movement of goods to the pierhead, onto the ship, and to the ultimate destination. The Maritime Administration might finance the foreign-domestic rate differential, but would have no basis for projecting amounts needed or for controlling the manner in which they were paid unless it also took charge of the shipping arrangements. The administrative dilemma in effect mirrors more basic anomolies and contradictions within the cargo preference program.[34]

Other Issues. Other areas in which the Maritime Administration's responsibilities overlap other agencies' missions include dealings with maritime labor, port development, and promotion of coastwise and intercoastal shipping. In each area the Maritime Administrator has appointed a special assistant to the administrator to act as liaison to the agency of primary interest and to represent the Maritime Administration's interests in these fields. The arrangement, however, is not a very effective one and is premised entirely on the principle that the government's overall program for the merchant marine can be integrated through voluntary cooperation.

The American shipping industry also has an important stake in the Treasury Department's administration of tax, inspection, and registry statutes. The tax program must clearly continue to be administered by the In-

---

[34] The difficulties arise because *shipments* rather than *ships* are subsidized. An alternative, discussed in Chapter 12, would be to authorize direct subsidies to a specified number of ships geared to carrying a suitable proportion of government-sponsored cargoes, but to contract for the shipments at world market rates.

ternal Revenue Service. However, Treasury's jurisdiction in ship safety inspection and registry matters appears to be more a product of historical accident than current needs and has caused some problems, particularly in planning for ship automation. Transfer of these functions to the Maritime Administration would appear to be a practical solution, which would also increase its ability to influence the development of American shipping, enhance its powers in dealing with the industry, and generally bolster its authority and prestige.

A final problem concerns protection of U.S. flag shipping against foreign discrimination and unfair competitive practices employed by foreign flag lines. Power to make rules and regulations to meet unfavorable competitive conditions was placed in the U.S. Shipping Board by Section 19 of the 1920 Merchant Marine Act. Because the section dealt with rule-making authorities, its administration was transferred to the Federal Maritime Board in 1950 and (apparently by inadvertence) to the Federal Maritime Commission in 1961. The commission as a regulatory agency does not have as direct an interest in correcting conditions unfavorable to American ship operators as does the Department of Commerce. Neither agency can act effectively in this area without the concurrence of the Department of State. A recasting of the 1920 procedure therefore appears indicated.

Integration of Shipping Policies. The large number of agencies with a legitimate interest in maritime policy formulation and administration complicates the coordination of their activities and integration of the total government program. For many years the difficulties of coordination were compounded by the independence of the principal maritime agency. This problem was particularly troublesome immediately following World War II when the commission's promotional objectives often conflicted with the Administration's overall strategy for European recovery and even with specific presidential requests for use of commission-controlled ships.[35]

The stipulation in the 1950 reorganization that the new Federal Maritime Board was to be "guided by the general policies of the Secretary of Commerce" was intended to overcome these difficulties without compromising the board's independence in deciding specific cases. It proved however, to be only partially effective and further reorganization (in 1961)

[35] One of the issues dividing the commission and the Administration, concerned with sales of tankers to European nations to meet critical fuel shortages during the winter of 1947-48, became so celebrated a case that the incident was recorded and included in the Herbert Stein casebook, *Public Administration and Policy Development* (Harcourt Brace, 1952) to illustrate the difficulties of program coordination.

was required to bring the promotional program fully within the control of the executive branch.

Statutory Powers. The need for coordination of the government's maritime programs has been explicitly recognized on several occasions by the Congress. As early as 1920 the Congress authorized and directed the U.S. Shipping Board to monitor other agency activities affecting shipping and to notify the responsible officials of any rule or regulation it wished modified, annulled, or promulgated. In the event of disagreement, the facts must be submitted to the President for decision. The force of the procedure was considerably diminished by exemption of the Public Health Service, Steamboat Inspection Service, and Consular Service, then the three most important activities outside the Shipping Board's immediate organization. In the memory of present agency staff, the 1920 procedure has never been used, perhaps because sufficiently serious disagreements can be taken to the President in any event.[36]

Congressional interest in effective inter-agency coordination was reaffirmed in the 1936 act, which directed the new commission to establish liaison with other government agencies in order to secure preference for U.S. flag ships. During World War II the commission was given power to coordinate and later to direct most public and private shipping activities.[37] Following the war, however, primary responsibility for traffic management reverted to the various shipping agencies. A 1954 effort by the House Merchant Marine and Fisheries Committee to restore the Maritime Administration's role as coordinator of cargo preference statutes accordingly met with only partial success.[38]

[36] The powers vested in the Shipping Board by the 1920 act were assumed by the Maritime Commission in 1936, by the Federal Maritime Board in 1950, and (apparently by error) by the Federal Maritime Commission in 1961. Inasmuch as the powers placed in the Shipping Board by the 1920 statute were conditioned upon their being used in the "accomplishment of the purposes of this Act"—an exclusively promotional statute—it is questionable whether they could even be invoked by the commission, in the unlikely event that a situation arose in which their use was desired.

[37] Beginning in July 1941, the commission (subsequently the War Shipping Administration) administered a comprehensive priority system applicable to both U.S. and foreign owned ships operating in U.S. foreign trade through powers placed in it by ship warrants legislation to set the conditions to be observed as a condition to receiving fuel and supplies. This emergency legislation was supplemented in March 1942, by permanent legislation (56 Stat. 171) authorizing the commission to coordinate public and private freight forwarding activities and directing other departments and agencies to follow its instructions.

[38] The House Merchant Marine and Fisheries Committee recommended that the Maritime Administration undertake to coordinate cargo preference administration, but failed to equip that agency with any statutory powers or other tools to aid it in

Interagency Committees and Agreements. Where responsibility is not clearly defined, as in cargo preference administration, policy coordination depends on voluntary methods. A popular, though frequently ineffective, method is the interagency committee. Occasionally, formal agreements are concluded between two or more interested agencies to define responsibilities and tie down policies.

The cargo preference problem illustrates both the uses and limitations of the committee device. In an effort to comply with the House committee's recommendation, the Maritime Administrator convened an Interagency Committee on Cargo Preference in 1955. The group initially was quite active and provided a useful vehicle for exchange of information and views. However, the committee had no authority and had little success in inducing the agencies represented to adopt consistent policies.[39] In fact, the committee was unable even to establish a uniform method of reporting. Although cargo preference continues to generate numerous and difficult problems requiring interagency coordination, the committee has been inactive since December 1963, although not formally discontinued.

✓ A second area in which committees are used for interagency coordination is in establishing a U.S. government position on matters being considered by international organizations. A permanent Shipping Coordinating Committee provides staff support to U.S. participants in the Inter-Governmental Maritime Consultative Organization. Other international activities are staffed through *ad hoc* working groups. This procedure has been effective within its limited frame of reference, but no attempt is made to oversee the many dealings which agencies administering maritime programs have with foreign governments.

A third major area requiring interagency coordination is the matter of defense requirements and availabilities. General policy guidance on logistic and strategic assumptions is provided through the National Security Council. Staff level liaison has been achieved through a Joint Navy-Maritime Administration Planning Group, co-chaired by the Deputy Mar-

---

this task. See *Administration of the Cargo Preference Statutes,* H. Rept. 80, 84 Cong. 1 sess. (1955), p. 22.

[39] The Interagency Committee on Cargo Preference is chaired by the Maritime Administrator. Other committee members are senior civil service personnel in charge of the shipping activities of their agencies. The problems of administering the cargo preference statutes are so sensitive that at one time or another they have personally concerned the heads of each of the major shipping agencies, who have been unable to agree on common policies. Under these circumstances, it has also been impossible to achieve agreement through their staff.

itime Administrator and Deputy Commander, MSTS.[40] Since 1962 the Commerce Department's Office of Emergency Transportation has provided an additional vehicle for drawing together civil and military data and for developing mobilization plans. Neither of these groups, however, is represented at the level at which critical Pentagon decisions regarding the role of sealift are made, with the result that it has been extraordinarily difficult to detail definitive plans compatible with the nation's overall defense strategy or to achieve a spirit of active and positive collaboration between the civil and military agencies concerned with the merchant marine.

Interagency committees have been more successful dealing with problems where there are fewer policy considerations. Several committees operate in specialized technical areas such as ship structures and nuclear technology. Others are concerned with such matters as document simplification, travel facilitation, and port utilization and control.

Aside from the documents establishing these various committees, there have been almost no formal agreements among the agencies concerned with merchant shipping to define their respective roles, assign responsibilities, or establish procedures for consultation on matters of mutual interest. There is, for example, no document to supplement Reorganization Plan Number 7 of 1961 to specify operating relationships even between such intimately associated agencies as the Federal Maritime Commission and Maritime Administration. In fact, the only interagency agreement of any programmatic importance is the 1954 Wilson-Weeks compact, which established a system for allocating MSTS shipments to liner and contract carriers, fixed the size of the MSTS nucleus fleet, and established procedures for its review.[41]

The lack of continuing interagency consideration of maritime policy issues has forced *ad hoc* coordination through the White House, the Exec-

[40] Although officially only for the guidance of the Secretary of the Navy and Maritime Administrator, analyses of active and reserve fleet requirements prepared by the Joint Navy-Maritime Administration Planning Group have also been made available to the Congress and to other government agencies. Although the group's findings have been without official status, they have naturally been regarded as authoritative by those whose predilections they confirmed and by others not informed as to their status. This has sometimes caused embarrassment to the Administration, most notably when President Eisenhower refused to support construction of new superliners despite the group's findings that the fleet was deficient in fast, modern troop carrying capability. The planning group is now inactive.

[41] The complete text of the Wilson-Weeks agreement may be found in *Operations of the Military Sea Transportation Service*, Committee Print, House Merchant Marine and Fisheries Committee, 83 Cong. 2 sess. (1955), pp. 22-23.

utive Office of the President, the congressional maritime committees, or interested private groups. At this level, however, it is exceedingly difficult to secure the concentrated, sustained attention necessary to unravel and solve complex issues. Furthermore, once an issue has been identified, it attracts the attention of groups having important private interests to defend, which complicates its solution. Finally, and perhaps most important, coordination of merchant shipping matters is made vastly more difficult by the lack of any general agreement as to the purposes of the program or even as to the current position of the U.S. merchant fleet.

The obstacles to shaping coherent, government-wide policies are illustrated by the substantial but fruitless efforts of President Kennedy's Ad Hoc Committee on Flags of Convenience and Cargo Preference. The committee, organized by the Secretary of Labor at the President's request in February 1962, was composed of policy-level representatives from each of the eleven agencies having significant interests in the problems to be considered.[42] Initial plans anticipated that a report would be rendered in March, following approximately six weeks of intensive study. The calendar for the Supreme Court's consideration of the flag of convenience issue established late summer as the absolute deadline on the committee's work. However, early in its deliberations, the committee concluded that it would be impossible to make any recommendations on the matters before it except in the context of broad national policies and of more data than was then available on the fleet's military role. By late summer the committee still did not have even a tentative position to guide the Solicitor General. An interim report to the President on the committee's activities was filed by the Director of the Bureau of the Budget in December 1962. There was no final report.

Administrative Operations

Administrative operations and procedures, such as budget, personnel, legislative reporting, and internal agency management and control, can contribute importantly to better integrated and articulated policies as well as to successful program administration. Selection of personnel sympa-

---

[42] Initial members of the committee were the secretaries of State, Treasury, Defense, Agriculture, and Commerce, the Attorney General, the Director of the Bureau of the Budget, and the Maritime Administrator. The group was subsequently expanded to include the chairman of the Council of Economic Advisers, the deputy special counsel to the President, and the chairman of the National Labor Relations Board. Actual attendance at committee meetings was usually at the assistant secretary level.

thetic and responsive to his objectives may in fact be the President's most effective mode of coordination.

Administrative Continuity. Some years ago the CIO Maritime Committee addressed itself to the question, "What is really wrong with American merchant marine policy development and administration?"[43] Its principal conclusion was that the program lacks continuity. The turnover rate among policy personnel has been extremely high. Between 1950 and 1964 there were eight Maritime Administrators; five additional men served an average of two and a half years each on the Federal Maritime Board. There also were six appointments to the position of Secretary of Commerce and eight as Under Secretary of Transportation. A total of one hundred and two different persons served on the House Merchant Marine and Fisheries Committee; forty-six on the Senate Commerce Committee.

This turnover rate obviously establishes a mammoth obstacle to consistent and coherent program development. Its effects, however, have been compounded by inadequate linkage between politically appointed personnel, among whom turnover is always high, and the civil service staff which renders continuing service to the maritime agency. As the CIO committee pointed out:

> Each new President, Director of the Bureau of the Budget, Secretary of Commerce, Under Secretary of Commerce for Transportation, and Administrator make their independent studies. More frequently than not, these studies are not completed in time for action by the persons for whom they were conducted. The successor seldom profits from the previous study. This despite the fact that their conclusions, if any, are frequently the same.[44]

In a relatively small agency, such as the Maritime Administration, the administrator customarily takes direct charge of the agency's work. Each new man appointed to the post has undoubtedly believed that he should give direction where his predecessors failed, and has felt justified in temporarily deferring policy changes under consideration until he has had an opportunity personally to assess his new job. However, because the men appointed maritime administrator have for one reason or another not remained in office as long as they expected, policy development has been in a condition of semipermanent suspension punctuated by occasional spurts of feverish but often non-productive activity.

[43] CIO Maritime Committee, *Merchant Marine Policies, Practices, and Problems,* a statement presented to the House Merchant Marine and Fisheries Committee, July 13, 1955.
[44] *Ibid.*

There is little even the best organized staff can do to relieve this condition. At most, the staff can seek to ease the transition and to maintain the agency's institutional learning process by educating each new administrator to his predecessors' objectives, methods and frustrations in an effort to build for the future upon the experience of the past. However, if the administrator is suspicious of his staff or the staff too inured by the frequent shifts in the agency's top personnel to really try to maintain the momentum of the previous administration, this learning process cannot take place and the opportunities for successful policy development are severely inhibited.

Personnel. An organization's ability to surmount the difficulties created by excessive turnover is one measure of the quality of both its appointive and civil service personnel. All the men who were appointed to the chairmanship of the U.S. Maritime Commission were persons of substantial prior accomplishments.[45] Although the chairmanship of the Federal Maritime Board within the Department of Commerce has been a less prestigious position, it has also drawn men of proven abilities and extraordinarily varied experience. The roster of chairmen includes the former Chief of the Bureau of Ships and the former Commander of the MSTS, a well-known clothing executive who chose to follow President Eisenhower to Washington, a former steamship company president, a member of the maritime bar who had been the agency's general counsel, and a career civil servant, who had served for four years as a member of the board. Appointments to these positions, and to the position of Maritime Administrator since 1961, have been "merit" appointments, made with the intention of providing effective leadership to the maritime program. In contrast, most of the appointments to associate membership on the commission and board appear to have been politically motivated, made with less concern for their effect on the agencies' operation.

Staffing of the government's maritime agencies has been adversely affected by the limited opportunities for new hires and promotions. Between 1946 and 1956 the size of the maritime agencies' administrative staffs fell from approximately 9,300 to only 1,150. In the succeeding years there has been modest growth, bringing the staff to 1,325 in 1961 and to approximately 1,500 persons (including the 240 employees of the Federal Maritime Commission) in 1964. Nevertheless, the agencies' two reorganizations have permitted some selectivity in filling senior positions and have thus prevented stagnation in the upper brackets.

[45] The men who have directed the government's shipping agencies and their qualifications for office are listed in Appendix D.

Both the 1950 and 1961 reorganizations protected the status of the agencies' civil service personnel. In 1950 the staff of the commission was transferred en bloc to the new agency. However, new personnel were brought in from outside the agency to direct nine of its fifteen major offices. Four deputy office heads and five division chiefs were also recruited from outside the agency and some thirty internal readjustments were made among key personnel.

In 1961 about half of the Maritime Administration's top staff transferred to the new commission, permitting a large number of new appointments to be made within the older organization. Those transferring to the commission tended to be the more senior members of the administration staff; the vacancies created by their departure were largely filled from within but by a much younger group.[46]

Budget. The postwar contraction in the maritime agencies' administrative activities has tended to insulate them from the budgetary pressures and controls applied to expanding programs.[47] In the administrative area the Maritime Administration has been able to plan its activities with reasonable confidence that funds will be provided in adequate amounts. Where backlogs have developed, as in the determination of subsidy rates, the delays have been caused by meticulous procedures rather than inadequate funds.

In other areas the agency's budget estimates have not been fully supported. Most notably, the subsidized vessel replacement program, so laboriously negotiated during the mid-fifties, has been significantly slowed through budgetary controls.[48] These appear to have resulted from a mix-

[46] Within the Maritime Administration there are twenty-two key career positions (chiefs of offices, coast directors, and key staff positions). Less than ten of the occupants of these key positions as of Dec. 31, 1964, had been employed by the Maritime Administration in a similar capacity prior to the 1961 reorganization. Six of the jobs have been filled from outside the agency. Over the ten-year period 1954-64, a total of sixteen senior personnel were brought in at the career executive level.

[47] The insulation from budgetary pressures has not extended to the new Maritime Commission, which has attempted a very rapid expansion of staff. Limitations on staff expansion are held by the chairman to have caused the commission to operate on a "crisis-to-crisis basis rather than in a planned and orderly fashion." *Department of Commerce and Related Agencies Appropriations, 1965,* Hearings before the Senate Appropriations Committee, 88 Cong. 2 sess. (1964), p. 1701.

[48] The date for replacement of each ship covered by subsidy is specified in the contract. Although enforcement of the replacement clause has never been attempted through the courts, it is presumed to impose a binding obligation upon the contractor. The grant of subsidy to assist in such construction, on the other hand, is at least technically at the discretion of the government. The government's failure to finance the replacement programs provided in the contracts accordingly is not a default of its obligations.

ture of programmatic and budget policy considerations, and the reduced level (which permits construction of about seventeen rather than twenty-five ships per year) has been alternatively supported and opposed by those immediately responsible for the program.[49] The research and development program has also been molded by the budget process. Here the budget has been used as an instrument for coordination and management, since many of the Maritime Administration's proposed projects are closely related to work in other agencies.

The budget process has not been an effective check on the operating subsidy program, although efforts have been made to control the growth of subsidies through special limitations on the board's contract authority.[50] Indirect cargo preference, tax, and credit subsidies are not even identified in the budget and usually completely escape review. Occasionally, however, the diversion of Agriculture appropriations to the merchant shipping industry provokes the subcommittee handling the Agriculture bill to insert a statement in the record which at least identifies the amounts involved.[51]

Legislative Reporting. The Merchant Marine Act of 1936 is explicit in requiring the administrative agency to report annually to the Congress with recommendations for improvements to the act. During its first several years of operation, the commission submitted a legislative program with

[49] Competition for funds was clearly the principal factor which forced stretchout of the replacement program. However, a number of industry and executive branch officials also questioned the economy of retiring ships with less than twenty to twenty-five years service, particularly at a time when construction prices were high and the industry appeared to be on the threshold of a major technological advance.

[50] Appropriations are required for operating subsidies only to liquidate obligations which the board can validly incur under the authority of the Merchant Marine Act, 1936 (see Comptroller General decision B-73381). Should the government refuse to honor these obligations, the contractors would have recourse to the courts for judgment. Judicially determined claims and judgments are financed through a separate appropriation, usually enacted without objection.

The use of limitations on the board's authority to contract for additional voyages is discussed in Chapter 6. The practical relationships between the House and Senate Appropriations and Merchant Marine subcommittees which have caused these limitations always to be set at a level which does not crimp existing programs are discussed in Chapter 11.

[51] Agricultural interests have become acutely sensitive to the size of agricultural subsidies and have consistently pressed for accounting techniques which segregate assistance made available through the price support program to other sectors of the economy. In reporting the department's 1965 bill, the House Appropriations Committee noted that from 1955 through 1966 Agriculture appropriations had provided $675 million indirect subsidy to the shipping industry and requested the department to develop ways for removing this cost from its bill. (*Department of Agriculture and Related Agencies Appropriation Bill, 1965,* H. Rept. 1387, 88 Cong. 2 sess. [1964], p. 54.)

its annual report. The practice was discontinued in 1941. Since the war, recommendations for new legislation have been relatively few and have been mostly limited to minor modifications of existing programs.[52]

The discipline of preparing a comprehensive legislative plan has been supplanted in the postwar years by less formal procedures for reporting to the Congress. Under Congressman Bonner's chairmanship, the House Merchant Marine and Fisheries Committee generally held hearings at least biennially to review the general status of the government's maritime program. These hearings were intended both to introduce new members to the committee's work and to glean suggestions for legislative changes from the Administration. Mr. Bonner regarded this device, however, as of marginal usefulness, and the hearings were discontinued in 1962.[53]

Research Activities. The government's maritime agencies have numerous research responsibilities. The Maritime Administration's Office of Ship Construction is continuously engaged in laying out new cargo ship designs and in improving structural features. Foreign and domestic cost studies, conducted annually by its Office of Government Aids, and trade route reviews, conducted on a three-year cycle by the same office, require fairly sophisticated techniques. The Division of Trade Studies (previously the Office of Statistics) maintains basic ship, manpower, and cargo data and periodically analyzes the data. However, none of these units has attempted to mount a comprehensive research or development program aimed at identifying and solving basic industry problems.

A major step in this direction was taken in 1960, when an Office of Research and Development was organized by the Maritime Administration pursuant to recommendations of a panel of the National Academy of Sciences. The office was charged with developing a technical research program to increase the competitiveness of U.S. flag shipping in international trade and specifically to reduce government subsidy costs. Except for carrying forward the N.S "Savannah" project, the office has concentrated on developing ship automation and sponsoring exploratory work on ad-

[52] In the 87th and 88th Congresses, the Maritime Administration proposed five significant substantive and six technical amendments to existing legislation. Four of these proposals were approved.

[53] A factor which probably contributed to the committee's discontinuance of its biennial reviews was the shift in Administration attitudes toward the merchant marine in 1961-62. Rather than providing an indoctrination compatible with the general views of the committee's senior members, the 1962 hearings publicized a point of view which the committee could not accept. It was during these hearings that Secretary McNamara reported that merchant shipping, although still necessary, made only a limited contribution to national defense, which did not justify any expansion of existing programs.

vanced ocean transportation concepts. In support of those projects the Office of Research and Development has contracted studies on such diverse subjects as the structure of steamship tariffs, the impact of automation on maritime labor, and the manner in which subsidy payments might be restructured to maximize incentive to increase efficiency. The program has received only lukewarm support from the maritime industry, which appears to regard much of the work as unrealistic.

The Maritime Administration's only professional economist for many years was the director of its Office of Statistics. In 1963, two economists were added to its Office of Program Planning to initiate an analysis of economic trends in the U.S. flag shipping industry and to perform other special studies. The following year an Office of Transportation Economics was organized by the Federal Maritime Commission to assist in its studies of freight rate differentials. However, even with this augmentation, the maritime agencies' resources for economic analysis remained woefully slim.

Internal Operating Procedures. The internal operations of the government's maritime agencies have been constantly criticized by outside groups. The key matters of concern were identified by Judge Landis in his 1960 *Report on Regulatory Agencies,* which describes the Federal Maritime Board as an agency which has "suffered from a lack of settled public procedures and standards of decision and has placed too much emphasis on bureaucratic details to the disregard of matters of large public importance."[54]

The two problems are interrelated. The maritime agencies' somewhat ponderous methods, attention to detail, and insistence on careful documentation are a logical defense to the hostile environment in which they operate.[55] To some extent, at least in past years, an accumulation of detail was permitted to substitute for decision making on basic issues. The agencies' inability to make basic decisions and general rules to guide administrative action, however, in part simply mirrored the continuing political

[54] James M. Landis, *op. cit.,* p. 65.
[55] The agencies' origin as an independent commission may also have contributed to their emphasis on legal procedure. Formal hearing procedures have been frequently used by both the Federal Maritime Board and Maritime Administration in order to establish a record on contentious issues. (Hearings are typically used in considering whether to withdraw ships from the reserve fleet, in considering construction contract appeals, and in examining the economic feasibility of non-routine proposals for mortgage guarantees.) Even when formal hearings are not held, careful documentation of all matters to be considered by the Maritime Administrator is required in important cases.

contest over the methods and purposes of the government's maritime programs.

The 1950 and 1961 reorganizations improved the maritime agencies' internal day-to-day operations but failed to cure underlying problems. Following the 1950 plan, formal manuals of procedure were prepared, backlogs were brought under control, confidence was re-established in the agency's ability to contrive reasonable approximations of foreign-domestic cost differentials, and a ship replacement program was organized. On the other hand, the agency still lacked tangible standards to guide its administration of its regulatory, promotional, and operating programs; performed no economic analysis of the industry it was charged to oversee; and had only the most elementary notion of its long-range problems and no plan (other than the subsidized ship replacement program) for meeting them.

Following the 1961 plan, emphasis was placed on evaluation of current operations and formulation of long-term plans. The operations research studies contracted under the Office of Research and Development were stepped up in order to identify means (including revision of government aid programs) of improving American shipping operations, reducing subsidies, and improving the fleet's competitive position. The Office of Program Planning was reorganized, placed under new direction, and given a mandate, which it had never previously enjoyed, to undertake policy research and substantive program development. This task was energetically tackled. By 1964, for the first time since before World War II, the Maritime Administration had an articulated long-range plan supported by the agency's top management. Although the plan had not by the end of 1965 been adopted as official government policy and lacked industry support, it had served to flush out basic issues and to force discussion of alternative approaches.

Interaction of Administration and Policy

The stimulus to development of new promotional policies given by revival of the Office of Program Planning, and the neglect of shipping regulation which resulted from commingling regulatory and promotional functions are dramatic examples of the interplay between administrative arrangements and policy. In other less clear-cut cases, relationships between the machinery for administration of the government's maritime programs and their policy content can also be identified.

The most damaging aspects of these interactions have been the imprecision of the maritime program's objectives and the fragmentation of its administration. The operating subsidy program was assigned to a multi-headed commission partly because it was believed that the program's equitable aspects required quasi-judicial considerations; however, the commission proved unable to operate effectively in either an executive or a promotional role. Its ineffectiveness enhanced the centripetal tendencies inherent in government organization.

The commission's difficulties in its postwar readjustment were compounded by the lack of procedures for orderly consideration of maritime problems by the President and the Congress and by the hiatus in the commission's leadership following World War II. The fact that its principal programs were not subject to appropriation controls removed these activities from the discipline of a periodic budget review. Because the commission was an independent agency, neither the President nor the Congress could force it to develop long-range plans or to formulate legislative proposals.

The commission's bipartisan membership and staggered terms of office were intended to preclude the vacuum of leadership which occurred from 1946 to 1949. However, the administrative arrangements not only failed to protect against the mass resignations which followed the war, but the statutory prohibition against removal of commission members except for cause made the subsequent problems even more difficult to cure.

One can only speculate what might have been the impact of a Commissioner Kennedy or an Admiral Land on the commission's program from 1946 to 1950 or 1955. However, independent regulatory agencies generally have been unable to attract or hold such men in normal times, when the need may be most urgent.

Excessive concentration on current problems has been the most marked deficiency in the postwar administration of the government's maritime program. Here, as in other regulatory programs, the pressures of an incoming caseload have been allowed to push program analysis and planning to the side. Policy studies requested by the President and by Congress have been months or even years in preparation.[56] For many years the field consequently lacked the ferment of ideas necessary to anticipate new developments and up-date old programs.

The maritime agencies' concentration on their immediate responsibil-

[56] For example, a study of alternatives to cargo preference requested by the President in 1954 was not completed until 1956. A study of the economics of the essential trade route system requested in 1959 was never officially submitted because a new administration was installed prior to its completion.

ities has limited their contacts with other agencies and cut off their staffs from broader policy considerations. As a result their staffs have developed somewhat insular attitudes which inhibit communication with outsiders and increase the difficulty of effective interagency coordination. During the 1950's, for example, there was no real communication between those preparing ship mobilization plans and those engaged in airlift studies. The barriers began to break down in the early 1960's.

Generally the procedures for program coordination across agency lines have been geared to too low a staff level. Responsible policy officials have attempted to overcome this difficulty by establishing new organizations and by using outside contractors and advisory groups. Both techniques have been helpful: the first because it has brought new personalities and a new sense of purpose to the administrative agency; the latter because it has permitted examination of maritime problems uninhibited by the usual institutional restraints. However, neither technique has been able to effect any basic redirection of federal maritime policies or even to create a sense of common purposes in pursuit of established goals.

10

Interest Group Policies and Politics

IN THE AMERICAN political system, a free interplay of active, well-organized, representative, and enlightened special interest groups is a necessary ingredient to effective policy development. If groups with a significant stake in public issues simply "stand on their principles" rather than participating in the give-and-take of the political process, development and implementation of new policies may be completely blocked.

Interest group policies are the product of many diverse influences. Although "pocketbook issues" dominate the government's shipping programs, the parties in interest are also influenced by ideological, geographic, and political considerations. Characteristics of the group itself—its cohesiveness, militancy, organization, leaders, and finances—also influence its activities.

The industry associations representing American shipowners, seafarers, shippers, and shipbuilders obviously do not represent the total national interest in U.S. shipping policy. However, the immediacy of their concerns properly gives them an important role in shaping that policy and in the program's administration. This chapter examines their stake in the government's program, how they are organized to defend their interests, and, in general terms, the impact of their participation in the political process.

The Interests at Stake

The U.S. merchant marine is a small industry with a very large stake in the government's promotional and regulatory programs. Since even minor shifts in public policy can have a major impact on individual firms, it is not surprising that the industry's apparatus for coping with political problems is disproportionate to its size, or that many independent, sometimes overlapping, associations have been organized to represent each segment of the merchant marine and each variation of opinion.

Two common interests bind all of the groups benefiting directly or indirectly from the government's shipping programs: the first is their common economic stake in the continued operation of a U.S. merchant marine, the second a genuine conviction that "what's good for the merchant marine is also good for the United States." Economic self-interest reinforced by a genuine belief in the rightness of the cause is a powerful combination which may cause shipping groups to magnify somewhat the problems of the industry and the importance of their solution. An appreciation of the interested parties' commitment to the existing system is necessary to understand the manner in which the system has developed and also to assess its tolerance to change.

Investment Commitments. Industry statements commonly stress the substantial investment in America's foreign trade merchant fleet, totaling in excess of $2 billion. As the subsidized operators replace their war-built ships, this investment will become even larger. These operators plus a few of the larger non-subsidized companies, are clearly in the business for the long pull. Tramp operations, in contrast, are financed chiefly by speculators who use heavily mortgaged, low-cost equipment, frequently assigned to paper corporations with virtually no collateral assets.

One of the central objectives of the 1936 act was to create a climate which would attract and hold long-term investment. Mutual confidence has been regarded as essential to the program's success. In order to reinforce this confidence the government has not hesitated to reaffirm its intention to provide continued aid. Banking on this assurance (and limited by restrictive regulations), the subsidized companies have done little to hedge their investments. Many of their ships have been designed for particular trades. The patronage of their clientele also partially depends on their U.S. flag affiliation.

Since risk has been understood to be intrinsic to tramping, those who have put their money into this business have retained maximum flexibility. U.S. flag tramps generally are easily adaptable to other trades; about 40 percent of the tramp fleet has at one time or another been operated under foreign flag. Should U.S. cargo preferences be withdrawn, these ships (but not their crews) could probably be shifted to foreign flag operation.

Contractual Commitments. The government's contractual commitments to ships supported through cargo preferences apply only to the period of their hire. Most contracts with subsidized operators, on the other hand, cover a twenty-year span and contain elaborate safeguards for both parties. All but three of the contracts currently in force extend through the latter portion of the 1970's.[1]

The obligations assumed by the signatories of a maritime subsidy contract have never been adequately defined. Escape clauses are included for both the government and the private operator. Under the 1936 act the government is authorized to adjust subsidy payments yearly to reflect changes in foreign-domestic cost differentials and other conditions affecting shipping. Each contract is further required to specify that:

> . . . if the Commission shall determine that a change in the service, route, or line, which is receiving an operating differential subsidy under this title, is necessary in the accomplishment of the purposes of this Act, it may make such change upon such readjustment of payments to the contractor as may be arrived at . . . [through] mutual agreement, or . . . after proper hearing, . . . determined to be fair and reasonable and in the public interest.[2]

Conversely, if any contractor is able to prove that he "cannot maintain and operate his vessels on such service, route, or line, with a reasonable profit on his investment," he is to be discharged of any further obligation under the contract and permitted to transfer his equipment to foreign registry.

There have been few cases involving either of these provisions.[3] Neither provision has ever been tested in court. The language of the statute appears to treat the subsidy contract as an instrument which defines the rights and obligations of the contracting parties only with respect to such voyages as the government may from time to time determine are required to maintain services essential to U.S. foreign trade. However, Maritime

---

[1] Passenger and freight contracts with the U.S. Lines will expire in 1967 and 1969 respectively. The Oceanic Steamship contract expires in 1972. The ten-year contract signed with the Bloomfield Line in 1953 has already expired and, because of special circumstances, is currently being extended on a year-to-year basis.(See the Maritime Subsidy Board's opinion, Nov. 4, 1964, in Docket A-7, Bloomfield Steamship Company, Proposed Long-Range Operating Subsidy Agreement.)

[2] 49 Stat. 2004.

[3] In two cases subsidized operators petitioned the government to discontinue unprofitable services (the Grace Lines' Great Lakes service, discussed in Chapter 6, and Arnold Bernstein's one-ship passenger service to Europe, resolved through the vessel's sale to the American Export Line for use in the Mediterranean). In only one episode has the government seriously considered cutbacks in subsidized operations (as a result of a congressional limitation on subsidized voyages stipulated in the board's 1952 appropriation); this episode is discussed in Department of Commerce, *Maritime Subsidy Policy* (multilith, 1954), p. 96.

Administration staff have informally indicated that the contract obligates both parties to maintain the service over the entire contract term.

Minor adjustments in subsidized services or in the methods of computing subsidy would not work a substantial hardship on America's subsidized lines, for with one or two exceptions they have built up sufficient financial strength to absorb temporary setbacks. On the other hand, termination of the subsidy program, either immediately or as existing contracts expire, would be extremely disruptive and costly to the participating firms. Although companies are permitted by law to transfer their ships to foreign flag, any attempt to do so would surely be met with massive labor resistance. Even if successful in shifting to foreign flag, most of the companies would have to build a new base for their businesses, which currently depend heavily on their U.S. flag affiliation. The subsidized operators would also have to pay substantial deferred taxes (running to as much as $170 million) on the reserve fund deposits required by subsidy contracts.

Career Commitments. Almost all of the personnel employed in the management and operation of U.S. flag ships have strong career commitments to the maritime industry. Over half of the work force first went to sea during or before World War II; more than half of the remainder entered the industry between 1946 and 1955. The average age of licensed officers is forty-seven; of unlicensed personnel, forty-four. Although no statistics are available, it is generally believed that this pattern is repeated among the industry's shoreside personnel.

From these data it is estimated that deaths, retirements, and voluntary separations will cause about 5,800 persons (6½ percent of the seafaring work force) to leave the industry each year over the next five years.[4] The industry's present attrition rate is about three times larger than the contraction in employment opportunities actually experienced over the past ten years and should adequately cushion any further loss of jobs which can reasonably be anticipated to result from shipboard automation. In fact, additional manpower will have to be recruited into the industry to maintain an adequate complement of skilled personnel.

Some limited efforts have been made to assess the career mobility of the maritime labor force, but in this field only qualitative judgments are

[4] Retirement plans for licensed engineers allow payment of benefits after twenty years' service regardless of age. Unlicensed personnel currently are eligible for full benefits of $150 to $200 per month only upon reaching age 65. Early retirement at a reduced payment is permitted by most of the plans. The subject is one which is currently receiving much attention, and further liberalization of benefits and age qualifications is anticipated.

possible. Personnel now serving in the steward's and engine departments should be able to find adequate shoreside employment opportunities, although probably not at their present rates of pay. Shipping management and sales personnel are probably somewhat less mobile, but should be able to use their skills in related activities such as freight forwarding, brokerage, or management of foreign flag operations. The most severe adjustment problems would be faced by the industry's deck officers and unlicensed personnel. For the older men particularly the transition to shoreside employment would probably cause both loss of income and considerable personal distress.

Unions' Stake. Among those maritime personnel with the most at stake in U.S. maritime policy are officials of the industry's thirteen major seafaring unions. These unions are substantial business organizations which pay their chief executive officers up to $86,000 per annum (plus many fringe benefits). Annual dues run from $100 up. The largest organization, the National Maritime Union (NMU), reported 1961 net assets (excluding pension, welfare, and other special funds) of $9.1 million—roughly $2,600 per member. Gross assets of its pension and welfare funds were reported to be $54.3 million or $15,000 per member.[5]

The maritime unions must continue to obtain substantial revenues from dues and assessments simply to meet their commitments to their members. Continued income is equally necessary to meet the unions' $3–$4 million annual payroll and continued payments must be made to pension and welfare funds to meet guaranteed retirement benefits.[6]

The union officers have responsibilities which extend beyond simply meeting the payroll. Their positions and prestige depend on an active and effective defense of their members' interests.[7] They can therefore be ex-

---

[5] Data from reports filed with the Bureau of Labor-Management Reports, U.S. Department of Labor. The financial position of the Seafarers International Union (SIU) appears to be commensurate with that of the NMU but is much more difficult to determine inasmuch as its constituent organizations have not reported on a consistent basis.

[6] Several of the major unions' retirement plans are not fully funded according to actuarial calculations, including the Maritime Engineers Beneficial Association retirement fund which is estimated by the Maritime Administration to have $85 million less than will be needed to finance its obligations. (See Docket A-14, Maritime Subsidy Board, July 13, 1965).

[7] Leaders of the principal maritime labor unions have enjoyed long tenure in office. Their success in retaining office can probably be related to the practice of limiting voting privileges to "book men," who have seniority and who are therefore somewhat insulated against the industry's loss of jobs.

pected to speak out vigorously for labor, and the more so because of their own personal stake in the industry.

Diversification. The adverse effects of a changing demand for U.S. ships and seamen can be ameliorated through diversification. Interestingly, this strategy has been adopted by both maritime management and labor.

Several of the leading U.S. flag operators have long been units of large, diversified industrial empires. The Grace Line is the arch-type of this group. Though corporately independent, the Lykes Steamship Company is closely associated with a wide range of other Lykes family enterprises in cattle, lumber, and sugar. The Prudential Line is a venture of movie magnate Spyros Skouras. Waterman Steamship Company from 1955 through 1965 was an affiliate of McLean Industries.

These and other operators are themselves diversifying. Lykes Steamship Company has organized a subsidiary capitalized at $2 million to develop non-shipping enterprises. Isbrandtsen, which for many years has traded in the products which it ships, has recently invested in such diverse activities as Chilean iron mines and the Liquifreeze Corporation of America. The Natomas Company, which controls the American President Lines and holds 36 percent of the outstanding stock of the Pacific Far East Lines, has established a partnership with a firm specializing in missile site construction. Matson Lines has built its subsidiary terminal company into the largest combined terminal and stevedore operation on the West Coast. The Moore-McCormack and American Export Lines have also recently announced their intention to diversify into non-shipping activities.

A particularly interesting diversification is that of Seafarers International Union (SIU), the union most severely hit by the postwar decline in maritime employment. In order to meet the very real threat to its institutional viability, the SIU has moved vigorously into a variety of alternative opportunities. In the late forties it established a Canadian district to rout the communist-dominated Canadian Seaman's Union from Great Lakes shipping. In the mid-fifties it established an affiliate, the United Industrial Workers, to organize shoreside workers in related trades. In the late fifties it pressed hard to win the right to organize seamen on PANLIBHON vessels.

As a result of its diversification efforts SIU now represents such diverse groups as taxi drivers and maintenance personnel, cannery workers, and marine repairmen. These affiliations have provided employment opportunities for SIU members between ocean voyages or upon retirement. The diversification has been so successful that about 25,000 of the SIU's claimed 80,000 membership are now principally employed ashore. Another 25,000 to 30,000 are employed on harborcraft or fishing vessels, and on the inland waterways.

Interest Group Organizations

There is no single organization, with the possible exception of the semi-social Propeller Club of America, which is broad enough to span the diverse interests of the many varied components of the U.S. merchant marine. The industry includes the usual groupings of owner, worker, user, and supplier interests. In addition, separate management and labor organizations have developed on the East and West coasts, which often adopt quite different points of view. The industry's trade associations are also differentiated functionally—one on each coast concentrating on labor-management negotiations, a second on political representation, and so forth. Fragmentation has been further compounded by the divisive effects of the government's shipping programs.

Shipowner Groups. Thirty-three U.S. flag steamship companies maintain offices in Washington, a city whose principal industry is not exports but government. Five shipowner associations have either their headquarters or supporting branch offices in that city. Approximately a dozen law firms make practice before the government's maritime agencies their principal business. Several foreign governments have appointed shipping attaches to their embassies. In total, there are approximately eighty to a hundred senior professionals in the city whose primary function is to represent the interests of U.S. and foreign flag shipping companies.

Both the size and diversity of the maritime industry's Washington lobby have increased enormously since the war. Prior to enactment of the 1936 act, the industry had supported only two associations—the American Steamship Owners Association, with members drawn principally from the East and Gulf coasts, and the Pacific American Steamship Association (PASA), which operated on the West Coast. Political representation was handled almost entirely through the eastern group, headquartered in New York. In 1938 this group dissolved. It was succeeded by two organizations —the American Merchant Marine Institute (AMMI), a broadly based trade association which also conducts collective bargaining on behalf of its members, and the Association of American Ship Owners, which is no longer active.[8]

[8] The Association of American Shipowners was organized in 1942 to represent non-subsidized companies in negotiating payment for requisitioned ships. It has been in-

Developments since World War II have led to the organization of additional groups. In 1949, the tramp segment of the U.S. flag merchant marine incorporated an Association of Tramp Shipowners, which retained Washington counsel to represent its unique interests. Labor union pressure in the late fifties caused owners of foreign flag ships to form a Committee for Flags of Necessity. New organizations have also been formed to meet specific needs. For example, the industry's efforts to obtain legislation sanctioning dual rates were channeled principally through an *ad hoc* American Steamship Committee on Conference Studies. The industry's response to the Joint Economic Committee's study of rate disparities has been carried by an Association of Steamship Traffic Executives.

From 1945 through 1953 the most politically active and influential of the industry's trade groups was the National Federation of American Shipping, an organization formed to represent shipowner interests during preparation of the Ship Sales Act of 1946. At its zenith the federation included all of the industry's subsidized companies and many of its non-subsidized liner and tanker operators. It collapsed in 1953 as a result of a variety of personality and political factors, including a feeling on the part of its subsidized members that their unique stake in the government program demanded more effective, separate representation. Prior to the federation's collapse its subsidized members had formed an informal committee to combat proposals advanced by a group of non-subsidized companies to replace the 1936 program with a direct wage subsidy payable to any qualified firm operating U.S. vessels in foreign trade. The informal committee was institutionalized in 1954 as the Committee of American Steamship Lines (CASL) and is now the industry's most prominent Washington-based trade association.

CASL provides a continuing point of contact between the subsidized lines and the administrative agencies. Its external activities are focused principally on assuring continuation of the existing subsidy program and on developing recommendations for its improvement.[9] Each year CASL adopts a legislative program, which it vigorously promotes, and offers testimony on a variety of subjects of interest to its member lines. From time to time it has sponsored economic research studies and policy reviews. It

---

active since the mid-fifties. Since that time, one of its members has been admitted to subsidy and two others have applied for admission to the program. Half of the remaining companies have maintained some interest in shipping, either chartering ships, operating tugs or barges, or operating on the Great Lakes. The others have either liquidated or shifted to entirely different businesses.

[9] Eleven of twelve proposals made by CASL to the 87th and 88th Congresses have been enacted. This record is substantially better than that achieved by the Maritime Administration, which batted less than .500, and of other industry groups.

also sponsors institutional advertising, collects and publishes statistics, and conducts a community visit program to sell American shipping to leading business and foreign trade groups.

CASL's effectiveness results in large part from the cohesiveness of its membership. The committee has no formal organization and only a small (four-man) full-time professional staff. However, the presidents of the fourteen CASL lines meet for at least four three-day conferences each year. Members of the group's executive committee devote a large share of their time to CASL business and are supported by five very active standing committees and a number of subcommittees, each of which also meets frequently. In addition, each of the subsidized lines maintains a Washington representative or sales officer whose many contacts significantly supplement CASL's own resources.

Three other shipowner associations, two based in New York and one in San Francisco, also maintain Washington offices. These are the AMMI and PASA, both well-established, general-purpose trade organizations dating from before World War II, and the American Maritime Association (AMA), organized as an outgrowth of the 1961 East and Gulf coast seamen's strike to advance the interests of the industry's non-subsidized dry cargo carriers.[10] In contrast to the two older groups, the AMA is both amply financed (it operates on a $700,000 annual budget) and oriented toward avowedly political objectives. Its principal programs are to press for extension of cargo preference and to prevent government grain cargoes from being diverted to supertankers from tramps. AMA also has sought to win construction subsidies for domestic carriers and a quota system which would require 50 percent of the nation's oil imports to be carried on U.S. ships. In its three years' existence, the AMA has proved a highly vocal, but frequently frustrated participant on the Washington scene.[11]

[10] A principal objective of the SIU group in the 1961 contract negotiations was to expose deficiencies in the established subsidy program and to lay the groundwork for revising existing law on terms more favorable to the non-subsidized lines and tramps. The settlement between the SIU-affiliated unions and the Atlantic and Gulf Coast Owners Association (a loosely-knit bargaining entity led by J. Max Harrison, an independent labor relations consultant) provided for a jointly financed labor-management committee to be directed by a joint board and mandated to press for subsidy revision. The arrangement was later declared illegal, and the American Maritime Association, which is financed and titularly controlled by management, established in its stead. Harrison was named president; a former president of one of the SIU-affiliated unions was made executive vice president. AMA's Washington office is staffed chiefly with former union men, its New York office chiefly by management men.

[11] A check of its *Annual Report for 1963* indicates that the AMA has been successful in only about one-third of the matters in which it has been engaged. In contrast to the established subsidized lines, the AMA is generally cast in an "underdog" role and seeks to make up with energy what it lacks in acceptance.

Labor Groups. Labor organizations interested in U.S. maritime affairs present, if anything, an even more complex pattern than the shipowners' associations. The history of the maritime labor movement, its personalities, and its extreme segmentation have been noted in Chapters 7 and 8. The rivalries among the thirteen major unions, their past difficulties with communism, occasional violence, raiding, and jurisdictional strikes have all contributed to seafaring labor's unusually poor public image. Nonetheless, maritime labor has proved to be a key element in the power structure which controls the industry's affairs.

The maritime unions' power rests basically on the industry's hiring hall system, through which the unions control the supply of men to crew U.S. flag ships.[12] Because a new crew is signed on for each voyage, the unions' hiring hall policies are of vital interest to their members, whose livelihoods depend upon the rules established to guide the selection of personnel and the fidelity with which they are enforced. Maritime unions, particularly the principal unlicensed groups, have consequently developed cohesive, aggressive, and well-financed organizations.

Over the past ten to fifteen years maritime labor's original incentive for organization—to win improved wages and working conditions through collective action—has gradually been supplanted by an interest in promoting and protecting the industry which it serves. The change in objectives has been accompanied by a shift in tactics from direct work action to political action. In order to be equipped for effective political action, the seafarers' unions have established alliances with one another, with other elements of the AFL-CIO, and with management groups.

Much of labor's political influence is exercised locally. Port maritime councils now operate in twenty-seven major port areas. These councils draw together longshore, deep-sea, and related unions and multiply the seamen's political leverage.[13] At the national level maritime labor's strength has been enhanced by its close affiliation with the parent AFL-CIO organization, of which both Hall and Curran are vice presidents. In the past, the rivalry between Hall and Curran has limited their effectiveness; however, when they have worked together to enlist the support of

[12] Hiring in the maritime industry is generally controlled through seniority rules, which have the effect of creating a preferential shop favoring senior union members. Union membership and voting rules are also arranged to favor senior men, who are thus able to perpetuate their preferred position.

[13] Seamen are not generally believed to be reliable voters and constitute only a tiny portion of the electorate even in the few cities in which they are concentrated. Longshoremen, on the other hand, are a highly organized and significant political force in a dozen or more major ports.

the AFL-CIO leadership in a common cause, as in the 1963-64 Russian wheat controversy, the maritime unions have been capable of staging a formidable show of political power. Since the wheat controversy, the major waterfront unions have continued to cooperate, at least in dealings with the federal government.[14]

The unions' influence has also been enhanced by its sophistication in the political arts. Labor's friends are strategically placed throughout the Congress, including such unlikely spots as the House Agriculture Committee, where they help ward off attacks on cargo preference.[15] Senator Warren Magnuson of Washington, generally regarded as a labor senator, has been a key figure in legislative matters concerning the merchant marine since 1950, when he was named chairman of the Senate Commerce Committee's merchant marine subcommittee. The maritime unions, whose dues are among the highest in U.S. labor organizations, are also well financed and therefore in a position to assist with campaign contributions to friendly congressmen.

User Groups. The most important shipper via U.S. flag ships is the U.S. government. Several of its agencies have consequently developed a strong user interest in maritime rules and policies. Of the three largest government shipping agencies, the Department of Agriculture has been most vocal in resisting cargo preferences, dual rate agreements, and other promotional devices which it regards as damaging both to its own programs and the interests of its clientele. The Military Sea Transport Service (MSTS), although strongly interested in obtaining low cost and flexible service, must also be alert to the Navy interest in promoting a larger U.S. flag fleet. Early in its existence, the MSTS also learned that it must avoid the active hostility of the privately owned merchant fleet in order to survive. The last of the three, the Agency for International Development (AID), makes maximum use of American vessels both to minimize dollar expenditures abroad and to build domestic political backing for its program. Although AID's predecessor agencies once strongly objected to the

---

[14] Since the Russian wheat incident, raiding and jurisdictional rows between the NMU and SIU are said to have ceased. More significantly, both Hall and Curran have agreed to participate with T. W. Gleason, president of the powerful International Longshoremen's Association (ILA), in a new Maritime Committee intended to provide an instrument through which maritime labor can speak with a single voice.

[15] Brooklyn Congressman Victor Anfuso is reported to have taken his assignment on the House Agriculture Committee partly to protect home district maritime interests. Another Brooklyn congressman, John Rooney, heads the House Appropriations Subcommittee, which acts on the Maritime Administration budget, and also strongly supports the cargo preference program.

rigidities of cargo preference, the agency now actively supports the U.S. flag industry.

In the private sector the leading shipper organization which has shown sustained interest in government maritime policies is the National Industrial Traffic League, a loosely knit association of about 1,700 members. The league works largely through a rather cumbersome committee process, which limits the number of issues on which it can establish institutional positions. However, on important issues, special *ad hoc* committees are often formed, which can effectively focus and apply the prestige of the parent organization.

National farm organizations have occasionally participated in maritime affairs in order to protect tramp shipping, which handles most agricultural products, from nationalistic regulation. Most farm organizations have carefully refrained from attacking the subsidy or promotional program per se. However, they have strongly resisted extension of cargo preferences, and in 1955-56 threatened to overturn the cargo preference act which had been placed on the books the previous year.

Since the organization of the independent Federal Maritime Commission in 1961, government contacts with individual shippers and shipper organizations have increased. The Maritime Administration has named an advisor for cargo promotion. However, there is still very little direct shipper influence on the Maritime Administration's trade route or adequacy-of-service determinations or any other facet of the direct subsidy program.

Supplier Groups. The most important suppliers of the U.S. flag merchant marine are the shipbuilding, ship repair, and steel industries. Their business depends on the preservation of the "buy America" principles of the 1936 act. Though their most direct and active interests—the government's construction subsidy and ship construction programs—lie beyond the scope of this study, the shipbuilding and repair companies have a significant secondary interest in supporting operating subsidies to assure that their customers remain financially healthy. Shipyards and operators share a common interest in sustaining general public support for an American merchant marine and specifically for the differential subsidy principle.

Supporters of an American shipping industry emphasize the large number of products, supplied from almost every state, which go into the making of a ship. Though the ship chandlers, ropewalks, turbine manufacturers, and steel fabricators are not organized on behalf of the U.S. flag fleet, the knowledge that curtailment of the program might cause contracts to be lost at home undoubtedly affects their congressmen's orientation toward the program.

Finally, it should be noted that a number of the merchant marine's staunchest congressional supporters have come from shipbuilding rather than ship operating districts.[16] Shipyard and steel workers, in contrast to the typical seaman, are voting residents of the localities in which they are employed. Their votes undoubtedly add muscle to a congressman's desire to represent energetically the interests of his district.

Business and Professional Groups. Over the years the American merchant marine has enjoyed the support of a wide variety of other organizations, including the Chamber of Commerce of the United States, the National Foreign Trade Council, the Mississippi Valley Association, the Defense Transport Association, the American Legion, and the Naval Reserve Officers Association. Meetings and publications sponsored by these groups have provided a medium for promotional statements and a forum through which criticism of the maritime program might be rebutted. Thus, their interest has provided an antidote to the adverse publicity which the industry's subsidy dependence sometimes generates.

Finally there are a number of individuals who have only a professional or personal interest in the merchant marine. Sometimes this interest is channeled through professional societies, such as the Maritime Administrative Bar Association, U.S. Naval Institute, or Society of Naval Architects and Marine Engineers. From time to time individual lawyers, ship brokers, economists, and others interested in the industry have acted on their own to call attention to a particular situation or to spur action on some matter. These informal, behind-the-scenes contacts, usually motivated only by a sense of equity and public service, have also influenced the development of the merchant marine program.

Patterns of Cooperation and Conflict

The large number of organizations interested in the government's shipping programs is both a result and symptom of the conflicts which have rent the industry since World War II. The industry's non-subsidized com-

---

[16] E.g., Congressmen Schuyler Otis Bland and Tom Downing of Newport News, Virginia; Congressman Edward Garmatz, present chairman of the House Merchant Marine and Fisheries Committee, of Baltimore, Maryland; Congressman Thor Tollefson (senior minority member of the House Merchant Marine and Fisheries Committee through 1964) of Tacoma, Washington; and Senators John Marshall Butler of Baltimore, Maryland, and Warren Magnuson of Seattle, Washington.

panies have fought bitterly with the subsidized lines; conference operators have scrapped with independents; tramp operators have tried to enjoin grain shipments via tankers; the NMU has opposed the SIU; and small shippers have sought added protection from abuses of the conference system and the big business organizations supporting it. In the shipbuilding industry, bitter battles have been waged between East and West coast yards and between the industry's public and private sectors.

The unique characteristic of these conflicts is that each involves a divergence of interests within a particular segment of the industry rather than a conflict between groups. Although inter-group conflicts are not entirely absent from the maritime industry—e.g., the sharp difference between labor and management groups regarding the imposition of compulsory arbitration—they have been increasingly restrained. At least in their dealings with government, the management, labor, users, and suppliers of each of the merchant marine's several sub-industries (i.e., the subsidized liners, non-subsidized liners, domestic operators, tramps, and tankers) have proved more cohesive than have the industry's management and labor as a whole. Thus the government's programs have operated to unify previously alien interests as well as to segment groupings which were previously homogeneous.

Labor-Management Coalitions. The convergence of labor and management interests is both the most dramatic and the most important political development in postwar maritime affairs. This development had its roots in World War II, which caused the two groups to put aside past enmities to work harmoniously for victory. When the war was over the unions realized that labor's continued prosperity depended on the industry's prosperity. Union leadership had also matured, and the radicalism of the late thirties was replaced by positive support for the subsidy program.[17]

Joseph Curran's realization that his union had a common stake with U.S. steamship owners in preserving the maritime subsidy system led in 1950 to the organization of a joint Labor-Management Maritime Committee, cosponsored by six subsidized shipping companies and the NMU. The committee was conceived as a fact-finding group to meet outside criti-

[17] From 1936 to 1940, maritime labor was largely indifferent or openly hostile to the proposed subsidy program. Some, like Harry Lundberg, believed that the companies could be reformed only by being bankrupted; others, like Curran, put their stock in constant and vigorous agitation (see "Maritime Labor Unions," *Fortune,* Vol. 16, No. 3, [Sept. 1937], p. 123). Following the war Lundberg softened his views; Curran undertook to purge alleged communists from his union and strongly supported the subsidy program.

cism. Its bylaws call for "continuing studies, objective and analytical in nature, of the problems of the maritime industry [covering] unemployment, the economics of shipping, comparative operating costs of American and foreign flag vessels, rate trends, their impact upon the American Merchant Marine, and worldwide subsidization of shipping." The committee has been particularly useful in technical matters, such as compiling foreign cost data and data on the seamen's medical program, but has also provided a useful liaison between the Washington representatives of management and the unions.

The second group developed to cut across labor and management interests—the Maritime Cargo Transportation Conference (MCTC)—has confined its activities to technical matters. This group was organized in 1953 by the Maritime Administration and MSTS to study means of improving port-turnaround time. Its board of directors is broadly representative of the entire industry and the organization has proved a useful vehicle for conducting a variety of maritime manpower and productivity studies.

The most recent example of labor-management cooperation was the 1961 organization of the American Maritime Association (AMA) as a result of collective bargaining agreements between SIU-affiliated unions and non-subsidized liner and tramp firms. In contrast to the two fact-finding groups, AMA was established to operate in a political role to win a larger share of government cargoes and increased aid for its sponsors. Although staffed partially with former union officials, the AMA also conducts collective bargaining on behalf of its member lines—an arrangement which is defended on the basis of the association's success in avoiding work stoppages or direct wage increases as large as those allowed in other sectors of the industry.[18]

Alliances with User and Supplier Groups. In a free market economy, the interests of American ship operators would tend to conflict with those of their customers and suppliers. In a subsidized economy, this principle does not necessarily apply.

Conference rate-making procedures tend to unite major shipper organizations and the conference lines against any alternative which might stiffen the competition faced by either party. Other elements of the business community have supported the U.S. merchant marine as a corollary to their broader support for increased foreign trade, a stronger defense, or

[18] For example, see Representative Bob Casey's interrogation of Paul Hall in *Maritime Labor Legislation,* Hearings before the House Merchant Marine and Fisheries Committee, 88 Cong. 1 sess. (1963), pp. 497-504.

enlargement of government aids to business. Since merchant shipping is a respected component of the business community, the subsidy program is almost never attacked by business organizations—or even listed in the U.S. Chamber of Commerce's annual budget trimming proposals.

A firm and effective alliance has been developed between the subsidized operators and shipbuilders, despite the fact that their economic interests in the construction subsidy program are often at odds. Clearly each has determined that the long-run political advantages of continued cooperation outweigh the possibilities of short-term gain at the expense of the other. However, within this broad framework of cooperation, the operators and yards have occasionally skirmished with one another over construction techniques and costs. Recent proposals to permit subsidized operators to build their ships abroad have also brought some policy conflicts to the surface.[19]

Political Affiliations. Since 1936 political parties have had little direct influence or interest in government shipping policies. Democratic and Republican platform pronouncements are virtually indistinguishable in their advocacy of a merchant fleet adequate for defense needs. Only in a few issues (notably the 1963 compulsory arbitration bill) have party loyalties had any decisive influence. Party organizations have not even been active in identifying persons for appointment to the maritime agencies. ("Political" appointments, when made, have usually been based on personal rather than party relationships.)

On the other hand, political connections are of prime importance to this obviously political industry. In general, industry groups have avoided becoming too closely identified with either political party and have sought to maintain the support of both. Within the industry, however, are a few in-

[19] During 1964 the Committee of American Steamship Lines sponsored an evaluation of the ship construction subsidy, published in December 1965, under the title *New Concepts for a Stronger Commercial Shipbuilding Industry.* The report does in fact contain a number of major, provocative proposals, including a proposal that shipyard subsidy in effect be divorced from the operating subsidy program by making a subsidy fund of fixed size available to assist the yards to obtain orders from both U.S. and foreign buyers, but freeing U.S. shipping companies to purchase abroad if a favorable bid is not received from a U.S. yard. The proposal was discussed with the shipbuilding industry prior to its publication. A statement by the Shipbuilders Council of America, included as an appendix to the CASL report, expresses the shipbuilders' unqualified opposition to any "build foreign" or "buy foreign" philosophy, "even if advocated as a remote alternative under certain circumstances." However, the Shipbuilders Council also reiterated its common interest with CASL in underlining the importance of sea power and of an American maritime industry to U.S. security.

dividuals who have participated actively and openly in party affairs.[20] Their participation, however, appears usually to have been a product of past affiliations or personal interest rather than a purposeful effort to use this avenue to advance company or industry interests.

Participation in the Political Process

The American merchant marine has such a large and obvious stake in government shipping policies that its participation in the political process inevitably arouses public suspicion and risks antagonizing rival industry groups. Government and industry personnel both approach their roles in the knowledge that the program must maintain public confidence in order to maintain public support. The hurly burly practices of the 1920's, which were reported in such agonizing detail to Senator Hugo Black's investigating committee in 1934-35, have long since been displaced by a wary and almost self-conscious decorum. In reaction to its free-booting past, the U.S. maritime industry has been scrupulous to avoid any taint of scandal and has been extraordinarily successful in this regard.[21]

The American shipping industry depends heavily on government aid. Perhaps slightly less obvious but equally true, the federal establishment depends on the U.S. merchant marine not only for ships and shipping services but also for information, cooperation, and advice in conducting the government aid program. The partnership this effort demands has been

[20] Industry personnel who have held public positions include George Killion, formerly treasurer of the Democratic National Committee and now president of American President Lines; Wilfred McNeil, an Assistant Secretary of Defense during the Eisenhower Administration, now president of Grace Lines; and Clarence G. Morse, who was briefly president of Pacific Far East Lines following his term as Maritime Administrator. At least Killion and McNeill have continued to be active in local and national politics (the latter served on a Goldwater committee to study defense policies).

[21] Suggestions of scandal have touched the postwar merchant marine on only three occasions, and have each time been successfully turned aside. The first problem arose in connection with fixing the sales prices for the three postwar superliners. The industry's standing was threatened a second time by the Celler Committee's report, *The Ocean Freight Industry,* H. Rept. 1419, 87 Cong. 2 sess. (1962), which documented a large number of alleged malpractices. A third incident concerned rates charged by two subsidized operators to move government-sponsored grains, found by the General Accounting Office to have been substantially higher than the rates charged on privately sponsored consignments on the same ships. One of the operators immediately paid reparations, protesting that the charges were nonetheless legitimate. Suit for recovery from the second operator was still pending in the U.S. District Court as of December 1963. (For a report of this case, see H. Rept. 1419, pp. 280 ff.)

particularly close in the industry's subsidized sector. Public policy is committed to the use of privately owned shipping if feasible. Private corporations own the ships, command the skills to run them, and hence have a large role in setting the conditions under which they will be operated.

Contacts with Government Personnel. Perhaps the most sensitive facet of government-industry relations is regulation of industry's access to the government's administrative apparatus. Only recently and after much difficulty has the government devised rules to guide its employees in their contacts with interested private parties.[22] The statutes defining conflicts of interest are still so ambiguous as to be inadequate guides.

The 1936 act included specific precautions to minimize conflicts of interest. No person who had been affiliated with the industry in any manner within the previous three years was eligible for appointment to the commission. No member, officer, or employee of the commission was permitted to have "any pecuniary interest in, or hold any official relationship [with any person or firm] . . . with which the Commission may have business relations."[23]

The exigencies of World War II demanded that industry personnel be brought into government, notwithstanding possible conflicts of interest. The War Shipping Administration was staffed largely with persons skilled in private ship operations. Following the war, most of these persons returned to industry. The pattern was repeated, on a much smaller scale, during the Korean conflict. Since the Korean conflict there has been very little recruitment for operating, inspection, or audit positions from the industry.

Abolition of the U.S. Maritime Commission by Reorganization Plan Number 21 of 1950 removed the prohibition against appointment of industry personnel. Appointments to the board since 1950 have included one former steamship executive and two admiralty lawyers, one of whom, Clarence G. Morse, was named chairman and subsequently took a position in the industry. Partially in reaction to the close working relationships with the industry developed during this period, the Democratic Adminis-

[22] The problem of ex parte contacts was the subject of extended hearings before the House Interstate and Foreign Commerce Committee during the 86th Congress and subsequently was further considered by the Administrative Conference of the United States. The latter group formulated a code of ethics to guide agency practice. As of December 1964, neither the Maritime Administration nor the commission had formally adopted the code.

[23] 49 Stat. 1985. This restriction was waived to permit Joseph P. Kennedy to accept appointment as chairman of the commission.

tration has leaned over backwards since 1961 to find persons to direct the Maritime Administration who have had no industry ties whatsoever and who could bring a "completely fresh approach."[24]

The industry's access to the Congress has historically been freer than its access to the administrative agencies. None of the congressional committees' full-time professional staff have had any known links with the merchant marine industry. However, these staffs have occasionally been supplemented by personnel drawn from the industry itself. For example, the Senate Commerce Committee's special counsel, hired in 1961 to prepare an alternative to the restrictive dual rate bill which had been passed by the House, was an attorney who had previously been the industry's principal Washington representative on the bill.[25]

Access to Records and Information. The maritime agencies in the course of their work acquire a great deal of sensitive information about the operations and financial status of the companies with which they deal and about the costs of foreign shipping companies and yards. In order to protect the companies' proprietary information, the government holds this data confidentially. Consequently, it is difficult for other parties in interest or for the press to obtain a full grasp of matters at issue or of the basis for government policy.

The problem is more severe in reference to military security information. Because the data on which ship requirements are based have been labeled "secret," it has been impossible to develop any intelligent public discussion on the real utility of an American merchant marine or even for the industry itself to gain an understanding of its national security role. Security classification has also contributed to intra-governmental misunderstanding on merchant shipping requirements and the industry's importance to the overall defense.

The maritime agencies have also gained a reputation for secretiveness in their handling of non-classified, non-proprietary information. During

[24] E.g., see *The New York Journal of Commerce*, March 31, 1961, p. 1. Although the Maritime Administration has been somewhat more aloof from the industry since 1961, the Democratic Administration has permitted closer ties between the Labor Department and maritime labor groups than characterized the previous eight years.

[25] Jack Anderson in *The Washington Merry-Go-Round*, Aug. 4, 1961, reported that the attorney, who had been executive secretary for the *ad hoc* Steamship Committee on Conference Studies, was recommended to Senator Engle, chairman of the Commerce subcommittee handling the bill, by George Killion, president of American President Lines. Killion, who had been treasurer of the Democratic National Committee prior to joining the San Francisco-based line, was reported to have also assisted in Senator Engle's election.

Mr. Morse's administration, communication between industry representatives and the agency staff flowed sufficiently freely that private groups were well informed as to the government's internal deliberations and reasoning and vice versa. More recently, Maritime Administration and Commission employees have been admonished to be on guard in their dealings with non-government personnel. Information on the status of matters pending within the agencies is released only through official channels; internal memoranda, general counsel's opinions, foreign cost estimates, and the like are held within the agency.

This shift in administrative policy has been criticized by industry officials, who contend that if the agency withdraws into a cloister, it will be unable to administer its program efficiently. Lack of information and access to pertinent records has been particularly irksome to the maritime bar, which has complained that the agencies' practices make it impossible to know the reasoning underlying administrative decisions and permit "unsupported assertion to be substituted for an articulation of public policy."[26] Actually, the maritime bar has been in a far more favorable position than the general practitioner, since until 1962 the agency failed even to bind and publish its official decisions dating from 1950.

Channels for Industry Advice. The many common interests of industry and government officials administering federal maritime programs necessitate frequent and effective communication between the two groups. Contacts between industry and government personnel take place for a variety of purposes, and within many different settings, ranging from ship launchings, Propeller Club meetings, and the like, to the formalized hearings required under the Administrative Procedures Act to allow all parties in interest to put their arguments and recommendations on the record.[27]

Formal Advisory Mechanisms. From the end of World War II through

[26] Testimony of Mark P. Schlefer, representing the Maritime Administrative Bar Association, in *Freedom of Information,* Hearings before a subcommittee of the Senate Judiciary Committee, 88 Cong. 1 sess. (1963), pp. 124 ff. Schlefer cites a number of "horrible examples" to support his case. His general thesis is supported by James M. Landis in his *Report on Regulatory Agencies to the President-elect* (Government Printing Office, 1960), p. 65, which asserts both that "a fog of secrecy surrounds many actions of the Board" and that it had established no standards to regulate ex parte presentations.

[27] At one time a fairly sizeable delegation of senior government officials attended all of the industry's major semi-official functions, such as launchings, Propeller Club meetings, and conventions. Under a rule laid down in 1962, however, the Maritime Administration limits its official representation to one individual. Any others wishing to attend are required to do so on their own time and at their own expense.

1964, adversary hearings provided the only formal means for the industry to advise on government shipping policies.[28] Semi-formal arrangements were available in such fringe areas as merchant marine research and development, documentation, and international affairs. Maritime industry members also participated in certain high-level panels (such as the Business Council and the President's labor-management committee) concerned with overall government-industry relations and public policy.[29] However, there were no formal advisory mechanisms focused directly on maritime policy problems.

The absence of any formal mechanism to assure that their viewpoint would be heard was strongly resented by those elements of the industry that felt their interests were being overlooked in the government program. The principal demand of the AFL-CIO as its price for lifting the 1964 Russian wheat boycott was consequently that high-level committees be established through which maritime labor could press its grievances at the highest levels of government and through which the industry could be more systematically involved in maritime policy making.

Much difficulty was encountered in organizing the two committees pledged by the President in his February 1964 conversations with George Meany, president of the AFL-CIO. Three months elapsed before a proposed organization for the Grievance Committee was released by the government. The proposal cast the industry's labor and management representatives in the role of advisors to the Maritime Administrator, who himself was only one of an all-government, five-man group. This arrangement was rejected by the labor members, who charged that it breached the President's pledge and insisted that the group be reorganized and given power to settle specific issues arising out of the cargo preference

[28] Although not usually regarded as an advisory mechanism, the whole purpose of the publication and hearing procedures of the Administrative Procedures Act (particularly in general rule-making proceedings) is to establish a fair and systematic method for soliciting the advice of interested parties. The act, however, pertains to only a small portion of the Maritime Administration's business.

[29] The 187-member Business Council (approximately 100 are active) was among the most influential private groups interested in governmental affairs during the 1950's. Its active membership included two steamship executives, General John Franklin, chairman, U.S. Lines, and Solon Turman, president of Lykes Bros. Lines, both subsidized companies. (John T. Connor was also a member before his appointment as Secretary of Commerce.) It is widely anticipated that the Council will regain its earlier position during the Johnson Administration. During President Kennedy's Administration, greater influence resided in the President's Labor-Management Advisory Council, a much smaller (23-member) group with joint labor-management representation. General Franklin also served on this committee as one of its six management members.

program.[30] A year later these issues were still unresolved and the committee had become inactive.

The Maritime Advisory Committee, organized later, is much more firmly established.[31] This committee is chaired by the Secretary of Commerce and is composed of seven government members, five labor representatives, five management representatives, and five representatives of the public at large. The committee is described in its organic order as:

> a forum within which the recommendations of the representatives of the public, labor, and management members . . . shall be presented to and discussed with the Secretaries of Labor and Commerce and such other Federal officials . . . as may be appropriate.[32]

Under Secretary Connor's chairmanship the Maritime Advisory Committee has assumed a significant role. Although the committee is an advisory body only, Secretary Connor has pledged that no significant new policy proposals will be advanced by the Administration until the committee has examined them fully. The circumstances leading to the formation of the committee and the character of its membership make this review power unusually potent. In addition, the Secretary has invited the committee to develop policy proposals of its own and has appointed several subcommittees. At least some of the committee's members interpret these steps as indicating that the Secretary feels "that the Committee should determine the [President's] policy and not the Maritime Administration alone."[33]

Informal Advisory Channels. Formation of the Maritime Advisory Committee has not displaced the long-standing need for informal techniques for obtaining industry advice. It has long been the Maritime Administration's practice to discuss important proposed changes in administrative policy with the affected parties. (In effect, the agency has followed formal rule-making procedures even where the Administrative Procedures Act does not apply.) The Maritime Administration also has from time to time sponsored general panel discussions of problems of general government-industry interest. Occasionally, selected industry representatives have been invited to join with government officials in *ad hoc* efforts to grapple with specific public policy problems.

The process through which proposals were developed to respond to the President's January 1965 State of the Union pledge that he would

---

[30] Grievance Committee on Cargo Preference Administration, "Transcript of Meeting Relating to Organization and Operation," May 13, 1964, p. 68.

[31] This committee was established by Executive Order 11156, June 17, 1964.

[32] *Ibid.*

[33] *Baltimore Sun,* Feb. 9, 1965, p. 30.

recommend "a new maritime policy" illustrates some of the proce-dures used and problems encountered when industry and government tackle a common problem.[34] Before the President made his statement, the Maritime Administration had advanced certain preliminary proposals within the Executive Branch. During February and March briefings were held to inform interested individuals of the agency's tentative thinking and obtain informal reactions. An effort was made to prepare the way for general industry acceptance through speeches probing the general issues involved in the new policy. However, no documents were released, no official positions taken. Furthermore, during the succeeding months while the Interagency Maritime Task Force of sub-cabinet level personnel tried to hammer out an acceptable and effective program, there was no further discussion of Marad proposals with the industry.

During these months, the Maritime Advisory Committee at the sugges-tion of its chairman, Secretary of Commerce John T. Connor, was also at-tempting to develop new policy recommendations. A subcommittee hav-ing representation from both maritime management and labor was formed in March 1965 under the direction of Theodore Kheel, a labor relations arbiter, to prepare draft proposals. It obtained general policy guidance from Secretary Connor, but no detailed information on the government's ship requirements. The subcommittee conducted its work in consultation with various industry groups but without government participation and completely independently of the Interagency Task Force.

A Task Force report, proposing many significant modifications of the existing subsidy programs, was completed and presented to the Maritime Advisory Committee for its review in October 1965. At its November meeting the Advisory Committee refused to consider the Task Force pro-posals and endorsed instead the more promotionally oriented recom-mendations drafted by the Kheel subcommittee. Both the Task Force and Advisory Committee reports were published and widely reported in the press, causing considerable controversy and speculation.

This sequence illustrates some of the hazards of both formal and in-formal advisory mechanisms. The former place industry representatives in a quasi-public role in which they may seek to exercise a veto power over Administration proposals. The latter at best can expose only a small portion of the interested groups to incubating policies and is likely to be

[34] In his 1965 State of the Union message President Lyndon B. Johnson stated that he would recommend a "new maritime policy" to the Congress, but gave no details regarding either content or timing. No reference to this new policy was made in the 1966 State of the Union address or in any intervening presidential statements.

a source of rumors, anxiety, and misunderstanding. Because the system is imperfect, proposed new policies frequently arouse unnecessary opposition or even take the industry completely by surprise.[35]

Role in Subsidy Administration. Government and industry cooperation is most readily achieved when public and private officials are able to work within a fairly well-defined framework toward accepted common goals. Subsidy contracts provide a vehicle for particularly effective collaboration. In working out the countless details which the program's administration entails, government and industry are equally concerned with furthering "the development and maintenance of an adequate and well balanced American marine." Both parties are cast in roles which lead them to assume that what's best for American shipping is best also for the United States.[36]

Specific characteristics of the subsidy contract which encourage government partnership with the subsidized lines have been discussed in Chapter 6. Over a period of years, these characteristics have been reinforced by the program's administration. For example, the subsidized operators' long-term commitment to the program has permitted them to establish highly effective liaison with senior government officials, particularly in the Congress where there has been more continuity of interest in mer-

[35] For example, the Maritime Administration once issued a circular letter (without making any prior checks) to inform subsidized operators of the justification it would thenceforth require in support of claims for subsidy against certain non-salary labor costs (sick pay, retirement benefits, and the like) which was interpreted by the industry as a statement that such costs would no longer be subsidized. After considerable news notice, the Maritime Administration was forced to issue a clarifying letter.

In another instance, the subsidized lines learned of a major policy proposal (for the 1961 reorganization) only a few days before the plan was actually transmitted. A series of hurried meetings ensued, in which the operators' representatives were referred from one official to another within the Commerce Department, Bureau of the Budget, and the White House. The latter informed the CASL group that it understood the industry had been consulted. An industry witness, who opposed the plan, later testified, "We have never learned who in the industry was supposed to have cleared the proposals." *Reorganization of the Civil Aeronautics Board, the Federal Trade Commission, and the Federal Maritime Board,* Hearings before the Senate Commerce Committee, 87 Cong. 1 sess. (1961), p. 113.

[36] The point is illustrated by a colloquy between Senator Paul Douglas and J. W. Gulick, Deputy Maritime Administrator, in which the Senator asked, "Do you regard your function as merely . . . maintaining the shipping lines in a prosperous condition, or the furthering of the best interests of the United States?" Mr. Gulick answered: "We conceive, inasmuch as we have a mandate in the 1936 Act, that anything which is done to implement that Act is in the interests of the United States." (*Discriminatory Ocean Freight Rates,* Hearings, 88 Cong. 1 sess. [1963], p. 127.)

chant shipping than in the Executive Branch. The frequency of contacts and the technical nature of many of the problems arising in the administration of contracts have also forced the Maritime Administration to work closely with the subsidized operators.

The precise pattern of the government's working relationships with its subsidized lines has varied from time to time. For example, some Maritime Administrators have wanted their staff to obtain the contractor's concurrence on administrative matters (such as foreign cost determinations) before they were sent forward; others have asked their staff to obtain industry reactions to staff recommendations; while still others have preferred to insulate their staff from the industry and conduct any necessary negotiations personally. However, the elements for close collaboration are built into the subsidy program. The Maritime Administration and its subsidized contractor by law are both signatories to ship construction contracts; both must approve deposits and withdrawals from the statutory reserves; both have an obligation to assure that operations are conducted in an efficient and economical manner, and so forth. Operating in this context, government and industry's perspectives tend to converge and almost inevitably their interests become interdependent.

Effects of the Industry's Power Structure

The comparative wealth and cohesiveness of America's subsidized lines, their established position on the Washington scene, and their quasi-public status as partners in a common enterprise have all contributed to their dominant position in the power structure of the U.S. maritime industry. Their position has occasionally been challenged by other elements of the industry, but without success. In recent years talk among the less advantaged groups of exposing the subsidy program has subsided in favor of using that program's defense and commercial justifications to win increased indirect aids for the nominally non-subsidized segments of the U.S. flag fleet.

The evolution of the government program since 1936 has had a distinctly maturing effect on its participants, who have learned that there is much more to gain in cooperation than conflict. Old rivalries have been patched over in an effort to achieve a more effective political posture, and a network of alliances has been established between management, labor, user, and supplier groups. Because these alliances are both delicate and potentially unstable, the industry has become unusually fearful of "rocking the boat."

The manner in which the various segments of the industry have been involved in the policy formulation process has generated negative reactions. Consultation has usually taken place, but often in a guarded or hostile atmosphere and with only partial knowledge of other conversations held or commitments given. Until very recently, there has been no broadly representative forum through which diverse elements of the industry might collaborate with government in a useful and creative way, and there is no assurance, even though an instrument now exists, that it will be useful.

The latent rivalries among the various participants in the government's maritime programs inhibit innovation. Rigidities which have consequently crept into the government program in turn contribute to the artificial divisions within the industry. The effect has been such a tangle of interrelated special interests that it is extremely difficult to dislodge any element of the program without setting in motion an essentially unpredictable chain of events. Thus, rather than creating a force for change, the contest of interests within the industry has tended to reinforce the status quo.

11

The Government of Merchant Shipping

PUBLIC REGULATION of private enterprise requires that general public interests be applied to issues which otherwise lie entirely within the domain of special interest groups. Thus in its shipping program the government is responsible both to the industry and to the public at large. The ultimate measure of its success is whether it can effectively translate general national objectives into programs suitable and acceptable to the American merchant marine. This chapter examines the interaction between the industry's "private government" and its broader political environment, and reports on the continuing struggle between special and general interests in the system.[1] It concludes with a brief analysis of the preconditions to effective regulatory performance.

Political Supervision of Maritime Administration

For all but six of the past fifty years the government's merchant shipping programs have been entrusted to nominally independent or quasi-independent agencies. The dominant theory has been that an independent commission of able and public-spirited men, guided by their own perceptions of the public interest, is the best means for determining policies to implement the broad purposes set out in the statutes. Theory has seldom been carried out in practice, however, since policy problems have consis-

[1] The concept of "private governments" functioning within the framework of the overall government of the United States has been developed by Walton Hamilton in his *Politics of Industry* (Alfred Knopf, 1957). As used by Hamilton, the term denotes the continuing activities of government and industry personnel working together to resolve problems solely within the context of industry concerns.

tently been of such importance that the administrative agencies have been drawn into the political sphere.

Congressional Supervision. Reporting to the Congress is among the most significant tasks of the maritime agencies' top management.[2] Comprehensive program reviews were conducted by the Senate Merchant Marine Subcommittee in both 1950 and 1953. Prolonged hearings on such facets of the program as vessel transfer policies, labor relations, cargo preference, or conference policies have been conducted almost annually by the House committee since 1954. Investigations by the House Committee on Expenditures in 1948-49, the Antitrust Subcommittee of the House Judiciary Committee in 1958-61, and the Joint Economic Committee in 1963-64 created major workloads and importantly influenced federal maritime policies.

The diversity of congressional interests in federal maritime activities creates a variety of both formal and informal demands upon the administrative agency. The maritime program is one for which the Congress appears to feel a special responsibility. In turn, some administrative personnel have considered good congressional relations even more important than ties within the executive branch.

Congress is not an innovative institution. Its effectiveness is further limited by the number of jurisdictional subdivisions and variety of opinion which it contains. Often in maritime affairs the wishes of one committee have been checked by another.[3] Sometimes these conflicts have been compromised or argued out on the floor, but more often their solution has been left to the administrative agency.

Role of the Merchant Marine Subcommittees. Of the various congression-

[2] The time required for reporting to the Congress varies significantly from year to year. From the late fifties through 1961, congressional relations imposed a heavy requirement. Since 1961 demands have been much lighter, taking only 5-10 percent of the administrator's time. Each year the agency's general counsel provides Congress with reports on up to two hundred bills. Testimony is required on about forty; action is usually taken on ten to fifteen.

[3] For example, the House and Senate merchant marine subcommittees have disagreed on maritime labor policy; the merchant marine and judiciary committees have disagreed on regulatory policy; the appropriations committees have curtailed research and construction plans; and the agriculture and armed services committees have been generally negative on cargo preference. A particularly vivid example of intra-congressional policy differences occurred in 1952-54 over whether additional tankers to carry military petroleum should be publicly or privately owned. This incident is fully reported in *Study of Operations of the Military Sea Transport Service,* Hearings before the House Merchant Marine and Fisheries Committee, 83 Cong. 2 sess. (1954), pp. 577-78.

al units involved in maritime affairs, only the House and Senate merchant marine subcommittees and their staffs have shown a continuing interest in the administration of the program. Where administrative performance is deemed unacceptable, these units can step in to obtain corrective action.[4] If there is a failure of policy or lack of coordination across agency lines, the merchant marine subcommittees can take direct action or force action by the executive branch.[5]

The merchant marine subcommittees have greater freedom of action than any other official organization concerned with maritime policy and administration.[6] Their senior members are thoroughly conversant with the industry, its problems, and its personnel. Their assent is regarded as necessary to any major innovation in the maritime program's administration.[7]

Although these subcommittees are extremely important to the maritime program, they are not major factors within the Congress.[8] Their work is of marginal interest to most members of Congress and is virtually unknown to the general public. Subsidy benefits are highly localized and governed by more or less inflexible formulas. The committees as a result

[4] Examples are the committees' work on wartime tax exemptions, foreign-domestic cost differentials, and cargo preference administration. The committees have forced the Maritime Administration to adopt more liberal rules in valuing vessels for war risk insurance and for certain other purposes than the Administration proposed to apply.

[5] This role is probably best illustrated by the work of the Senate Commerce Committee in forcing more extensive use of U.S. flag ships to carry quasi-governmental cargoes. These activities are documented in two reports issued by the Committee, *Implementation of the Cargo Preference Laws*, S. Rept. 2286, 87 Cong. 2 sess. (1962) and S. Rept. 871, 88 Cong. 2 sess. (1964).

[6] The freedom of action enjoyed by the subcommittees results from the way in which the Congress as a whole is run. Congress almost never questions the activities of its committees. Relationships between the committee chairmen and between the chairmen and the leadership often make it difficult for even a majority of the committee members to control committee actions. Both the House and Senate merchant marine subcommittees have usually been chaired by the chairmen of the full committees.

[7] The need to win the congressional committees' assent to any major policy innovation is a result partly of the detailed character of maritime legislation, which requires that the statute be amended in order to initiate most new departures. Even where the statute does not require it, however, the committees have from time to time made it clear that they expect to be consulted, and the administrative agencies have complied.

[8] Merchant Marine and Fisheries is one of the less prestigious and less powerful of the twenty standing committees of the House. Many of its members have a second committee assignment (typically on Science and Astronautics). An assignment to the Merchant Marine and Fisheries Committee is usually available to any congressman who requests it. Actually, most new men who are assigned have not listed the committee among their first three choices.

control little patronage and have little leverage with which to force unpopular measures on Congress.

The House Merchant Marine and Fisheries Committee has been particularly sensitive to its peripheral position and consequently has avoided unnecessary controversy. The committee has operated in an almost completely nonpartisan manner. Junior members are given a reasonable opportunity to participate in its business. If at all possible, its chairman settles differences of opinion within the committee. Where differences persist, members are encouraged to file minority reports presenting their position rather than initiating a floor debate. Almost all of the committee's business can consequently be handled on the consent calendar.[9]

When controversial legislation must be taken to the floor, the Merchant Marine and Fisheries Committee often enlists the industry's aid in lining up support. This task is eased by the large number of members who have served on the committee sometime in their careers and who have confidence in its recommendations.[10]

The House and Senate committees' effectiveness is enhanced by cooperation between them. They observe an informal division of labor to save time and minimize friction. The Senate group with its wider jurisdiction and smaller membership has usually allowed the House to initiate legislation. The Senate committee typically operates as an appeals board, which considers grievances and perfecting amendments. Although the two committees have quite different viewpoints on several important issues, direct clashes have been avoided.[11]

Conference committees dealing with maritime legislation are consti-

[9] Rules governing the use of the consent calendar are published at the opening of each Congress by the informal Committee of Objectors, appointed by the House leaders. Four rules have usually governed: (1) the legislation should not involve an aggregate expenditure of over $1 million, (2) it must not change established policy, (3) it should have only limited, local application, and (4) it should have been cleared by the Bureau of the Budget and affected agencies, or if not approved by them, at least be fully explained on the floor. In the period 1959-61, over 80 percent of the maritime bills acted on by the House were brought up on the consent calendar. A member of the Merchant Marine and Fisheries Committee is a member of the objectors group. (*Congressional Record*, Vol. 111, No. 38, p. 3752.)

[10] Turnover on the committee is very high. For example, of the 28 who were members in 1955, only 10 were still members in 1963, although 6 of the remaining 18 were still in Congress. In total, the House may include some 30 to 50 committee alumni, who generally support its recommendations.

[11] Of the two, the House committee has been the more conservative in its economic outlook, its attitude toward the use of its powers, and its attitude toward maritime labor relations. The House committee is generally management-oriented and slightly weighted toward the East Coast. The Senate committee is labor-oriented and weighted toward the West Coast.

tuted entirely of members of the merchant marine committees, thus minimizing the possibility that delicate legislative compromises may be obstructed by outside groups. However, because House members have seemingly found it difficult to roll back the provisions of the upper chamber, legislation typically mirrors the Senate position more nearly than that
of the House.[12]

In sum, the committees dealing with the merchant marine can operate
effectively so long as they stay within their area of jurisdiction and avoid
controversy. Although much of the legislation is of limited importance, the
committees have processed a large volume of bills and won congressional
acceptance for a high proportion of their recommendations.[13] They have
also won enactment of enough controversial legislation to prove that they
can wield significant influence when it is needed.

Checks and Balances Within Congress. The merchant marine committees
are not bound by any moral or statutory obligation, as are the government's administrative agencies, to promote an American merchant marine.
Nevertheless, because of their composition and their exposure to industry
interests, they almost inevitably play a promotional role.

Other congressional committees view the government's maritime programs from wholly different perspectives. The appropriations committees
consider it their duty to limit expenditures, the government operations
units to expose waste, the judiciary committees to attack monopoly, the
agriculture committees to protect the interests of their constituency, and
so forth. Although none of these committees, with the possible exception
of appropriations, can continuously oversee the total merchant marine
program, they can study certain phases in depth and exert substantial
pressure to secure the changes that they desire.[14]

[12] During the 86th and 87th Congresses, 48 maritime bills were enacted. Fourteen
House-Senate conferences were required. In eight cases the House conferees ac-
ceded to the Senate position; in four, the Senate to the House. Two bills represented
a mix of House and Senate provisions. The most important bill handled during these
sessions, the dual rate bill, was accepted in its entirety as written by the Senate (see
Chapter 7). The frequency with which the House has yielded to the Senate raises a
question whether the senior members of the House committee may not as a matter
of policy frame more restrictive measures for presentation to the House than they
themselves personally support, expecting the Senate to liberalize the bill.

[13] Of some two hundred shipping bills enacted since the end of World War II,
only three (the 1946 Ships Sales Act, the 1954 cargo preference legislation, and the
1961 dual rate bill) have had a major and lasting impact on the industry's operations.

[14] These committees' effectiveness in obtaining desired changes in the maritime
program has resulted in part from their superior position in the congressional hier-
archy and in part from the strategic advantage always enjoyed by the party in a
debate who has been able to define its issues and marshal the most evidence in

The general disfavor with which subsidies are regarded has made the merchant marine program a particularly attractive target for investigatory groups. Some phase of the program has been under investigation almost continually since World War II. These formal investigations have been supplemented by the individual activities of such senators as John J. Williams and Frank Lausche, for whom curtailment of shipping subsidies has been a personal crusade.

Special investigations, which have approached long-standing problems from new perspectives, have been responsible for most of the major legislatively sanctioned innovations in the postwar program.[15] The potency of investigations makes relationships between the merchant marine committees, other rival congressional units, and the leadership especially important. These relationships are highly volatile. On some matters the merchant marine committees have been able to seize the initiative and ward off threatened attacks. On others they have not felt that they were in a position to take jurisdiction or have made only weak efforts to counter adverse publicity through friendly hearings.[16]

---

support of its position. The Hardy, Celler, and Douglas committees, which conducted the most important postwar investigations of shipping policies, were able to get action because the data they assembled seemed to demand action and their quarry was relatively weak.

[15] A special investigatory subcommittee of the House Merchant Marine and Fisheries Committee chaired by Congressman (now Senator) Henry Jackson forced the revision in the taxation of subsidized operators negotiated by the Treasury in 1947. A subcommittee of the House Government Operations Committee developed the record on superliner subsidies which precipitated the 1950 reorganization of the Maritime Commission. The Celler Committee was a major factor in the 1961 reorganization and the Douglas committee to the reorientation of the commission's work which followed in 1963. Even Senators Williams and Lausche have achieved occasional victories, the most notable being legislation restricting grants of free and reduced rate passage to government employees (including congressmen) by U.S. shipping lines.

[16] For example, the House Merchant Marine Committee has successfully defended cargo preferences and persuaded the appropriations committees to relax voyage limitations before proposed restrictions took effect.

However, the committee decided not to challenge the Celler Committee's authority to investigate steamship conference practices and cooperated by drawing up a reorganization of the Federal Maritime Board-Maritime Administration and by preparing the dual rate bill. Merchant Marine and Fisheries subsequently conducted hearings on President Kennedy's reorganization proposal per agreement with the Government Operations Committee and in order to secure a pledge from Secretary of Commerce Hodges that an administrative board would be established to hear subsidy cases. The committee has recently tried to offset some of the unfavorable publicity being given the steamship industry through the Joint Economic Committee investigation by sponsoring hearings in which the industry's position could be placed on the record. This tactic, however, appears to have had little effect.

The onslaughts of congressional investigatory groups serve to force consideration of a variety of more general public interests in administration of the maritime program. But they are intermittent, somewhat random, and unpredictable. They clearly do not provide a mechanism for comprehensive re-examination of the purposes and policies of government aid. Because the Congress is pluralistic, its impact on the program is also pluralistic.

Executive Supervision. Executive supervision of maritime activities is also fragmentary, intermittent, and dispersed. As an independent agency, the Federal Maritime Commission is directly exposed to the often contradictory interests of the Departments of Justice, Commerce, and State, other transportation regulatory commissions, and the Executive Office of the President. The Maritime Administration, despite its location within the Department of Commerce, is scarcely less shielded from the competing demands of these and other executive agencies.

Presidential Interests. The variety of executive branch interests in merchant shipping, together with the industry's importance to defense and foreign affairs, brings a substantial number of maritime problems to the Executive Office and even to the personal attention of the President himself. These contacts, however, are sporadic. No president since Franklin Roosevelt has taken a sustained interest in merchant shipping, considered the industry's problems comprehensively, had frequent personal contacts with the Maritime Administrator, or used personal leadership to achieve desired changes in this field.[17] Although a number of postwar shipping problems have required the President's attention, his preoccupation with other duties has usually kept him from giving it. Decisions often have therefore been made anonymously by members of the President's staff or not at all.

Each new postwar administration has sponsored a special study of maritime affairs to chart its policy. The first postwar advisory committee was appointed by and reported to President Truman. The next two studies, a 1954 in-house survey directed by Under Secretary of Commerce Robert Murray and the 1962-63 Maritime Evaluation Committee report, were organized by and reported to the Secretary of Commerce. The most recent effort, the Interagency Task Force on Maritime Policies, was

---

[17] Both Presidents Truman and Eisenhower indicated certain personal objectives (for example, to close tax "loopholes" and limit subsidy growth), which they were unable to fulfill.

organized by the White House staff in cooperation with the Under Secretary of Commerce to follow through on a presidential commitment.

Postwar presidents have generally been satisfied to delegate legislative initiative in maritime matters to their department officers or the Congress.[18] During the past ten years the only presidential request for revision of the maritime statutes was President Eisenhower's proposal to construct a nuclear ship, stimulated by his desire to demonstrate peaceful uses of atomic energy. No maritime legislation has been vetoed by any of the postwar presidents, although several bills that they approved were incompatible with their general political position.[19]

The appointment power has also been neglected. Only three of the eighteen presidential appointees to the Federal Maritime Board, Federal Maritime Commission, or Maritime Administration (1950-1964) were personally known to the President or his immediate associates prior to their appointments. In some cases professional qualifications were deficient. The judgment of the House Merchant Marine Committee's chairman is that most of the appointees to the Federal Maritime Board "took nothing to the Board" and contributed nothing while serving.[20] President Kennedy's initial appointments to the Federal Maritime Commission, whose organization was the product of real reforming zeal, were particularly disappointing to its sponsors.[21]

Participation of Executive Officials. Ranking executive officials who have stepped in to help resolve specific maritime policy problems bearing on their general field of interest include Secretaries of Agriculture, Defense, and Labor, the Attorney General, the Under Secretary of State, and the

---

[18] Presidential State of the Union and budget messages delivered between 1956 and 1965 make only five references to maritime affairs, four of which were confined to pledges, not yet fulfilled, to offer recommendations at a later date.

[19] Legislation incompatible with presidential views but nonetheless approved includes the 1954 cargo preference legislation, the 1958 bill authorizing construction of two superliners, and the 1961 dual rate legislation. This last bill had been strenuously opposed by the President's brother, Attorney General Robert Kennedy. Vetoes have also been proposed to the President on a number of other maritime bills offensive to one or more executive agencies, but these have involved relatively minor matters.

[20] Letter from Congressman Herbert C. Bonner to President-elect John F. Kennedy, Dec. 15, 1960, printed in *Reorganization Plan Number 7 of 1961*, Hearings before the House Merchant Marine and Fisheries Committee, 87 Cong. 1 sess. (1961), p. 10.

[21] The President's nominee for chairman, Thomas E. Stakem, was a career civil servant who had previously chaired the Federal Maritime Board and who had supported both the compromise House dual rate bill and the 1961 reorganization proposal. None of the remaining nominees had had any significant experience with either merchant shipping or federal regulation; they appear to have been selected entirely on the basis of political recommendations. Stakem was also the only lawyer.

Director of the Bureau of the Budget. Although these officials' contacts on merchant marine matters are nominally through the Secretary of Commerce, they have often worked directly with his Under Secretary for Transportation and the Maritime Administrator. Thus, the Maritime Administrator and the Secretary of Commerce were co-equal members of the Committee to Study Cargo Preference and Flags of Convenience established by President Kennedy in 1962 under the chairmanship of the Secretary of Labor. Routine day-to-day contacts are maintained between the Maritime Administrator and officials at the assistant secretary level of the Labor, State, Treasury, Agriculture, and Defense departments.

When secretarial officers become engaged in a maritime policy problem, it is usually to prod the government into action. Sometimes, however, the result is exactly the opposite. Signs of interest on the part of one secretarial officer typically arouse others. This tends to divert attention from the problem immediately at hand and to postpone its solution. Meanwhile, the multiplication of supervisory relationships complicates the Maritime Administrator's position and discourages action on his part.

The very real difficulties that have been encountered in attempting to harmonize maritime policy with other government programs and objectives tend to cast executive officials in a negative role when dealing with the merchant marine. The congressional subcommittees, in contrast, are seldom forced to consider merchant shipping in reference to the government's program as a whole and therefore chafe at the restraints imposed on the maritime agency by the President and the Secretary of Commerce. In order to lessen these restraints, many of the industry's strong congressional supporters favor removing the Maritime Administration from the Department of Commerce and establishing it either as an independent office, similar to the Federal Aviation Agency, or as an independent commission combining promotional and regulatory functions, similar to the Civil Aeronautics Board. (Eleven bills to accomplish one or both of these changes were introduced in the first session of the 89th Congress, including six by ranking members of its merchant marine committees.) But in order to make coordination more effective, the President has instead proposed that the Maritime Administration be incorporated in a new Department of Transportation.

Public Attention to Merchant Shipping. Since World War II there has been little public interest in merchant shipping to moderate the sharpness of special interest and intra-governmental conflicts. Little news of shipping is available in newspapers and periodicals; the occasional editorials and interpretative articles usually reflect such uncompromising attitudes that they are of little value in promoting public debate of the shipping program. The field, furthermore, has developed its own special language and expertise so that issues are often couched in such complex and mystifying terms that even responsible officials find it difficult to determine what action would be consistent with their general political position. These characteristics have tended to isolate the government's maritime program from the mainstream of national concern and make it impossible to conduct this public program within the purview of a vigilant and informed citizenry.

The Contest for Power

The lack of public interest in merchant shipping tends to push maritime policy decisions down to the second and third echelons of the governmental structure. Here, two, three, or a dozen public agencies as well as many private groups, may have a significant stake in a particular problem. Operating much of the time outside the government's formal machinery for policy development, and with only limited access to the President and the Congress as a whole, the parties in interest are forced to settle their differences as best they can.

The American system for "muddling through" sets the stage for a continuing struggle for public recognition and influence which may be observed in the jurisdictional rivalries of federal agencies, in executive-congressional relations, within the Congress, in the use of publicity, and in the selection of personnel to serve in official positions. Superimposed on these tussles is a more profound contest between the industry establishment, which seeks to shield its "private government" from outside interference, and the disaffected groups within the industry and out, who seek to nudge the program more into the mainstream.

Politics of Administrative Organization. Most government agencies are obligated either by statute or circumstance to represent the interests of some clientele group, and many have very close relationships with their customers. The desire of the clientele to increase or extend its influence over government programs fuels most bureaucratic battles over administrative organization.

American shipping supported the organization of the U.S. Maritime Commission in 1936 because it realized that a vigorous new administrative agency was needed to restore public confidence in the promotional program. Except for a few disaffected lines, the industry has fought the postwar erosion of the commission's powers and prestige.

When it was first organized, the Maritime Commission was delegated broad powers to rehabilitate the U.S. maritime industry. It regulated rates and services of all domestic deep water carriers, operated four transoceanic lines, held a majority interest in two other major companies, established wage rates on ships operated under subsidy contracts, and engaged in a major construction program. Although other agencies had charge of ship documentation, health, and safety, the commission's paramountcy over the industry's business operations was unchallenged.

Fragmentation of responsibility for American shipping began even before World War II when, because of the industry's militant unionism, the commission recommended a separate Maritime Labor Board be established to develop collective bargaining procedures. Although the board was disbanded in 1942, the commission never regained its earlier influence in labor affairs.

The commission's regulatory jurisdiction was also reduced prior to World War II. In 1938 the commission yielded its potential jurisdiction over international air transport to the newly organized Civil Aeronautics Board.[22] Two years later responsibility for regulating coastwise and intercoastal shipping was shifted by the Transportation Act of 1940 to the Interstate Commerce Commission. This transfer was vigorously resisted by the domestic lines, which feared (correctly) that their interests would receive a less sympathetic hearing in this new forum than before the Maritime Commission.[23]

Since World War II, successive reorganizations have seriously diminished the maritime agency's prestige and have erased its independent promotional powers. This trend has also been resisted by the industry. How-

[22] Prior to 1938 international air transportation was not subject to any economic regulation. The Merchant Marine Act of 1936 directed the commission to "determine what provisions of this Act and other Acts relating to shipping should be made applicable to aircraft engaged in foreign commerce". The Civil Aeronautics Act was enacted before the commission completed its report.

[23] Prior to 1940 the reasonableness of coastwise and intercoastal shipping rates had been examined principally in relation to cost. The Transportation Act of 1940 embarked the government on an exacting experiment of trying to examine land and water rates in relation to each other in order to encourage the development of a balanced transportation system. This experiment was abandoned in 1958 through repeal of the Interstate Commerce Commission's power to hold up rates in order to protect any particular mode of transportation unless required for the national defense—a proviso which the courts have indicated they will interpret very restrictively and recognize only if based on findings of fact (72 Stat. 572, interpreted by the Court in *ICC v. New York, New Haven and Hartford RR.* [372 U.S. 744]).

ever, neither the 1949 nor 1950 reorganization plan nor those portions of the 1961 plan which separated regulatory and promotional programs were overtly opposed by the industry.

The 1950 plan, which established the semi-independent Maritime Board within the Department of Commerce, aroused widespread fears that the Administration might be planning to abandon independent regulatory commissions and give the President responsibility for all transportation policy functions.[24] All of the major transportation organizations, including even the powerful Association of American Railroads, lined up against the proposal. The merchant shipping industry, which had been too closely associated with the commission's past derelictions to defend it effectively, did not testify. However, it was reported that most ship operators violently opposed the plan and were doing all in their power to ensure its defeat.[25]

The publicity given to the Celler Committee's findings made it impolitic for American shipowners to oppose the 1961 reorganization proposal to establish a new agency to administer the regulatory portion of the federal maritime program. However, the industry clearly had little taste for separating regulatory from promotional functions, since the existing arrangement suited its interests far better. Although the industry allowed the reorganization to take effect, it immediately set to work to limit the new agency's powers—a project which was successfully climaxed by enactment of the Senate-drafted dual rate bill.[26]

Most U.S. flag operators opposed the portions of the 1961 reorganization which transferred the quasi-independent Federal Maritime Board's promotional responsibilities to the Secretary of Commerce. In fact, the only firms supporting the plan were two coastwise carriers who claimed

[24] Industry fears that the President wished to dominate transportation policy had been aroused by the 1949 Hoover Commission Report on Transportation and its supporting documentation. Transportation groups had opposed creation of a Department of Transportation and also opposed naming of an Under Secretary for Transportation as provided by the plan. Its chief objections, however, were that the plan brought regulatory as well as administrative functions into the Department of Commerce. This feature of the plan was thought to threaten the status of all the transportation regulatory agencies. (See *Reorganization Plan Number 21 of 1950,* Hearings before the Senate Committee on Expenditures in the Executive Departments, 81 Cong. 2 sess. [1950].)

[25] For example, see testimony of J. J. O'Conner and the staff memorandum of the Committee on Executive Expenditures, *ibid.*

[26] For example, compare industry testimony before the House Government Operations Committee (June 27, 1961) in *Reorganization Plan Number 7,* Hearings, pp. 59-64, with the Senate report on the dual rate legislation, *Steamship Conferences with Dual Rate Contracts,* S. Rept. 860, 87 Cong. 1 sess. (1961), issued two months later.

that "things couldn't get any worse, and might be improved" under the new arrangement.[27] Objections stressed by the subsidized lines were that "politics" might creep into the program, that sound precedent and judicial procedure might be ignored by a single administrator, and that the plan vested the Executive with functions previously reserved to the Congress. However, the result most feared by the subsidized operators but never stated for the record was that bringing the agency unequivocally under the Commerce Department's control would diminish their influence over its policies. The shake-up, of course, also threatened to rupture the close working relationships these operators had enjoyed with the predecessor organization.[28]

Congress Versus Executive Branch. The House and Senate merchant marine subcommittees see themselves as a counterpoise to the administrative agencies. For the industry, they have provided a vehicle through which administrators could be called to account and administrative actions reversed if necessary.

During most of the postwar period, relatively good relations have been maintained between the subcommittees and the maritime agencies. On a few problems, such as establishing the ship replacement program, there has even been active collaboration. However, because each unit exercises independent powers, there has been tension below the surface, which has occasionally broken out into active competition.

Relationships between the merchant marine subcommittees and the maritime agencies have been more sensitive to the personalities and interests of the principals than to any other factor. During the early fifties, for example, both Warren Magnuson and John Marshall Butler were active members of the Senate subcommittee. However, Senator Butler's influence waned when he lost the chairmanship in 1955, and the press of other business has limited Senator Magnuson's direct participation to po-

[27] Sea Train and Sea Land Lines criticized the board for its neglect of domestic carriers and its ineffective regulatory methods. The Plan was also supported by a group of independent tanker firms. (See *Reorganization Plan Number 7*, Hearings, p. 68.)

[28] Reorganization Plan Number 7 escaped defeat for three reasons: (1) these plans are all referred to the Government Operations Committee, which is generally disinterested in their subject matter and inclined to support a president of the same party, (2) Congressman Bonner, who probably could have engineered the plan's defeat, was reluctant to challenge a fellow North Carolinian, Secretary of Commerce Luther Hodges, and (3) the administrative board pledged by the secretary to hear all subsidy matters formerly brought before the Federal Maritime Board disarmed the industry of most of its technical objections to the plan.

licing the cargo preference statutes. Nevertheless, since the committee's next ranking Democrat, Senator Frank Lausche, opposes the subsidy program, Magnuson has continued to chair the Commerce Committee's merchant marine group as well as the full committee. On the House side, Congressman Bonner, who gave a great deal of time and energy to maritime affairs during his first four terms as chairman of the Merchant Marine and Fisheries Committee, later indicated he was tiring of trying "to bail out" the U.S. flag shipping industry.[29]

The role played by individual congressmen and the several congressional committees in maritime affairs is a function of their interest and political position. Though the Senate Commerce Committee has not taken as active an interest in this field as the House committee since the mid-fifties, Magnuson's seniority in the Senate, his membership on the Appropriations Committee, and his key position as chairman of the full Commerce Committee in relation to all Commerce Department legislation give his committee greater power than the companion House group. On the other hand, membership of the Senate subcommittee is less homogeneous than the House merchant marine subcommittee and is exposed to a greater range of conflicting pressures.[30]

Over the years both Congress and the Executive have occasionally preempted functions traditionally reserved to the other. An executive branch decision to curtail maritime training programs in the mid-fifties, for example, was met by legislation placing these activities on a permanent basis.[31] In 1956 Mr. Bonner challenged the Maritime Administration's authority to construct a demonstration nuclear ship, proposed by the President, and urged that his committee should review and authorize the project before the Appropriations Committee acted on it.[32] Apparently fearing

[29] Note Congressman Bonner's remarks in *Review of Merchant Marine Policy, 1962,* Hearings before the House Merchant Marine and Fisheries Committee, 87 Cong. 2 sess. (1962), p. 55. Bonner became seriously ill early in the 89th Congress' first session and died in November 1965.

[30] The committee's membership in 1964 included such diverse personalities as Senators Lausche, Bartlett, Pastore, Thurmond, and Magnuson. A fascinating case study of its work is provided in its 1962 action on proposals to waive cabotage in order to aid the Pacific Coast lumber industry. A legislative compromise involving four highly controversial maritime bills was required to resolve this problem (*Congressional Record,* Vol. 108, No. 15, pp. 20424 ff. and P.L. 87-877 [76 Stat. 1200]).

[31] The Maritime Administration first considered closing the Merchant Marine Academy at King's Point, but was stopped by legislation establishing the Academy as a permanent federal institution. It then sought to curtail aid to state maritime academies and was met by legislation authorizing long-term contracts with those schools.

[32] This incident is reported in *Department of Commerce and Related Agencies Appropriations for 1957,* Hearings, 84 Cong. 2 sess. (1956), pp. 995 ff.

that the Maritime Administration's research and development program might "get out of control," the committee informally indicated that it also wished to authorize any future experimental ships prior to their construction.[33]

The Senate committee has focused its attention principally on the cargo preference problem, and has engaged in an extensive correspondence to prod Executive agencies to extend the applicability of the statute. Both House and Senate groups have held out for a more liberal approach to construction subsidy allowances than has been recommended by the Executive. Recently the Maritime Administration was deterred by the committees' obvious hostility to its proposal from adopting a procedure that would have reduced construction subsidy payments.[34]

The committees, in turn, have been nettled by the Executive's failure to implement 1958 legislation authorizing construction of two superliners. Several congressmen also feel strongly that the maritime agencies have not supported domestic shipping (particularly to Alaska, Puerto Rico, and Hawaii) with sufficient energy or funds. Others have challenged the Executive decision to support flags of convenience, a policy which has never received legislative endorsement.[35]

Friction between the congressional and executive agencies concerned with merchant marine affairs enhances the industry's opportunities to wield a decisive influence in the policy making process. Playing off one group against another can be an effective technique for maintaining the status quo, while the possibility that any unpopular action may be reversed

[33] *Ibid.*, particularly p. 998.

[34] The Merchant Marine Act, 1936, authorized the government to pay up to one-third the U.S. cost of construction or up to 50 percent "in cases where the Commission possesses convincing evidence" (49 Stat. 1996). The 50 percent limit was raised to 55 percent in 1960 over Administration objections. In 1964 the 55 percent limit was extended for two years despite the Maritime Administration's recommendation that the extension be limited to one year. Maritime recommended the shorter period because it believed that a revision in its procedure for computing the foreign-domestic cost differential would both provide a more equitable measure of the true differential and reduce subsidies to 50 percent of domestic cost or less. (Maritime's proposal was to base the subsidy on the *average* price of five low-price foreign yards rather than the single lowest-price yard as had been its previous practice. The effect obviously would be to increase slightly the estimated foreign cost and to reduce the subsidy.) Congressman Bonner responded cooly to this proposal and noted that he did not wish the Maritime Administration to implement it until the committee had had an opportunity to hear industry views. (*Construction Differential Subsidies*, Hearings before a Subcommittee of the House Merchant Marine and Fisheries Committee, 88 Cong. 2 sess. [1964], p. 24.)

[35] Hearings on the flag of convenience issue were held by both the House and Senate subcommittees during the late 1950's, but no reports were issued or legislation proposed.

by the other body causes all concerned to move cautiously in pushing for reform.

Jurisdiction Within the Congress. The operation of checks and balances within the congressional sytem is complicated by the overlapping jurisdictions of the twenty standing committees of the House and the sixteen Senate committees. Referral of new business, which is of crucial importance to the manner in which it is likely to be handled, is determined largely by the way in which proposed legislation is packaged. Bills in which a merchant marine matter is incidental to a more general tax, foreign aid, or defense proposal are assigned to committees which give the maritime industry's interests scarcely any special attention. Each year at least one or two items of major importance to the industry have been brought up in a context which has removed the matter from the House Merchant Marine and Fisheries and the Senate Commerce committees' jurisdiction.[36]

The volume of legislative activity escaping the merchant marine committees' jurisdiction would probably be much larger if the basic legislation in this field were not so broad in scope. Amendments to the merchant marine acts are almost invariably considered the business of the merchant marine committees, even if they deal solely with a tax, labor, or defense issue. The merchant marine committees also receive all matters bearing on maritime subsidies and economic regulation.[37]

Resolution of jurisdictional questions is a responsibility of the President of the Senate and the Speaker of the House. Access to these officials and their associates is important to a committee's standing and effectiveness since committee business generates a number of problems (relating to order of business, legislative calendars, referrals, and assignments) which can be settled only by the leadership. However, committees sometimes arrange to share jurisdiction by holding joint hearings, issuing joint reports, or arranging for one committee to report formally to another. By such means, open clashes between congressional groups concerned with the merchant marine have been avoided.

[36] For example, in the 88th Congress the Ways and Means Committee reviewed proposals to tax earnings of American-owned vessels operated under foreign flags; the Foreign Affairs Committee amended P.L. 83-480 to require that nations purchasing grains pay all shipping costs in their own currency, subject to reimbursement by the United States of the excess cost of shipping via U.S. flag vessels.

[37] The Legislative Reorganization Act specifies that all matters bearing on "the merchant marine generally" shall be referred to the House Merchant Marine and Fisheries and Senate Commerce committees. The act also confers specific jurisdiction over merchant marine officers and seamen, regulation, navigation, licensing, and pilotage of vessels.

Relationships between the merchant marine and appropriations committees merit special comment. The 1936 act as originally passed minimized appropriation restraints on the commission's programs, which were financed entirely from a generously capitalized revolving fund. No significant restrictions were imposed on the commission's use of this fund until 1946. The 1947 Appropriation Act specified maximum amounts to be expended for each major program. The following year the revolving fund was abolished altogether in favor of direct appropriations for operating and construction subsidies. When the Comptroller General ruled that the commission could incur operating obligations regardless of whether an appropriation had been made, the House Appropriations Committee experimented with other techniques (ship and voyage limitations) to bring this program under budgetary control. These efforts, however, have had no real effect because House-Senate conferees have always compromised the limitation at a level which avoided seriously restricting the program.

The House Appropriations Committee, which initiated all of the above actions, typically pursues more independent policies than its companion Senate group. The latter includes men of broad interests, who more often seek to promote than to restrict government programs. Senator Magnuson, for example, has been a member of the committee since 1953, and his presence has been an important factor in protecting the maritime program from more onerous appropriation controls.

Use of Publicity. Merchant shipping is a little known industry. Even at the World War II peak of American maritime power, less than half the general public are reported to have recognized the term "merchant marine."[38] The industry's problems and the steps that the government has taken to alleviate them are probably not known to one person in ten thousand.

Knowledge of merchant shipping is also limited within government. It is doubtful that more than 10 percent of the 535 members of Congress have an intimate knowledge of the industry or of the subsidy program. The hierarchies of both the executive branch and the Congress, because only occasionally in contact with maritime affairs, are only superficially informed on these matters.

General news coverage of shipping affairs is also limited. Maritime news is reported in the business sections of about half a dozen metropoli-

[38] Survey cited by Harvey Klemmer in "Post War Planning Committee of the U.S. Maritime Commission," *Proceedings of the American Merchant Marine Conference, 1944* (Maritime Administration library).

tan dailies; only three or four papers have reporters who specialize in this field. Their readership, like that of the industry's trade press, is limited largely to persons directly involved in the industry.

Merchant shipping is front page news only when the industry is strike-bound or involved in an international crisis. These occasions highlight industry weaknesses and inspire critical editorials. From time to time the industry is also excoriated in national periodicals.[39]

The U.S. flag shipping industry is acutely sensitive to the need to improve its public relations. Each of the several owners' associations employs public relations personnel and cooperates in sponsoring such activities as Maritime Day dinners and poster and essay contests. The Committee of American Steamship Lines (CASL) has produced a film, *Lifelines, U.S.A.*, and a variety of slide presentations and factbooks. These materials emphasize the industry's defense role and base their appeal for public support on patriotism.

The industry's most important public is the Congress. Its most costly single public relations project in 1963-64—a thrice-weekly newscast of congressional activities—was designed especially for this audience. Through this service and the spot announcements on CASL activities which accompanied it, the subsidized operators hoped to establish a climate of acceptance and win the cooperation of congressmen who had no direct knowledge of the industry.

The image the industry projects of itself is obviously keyed to its political goals. Thus for many years subsidized and non-subsidized operators alike stressed that only a tiny share of the nation's total export-import cargo was carried by U.S. flag ships but failed to point out that the greatest part of the total cargo tonnage was bulk ores and oils, transported almost entirely in foreign flag vessels. But in 1964 the subsidized lines began to stress instead the substantial share of total freight revenue earned by U.S. flag liner operators. The purpose appears to have been to prove the success of the 1936 program and to head off proposals to extend subsidies to bulk carriers so that U.S. flag vessels might carry a larger share of U.S. foreign trade.

Publicity can also be used as a weapon for winning specific goals. In 1964 the National Maritime Union distributed 100,000 copies of a *Handbook for Saboteurs* designed to warn good Americans against such subversive doctrines as that passenger ships might no longer be required for na-

[39] *Barron's Weekly* frequently features editorials which muckrake the merchant marine. *Fortune* and the *Reader's Digest* also occasionally carry critical materials. For example, see "Let's Give Subsidies the Deep-Six," *Fortune* (Oct. 1961), and "Our Strike-Strangled Merchant Marine," *Reader's Digest* (Feb. 1963).

tional defense. The *Handbook* delivered a clever attack on merchant marine policy reforms then under consideration and may have deterred their adoption. Although shipowner groups have never attempted similar mass campaigns, they have frequently been charged with "drumming up" shipper support for legislation which they favor.[40] Prestigious members of the business community and retired military officers have also occasionally been persuaded to lend their weight to the industry's cause.

The merchant marine and the Navy have a common interest in publicizing the importance of seapower to the nation's defenses and they work cooperatively to this end. The Navy's annual statements on merchant ship requirements, its limited alert of merchant vessels during the Cuban crisis, and even Secretary McNamara's 1962 testimony before the House Merchant Marine and Fisheries Committee have been used for their publicity value by the industry. In 1964, private ships joined the Military Sea Transport Service in a naval amphibious exercise which yielded both data on sealift's effectiveness relative to airlift and a handsome illustrated brochure. In January 1966, a circular letter from the Chief of Naval Operations to senior commissioned personnel, released by a retired admiral who heads one of the subsidized lines, served to announce the Navy's concern regarding the adequacy of the U.S. merchant fleet.[41]

Publicity also is a potential threat to the industry, whose political support rests on so narrow a base that it might be swept away by a shift in the political wind. Many industry personnel are fearful that the Celler and Douglas investigations, topped by the unfavorable publicity associated with the 1964 wheat boycotts, have weakened the industry's political support. A well-publicized scandal could be disastrous.

Personal Relationships. Ultimately it is individual officials who shape the government's decisions, not anonymous agencies and institutions. Thus the industry's personal relationships, rather than its public relations, count most.

The government personnel with whom the industry deals include congressmen, cabinet officers, and their assistants; senior administrative officials and their staffs; and military officers. The industry is represented by company presidents, trade association officials, union officers, attorneys, contractors, and staff personnel.

[40] *Index to the Legislative History of the Steamship/Dual Rate Law*, S. Doc. 100, 87 Cong. 2 sess. (1962), p. 316.

[41] The Chief of Naval Operations' letter, released January 19, 1966, with official clearance received wide publicity and was generally interpreted by the press as repudiating Secretary McNamara's earlier assertions that America's shipping programs were adequate to U.S. military needs. This was denied by McNamara. See Chapter 5.

Contact is least inhibited at the top levels of industry and government. Congressmen and cabinet officers expect to service their constituencies, are generally anxious to give assistance when they can, and welcome any support that is given in return. For most of these officials, however, merchant shipping is a marginal interest, whose claims must be weighed against a hundred competing priorities. In the entire Congress there are probably not more than a dozen members who need the maritime industry's support in order to retain their seats.

Contacts with senior administrative officials, such as the Maritime Administrator, the commander of the Military Sea Transport Service, and the chairman and managing director of the Federal Maritime Commission, are more reserved. These officials must protect their administrative integrity, but they must also serve as ambassadors to the merchant marine. Either from choice or from a feeling of obligation, they attend at least the major quasi-social functions sponsored by the industry and have frequent official contacts with its representatives. This exposure may influence an official's orientation without creating any bias. In any event, these officials have had sufficiently strong ties with the shipping industry that eight of the seventeen persons who have held these positions since 1952 have continued some relationship with the industry after leaving public service, although only two had had prior maritime employment.

Civil service personnel in the administrative agencies are generally well shielded from industry influence. The Maritime Administration rule, welcomed by most of the agency's employees, allows complete freedom to meet and talk with industry representatives, but bars giving or receiving any favors or revealing any administrative information.[42]

In World War II, government and industry personnel worked side by side. Many close friendships were formed that persisted for years after the joint effort had been dissolved. Over the past decade, however, a new group of federal executives, whose contacts with industry have always been in an official framework, have moved into the key positions in the maritime agencies. Relationships between government and industry at this level have accordingly been increasingly depersonalized and professional.

Public Responsibilities and Private Interests

For a game with such high stakes, the political contest has few well-defined rules. Bribery and blackmail are obviously not tolerated but

[42] Prior to the 1961 reorganization, there were fewer explicit rules to regulate administrative conduct, and information on internal agency operations was much more freely available to the industry.

promises of future reward and threats of punishment sometimes are. Occasionally the industry claims the scalp of a government official who threatens its interests, or government is forced to release an employee found to be too responsive to private groups. The maritime agencies face the usual difficulties in safeguarding administratively confidential information and must cope with the usual pressures for preferential treatment of favored personnel and parties in interest.

The glare of publicity provides the best assurance that the contest will remain within the rules. In the executive branch this assurance is reinforced by conflict-of-interest laws, codes of ethics, requirements for hearing and public counsel, and judicial review. In Congress the rules of fair play rest on the integrity of each member.

The rules are imprecise partially because of the difficulty of distinguishing clearly between public and private interests. Government regulatory agencies are in business to adjudicate conflicting private claims, and their most immediate responsibilities are to the claimants. However, they also are charged with a mission of broader national significance against which the private claims must be considered. Basically, the question is whether general considerations of the national good or the private concerns of the regulated industry will dominate the agency's work—that is, whether there will be "public control or private government of an industry."[43]

How this issue is resolved depends largely on the agency's charter. If the agency's mission is clear-cut and relevant to current national needs, a high sense of public responsibility is likely to ensue. If its mission has lost its national significance or been obscured by other programs, its administrators will tend to become preoccupied with the industry's private problems.

Administrative agencies are closely attuned to their political environment. If there is broad knowledge of, and interest in, an agency's work, the agency will be exposed to a wide range of pressures and its outlook stretched to encompass truly national interests. On the other hand, if the administrative agency's external contacts are limited, its program is likely to draw inward and concentrate only on matters deemed important by those immediately concerned.

The third principal factor in an administrative agency's orientation is its location within the federal organization. It is generally agreed that broad national objectives are more likely to be pursued if programs are administered by Executive departments than by independent commissions, for the latter can easily become detached from government's mainstream.

[43] Hamilton, *op. cit.* p. 43.

Procedures within Executive agencies are also important. Planning staffs and public counsel are useful for pointing up the long-term public implications of agency decisions. Broad national interests can also be adduced through staff studies, general agency investigations, and rule-making proceedings. On the other hand, case-by-case adjudication, such as has typified most regulatory commissions, tends to concentrate attention on the claims of private parties.

The contest for control of the government's maritime program has mirrored these facts of political life. The industry has stressed the need to strengthen the privately owned merchant marine as the program's first, immediate, and most important objective, leaving until later decisions as to how this fleet is to be used as an instrument of public policy. It has sought to keep consideration of the program within the merchant marine committees and channel public debate. Transfer of the government's promotional programs from an independent commission to the Commerce Department was resisted, but without success.

The contest for dominance of America's merchant marine program has been an uneven and indecisive struggle, complicated by side issues, intra-industry divisions, and contradictions to the general thrust. The spirit of reconstruction and reform which activated the prewar commission has long worn away, and the patriotism associated with the program's defense role has lost its wartime glitter. There have been difficulties both in retaining key administrative personnel and in getting rid of less capable aides. The program is highly technical. In many respects it has been uniquely vulnerable to an excessively private orientation.

However, the political system has self-correcting qualities, as illustrated by the chain reaction following the 1958 Supreme Court decision outlawing the dual rate contracts used in the Pacific trades.[44] The decision drew a strong response from the industry, which "demanded" enactment of legislation to correct the Court's "ill-considered decision." However, the industry's demands also aroused Congressman Celler's investigatory instincts. The rest is history. Although the conference lines succeeded in obtaining passage of a more moderate dual rate bill, the price they paid included both creation of a new agency, dedicated to regulating the industry, and the loss of a quasi-independent promotional agency to the Depart-

---

[44] *Federal Maritime Board v. Isbrandtsen*, 356 U.S. 481. The example is drawn from Julian Singman, a former member of the Celler Committee staff, who has compared the industry's effort to overturn the Supreme Court's decision with "hubris—the insolent, overweening pride of the heroes of Greek tragedy." His analysis of the industry's reaction and its effect is presented in H. C. Reese (ed.), *Merchant Marine Policy* (Cambridge, Maryland: Cornell Maritime Press, 1963), p. 180.

ment of Commerce. Evidence also strongly suggests that it was the sting of defeat in the 1961 Senate floor fight on dual rates that led Senator Douglas two years later to reopen the regulatory issues.[45] His hearings, in turn, sharpened the President's interest in maritime affairs and caused new appointments to be made to the regulatory agency. Thus by 1965 the pendulum had swung again and the industry seemed on the defensive.

Concluding Remarks on Part III:
Innovation and Politics

The United States merchant marine is frequently described as the "world's most studied industry." The studies, however, have exposed problems without resolving them. Rather than leading to action they typically add to the sense of frustration and irresolution which pervades the industry and the maritime program.

There are many interacting causes for the government's inability to update its maritime programs. Executive turnover has been excessive, and organization often inappropriate and confused. Resort to indirect aids has unduly complicated administration and increased the difficulty of establishing a single coherent government policy. Because the program is marginal to the government's main concerns, it has not commanded the sustained attention of the officials whose power and prestige are required to coordinate activity across agency lines and within the Congress or to force change.

Divisions and alliances within the industry have also hampered the program. The industry's disaffected elements have perceived that nothing is to be gained by overturning existing programs and have concentrated instead on expanding the applicability of cargo preference, in which both the subsidized and non-subsidized firms have a stake.

The structure of the political system supports the industry's strategy. Because responsibility is diffused and widely dispersed, no single government agency has sufficient power to seize the initiative to overcome the status quo. Operating at the periphery of government, the administrative agencies and congressional subcommittees concerned with maritime affairs have attempted to resolve problems through negotiation rather than referring them to the President or the Congress as a whole. Fre-

---

[45] Douglas was personally involved in the 1961 dual rate debate. The fact that he used the same evidentiary material to embark on his 1963-64 investigation strongly suggests that he had never abandoned either his files or his resolve to reopen the question of monopoly abuse as soon as a more suitable political climate prevailed.

quently they have been forced to compromise on the industry's terms. Higher political echelons, when they have become involved, usually have acted as peacemaker between dissident groups. They have often allowed the cost of the government's program to increase rather than risk alienating any immediately affected group. In effect, creeping liberalization of government aids has substituted for hard decisions and real innovation.

There are some who believe this to be a chronic condition of government. However, the maritime program has unique characteristics. First, merchant shipping throughout the world is a tradition-minded industry. Most shipping firms are family enterprises which have difficulty attracting the most able young men. Most are too small to sponsor research and development. Dependence of liner firms on conferences to establish rates and services discourages innovation. The industry generally suffers from wide cyclical swings. The U.S. industry expanded enormously to meet World War II needs and then slowly and painfully had to contract to peacetime levels.

Administration of government shipping programs has been handicapped by the confusion of regulatory and promotional and of military and commercial objectives. Agencies have been given poorly articulated, contradictory, and overlapping missions, which forces collaborative decision-making, undermines accountability, creates opportunities for jurisdictional squabbles and confusion, and increases the difficulty of attracting and retaining qualified personnel.

The sheer number of people involved in maritime policy development tends to retard policy formulation. Because the machinery is ponderous, delay is a potent weapon for fending off undesired change. Procedures designed to allow a full airing of issues have been used to postpone decision-making indefinitely. The agencies themselves have been so immersed in day-to-day affairs that they have seldom offered the sustained leadership necessary to push policy proposals through to a top-level decision.

The complexity of the subsidy program has also retarded innovation. The program provides a patchwork of aids, interwoven and interdependent. Every issue is a potential Pandora's box. As a result, even dissident groups have hesitated to raise basic questions, and the program's opponents can be easily overwhelmed by obfuscating detail.

The program's complexity has helped to protect it from outside interference. However, it has also impeded communication between the program's administrators and others in the political superstructure within which it operates. Experts in the intricacies of the maritime subsidy programs and shipping operations have developed their own special language, which tends to isolate them. Isolation in turn tends to intensify beliefs, to abet the development of orthodoxies, and to deny the participants the stimulus of detached criticism of disinterested third parties.

The purpose of public regulation is to overcome the natural penchant of private enterprises to regulate their affairs in their own interests. Regulation can be justified only if significant national interests in the industry's activity require use of governmental power. To sustain an effective program, these public interests must be translatable into concrete, attainable, and politically meaningful objectives.

The government's maritime programs have lacked clearly defined objectives. Despite frequent blue-ribbon studies, the programs have failed to generate any intelligible public debate. Even policy officials find it difficult to thread through the programs' ambiguities to evaluate their achievements or alternatives to the present subsidy scheme. Their inability to grasp policy issues inhibits their participation in the political process and contributes to the sense of drift which permeates this field.

Political support of the merchant shipping industry consequently depends on a very narrow base of informed persons. This small core of trade association, executive, and congressional officials who are friends of the industry has been able to use its friendships and position to safeguard the industry's prerogatives, but it has not been strong enough to introduce any real innovations in established programs. This situation immobilizes the political process. Those favored by the subsidy program have reason to avoid any action which will disturb the equilibrium. Those not so favored tend to be so disorganized that they cannot act effectively to win a larger share. Furthermore, the fragmentation of power within the U.S. political system relieves the shipping industry of any sustained external pressure to introduce innovations.

12

Problems, Proposals, and Prospects

AMERICA'S MARITIME PROGRAMS have wandered a long way from the model laid out in the Merchant Marine Act of 1936. This is as it should be in a world in which changing conditions demand new and original responses. However, the programs have not developed as planned or compatibly either with the basic principles established in the 1936 act or the aspirations of its authors. Shaped largely within its own "private government," where opportunities to introduce new departures and constructive policy innovations have been severely limited, the programs' long-range public objectives have too often been sacrificed to immediate needs. These developments have diluted the programs' sense of public purpose and gradually undermined the industry's ability to respond to public needs.

Problems

The seemingly uncontrolled drift which has marked U.S. maritime programs over the past ten years has been frustrating to many supporters of a strong and vigorous U.S. merchant marine and to the program's opponents as well. It has generated a feeling that it is time for a change, but has failed to develop a sense of common purpose or to identify objectives for new maritime policies. The impasse which has ensued lies at the heart of America's maritime problem.

A general frustration over maritime affairs has bred a tendency to overestimate the difficulties we face. Actually the government program has operated reasonably well in certain areas. Its principal beneficiaries, the subsidized liner companies, have acquired some of the world's finest vessels and are well-established in their trades. However, the postwar drift of federal maritime policies has also created certain very real and tangible problems which seriously hamper achievement of national mari-

334

time objectives. These problems are troublesome and costly to the industry, to other sectors of the economy, and to the public at large.

To the industry the most important problems arise from its excessive dependence on government patronage and the vicissitudes of the political process:

1. U.S. flag carriers lack the flexibility necessary to successful steamship operations. Subsidized companies are restricted by a trade route system which has outlived its initial purpose and are committed to a mode of operation that appears increasingly vulnerable to competition from alternative transportation systems. Non-subsidized companies are at the mercy of unpredictable shifts in the volume of government shipments or locked into specific protected trades.

2. Almost half of America's foreign trade merchant marine is denied any practical opportunity to obtain new ships. Because there is no plan for replacing the war-built vessels now used in most non-subsidized operations, a large portion of the U.S. merchant fleet will eventually have to discontinue operations or transfer to foreign flag.

3. The entire industry suffers from unsatisfactory labor-management relations, which have been exacerbated by the government program. The divisive effects of direct and indirect subsidies have complicated negotiations between rival industry groups and the seafaring unions. Subsidies also have helped escalate maritime wages to a level which has encouraged more workers to remain in the industry than it can efficiently support. This has heightened job issues and increased the difficulty of adjusting to new technology.

4. Unsatisfactory labor-management relations have also made it more difficult for U.S. flag firms to obtain commercial cargoes or to attract the capital needed to expand their trade. Frequent strikes, increased costs, and the consequent loss of private clientele have given the industry an unfavorable public image, which further contributes to its difficulties.

5. Payment of subsidies has led many political figures to conclude that some *quid pro quo* should be extracted from the industry. This attitude has forced the subsidized companies to assume certain burdens (for example, the inconvenience of having virtually all repairs made in U.S. ports) and has contributed to the government undertaking regulatory activities which the industry believes weigh more heavily on U.S. than foreign lines.

6. Pressures and resentment created by U.S. subsidy, regulatory, and cargo preference programs threaten to undermine the continued tenability of flags of convenience. If nationalism in shipping is allowed to run full course, the government will eventually be forced to choose between repa-

triating PANLIBHON vessels to U.S. flag at very high cost or allowing these ships to transfer to other foreign flags over which the United States can exercise less effective control.

7. Government's involvement in American shipping has made it more difficult for the industry to develop long-range plans, experiment with new equipment and services, and attract young imaginative personnel. Whereas subsidies have permitted selected companies to acquire fine, modern equipment, their deadening effect on the industry as a whole has contributed to the basic problem—excessive dependence on government aid.

To other sectors of the economy the American merchant marine has become a drag rather than a positive element in economic development and trade:

1. Sales of surplus agricultural products have been made more difficult and in a few cases have been prevented by the requirement that 50 percent of the produce be carried by American flag ships. The cargo preference statutes have also occasionally complicated the administration of foreign aid and negotiation of sales financed by the Export-Import Bank.

2. The high costs of U.S. flag ship operations have necessitated a rate structure which America's non-contiguous states and possessions claim has unduly burdened their economic development. Certain domestic industries (for example, the lumber industry in the Pacific Northwest) have also asserted that in some instances the high cost of ocean freight in domestic services has prevented sales in competitive markets.

To the public at large the government's maritime program has appeared to be the source of factional disputes which have spawned troublesome strikes and international friction. Occasionally, as in the Russian wheat sales, promotion of American shipping has directly conflicted with specific national goals. And in general the ship subsidy program has failed to achieve its stated defense and foreign trade aims:

1. Though the program has supported operation of roughly the number of vessels stated by the Defense Department to be necessary to meet military requirements, many of these ships have been of inferior quality. Furthermore, the emphasis on the defense role of an active, privately owned merchant fleet has deflected attention from the need to maintain adequate reserves of mothballed vessels and trained personnel and has deterred acquisition of new tonnage for the Military Sea Transport Service.

2. The promotional program is alleged to have impaired U.S. foreign commerce by encouraging excessive allegiance to the conference system

and, as an indirect result of cargo preferences, by permitting higher rates on U.S. exports than on imports.

3. The program's tendency to abet cost inflation has not only caused U.S. shipping to be noncompetitive with foreign flags but also to become relatively inefficient compared to domestic industries and a highly inefficient means for earning foreign exchange. The industry, in short, is uneconomic in every sense. Although the United States is easily able to maintain it, the industry's excessive costs are a drain on U.S. economic strength as well as a source of trouble in international affairs.

In the political arena, the U.S. flag fleet's dependence on subsidies has hindered the efforts of the industry and its supporters to win needed improvements in the subsidy system:

1. The industry's vulnerability has made it defensive, cautious, and reluctant to risk any thoroughgoing re-examination of the government program. Apprehensive that they could not win support for sufficient direct aids, the industry and its supporters have resorted to indirect subsidies which have exacerbated basic problems.

2. The disrepute of maritime subsidy programs has caused those with a stake in the industry or an interest in its welfare to keep close control of the program, even at the cost of further narrowing its base of political support.

3. This condition has tended to quash any intelligible public debate of the government's merchant marine programs. Supporters and opponents of the program have each tended to adopt extreme, uncompromising positions in an effort to repel the arguments of the other. But since neither is strong enough to silence the other, the effect of the debate has been chiefly to confuse and obscure the program's basic objectives and to checkmate any real updating of the promotional program.

Proposals

In order to break the impasse in U.S. maritime policy it is essential to define goals for the maritime industry which will arouse the enthusiasm of the parties in interest and win broad public support as well. A practical program for the merchant marine can neither be aimed at the abolition of subsidies (at least until restrictive practices generally are removed from international trade) nor involve any significant increase in government outlays unless tangible benefits to the nation as a whole can be shown to justify the cost. In sum, proposals to update maritime promotional programs must be challenging but realistic and compatible with the nation's general political philosophy so that a consensus can develop in their support.

The three broad alternative goals toward which America's maritime policies might be aimed are: (1) to enlarge the U.S. flag merchant fleet (without too much regard for cost) in order that sufficient ships will be available to provide a margin of military safety and to carry a substantial portion of the nation's foreign commerce; (2) to reduce shipping subsidies (without too much regard for this action's effect on the industry) on the basis that the national interest no longer justifies subsidies to a national flag merchant marine; or (3) to place major emphasis on increasing the competitiveness of U.S. merchant ships (without being excessively meticulous as to the exact size of the program) so that the United States may be creditably represented among the world's merchant fleets and will have a nucleus of skills in the event of a future mobilization.

Of these three alternatives, the first—simply because it is the most familiar—now enjoys the widest support. The traditional military and commercial objectives of U.S. maritime policy continue to be sufficiently credible that the statement of policy incorporated in the 1936 act is seldom challenged. Furthermore, enlarging the U.S. flag fleet is an attractive way to offset the loss in shipboard job opportunities expected to result from increased automation.

The second alternative is the most coldly logical objective for U.S. maritime policy if it is assumed that (a) the United States can continue to exercise effective control over ships registered under flags of convenience and (b) alternate job opportunities can be developed for the men currently manning the U.S. flag fleet. However, there is sufficient political attraction to continuing subsidies and doubt regarding the validity of the above assumptions that this alterntive is highly unlikely to be acceptable to the Congress. Furthermore, its adoption would be so completely unacceptable to organized labor that its implementation would almost certainly be complicated by direct action.

The third alternative accepts the necessity of subsidies, but insists that they be restructured to encourage lower costs and more effective performance. In recent years this objective has won increasing support. Exhausted by years of labor-management conflict and alarmed at the persistent inflation in subsidy costs, many industry officials have concluded that something must be done to make the industry more responsible, self-reliant, and competitive. Public officials have also recognized these qualities to be essential to the merchant marine's effectively fulfilling its military and commercial roles.

An absolute commitment to maintain a U.S. flag fleet at some given size, which is sometimes construed to be the intent of the 1936 act, is fundamentally incompatible with that legislation's objective to develop an efficient, innovative, and viable U.S. merchant marine. The doctrine of essentiality implies unlimited government support. In contrast, if the government is to create a more efficient, tough, self-reliant, and independent U.S. merchant fleet, it must establish and strictly administer standards which limit the amount of its aid, since increased efficiency depends upon convincing the industry's management and labor that the government's interest *is* limited and that they cannot rely on government to solve their problems.

Currently the government is attempting through its subsidy programs to meet a variety of objectives, but failing to fulfill any of them satisfactorily. A subsidy program aimed at increasing the competitiveness of U.S. merchant shipping should be targeted on that objective alone. The program should permit the more efficient U.S. flag operators to expand and force the less efficient companies either to improve their operations or leave the business. Whether the U.S. flag industry as a whole expands or contracts should depend on how well it responds to the program's terms. Within rather broad limits, the precise size and composition of the U.S. merchant fleet are no longer relevant to the nation's military and commercial needs; but its competitiveness is.

The number of ships and jobs to be supported through the government aid program is, of course, of crucial interest to the industry's labor and management, and a strategy for satisfactorily answering these questions crucial to winning their cooperation in strengthening the U.S. merchant fleet. The National Maritime Union, for one, has served notice that it does not intend to be party to "automating a corpse." Yet, if the government gives unconditional assurances of job protection, it is questionable whether the industry will automate at all. There are also limits to the government's ability to create new shipboard jobs to offset the impact of automation.

Expansion of the U.S. merchant marine can be accomplished only if a market can be developed for its services. This additional business cannot be created by government fiat without provoking retaliatory actions which in the long run will harm the American merchant marine. However, new markets can be won by the industry on its merits, through lower costs and better service. If such improvements can be achieved, it will be practical to increase the size of the subsidized fleet and possible to do so without increasing subsidy costs. Thus, if a firm formula can be established to relate government aid to operating efficiency, the subsidy program's scale should be more or less self-regulating and continue approximately the present level of expenditure.

The objective of increasing the U.S. flag fleet's competitiveness requires clarification of the government's and industry's respective roles. Conceivably, increased efficiency might be sought through socializing the private industry or by bringing privately owned companies under the direct or indirect control of one or more government corporations. None of the parties at interest, however, desire these arrangements, nor is there any convincing argument to compel abandoning the United States' historic preference for private enterprise in this field.

The present partnership between the government and its subsidized lines, however, is unsatisfactory. The experience of the past twenty years suggests that it simply is not tenable to expect an administrative agency to rule on the reasonableness of wage settlements and the many other facets of subsidized ship operations. Partnership also has thrust the government too intimately into the industry's operations, bred excessively detailed regulation, weakened private initiative, blurred responsibility, and permitted companies holding operating subsidy contracts to gain a favored position among U.S. flag firms.

Revival of American shipping requires that the industry be allowed maximum flexibility and a maximum opportunity to improve its operations. Since some government subsidy is necessary to the survival of U.S. flag operations in foreign commerce, there must be some government involvement to assure that public funds are not diverted from their intended purpose. However, if the private industry is to win its own way in a highly competitive market, it must (to the maximum extent possible) be permitted to deal with its own problems on its own terms. In short, in lieu of the present partnership, the government should extricate itself as completely as possible from the industry's affairs.

There are other important reasons for clearly distinguishing the government's and industry's respective responsibilities. First, clarification of the public and private roles permits a clearer perception of the public interest in American shipping and should tend to direct greater attention to the program's public purposes. Second, a policy of disengagement minimizes the possibility that one or another portion of the industry will receive preferential treatment and limits opportunities for malpractice or collusion. Third, this policy releases government agencies from any obligation to operate exclusively through private channels to meet their own ocean shipping needs. Making it clear that the government's shipping agencies (including the military) are responsible for meeting their shipping needs in the most effective way, without regard to whether vessels are publicly or privately owned, liners or tramps, can also help to protect both parties from the misunderstandings and recriminations which have sometimes infected this field.

Disengagement of government from the industry's operations does not imply abandoning the U.S. merchant marine. It does require revising the existing subsidy system. The problem is not to eliminate subsidy, but to design a subsidy formula which interferes as little as possible with the natural, healthy functioning of both the private industry and the agencies of government.

A completely satisfactory means of enlisting government and industry's respective talents in building a lean and efficient U.S. merchant fleet is unlikely ever to be devised. However, a thorough overhauling of the present system is clearly necessary if real progress is to be achieved. Simply "trying harder" within the framework of present policies is not enough. The situation instead requires, as President Johnson has indicated, "a new maritime policy," new arrangements for its administration, and improved procedures to appraise the program as it develops and to assure it is appropriately updated to meet changing needs.

A new maritime policy aimed at increasing the competitiveness of the U.S. flag fleet should be based on a single comprehensive subsidy system covering all U.S. registered vessels in foreign trade. It should be geared initially to supporting the present U.S. flag fleet. However, in order to encourage those participating in the system to up-grade their equipment and improve operations, the present program's structure must be substantially modified. The new system should be designed to be as simple, easy to administer, neutral in its economic effects, and impervious to political manipulation as possible. The following new policies are proposed:

1. An explicit judgment should be made regarding the amount the government will invest in shipping subsidies in relation to the overall size of the fleet to be supported. The present system generally evades these key determinations; ships are operated and subsidies paid as an incidental by-product of foreign assistance and agricultural programs. Though conditions are studied on individual trade routes, there is no mechanism for determining total national needs and acting to fulfill them. The new system must correct this basic deficiency through procedures to compel periodic reconsideration of the overall scale of the government assistance program in relation to the industry's performance and national needs. These matters should be continuously subject to Executive review so that

recommendations regarding program level may be periodically made to the Congress for its review and approval. This program authorization, translated into specific authority to incur subsidy obligations, would establish the maximum amount of aid which might be provided to privately owned U.S. flag shipping during the year. Arrangements could be built into this authorization procedure to protect the participants in the program against undue fluctuations in the overall size of the program consistent with the need to provide the government some flexibility to adjust its size to changing needs.[1]

2. Within this overall authorization control, there should be a minimum of administrative restraints on eligibility to participate in the program and on subsidized shipping operations, consistent with reasonable prudence to protect the government's investment. Eligibility to participate in subsidy should be extended to any citizen or citizen-controlled corporation that owns ships meeting Coast Guard standards, employs qualified citizen crews, and is adequately financed. Trade route restrictions should be relaxed in favor of broad trading areas or perhaps eliminated.[2] Companies should be allowed to operate liners, bulk carriers, tramps, or any other vehicle (such as hydrofoils and barges, and perhaps even tankers) that produces revenue by carrying cargo in foreign trade. However, means would have to be devised to assure that subsidies were not diverted into domestic competition or to foreign flag operations. Further-

[1] The key importance of the overall authorization and review procedure would require careful attention to be given to its specific design. Among the variables requiring consideration are: the respective roles of the executive branch and the Congress and of elements within both (for example, the role of the substantive versus appropriations committees and of the Defense versus Commerce departments); the specific components of the program to be controlled (for example, subsidy obligations, expenditures, ships, or shipping services); the time period over which controls should apply; the manner in which service and money targets should be related and the character of the in-depth economic studies needed to establish these relationships; and the checks which might be built into the procedure to prevent its having an erratic result. The last is a particularly difficult, but nonetheless solvable problem. For example, the program authorization could be expressed as a lump sum total to be applied over a number of years, to be up-dated from time to time but always with at least three years' lead time. Alternatively, the authorization might include a stipulation that in the absence of a national emergency the total expenditure for subsidies would not be increased or decreased by more than 10 percent in any one year. Future year authorizations might also be geared to an index of overall foreign-domestic price differentials so that the overall subsidy available to the industry would in some measure reflect changing relationships between the dollar and foreign currencies.

[2] Subsidies for services to relatively remote areas, such as Micronesia and Africa, might be administered separately if necessary to insure continuance of the services. Alternatively, the Secretary of Commerce might be empowered to make supplementary contracts with subsidized lines to assure minimum services are maintained.

more, all participating companies should be subject to audit of their accounts.

3. The system should not attempt to extract any "bonus values" or *quid pro quo* from its participants other than a commitment to cooperate with U.S. regulatory authorities and to make ships available to the government in the event of national emergency. Shipowners should neither be required to participate in conferences and pools nor prevented from doing so simply on the grounds that they are favored with subsidy. However, like any other U.S. corporation, subsidized shipping firms should be willing to consult with their government on competition and price policy if national interests are at stake.

4. "Buy America" restrictions should be relaxed to permit U.S. flag operators to obtain at least half of their supplies, maintenance, repairs, and other services (such as insurance) from foreign sources.

5. Shipyard subsidies should be disassociated from ship operations. All firms eligible for the operating program should be equally eligible to acquire new ships on equal terms at world market prices.

6. Operating subsidy payments to participating companies, within the total authorized expenditure level, should be determined through procedures which are based insofar as possible on normal economic incentives rather than administrative determinations.[3] Two methods for distributing the subsidy to qualifying companies are available: eligible companies

[3] Various alternative methods of computing subsidy to enhance economic incentives have been proposed, but each has certain disadvantages and ambiguities. For example, the Maritime Evaluation Committee proposed payment in a lump sum of the estimated foreign-domestic cost differential for the succeeding three years (Maritime Evaluation Committee, *Maritime Resources for Security and Trade* [mimeograph, Jan. 1963], p. 43). This would have required the government to make even more difficult judgments than presently as to the costs that should be considered "fair and reasonable," and would have failed to overcome other deficiencies of the cost parity system. The Interagency Task Force proposed payment of subsidies on the basis of a rate geared to past cost differentials in amounts (up to some maximum) proportional to revenues earned on commercial cargoes (Interagency Maritime Task Force, *The Merchant Marine in National Defense and Trade* [multilith, Oct. 1965], p. 15). This requires judgments both as to the size of the differential and as to what may be considered a "normal" cash flow from commercial business. Both proposals assume a restricted number of ships and companies will be permitted to participate in the program.

The Committee of American Steamship Lines, noting these deficiencies, has recommended retaining the present cost parity system. This recommendation overlooks inadequacies of the existing system which (a) pledges the government to an essentially open-end subsidy, which is inconsistent with the proposed overall expenditure control; (b) assumes more data on U.S. and foreign operating costs than is available or, if available, could be economically processed; (c) nullifies differences in the real factor prices of U.S. versus foreign firms; (d) is calculated retrospectively and there-might bid for the privilege of performing specified services (as commodity dealers now bid on subsidized grains), or the subsidy might be distributed after the fact in proportion to net revenues earned during the year in foreign trade. The distribution could embrace all qualifying U.S. ship operators or be administered within administrative allocations for such broad service categories as liner services to the Far East or worldwide voyage charter operations.

Either alternative for distributing a predetermined subsidy total would place U.S. flag firms in competition with one another to maximize their subsidy shares. This competition should induce introduction of more efficient equipment and operating methods and place profits under normal economic controls. In effect, marketplace judgments would be substituted for the present attempt to determine parity administratively. Assuming the total authorized subsidy is held constant, both alternatives would encourage activation of additional vessels in good years and retrenchment in bad. (The subsidy per vessel would thus automatically be reduced when business is good and augmented when freight revenues fall off.) The principal defect in the bid alternative would be the difficulty of specifying the services on which bids are requested; and of the revenue system, of assuring a faithful accounting of revenues, net of longshore and brokerage expenses, earned in U.S. foreign trade.[4] The systems also have two characteristics which may be regarded either as virtues or deficiencies: they require politically responsible officials to reach a judgment as to the appropriate overall level of subsidy expenditure, and they deny individual companies advance assurance of the portion of the total subsidy fund they will receive.[5]

7. American ship operators should be free to transfer ships to foreign flag (subject only to a requirement that the government first be given an

---

fore passes on to the government all increases or decreases in the subsidizable costs of U.S. flag firms; (e) is geared entirely to maritime industry costs, ignoring trends in other sectors of the economy; and (f) involves the government too intimately in every change in shipboard operations.

[4] The revenue shares alternative would be the simpler to administer, but probably also the simpler to abuse, since ocean transportation costs are not always easily differentiated from cargo handling and brokerage expenses and because there are various ways in which revenues can be padded. Administration of the bid system would require that quantities to be bid upon be carefully specified; the invitations to bid would also need to be arranged to permit the government to evaluate quotations for alternate levels of service.

[5] A competitive system cannot guarantee future subsidy payments, but does provide reasonable assurance that efficient operators will continue to receive a fair share of the government's aid. (Methods for holding fluctuations in the total subsidy budget within tolerable limits have been discussed at p. 342, footnote 1.)

opportunity to purchase them); however, in order to protect companies retaining their ships under U.S. flag and to encourage them to acquire new equipment, some tariff or other restraint should be placed on imports of used vessels.

8. American companies should receive a fair share of government shipments. However, the proposed comprehensive subsidy will remove any basis for continuing the present preferential rates on government cargoes. Either of two approaches to assuring U.S. operators a fair deal within a competitive system appears reasonable: (a) the government could deal on equal terms with U.S. and foreign flag carriers in negotiating each separate shipment, but continue a reporting system so that corrective action might be taken if over a period of time it appeared American carriers were not receiving a fair share, or (b) the government could allow a small (6 percent) "buy America" differential and withhold any guarantee as to how its overall business would be split.

9. The government should assume more direct responsibility for shipments made for its account. Any special preference arrangements should apply only to cargoes owned by the government while in transit and therefore clearly under government control. This policy would require that closer attention be given to the transportation terms of purchase and sales agreements in government procurement, agricultural, and foreign aid programs than is current practice, but would reduce international frictions over U.S. cargo preferences.

10. Government should not be constrained by mandatory rules to use privately owned merchant vessels if government-owned facilities would better meet its transportation needs. However, government-owned vessels should not compete for private cargoes except under lease arrangements which equalize the position of lessees and private shipowners.

11. Increased emphasis should be given by government to supporting investigations of new marine transportation technologies which lack sufficient promise of immediate financial return to merit investment of individual company funds. However, the industry as a whole should share in the cost of this research in order to insure proper attention to its results and to improve the selection of projects.

12. The United States should give greater attention to the international character of the merchant shipping industry and recognize that its special interests are unlikely to be successfully imposed on the industry through unilateral regulation. De-emphasis of U.S. cargo preferences should place the United States in a better position to insist on removal of preferences by other nations. Relaxation of "buy America" restrictions, including those on ships built abroad, would reduce U.S. dependence on

flag-of-convenience registries and might even cause a portion of the U.S.-owned foreign-registered fleet to return to U.S. flag.

New administrative arrangements will be required to implement the proposals outlined above, to overcome the confusion of objectives which has immobilized the present program, and to equip the government to meet future problems. Two principles should be observed: first, administrative arrangements should be kept as simple as possible; and second, the responsibilities of each agency participating in the program's administration should be precisely defined, internally consistent, and fully compatible with the agency's principal mission. Experience in the administration of federal maritime programs has proved that coordination of activities across agency lines is preferable to administering the diverse aspects of the government's shipping program through a single federal agency. However, a major advantage of shifting from the present patchwork of direct and indirect aids to a single comprehensive subsidy system is that it reduces requirements for interagency coordination.

A comprehensive subsidy program would provide the basic support needed to sustain a U.S. flag merchant marine. Various agency interests in U.S. merchant shipping can and should be considered in reviews of the overall level of subsidy support to be provided. More specialized needs not accommodated through the basic program should be met through supplementary programs sponsored by the interested agencies. Within this general framework the following specific arrangements are proposed:

1. Responsibility for administering the proposed new single subsidy system should be placed in the Department of Commerce (or, if approved, the new Department of Transportation). Program emphasis, however, should be shifted from detailed supervision of shipping operations to studies of shipping economics in order to assess more realistically the industry's efficiency, to advise on the proper level of overall subsidy aid, and to plan future programs. Although it should avoid all unnecessary involvement in industry operations, the Department might sponsor and assist in financing cooperative research associations and participate in other special studies. Its maritime agency should provide a point of contact with the U.S. flag industry for discussion, as appropriate, of steamship rates and practices, labor-management problems, and foreign discrimination. It should also coordinate the activities of other agencies in such matters as shipping documentation, contracting procedures, and the like, and should sponsor work to simplify shipping tariffs, reduce the number of freight rate classifications, overhaul shipping statistics, lay down some

basic rules regarding corporate organization, and standardize terminology.

The Maritime Administration would be strengthened if the Treasury Department's merchant marine inspection and documentation functions could be transferred to it. Administration of international shipping programs would also be facilitated by their colocation with international air transport activities in a new Department of Transportation.

2. The Office of Emergency Transportation, Department of Commerce, has overall responsibliity for monitoring potential emergency requirements and the mobilization readiness of U.S. transportation industries, including shipping, and is authorized to request the President (through the Office of Emergency Planning) to take corrective action if foreign competition or insufficient subsidies appear to threaten the industry's ability to fulfill its defense role. These procedures permit the Maritime Administration to concentrate its attention on increasing the efficiency of U.S. maritime operations.

3. The Department of Defense should be given clear responsibility for whatever action it deems necessary to meet its sealift requirements to support its active and priority reserve forces, after considering the present and anticipated capabilities of the privately owned merchant fleet. The Defense Department should plan and pay for defense features incorporated into commercial ships. Consideration should also be given to transferring the National Defense Reserve Fleet to the Department of Defense, including responsibility for obtaining whatever new or used tonnage it believes should be added to the reserve. (The transfer should be accompanied by arrangements permitting ships to be withdrawn from reserve by the Secretary of Commerce in the event of a non-defense emergency and specifying arrangements under which Defense-owned ships might be leased or sold for private operation.)

4. The Federal Maritime Commission should limit its activities to regulation of shipping rates and practices and should be scrupulously neutral in dealing with U.S. and foreign flags. The regulatory program is not an appropriate instrument for promoting U.S. flag shipping and should not be employed in this manner. If further experience should demonstrate that unilateral regulation is not a practical method for supervising foreign trade rates and practices, emphasis should be shifted to negotiating agreements to supervise international shipping cooperatively with other nations and the present commission either be phased out or redirected to attend only to domestic shipping affairs.

5. The State Department has a potentially important role in promoting acceptance of American shipping policies, minimizing adverse foreign practices, and facilitating negotiation of improved international procedures. The Department also has a responsibility to assure that the actions of other agencies concerned with the U.S. merchant marine do not rupture U.S. foreign relations.

6. Recommendations frequently are made for a cabinet-level committee or similar group to coordinate the government's merchant marine affairs. Experience indicates, however, that it would not be likely to be effective in this field. Instead, procedures should be established to require other agencies to notify the Secretary of Commerce of any intended actions bearing on merchant shipping significant enough to be of potential secretarial interest. This would permit the Secretary informally to coordinate most maritime matters and bring to the President those which require his attention.

7. Administration of U.S. maritime affairs is ultimately a presidential responsibility. Certain aspects of the program require bringing a span of interests to bear that is possible only through his office. For example, a decision to invoke retaliatory tariffs must balance foreign and domestic policy considerations. The proper level of subsidy investment must be determined in reference to competing budgetary priorities and the President's overall economic strategy. The President is likely also to provide the only effective channel of communication between the administrative agency and the congressional leadership. These channels must be kept open if direction of the program is not to slip from politically responsible public control into the hands of lower-level civil service and industry personnel.

Political responsibility for the conduct of the government's merchant marine affairs can be enforced only if reasonably clear-cut alternatives, which are framed in reasonably simple terms, can be brought to the government's top policy levels. Heretofore, the program's complexity has made impossible any meaningful public debate or useful direction from the President and the Congress, whose participation has been largely confined to peripheral issues and minor amendments to the 1936 statute. To achieve more effective political direction of the new program, the following actions are proposed:

1. A new maritime policy merits a fresh beginning. Even though many of the proposals advanced above could technically be accomplished within existing law, a new statute is required to secure the program the broad support needed for thoroughgoing change. It should specify objectives for a new maritime policy and give the administrative agency a fresh, up-to-

date, and clear mandate of its duties. It should state general standards and procedures to be followed in the program's administration but avoid specifying details. Obsolete statutes should be repealed.

2. The program should be supported by carefully devised procedures to assure systematic top-level review and updating as necessary of the program's objectives, scope, methods, and administration. Current efforts in the executive branch to systematize planning, programming, and budgeting of federal functions promise to provide an effective framework for updating and review. However, effective congressional participation in this process is clouded by the extremely loose linkage and diverse viewpoints among its substantive, investigatory, and appropriations committees.

3. Conscious provision also should be made to obtain a balanced sampling of industry and public views through public committees advisory to the Maritime Administrator and/or the Under Secretary of Commerce for Transportation. The effective functioning of these groups requires free give-and-take between their public and official members, which is possible only if all concerned clearly understand that the committees' role is solely advisory and that they must carefully avoid derogating to themselves the government's policy-making functions.

4. These mechanisms can be usefully supplemented from time to time by a thoroughgoing re-evaluation of the program's purposes and procedures by an *ad hoc* blue-ribbon public committee. This re-evaluation in depth is probably most usefully timed to orient and provide advice to policy officials of a newly elected administration.

Prospects

In view of the rigidity of the government's relationships with the U.S. merchant marine, are proposals for changes in the government program, such as those outlined above, realistic? How would such changes affect the parties in interest? What would be their cost? Who would organize such a program, and how could the political process be activated?

Basic changes are unlikely in the immediate future. Attitudes are now too diverse and positions too tenaciously held to permit the process of accommodation and compromise that is essential to building a consensus of realistic and informed opinion. Few reforms, however, are possible without a period of preparation. This has already begun. Government officials in their public statements have been stressing the need for a more enlightened approach to the industry's problems, for re-examination of old beliefs, and, where necessary, a change of attitudes. The President has pledged a new maritime policy. Much of the industry is in ferment, anticipating that in due course there will indeed be change.

The proposals made above call for major changes in subsidy procedures. However, their immediate impact on the parties in interest would be relatively minor. The fleet would be maintained at approximately present size. Most government cargoes would continue to be handled by U.S. flag carriers. There would be no immediate displacement of seafaring labor.

Their long-run significance, on the other hand, is substantial. The maritime industry *is* at a crossroads, and the slow physical deterioration of its equipment requires that a decision as to its future be made very soon. Simply to hold the U.S. fleet's present position within the framework of present law would require expenditures of $1–$2 billion per year by 1975.[6] This course would also involve the government so intimately in the industry's operations and force it to assume so large a responsibility for its affairs that it would bring de facto if not de jure nationalization of the American merchant marine.

Nobody wants this result. American seamen do not wish to be impressed into government employment any more than management wishes to lose title to its ships. Management and labor therefore share a common long-term interest in stemming the tide toward increased government subsidization and increased government control.

Disengagement of government and industry through a new maritime policy also offers the only real hope of expanding the American merchant marine. Jobs cannot be created by the government's simply forcing more ships into already overtonnaged foreign trades without precipitating violent international reactions. They can be created by a private industry whose excellence, respected by its customers and competitors alike, enables it to capture the business.

A reforming program aimed at reviving the flexibility and vitality of the U.S. merchant marine is therefore labor's best strategy for minimizing job attrition due to automation. It should also appeal strongly to those in-

[6] A $2 billion estimate was cited by the Maritime Administrator in a press briefing in the spring of 1965 (*Washington Post*, March 3, 1965, p. 2). A more modest projection, however, is indicated by figures developed by the Interagency Task Force, *op. cit.*, pp. 45 ff. The Task Force figures indicate an average subsidy cost of roughly $15,000 per berth in the subsidized fleet by 1975. Maintenance of the industry's present employment using this factor would require $570 million in direct operating aids and construction of 600-700 new ships by 1975 at a subsidy cost, if all built in U.S. yards, of $400-$500 million per year.

dustry leaders who have been urging that they be given a freer hand in managing their operations. A reordering of the subsidy system might force some firms to leave the industry and cause some mergers and temporary losses, but it would also permit the industry's more efficient firms to expand, acquire new equipment, and enhance their profits. Over the long term, a new program is clearly the best hope for the American merchant marine.

A new program for American shipping need not and should not increase overall program costs. Relaxing restrictions now built into cargo preference and the trade route system creates many opportunities for increased efficiency, which should reduce requirements for subsidy as well as increase profits. The calculations in Chapter 8 indicate that direct payments to U.S. flag bulk carriers and tramps would actually require a smaller outlay than the present indirect payment through cargo preference and would ease disposal of surplus agricultural products (presumably at higher prices) as well. Payments to the non-subsidized liners would probably be somewhat larger than the indirect aid now received, but are needed to build up reserves for replacement of their ships. The impact on presently subsidized operators would vary depending on their particular situation (subsidies now range from 15 to 30 percent of freight revenues), the exact terms of the new program, and, most importantly, whether an option is allowed on converting from present contracts.[7]

The most important question bearing on the costs of a new maritime program is whether eligibility for operating and construction aids can be severed. (Present law requires that vessels receiving operating subsidies and cargo preferences be constructed in U.S. yards, but allows vessels to be imported for non-subsidized operation in foreign trade.) The pool of war-built ships which has sustained the non-subsidized portion of the industry for the past eighteen years will soon no longer be adequate. Continuation of the requirement that a shipyard subsidy be appropriated to accompany the introduction of every new ship into U.S. flag operations would severely throttle any program to revive American merchant ship-

---

[7] Equity could be construed to require either that existing contracts be allowed to run until their expiration or that the presently subsidized and non-subsidized segments of the U.S. merchant marine be placed immediately on an equal basis. The difficulties which have been encountered in past years due to the subsidized carriers' preferred position argue strongly for applying the new system immediately to all operators, indemnifying for any damages which can be demonstrated to have resulted from breach of contract through the usual legal processes. (Actually, an argument can be made that there is no breach of contract so long as the government deals fairly with the recipients of subsidy aid. See pp. 824-86.)

ping. If the United States seriously intends to maintain a first class merchant marine, it must either quadruple appropriations for construction subsidies or allow its shipping firms to acquire vessels from shipyards located abroad.

American maritime policies have been drifting toward increasing government involvement because none of the participants in the political process has had the strength or the inclination to stem the tide. Internally divided, the parties in interest have been unable to get together on the terms of a new maritime policy. Other groups and public officials have failed to give the program the sustained interest and leadership necessary to set a new course.

However, with the industry's support, improvements can be achieved. The deterioration of America's maritime position, the industry's failure to update its operations apace with foreign flags, and the fractiousness of its labor relations have generated wide concern. Influential members of both the Congress and the executive branch have indicated that they would welcome constructive proposals for reform. The President himself has pledged that changes will be proposed.

If the industry resists an updating of subsidy programs, only a strong effort, led by the President himself, is likely to be sufficient to crack the mold in which America's maritime policy has been cast. But no President can be expected to undertake so time-consuming and politically thankless a task unless he is personally persuaded that there is a real and urgent national need which demands his attention or for some personal reason is aroused to give the project his full support.

In the ordinary course, subsidies to merchant shipping are too marginal to the nation's main affairs to compel sustained public attention. The government can assist in developing and enforcing a new subsidy system. But in the American system, the industry itself enjoys the privilege and bears the chief responsibility for choosing whether to make the adjustments necessary to move ahead or to preserve the status quo.

Appendixes

APPENDIX A

Statistical Tables

TABLE A1. *Tonnage of Active World Merchant Fleets: 1939, 1948, and 1962*

(Gross tons, in thousands, of ships 1,000 gross tons or over)

Registry	Dry Cargo and Passenger			Tanker			Share of World Tonnage (Percent)	
	1939	1948	1962	1939	1948	1962	1939	1962
United States[a]	4,653	8,590	6,083	2,704	4,538	4,307	12.8	8.7
(U.S. including effective control)			(7,497)			(9,483)		(14.9)
United Kingdom, its colonies, and dominions	14,556	14,953	15,720	3,215	3,788	7,715	30.9	19.6
Northern Europe	11,094	7,470	18,582	3,232	2,977	11,750	24.9	25.2
France, Spain, and Mediterranean	8,335	6,274	15,010	819	1,265	6,475	15.0	17.0
Japan, China, and Southeast Asia	4,943	1,714	6,718	448	242	2,550	9.4	7.7
Communist bloc[b]	1,635	1,950	5,692	145	140	1,510	3.1	6.0
PANLIBHON[c]	324	1,606	5,554	477	1,490	8,911	1.4	12.0
All other	701	1,624	1,948	219	427	1,565	1.6	2.9
Total	46,241	44,181	75,307	11,259	14,867	44,783	100.0	100.0

Source, U.S. Maritime Administration.

[a] Excludes reserve fleet, Military Sea Transport Service vessels, cable and picket ships, and others not in commercial transport service.

[b] Nations identified as Communist bloc, excluding Yugoslavia, but including (in 1948 and 1962) approximately 500 tons lend-leased to Russia.

[c] Panama, Liberia, and Honduras. Other states having unusually liberal registry laws (i.e., Costa Rica, Morocco, Tunisia, and Lebanon) had enrolled 1,026,000 gross tons as of December 31, 1962; their inclusion with PANLIBHON would raise the current percentage of world shipping registered under flags of convenience from 12 to 13 percent.

TABLE A2. *Employment of U.S. Merchant Ships: 1936 Versus 1963*
(Number and deadweight tonnage, in thousands of tons, of ships 1,000 gross tons or over)

	Passenger and Combination				Dry Cargo				Tanker			
	1936		1963		1936		1963		1936		1963	
	Number	Tons	Number	Tons	Number	Tons	Number	Tons	Number	Tons	Number	Tons
Total active ships	171	1,083	30	274	694	5,071	618	7,157	343	3,541	282	6,365
Foreign trade:												
Overseas liner services	65	615	23	220	208	1,897	387	4,454	24	276	12	215
Nearby foreign	39	155	6	50	42	189	27	199	52	582	7	181
Domestic trade:												
Coastwise	46	170	...	...	243	1,226	29	317	248	2,481	225	5,060
Intercoastal	7	78	...	...	150	1,392	21	246	15	169	6	115
Non-contiguous	14	64	1	4	49	341	47	520	4	33	9	172
Irregular, tramp, and industrial[a]	0	0	...	...	2	25	107	1,420	0	0	23	622
Total inactive ships	30	197	263	1,679	313	2,332	1,384	13,786	12	95	106	1,418
Privately owned	26	156	4	39	119	644	39	461	12	95	26	439
Government-owned (including reserve fleet)	4	42	259	1,640	194	1,690	1,345	13,325	...	...	80	979

Sources, U.S. Maritime Administration and S. Rept. 2494, 81 Cong. 2 sess. (1950), p. 152. Includes both government and privately owned ships. 1936 data as of June 30; 1963 as of March 31 to avoid temporary strike effect.

[a] Includes MSTS charters and estimated foreign-to-foreign operations. The extent to which the prewar fleet was used in irregular operations is not reported, but is thought to have been very small. (See U.S. Maritime Commission, *Report on Tramp Services*, H. Doc. 520, 75 Cong. 2 sess. [1938].)

TABLE A3. *Trends in Tonnage and Number of U.S. Registered Ships, 1950-63*

(Number and gross tonnage, in thousands of tóns, of ships 1,000 gross tons or over, excluding U.S. reserve fleet)

Year	Privately Owned		Government-Owned		Total		Number Engaged in		Number Temporarily Inactive
	Number	Tons	Number	Tons	Number	Tons	Foreign Trade	Domestic Trade	
Passenger and Combination:									
1950	44	394	11	180	55	574	41	4	10
1955	34	414	13	132	47	546	38	1	8
1960	37	507	2	20	39	527	30	2	7
1961	35	489	0	0	35	489	29	1	5
1962	34	474	1	14	35	488	24	2	9[a]
1963	32	465	1	14	33	479	30	1	2
Dry Cargo:									
1950	600	4,229	64	468	664	4,697	447	175	42
1955	679	4,985	33	234	712	5,219	538	141	33
1960	633	4,844	37	263	670	5,107	517	115	38
1961	611	4,816	41	300	652	5,116	508	104	40
1962	637	5,207	31	233	668	5,440	469	73	126[a]
1963	645	5,431	15	105	660	5,536	520	90	50
Tankers:									
1950	443	4,173	1	7	444	4,180	158	274	12
1955	362	3,778	...	...	362	3,778	77	277	8
1960	338	4,259	...	...	338	4,259	47	246	45
1961	327	4,311	...	...	327	4,311	38	258	31
1962	314	4,301	...	...	314	4,301	43	232	39[a]
1963	297	4,180	1	13	298	4,193	57	214	27
Total:									
1950	1,087	8,796	76	655	1,163	9,451	646	453	64
1955	1,075	9,177	46	366	1,121	9,543	653	419	49
1960	1,008	9,610	39	283	1,047	9,893	594	363	90
1961	973	9,616	41	300	1,014	9,916	575	363	76
1962	985	9,982	32	247	1,017	10,229	536	307	174[a]
1963	974	10,076	17	132	991	10,208	607	305	79

Source, U.S. Maritime Administration, vessel employment reports.
[a] Temporarily augmented by New York dock strike.

TABLE A4. *Estimated Overall Size and Composition of U.S. Owned and/or Controlled Shipping, 1962*

(Number and deadweight tonnage, in thousands of tons, of ships 1,000 gross tons or over)

Item	Total	U.S. Flag		U.S. Owned, Foreign Flag			Foreign Owned U.S. Control		U.S. Reserve Fleet
		Domestic Trade	Foreign Trade	Effective Control	Other, Marad List[a]	Other, Estimated	Effective Control	Other, Marad List[b]	
	(1)	(2)	(3)	(4)	(5)	(6)	(7)	(8)	(9)
Number of ships:									
Passenger and combination	300	2c	32c	6	-0-	-0-	-0-	2	258
General freight	}2,542	}103c	}587c	50	19	125	}29	}74	1,355
Bulk dry				57	12	131			-0-
Subtotal	2,842	105	619	113	31	256	29	76	1,613
Tanker	1,152	273	43	237	184	299	28	8	80
Total	3,994	378	662	350	215	555	57	84	1,693
Deadweight Tons:									
Passenger and combination	1,983	14	300	27	-0-	-0-	-0-	15	1,627
General freight	}30,447	}1,185	}6,684	441	106	1,597	}351	}796	13,425
Bulk dry				1,801	152	3,909			-0-
Subtotal	32,430	1,199	6,984	2,269	258	5,506	351	811	15,052
Tanker	30,905	5,831	1,061	7,626	4,788	9,760	728	132	979
Total	63,335	7,030	8,045	9,895	5,046	15,266	1,079	943	16,031

Sources, Maritime Administration data, all columns except (6) which is based on the tabulation of ships ordered for construction or conversion abroad by U.S. citizens and corporations printed in *Marine Engineering Log*, Vol. 68, No. 7 (June 15, 1963) and should be construed as an order-of-magnitude estimate only. Column (1) therefore also an order of magnitude estimate.

[a] U.S. Maritime Administration, *Foreign Flag Ships of 1,000 Gross Tons and Over Owned by U.S. Parent Companies, June 30, 1962.*

[b] Ships transferred to foreign registry, owned by foreign citizens, which are pledged to the United States in the event of emergency but which are not considered by the Navy to be under "effective U.S. control" because of restrictions on transfer imposed by the country of registry.

[c] Privately owned ships laid up and temporarily inactive were prorated in same proportion as actively employed fleet.

TABLE A5. *Participation of National Flags in National Foreign Trade, 1953-62*

(Percent of total foreign-trade tonnage carried)

Registry	1953	1954	1955	1956	1957	1958	1959	1960	1961	1962
Argentina	23.8	17.0	20.7	18.6	17.8	...	...	15.0	...	...
Belgium	10.1	9.7	9.9	8.9	8.8	8.2	...	8.8	...	...
Brazil	...	...	...	5.7	...	...	...	...	12.0	...
Canada[a]	40.2	34.0	34.4	32.6	33.1	...	...	...	27.2	26.2
Chile	...	...	...	...	20.4	...	23.0	...	...	...
Denmark	29.0	28.4	26.6	24.3	26.6	24.7	...	...	...	...
Finland	57.6	54.0	50.0	45.9	45.7	...	...	48.4	...	54.2
France	51.3	51.6	52.5	49.9	49.6	57.9	61.8	62.6	57.0	58.7
West Germany	31.5	27.2	38.2	39.3	38.3	41.4	41.2	38.4	36.0	37.0
India	4.5	5.0	5.5	19.9	20.1	...	...	9.3	...	12.0
Israel	...	29.0	27.0	32.1	30.0	29.2	34.0	38.5	39.0	...
Italy	41.9	45.5	48.5	49.2	47.7	45.4	37.6	34.6	39.0	32.6
Japan	44.4	48.3	50.4	47.0	44.0	58.2	53.2	48.5	47.5	46.2
Netherlands	26.5	20.6	20.8	16.7	19.0	17.2	18.7	17.2	...	13.0
Norway[b]	56.9	43.4	43.2	40.7	45.0	54.0	49.1	49.2	43.8	42.7
Peru	...	...	...	6.2	5.0	...	...	4.6	6.2	...
Spain	...	...	...	...	...	38.0	...	...	...	...
Sweden	...	...	...	41.1	39.4	39.2	42.5[c]	37.0[c]	...	...
Turkey	...	...	...	35.5	42.0	...	...	...	...	...
United Kingdom[d]	...	56.8	55.4	57.6	53.9	53.5	55.1	53.0	54.0	52.0
United States	29.5	27.8	23.6	20.5	17.8	11.7	9.7	10.5	8.8	8.9
Yugoslavia	...	...	...	...	42.0	51.0	...	52.5	...	...

Source, various publications and trade sources, collected by the U.S. Maritime Administration.
[a] Includes Great Lakes.
[b] Excludes Swedish iron ore shipped through Narvik.
[c] Arithmetic average of exports and imports reported.
[d] Participation data based on net tonnage of vessels clearing British ports with cargo.

TABLE A6. *Participation of U.S. Flag Ships in U.S. Foreign Trade, 1938 Versus 1962*

(Number of long tons, in thousands of tons, carried in U.S. trade and percent of total carried U.S. flag[a])

Cargo	Tonnage Carried						U.S. Flag Participation (*Percent*)	
	U.S. Flag		Foreign Flag		Total			
	1938	1962	1938	1962	1938	1962	*1938*	*1962*
Liner cargoes								
Essential trade routes from U.S. to:								
Europe and North Africa	4,005	3,597	6,903	14,310	10,908	17,907	*36.8*	*20.1*
Far East, Southeast Asia, and Oceana	843	3,624	4,870	10,145	5,713	13,769	*14.7*	*26.3*
Central and South America	3,234[b]	2,487	3,415	5,033	6,649[b]	7,520	*48.5*	*33.7*
Africa (other than Mediterranean)	530	1,503	321	1,022	851	2,525	*62.1*	*59.5*
South Asia	201	1,797	727	1,769	928	3,566	*21.7*	*50.4*
Routes not designated essential	587	197	564	1,532	1,151	1,729	*51.0*	*11.4*
Total, liner cargoes	9,400	13,205	16,800	33,811	26,200[b]	47,016	*36.6*	*28.1*
Other dry cargoes[c]								
Irregular operators	2,200[b]	5,783	15,700	85,254	17,900[b]	91,037	*12.2*	*6.3*
Industrial carriers (import only)[d]	–0–	1,972	–0–	31,527	–0–	33,499	...	*5.9*
Tankers	–0–	1,639	–0–	3,917	–0–	5,556	...	*29.4*
Total, other dry cargoes	2,200	9,394	15,700	120,698	17,900[b]	130,092	*12.2*	*7.2*
Liquid cargoes carried by tankers, total	7,800	3,447	22,700	111,181	30,500	114,628	*25.6*	*3.0*
Total, all cargoes	19,400	26,046	55,200	265,690	74,600	291,736	*26.0*	*9.0*

Source, U.S. Maritime Administration.

[a] Excludes shipments within the Great Lakes and about 3 million tons of "special category" military cargoes (carried almost exclusively via U. S. flag) routed via commercial carriers, chiefly liner. Inclusion of these cargoes would raise U.S. flag liner participation by four percentage points.

[b] Maritime Administration data adjusted to shift an estimated 1.5 million tons of bulk commodity imports on ships used chiefly as industrial carriers inbound, common carriers outbound, from liner to non-liner category. Actual data not available.

[c] Includes a small amount of liquid cargoes carried by dry cargo ships.

[d] Included in irregular in 1938.

TABLE A7. *Estimated Government Dry Cargo Tonnage Carried by U.S. Flag Ships, 1955-62*[a]

(Number of long tons, in millions of tons carried)

Year	Total Government Cargoes		Carried by U.S. Liners				Carried by U.S. Tramps			Carried by U.S. Tankers	
	Total	U.S. Flag	De-fense[b]	Agri-culture	AID[c]	Other[d]	Agri-culture	AID[c]	Other[e]	Agri-culture	AID[c]
Outbound:											
1955	12.3	8.2	2.1	.3	1.7	.4	1.0	2.3	.3	f	f
1956	14.1	8.5	2.2	.8	1.9	.4	1.6	1.4	.2	f	f
1957	15.3	9.2	2.1	.7	1.2	.5	3.0	1.4	.1	.1	f
1958	15.0	9.3	2.1	1.1	1.0	.7	2.8	1.1	.1	.5	...
1959	13.9	8.3	2.1	1.1	.9	.4	2.3	.6	.1	.8	f
1960	17.2	10.0	1.9	1.3	.9	.4	2.6	.4	.1	2.3	f
1961	17.7	11.2	2.2	1.1	1.6	.5	2.9	1.1	.2	1.6	.1
1962	19.8	13.6	2.4	1.3	3.1	.6	3.3	.9	.4	1.7	f
Inbound:											
1955	.7	.5	.1	f	...	.2	.1	...	.1	...	...
1956	1.4	1.0	.2	.2	...	.2	.1	...	.3	...	...
1957	2.0	1.4	.3	.3	...	.2	.2	...	.4	...	...
1958	2.7	1.8	.5	.2	...	.2	.5	...	.4	...	...
1959	2.0	1.5	.5	.1	...	.2	.6	...	f	...	...
1960	2.6	1.9	.5	.2	...	.2	1.1	...	f	...	...
1961	2.9	1.9	.4	.1	...	.2	1.1	...	f	...	...
1962	5.0	2.8	.4	.1	...	.2	2.0	...	.1	...	...

Source, various government agencies.

[a] Excludes: (1) shipments of government cargoes between foreign ports, (2) shipments of certain privately owned cargoes out of U.S. ports which are considered to fall within the cargo preference program since the cargoes are for the use of U.S. forces overseas, and (3) other quasi-governmental shipments out of U.S. ports, such as shipments by voluntary relief agencies and international organizations, which are not formally covered by the preference statute although significantly influenced by U.S. preferential policies. (For example, in fiscal year 1963 approximately two-thirds of the 1.2 million tons shipped by voluntary relief agencies under Title IIIA of P.L. 83-480 was consigned to U.S. flag carriers, chiefly liners.)

[b] Measurement tons converted to long tons by assuming 2.6 measurement tons per long ton.

[c] Includes shipments financed through the Development Loan Fund and the Social Progress Trust Fund of the Inter-American Development Bank, estimated at 504,000 tons in 1962.

[d] Shipments financed by Export-Import Bank long term credits and project loans and other direct government bill of lading shipments. Tonnage estimates based on reported freight billings, assuming an average revenue of $60 per ton.

[e] Chiefly shipments of military cargoes in vessel lots on privately owned freighters chartered to MSTS.

[f] Less than 50,000 tons.

TABLE A8. Contribution of Preference Cargoes to Total Tonnage Handled by U.S. Flag Ships, 1955-62

(Number of long tons, in millions of tons carried)

Year	Total Dry Cargo[a]			Carried by Liners			Carried by Tramps			Carried by Tankers	
	All Cargoes	Preference Cargoes	Preference Share (Percent)	All Cargoes	Preference Cargoes	Preference Share (Percent)	All Cargoes	Preference Cargoes	Preference Share (Percent)	All Cargoes	Preference Cargoes
Outbound:											
1955	16.5	8.2	50	12.6	4.6	36	3.8	3.6	95	NA	b
1956	19.1	8.5	45	13.7	5.2	38	5.3	3.2	60	NA	.1
1957	20.5	9.2	45	13.8	4.6	33	6.6	4.5	68	NA	.1
1958	15.5	9.3	60	10.9	4.9	45	3.3	4.0c	...	NA	.5
1959	13.9	8.3	60	9.9	4.5	45	3.0	3.0	100	NA	.9
1960	16.8	10.0	60	11.1	4.6	41	3.3	3.0	90	2.2	2.4c
1961	16.8	11.2	67	10.7	5.4	50	4.4	4.1	93	1.5	1.7c
1962	17.5	13.6	78	11.2	7.4	66	4.6	4.5	98	1.6	1.7c
Inbound:											
1955	16.0	.5	3	6.8	.4	6	9.2	.2	2	...	...
1956	17.0	1.0	6	7.3	.6	8	9.7	.4	4	...	...
1957	15.9	1.4	9	7.0	.8	11	8.9	.6	7	...	...
1958	11.4	1.8	16	6.1	.9	15	5.3	.9	17	...	...
1959	11.1	1.5	14	6.5	.8	12	4.6	.7	15	...	...
1960	10.5	1.9	18	5.9	.8	14	4.6	1.1	24	...	...
1961	8.0	1.9	24	4.7	.7	15	3.3	1.2	36	...	...
1962	8.4	2.8	33	4.9	.7	14	3.5	2.1	60	...	...
Total Inbound and Outbound:											
1955	32.5	8.7	27	19.4	5.0	26	13.0	3.8	29	b	b
1962	25.9	16.4	63	16.1	8.1	50	8.1	6.6	81	1.6	1.7c

Source, U.S. Maritime Administration cargo data reports adjusted to include estimated "special category" military shipments (estimate based on MSTS measurement ton shipment data converted at 2.6 measurement tons per long ton, net of military cargoes included in the Maritime Administration report). Tonnage of government sponsored cargoes from various agencies.

[a] Represents all cargoes (including some liquids) carried by U.S. flag liners and tramps on trans-oceanic voyages inbound or outbound from the United States plus dry cargoes carried by U.S. flag tankers (1955–59 estimated).

[b] Less than 50,000 tons.

[c] Total cargoes reported by U.S. Maritime Administration exceed shipments reported by government agencies due to differences in the timing of reports. (Marad data records tonnage when shipped; Agriculture records tonnage when booked; AID records tonnage when billed, although an effort is made to make the posting to the fiscal year in which the shipment was made.)

TABLE A9. *Estimated U.S. Flag Revenue from Preference Cargoes, 1962*

(Freight revenues, in millions of dollars earned, and cargo tonnage, in thousands of long tons carried)

Program	Total, All Categories		Liner		Tramp and Industrial		Tanker	
	Tons Carried	Revenue Earned	Tons Carried	Revenue Earned	Tons Carried	Revenue Earned	Tons Carried	Revenue Earned
Agriculture P.L. 83-480:								
Titles I and IV	6,290	$150.8	1,309	$ 40.0	3,262	$ 76.4[a]	1,719	$34.4[a]
Title IIIB (barter)	2,048	14.1[a]	65	.1[a]	1,983	14.0[a]	...	...
Agency for International Development:								
P.L. 83-480 programs:								
Title II (emergency relief)	1,000[a]	23.9	514[a]	15.1	486[a]	8.8	...	...
Title IIIA (voluntary aid)	777	28.2	777[a]	28.2[a]	...	...	...	...
Loans and grants:								
Outbound	3,000[a]	73.0	2,628[a]	66.0[a]	367[a]	6.5[a]	5	5
Offshore	1,135	7.0	158	2.0[a]	433	2.5[a]	544	2.5
Military Sea Transport Service:								
Shipping contract	2,643	162.9	2,643	162.9	...	...	...	...
Berth term	192	18.4	192	18.4	...	...	...	...
Time and voyage charter	427	16.1	...	...	427	16.1	...	...
Export-Import Bank Credits	430[a]	28.0	430[a]	28.0	...	...	...	...
General Services Administration—Stockpile	25	.4	25	.4	...	...	...	...
Government Bill of Lading:								
Department of Defense	200[a]	15.0[a]	200[a]	15.0[a]	...	...	...	...
Other	200[a]	12.0[a]	200[a]	12.0[a]	...	...	...	...
Total Government Cargoes[b]	18,367	$550.0	9,141	$388.1[a]	6,958	$124.3[a]	2,268	$37.4[a]
Less offshore	1,135	7.0	158	2.0	433	2.5	544	2.5
Government sponsored cargoes in U. S. foreign trade	17,232	$543.0	8,983	$386.1[a]	6,525	$121.8[a]	1,724	$34.9[a]
Commercial cargoes in U. S. foreign trade[c]	8,743	381.3	7,086	361.9[a]	1,657	15.7[a]	...	...
Total	25,975	$924.3	16,069	$748.0[a]	8,182	$137.5[a]	1,724	$34.9[a]

Source, author's estimates based on data compiled from various government agencies. In general, payments for fiscal year 1963 are considered to represent cost of calendar year 1962 shipments. Total payments for U.S. flag shipping services are regularly reported for all programs except the Agriculture Department P.L. 83-480, Title IIIB shipments, for which an estimate was constructed through inspection of cargo and destination data. Payments for government bill of lading shipments, which typically include packing and land transportation costs as well as ocean freight, were adjusted on the basis of sample studies to exclude these factors. The distribution of revenues from Agriculture cargoes by class of carrier also is estimated on the basis of commodity and shipment data.

[a] Approximation based on available data.

[b] Cargo tonnage, net of offshore shipments and shipments pursuant to P.L. 83-480, Title IIIA, equals total government-sponsored inbound and outbound tonnage shown on Tables A7 and A8. Freight revenue equals total payment to U.S. operators shown on Table A10.

[c] Tonnage data derived by deducting government shipments (including shipments under P.L. 83-480, Title IIIA), from Maritime Administration reported cargo totals, adjusted to include all military shipments. Revenue estimates based on reports to the Commerce Department's Office of Business Economics, adjusted to include revenues from military cargoes and distributed by class of carrier on the basis of approximate information on average revenues earned per ship reported to the Maritime Administration and average revenue per ton data developed by the Committee of American Steamship Lines.

TABLE A10. *Estimated Costs of Cargo Preference, 1962*

(In millions of dollars)

Program	Total Payment to U.S. Operators	Indirect Subsidy to U.S. Flag	Other Costs	Approximate Distribution of Indirect Subsidy[a]		
				Liner	Tramp	Tanker
Agriculture P.L. 83–480:						
Titles I and IV	$150.8	$ 80.9	$48.8[b]	$15.0	$47.9	$18.0
Title IIIB (barter)	14.1	4.0[c]	...	...	4.0	...
Agency for International Development:						
Title II, P.L. 83–480	23.9	9.4[d]	...	5.0	4.4	...
Title IIIA, P.L. 83–480	28.2 }	7.5[e]	...	...	5.5	2.0
Loans and grants	80.0 }		...	...	...	...
Military Sea Transport Service:						
Shipping contract	162.9	50.0[f]	...	50.0	...	...
Berth term	18.4	...	...	...	...	...
Time and voyage charter	16.1	8.0[g]	...	...	8.0	...
Other government shipments	55.6	[h]	...	...	...	...
Total	$550.0	$159.8	$48.8[b]	$70.0	$69.8	$20.0

Source, same as Table A9.

[a] The distribution of indirect subsidy by class of carrier is an approximation geared principally to certain assumptions regarding rate differentials applying to P.L. 83–480 cargoes. The $15 million assigned to liners, which is only 38 percent of their freight billings for this business, is a derived figure which assumes that U.S. flag tramp rates were 2.6 times world market rates and U.S. tanker rates twice the world market.

[b] "Other costs" are losses incurred by the United States because purchasers of P.L. 83–480 products were permitted (until 1964) to reimburse the U.S. for the estimated world market costs of the shipments made on U.S. flag vessels in nonconvertible currencies. The amount shown, which is not counted as "subsidy" to the U.S. maritime industry, is the amount of reimbursement received in 1962 in nonconvertible currencies which had officially been declared excess to U.S. needs.

[c] Estimated foreign-domestic rate differential based on inspection of cargo and shipment data.

[d] Indirect subsidy assumed to be approximately same percentage of total payment to U.S. liners and tramps as Title I.

[e] Cargoes are mostly carried by liners, move in small volume, and are under tariff rates. There is no way of identifying the indirect subsidy these rates may provide U.S. liners, if any. Estimates assume $2 million Title IIIA business and $9 million loans and grants shipped via tramp and that 50 percent differential pertains.

[f] MSTS offers unique cargoes, so that there is no real way to measure a differential. The estimate is based on (1) comparison of average rate per measurement ton on MSTS versus other cargo, and (2) estimated cost of shipping 70 percent MSTS cargoes via foreign tramps rather than U.S. liners. See Chapter 8 for further discussion.

[g] Assumes a 50 percent differential.

[h] Although this business is much sought after, no reasonable technique is available for estimating the differential, if any.

TABLE A11. *Selected Financial Data, Subsidized Operators*

(In millions of dollars)

Balance Sheet Items

Year	Total Assets	Statutory Reserves[a]	Capital Necessarily Employed	Retained Earnings	Net Worth
1937	$ 110[b]	–0–	$ 23	$ 2	$ 66
1941	c	$ 51	85	100	173
1945	c	147	c	180	255
1949	c	86	244	301	400
1954	c	195	318	413	522
1959	1,106	205	508	562	729
1960	1,202	275	537	576	747
1961	1,246	244	602	602	774
1962	1,309	210	624	629	804

Income and Expense Items (Annual Average)

Year(s)	Revenue from Ship Operations	Operating Differential Subsidy[d]	Operating Earnings Before Tax	Federal Taxes	Net Earnings	Capital Gains[e]	Net Profit	Dividends
1937–41	c	$ 12	$25.5	$ 1.4	$24.2	$ 6.4	$30.6	$ 4.4
1942–45	c	–0–	26.2	7.8	18.5	10.3	28.8	6.4
1946–49	c	46	63.0	15.4	47.6	1.4	49.0	15.1
1950–54	$491	71	59.0	17.6	41.4	[0.3]	41.1	15.3
1955–59	625	126	73.5	18.2	55.3	5.7	61.0	18.2
1960	633	164	42.4	15.2	27.2	2.8	30.1	14.4
1961	604	170	39.3	10.8	28.5	9.8	38.3	11.3
1962	672	188	55.8	17.9	37.9	5.3	43.3	13.2

Sources, 1960–61, *Combined Financial Statements*, Wayne Kendrick & Co., CPA (1962); 1954–59, *Combined Financial Statements*, Warwick and Mitchell & Co., CPA (1959); 1937–53, *The Scope and Effect of Tax Benefits Provided the Maritime Industry*, H. Doc. 213, 83 Cong. 1 sess. (1951), and *Amending the Merchant Marine Act, 1936, as Amended*, Supplement to Hearings before the House Merchant Marine Committee on H.R. 3289 and Other Bills, 81 Cong. 1 sess. (1949), pp. 132 ff.

[a] Excludes amounts estimated to be due for deposit and subsidy payments withheld against anticipated recapture.

[b] Estimated (1939 gross assets were reported at $148 million in U.S. Maritime Commission, *Postwar Outlook for U.S. Shipping*, p. 108).

[c] Not available.

[d] Net of estimated recapture.

[e] Net of estimated federal taxes, if any.

TABLE A12. *Selected Financial Data, Non-subsidized Operators*
(In millions of dollars)

1937–48: Total Non-subsidized Fleet

Years	Coverage Number of Firms	Coverage Number of Ships	Net Worth Beginning of Period	Operating Earnings	Annual Average Capital Gains	Annual Average Federal Taxes	Annual Average Net Profit	Annual Average Dividends	Net Worth End of Period
1937–41	80	497	$352.2	$46.3	$ 3.7	$15.6	$34.4	$24.8	$408.3
1942–45	78	387	408.3	69.3	12.3	38.6	43.2	27.0	456.9
1946–48	75	239	456.9	97.1	11.3	30.0	78.4	42.8	585.0

1946–51: Major Non-subsidized Lines

Years	Number of Firms Covered	Net Worth Beginning of Period	Annual Average Operating Earnings and Gains	Annual Average Federal Taxes	Annual Average Net Profit	Dividends	Net Worth End of Period
1946–48	14	$214.9	$18.4	$ 8.9	$ 9.5	$7.1	$223.2
1949–51	16	223.2	30.5	13.7	16.8	6.1	250.8

1961–62: Major Non-subsidized Firms

Year	Number of Firms Covered	Total Assets	Operating Earnings	Capital Gains and Adjustments	Federal Taxes	Net Profit	Dividends	Net Worth End of Period
1961	27	$365.0	$ [7.3]	$22.3	$3.4	$11.6	$ 2.4	$153.4
1962	25	350.3	17.3	3.9	4.1	17.1	15.3	145.4

Source, 1937–48, *Amending the Merchant Marine Act, as Amended*, Hearing before the House Merchant Marine Committee, 81 Cong. 1 sess. (1949), pp. 202 ff.; 1946–51, U.S. Treasury Department, *Scope and Effect of Tax Benefits Provided the Maritime Industry* (mimeograph, 1952), App. B; 1961–62, U.S. Maritime Administration, *Combined Financial Reports*. The 1946–51 data is confined to major liner companies, listed in the Treasury report, *op. cit.*, p. 37. Data includes results from both shipping and non-shipping operations, is unaudited, and not identical in coverage from year to year. In all, about 200 dry cargo ships are covered in the Maritime Administration report, including virtually all non-subsidized liners and a very few tramps.

TABLE A13. *Comparative Rates of Return, Subsidized and Non-subsidized Lines*[a]

(Profit as a percent of net worth)

Year	Subsidized Lines			Non-subsidized Lines	
	Before Tax		Net After Tax, Subsidy Included	Before Tax	Net After Tax
	Subsidy Excluded	Subsidy Included			
1946	19.5	19.5	12.2	9.6	5.6
1947	25.8	27.1	20.7	13.0	7.0
1948	10.0	14.7	12.5	3.3	0.6
1949	7.0	14.8	11.6	8.6	5.8
1950	− 0.6	10.1	7.1	10.8	6.1
1951	7.3	15.7	11.5	18.3	9.0
1952	7.0	19.0	14.5	14.7	7.9
1961	−16.8	5.2	3.8	− 4.7	−6.9
1962	−15.3	7.1	4.8	11.9	9.1

Sources, same as Tables A11 and A12.

[a] Rates of return are calculated on average net worth, beginning and end of year, and exclude capital gains and losses.

TABLE A14. *Comparative Operating Results, U.S. Subsidized Lines Versus Selected Foreign Lines, 1958-61*
(In thousands of dollars)

| | Number of Ships | Net Book Value of Fleet[a] | Vessel Operating + Profit | Capital Gain; Other Income | − Interest and Taxes | = Cash Flow (Net) | − Depreciation and Special Funds | = Net Earnings | Dividends | Financial Results Per $1 Million Book Value | | |
										Cash Flow	Earnings	*Percent Return[c]*
U. S. Subsidized Lines	312	$346,000	$ 78,476	$22,285	$21,200	$ 79,561	$36,316	$43,245	$15,551	$230	$125	*4.5*
Eight Foreign Lines	781	888,000	115,722	12,067	14,825	112,963	93,922	19,046	10,450	127	21	*1.2*
Cunard	84	137,000	11,469	1,353	48	12,774	12,256	518	1,453	93	4	*1.1*
Furness	80	98,000	12,446	2,091	1,406	13,131	8,854	4,281	1,748	133	43	*1.8*
Peninsula and Orient	390	409,000	53,387	3,805	6,712	50,480	39,589	10,890	5,192	123	27	*1.3*
Hansa	50	54,000	6,700[b]	670[b]	2,300	5,069	4,860	206	176	94	4	*0.3*
North German Lloyd	45	57,000	9,420	647	2,990	7,677	7,500	181	167	135	3	*0.3*
Holland-America	35	24,000	6,180	2,180	netted	8,360	6,947	1,412	1,317	348	59	*5.5*
Norwegian-American	17	15,000	3,333	42	19	3,356	3,156	200	176	210	13	*1.2*
French	80	93,000	12,787[b]	1,279[b]	1,950	12,116	10,760	1,358	280	130	15	*0.3*

Source, data from *Moody's Industrials*, 1958–61. Table reports annual averages over the four-year period.
[a] Data for certain foreign flag companies include net book value of equipment other than vessels used in shipping operations. Amount shown is average over four-year period.
[b] Vessel operating profit and other income not separately reported. Distribution is arbitrary.
[c] Dividends as a percentage of estimated book value of fleet.

APPENDIX B

Statutory Statements of U.S. Maritime Objectives

The objectives of U.S. maritime policy were declared in the preambles to the Merchant Marine Acts of 1920, 1928, and 1936, and to the Ship Sales Act of 1946. The 1920 declaration, the first statutory expression of U.S. maritime objectives, was simply reaffirmed in 1928 but supplanted by a slightly modified statement in 1936. The 1946 declaration elaborated on but did not repeal the 1936 statement. Hence, both the 1936 and 1946 declarations express official government policy. The 1946 statement supersedes the preamble of the 1936 act wherever it is inconsistent with the earlier statement. However, the 1936 preamble is better known and more frequently cited. Its complete text is as follows:

> It is necessary for the national defense and development of its foreign and domestic commerce that the United States shall have a merchant marine (a) sufficient to carry its domestic waterborne commerce and a substantial portion of the waterborne export and import foreign commerce of the United States and to provide shipping service on all routes essential for maintaining the flow of such domestic and foreign waterborne commerce at all times, (b) capable of serving as a naval and military auxiliary in time of war or national emergency, (c) owned and operated by citizens of the United States insofar as may be practicable, and (d) composed of the best-equipped, safest, and most suitable types of vessels, constructed in the United States and manned with a trained and efficient citizen personnel. It is hereby declared to be the policy of the United States to foster the development and encourage the maintenance of such a merchant marine.

The 1936 declaration made the following major modifications to the 1920 act:

(a) it substituted the qualitative phrase "sufficient to carry . . . a substantial portion of the waterborne export and import foreign commerce" for the quantitative statement in the 1920 act that the U.S. flag fleet should be large enough to carry the "greater portion" of all American commerce.
(b) it specified that the U.S. flag fleet should provide shipping service on all essential trade routes, and
(c) it further stipulated that the fleet should be composed exclusively of U.S.-built ships manned with trained and efficient citizen personnel.

369

The 1946 Ship Sales Act used language nearly identical to the 1936 act, but included a fifth subpart, "(e)," to declare that the U.S. flag fleet should be "supplemented by efficient, American-owned facilities for shipbuilding, ship repair, marine insurance, and other auxiliary services." The 1946 act deleted the qualification "insofar as may be practical" from subpart "(c)" and placed additional emphasis on the need for an "efficient and adequate" U.S. flag fleet for U.S. "national security."

APPENDIX C

Agencies Administering Government Shipping Programs, 1916-65

1916–33 U.S. SHIPPING BOARD
An independent bipartisan board vested with promotional, administrative, and regulatory functions. Membership on the board was raised from five to seven by the Merchant Marine Act of 1920 and reduced to three by the Independent Offices Appropriation Act for 1934. The 1916 act required regional representation on the board.

1917–27 EMERGENCY FLEET CORPORATION
Chartered by the Shipping Board as a wholly owned government corporation under section 11 of the 1916 act to own and operate vessels acquired or constructed by the board. The corporation was directed by a separate seven-man board of trustees with overlapping membership with the Shipping Board. From 1917 to 1920 its operations were directed by the Shipping Board's chairman, assisted by a general manager. From 1921 to 1927, the corporation was directed by a separate individual under the Shipping Board's general direction.

1927–36 MERCHANT FLEET CORPORATION
Succeeded the Emergency Fleet Corporation; at about the same time direction of the corporation was returned to the Shipping Board, which acted as the corporation's trustees.

1934–36 U.S. SHIPPING BOARD BUREAU
A bureau constituted within the Department of Commerce to conduct functions transferred from the Shipping Board to the Department by Executive Order Number 6166 pursuant to authority contained in the Independent Offices Appropriation Act for 1934. The bureau, headed by a three-man board, operated under direction of the Secretary.

1936–50 U.S. MARITIME COMMISSION
An independent bipartisan agency of five members (six-year terms) established by the 1936 act and vested with promotional, operating, and regulatory functions. Authority to oversee the commission's internal administration was transferred to the chairman by Reorganization Plan Number 6 of 1949.

1942–48   WAR SHIPPING ADMINISTRATION
An independent agency responsible to the President and directed
by the chairman, U.S. Maritime Commission, acting ex officio. The
agency was established by Executive Order 9054, February 7,
1942, and was responsible for wartime ship operations and administration of shipping priorities. (Management of the construction program was retained by the commission.)

1950–61   FEDERAL MARITIME BOARD
A bipartisan board of three members appointed for four-year terms,
established by Reorganization Act Number 21 of 1950. The board
was charged with administering the regulatory program established
by the Shipping Act of 1916 and with quasi-judicial functions related to the subsidy program. It was located within the Department of Commerce for administrative purposes and was to be
"guided by the general policies of the Secretary" when acting in
its promotional capacity but to be completely independent when
acting in a regulatory capacity. However, the Secretary was without power to reverse or specify any decision made by the board.

1950–   MARITIME ADMINISTRATION
Established by Reorganization Plan Number 21 as an agency within the Department of Commerce to carry out administrative functions previously exercised by the commission and not specifically
transferred to the Federal Maritime Board. (The plan vested these
residual powers in the Secretary in the expectation that they would
be delegated to the Maritime Administrator subject to his general
supervision.) Through 1961 the Maritime Administration was
headed by the chairman of the board acting ex officio. Reorganization Plan Number 7 of 1961 terminated this arrangement and
provided for a Maritime Administrator, appointed by the President
and confirmed by the Senate, to direct the agency.

1951–   NATIONAL SHIPPING AUTHORITY
Established by Executive Order Number 10219, February 28, 1951,
to exercise functions parallel to those exercised during World War
II by the War Shipping Administration. The authority is directed
by the Maritime Administrator, acting ex officio.

1961–   FEDERAL MARITIME COMMISSION
An independent, bipartisan agency of five members appointed for
four-year terms, created by Reorganization Plan Number 7 of 1961
(75 Stat. 840). The commission conducts the regulatory program
established by the 1916 act and certain other related activities.

1961–   MARITIME SUBSIDY BOARD
Reorganization Plan Number 7 transferred the Federal Maritime
Board's subsidy award functions to the Secretary of Commerce. In
order to secure approval of the plan, the Secretary pledged that
these functions would be delegated to an administrative board (the
Maritime Subsidy Board, established by Department Order Number 117, August 11, 1961) chaired by the Maritime Administrator
and composed of three members drawn from that organization.

Chairmen—Administrators of
Government Shipping Agencies, 1936-65

Chairman	Tenure	Prior Experience
U.S. Maritime Commission:		
Admiral Henry A. Wiley (interim)	1936–37	Retired naval officer
Joseph P. Kennedy	1937–38	Former chairman, Securities and Exchange Commission; business executive
Admiral Emory S. Land	1938–46	Naval officer and engineer
Admiral W. W. Smith	1946–48	Retired naval officer
General Philip S. Fleming	1949–50	Former administrator, Federal Works Administration; Army engineer
Federal Maritime Board–Maritime Administration:		
Admiral Edward L. Cochrane	1950–52	Former chief, Bureau of Ships; Dean, Department of Naval Architecture, MIT
A. W. Gatov	1952–53	Former president, Pacific, Argentine, and Brazil Line; member, Federal Maritime Board
Louis S. Rothschild	1953–55	Former president, clothing firm; Chairman, Inland Waterways Corporation
Clarence G. Morse	1955–60	Admiralty lawyer; General Counsel, Maritime Administration
Admiral R. E. Wilson	1960–61	Naval officer; Commander, Military Sea Transport Service

| Thomas E. Stakem | 1961 | Civil service (FBI and Maritime Administration); member, Federal Maritime Board |

Federal Maritime Commission:

| Thomas E. Stakem | 1961–63 | (see above) |
| Admiral John Harllee | 1963– | Retired naval officer; aide to Senator J. F. Kennedy; member, Federal Maritime Board |

Maritime Subsidy Board—Maritime Administrator:

Donald W. Alexander	1961–63	Business executive; graduate, U.S. Naval Academy
Robert Giles (acting)	1963–64	Lawyer; General Counsel, Department of Commerce
Nicholas Johnson	1964–	Lawyer; instructor, University of California

Selected Bibliography

Boczek, B. A. *Flags of Convenience: An International Legal Study.* Cambridge: Harvard University Press, 1962.

Clones, H. J., and MacKay, G. C. "Transportation Transactions in the U.S. Balance of Payments," *Survey of Current Business,* U.S. Department of Commerce, Vol. 43, No. 8, August 1963.

Committee of American Steamship Lines. *Government Aids to Foreign Competitors.* Washington, 1964.

——. *Studies Re-examining National Maritime Policies and Requirements.* 6 vols. Washington, 1964–65.

Dye, Captain Ira. "Sealift for Limited War," *U.S. Naval Review,* Frank Uhlig, ed., Annapolis, 1963.

Eversheim, F. *Effects of Shipping Subsidization.* Bremen, 1958.

Ferguson, Allen, and associates. *The Economic Value of the U.S. Merchant Marine.* Chicago: Northwestern University, The Transportation Center, 1961.

Goldberg, Joseph. *The Maritime Labor Story.* Cambridge: Harvard University Press, 1957.

Gorter, Wytze. *United States Shipping Policy.* New York: Harper Brothers, 1956.

Grossman, William. *Ocean Freight Rates.* Cambridge, Maryland: Cornell Maritime Press, 1956.

Harvard Business School. *Case Study of the Moore-McCormack Line.* Material prepared for use in the curriculum of the Graduate School of Business Administration. 1963.

——. *The Use Disposition of Ships and Shipyards at the End of World War II.* Washington: Government Printing Office, 1945.

Interagency Maritime Task Force. *The Merchant Marine in National Defense and Trade.* Washington, 1965.

Maritime Evaluation Committee. *Maritime Resources for Security and Trade.* Washington, 1963. (Multilith.)

"Maritime Subsidies," *Fortune,* Vol. 16, No. 3, September 1937. (This entire issue is a report on the U.S. merchant marine.)

Marx, Daniel. *International Shipping Cartels.* Princeton University Press, 1953.

McDougal, Myers S., and Burke, William T. *The Public Order of the Sea.* New Haven: Yale University Press, 1962.

McDowell, Carl, and Gibbs, Helen. *Ocean Transportation.* New York: McGraw-Hill, 1955.

National Academy of Sciences—National Research Council. *Proposed Program for Maritime Administration Research.* 2 vols. Washington, 1960.

President's Advisory Committee on the Merchant Marine. *Report of the President's Advisory Committee on the Merchant Marine.* Washington: Government Printing Office, 1947.

Reese, H. C., ed. *Merchant Marine Policy.* Proceedings of the Symposium of the Fifteenth Ocean Shipping Management Institute of the American University's School of Business Administration. Cambridge, Maryland: Cornell Maritime Press, 1963.

Sturmey, S. G. *British Shipping and World Competition.* London: The Athlone Press, 1962.

U.S. Congress. House. Judiciary Committee. *The Ocean Freight Industry.* H. Rept. 1419, 87 Cong. 2 sess. Washington: Government Printing Office, 1962.

——. House. Merchant Marine and Fisheries Committee. *Report on Steamship Agreements and Affiliations in American Foreign and Domestic Trade.* Printed as vol. 4 of the Hearing, same title, 63 Cong. 1 sess. Washington: Government Printing Office, 1914.

——. Joint Economic Committee. *Discriminatory Ocean Freight Rates and the Balance of Payments.* S. Rept. 1, 89 Cong. 1 sess. Washington: Government Printing Office, 1965.

——. Senate. Committee on Interstate and Foreign Commerce. *Final Report on Merchant Marine Study and Investigation.* S. Rept. 2494, 81 Cong. 2 sess. Washington: Government Printing Office, 1950.

U.S. Department of Commerce, Under Secretary for Transportation and the Maritime Administration. *Maritime Subsidy Policy.* 1954. (Multilith.)

U.S. Maritime Advisory Committee. *Maritime Policy and Program of the United States.* Washington, 1965. (Includes dissent of H. Lee White to the Majority Report.)

U.S. Maritime Commission. *Economic Survey of the American Merchant Marine.* Washington: Government Printing Office, 1937.

U.S. Navy. Bureau of Personnel. *Military Sea Transportation and Shipping Control.* Manual 10829-A. Washington, 1954.

U.S. Treasury Department. *Scope and Effect of Tax Benefits Provided the Maritime Industry.* Supplementary Report, 1952. (Mimeograph.)

Zeis, P. M. *American Shipping Policy.* Princeton University Press, 1938.

Index

Index

Greene, Horace, 39*n*, 76
Grievance Committee on Cargo Preference Administration, 303, 304*n*
Grossman, W. L., 12*n*
Guffey, Joseph, 76
Gulf Line, 134*n*
Gulick, J. W., 306*n*

Haag, A. H., 48, 63*n*
Hall, Paul, 92, 190, 214, 292, 293*n*, 297*n*
Hamilton, Walton, 309*n*, 329*n*
Handbook for Saboteurs, 326-27
Hardy Committee, 314*n*
Harrison, J. Max, 291*n*
Hart, Edward J., 138*n*
Harvard Business School, 74*n*, 75*n*, 219*n*
Hawaii, 85, 98, 109, 323
Henry, J. J., 213*n*
historical development of U.S. maritime policy. *See under* maritime policy, U.S.
Hodges, Luther H., 239-40, 241, 241*n*, 314*n*, 321*n*
Holland. *See* Netherlands
Honduras (*see also* PANLIBHON), 98*n*
Hoover, Herbert, 43*n*, 45*n*
Hoover Commission, 250, 256, 264, 320*n*

ICC. *See* Interstate Commerce Commission
ICC v. New York, New Haven and Hartford Railroads, 319*n*
ILA. *See* International Longshoremen's Association
IMCO. *See* Inter-Governmental Maritime Consultative Organization
Incres Steamship Company v. International Maritime Workers Union, 184*n*
"Independence," S.S., 140, 256
Independent Offices Appropriation Act (1933), 45
India, 27*n*, 88, 96, 100*n*, 110*n*, 154
industrial carriers, 10, 11-12; extension of subsidies to, 136-39
insurance, war-risk, 188*n*
intelligence activities, use of merchant shipping in, 26
Interagency Committee on Cargo Preferences, 271, 271*n*
Interagency Task Force on Maritime Affairs, 2, 153*n*, 305, 315-16, 343*n*, 350*n*
Inter-American Development Bank, 173*n*
Interdepartmental Committee on Shipping

Policy, 54, 63*n*
interest group policies and politics, 283-308:
cooperation and conflict, patterns of, 295-99:
labor management coalitions, 296-97;
political affiliations, 298-99;
user and supplier groups, alliances with, 297-98;
interests common to all groups, 284;
interests at stake in government program, 283-89:
career commitments, 286-87;
contractual commitments, 284-86;
diversification, 288-89;
investment commitments, 284;
of unions, 287-88;
organizations, 289-95:
business and professional, 295;
labor, 292-93;
shipowner, 289-91, 327;
supplier groups, 294-95;
user groups, 293-94;
political process, participation in, 299-307:
government personnel, contacts with, 300-301, 327-28;
industry-government cooperation, 302-7;
records and information, access to, 301-2, 328;
power structure of maritime industry, effects of, 307-8
Inter-Governmental Maritime Consultative Organization, 18, 18*n*, 147*n*, 167, 271
Internal Revenue Service, U.S., 268-69
International Bank for Reconstruction and Development, 173*n*
International Brotherhood of Teamsters, 92
International Commerce, Bureau of, 252
International Federation of Transport Workers, 184
International Labor Organization, 184
International Longshoremen's Association, 190, 191*n*, 293*n*
International Monetary Fund, 94*n*
International Trade Organization, 99
Interstate Commerce Commission, 38,

and politics; investment; labor; legislation; maritime policy; policy development and administration; rates; registry; regulation; steamship conferences; subsidized lines; subsidy program; tonnage data):

agencies administering government program *(see also agency in question)*, 128-29, 319-21;

changes in, after World War II, 83-104:

capital investment, 93-94;

demobilization of government ships, 84, 84n;

deployment of U.S. shipping, 85-86;

flags of convenience *(see also s.v.)*, 101-4;

foreign trade, composition of, 87-88;

foreign trade, increase in, 86-87;

freight rates, 90;

government shipments, 88-90;

impact of, on maritime policy, 103-4;

labor, shipboard, 91-93;

modes of transport, 97-98;

national flag preferences, 99-101;

national flags, growth in number of, 98-99;

rates of exchange, 94-95;

ship sales program *(see also* Merchant Ship Sales Act of 1946), 83-84;

technology, marine, 95-97;

Cold War, role in, 98, 124-25, 126, 127, 236-37;

commercial role of, 22-24, 77, 78, 82, 117-22, 230, 233-36;

dual functions of, 77-78, 230, 241, 266-67, 338;

economic development, national, impact on, 32-33;

economic and foreign policy roles of, 26, 122-25;

employment in, 9, 74;

government involvement in, summary of, 202-4;

government restrictions on *(see also* registry, U.S., *s.v.* requirements), 29, 34-36;

innovation, obstacles to introducing, 308, 331-33;

losses during Civil War, 32-33;

military role of, 24-26, 41, 66-67, 77-78, 81-82, 105-17, 229-33, 266-67;

military and commercial roles, conflicts of, 230;

nuclear war, role in, 108n-109n;

ownership of *(see s.v.)*;

physical condition of, 225-26;

political support of, summary, 331-33;

power structure of, effects of, 307-8;

private investment in *(see* investment, private capital);

public attention to, 317-18;

public obligations of flag lines, 11, 11n;

and public relations, 325-27;

public support of, 1;

registry requirements *(see under* registry, U.S.);

regulation of *(see s.v.)*;

replacement program, 63, 136, 143, 145, 145n, 225, 226, 276-77, 276n, 277n, 280, 335;

representational role of, 26-27;

revival of maritime interests in (1890's), 33-34;

scandal, success in avoiding, 299, 299n;

ships and services, types of, 10-12, *Table,* 10;

size of flag fleet in 1945 *(see also* tonnage data), 83, 83n;

status, current, of U.S. fleet, 237-40;

strength of, after World War II, 218-20;

total number of U.S.-owned or controlled ships, 105, 115n, *and* App. A, *Table* A4;

world affairs, present role in, 126-27

merchant ships, world, classification of, by types and services, 10-12, *Table,* 10

Merchants Parcel Delivery v. Pa. Public Utility Commissions, 11n

mergers, company, 71

Micronesia, 342n

Military Air Transport Service, 110, 111n

Military Sea Transport Service, 27n, 105, 112-13, 112n, 117, 155, 155n, 169n, 179, 208, 222n, 231, 232, 233, 252, 272, 293, 297, 327, 328, 336;